TAKING⟳SIDES

Clashing Views on Controversial
Issues in Secondary Education

D1535152

TAKING SIDES

Clashing Views on Controversial

Issues in Secondary Education

Selected, Edited, and with Introductions by

Dennis L. Evans
University of California–Irvine

McGraw-Hill/Dushkin
A Division of The McGraw-Hill Companies

To my love and best friend Kris and the family's best writers, Mark and Suzy

Photo Acknowledgment
Cover image: © 2002 by PhotoDisc, Inc.

Cover Art Acknowledgment
Charles Vitelli

Manufactured in the United States of America

First Edition

123456789BAHBAH5432

Library of Congress Cataloging-in-Publication Data
Main entry under title:
Taking sides: clashing views on controversial issues in secondary education/selected, edited, and with introductions by Dennis L. Evans.—1st ed.
Includes bibliographical references and index.
1. Education, Secondary. I. Evans, Dennis L., *ed.* II. Series.
373

0-07-248044-0
ISSN: 1537-0720

Printed on Recycled Paper

Preface

I t risks tautology to suggest that education evokes controversy. And while controversies in any field often involve conflicting values and belief systems; it is the fact that the lives of our children are so singularly impacted by the quality of what transpires in the schools that generates the vehemence and volatility characteristic of controversy in education. The volume of voices regarding what should or should not happen in our schools speaks well of our commitment and our concern regarding our most precious commodities. Also contributing to the heritage of controversy in American public education is its democratic structure both in terms of governance and the reality that it deals with "all of the children of all of the people." Controversies created by our democratic approach to public schooling are controversies worth having.

Plan of the book This volume contains 20 issues in secondary education, supported by 40 selections that are presented in a pro-con format. These issues represent dichotomous, or at least widely divergent, viewpoints on important educational issues. While a particular focus is placed on issues in secondary education, most such issues are also found in other levels of education and, thus, this book can inform anyone interested in the state of schooling in America.

Part 1 of the book presents five topics that generate conflicting views regarding the fundamental purposes of secondary education: universal compulsory education, citizenship education, education through a common core curriculum, ethnocentric considerations, and education for the workplace. Part 2 focuses on seven contemporary educational policy and/or legal/organizational issues: religion in the schools, school uniform policies, zero tolerance policies, achievement level grouping, high stakes standardized testing, merit pay for teachers, and the school principalship. Part 3 deals with eight controversies related to curricular and instructional practices: block scheduling, homework, grading practices, the role of technology, service learning, globalization as an emphasis in the study of history, the role of the classics in the English curriculum, and high school athletics.

Considerable care has been taken to not only select issues that are of current interest (although many of these have long histories of controversy), but also to provide selections that are representative of the divergent views on each issue and that are authored by a full panoply of those who care about education: advocates, critics, philosophers, practitioners, commentators, political/historical figures, and provocateurs.

The format for each of the 20 issues involves an *introduction* that outlines the controversy, the presentation of the opposing articles, and a *postscript* that summarizes the arguments and presents related views and works. Additionally, at the beginning of each of the three parts, *(Purposes, Policies, and Practices)*, there is an *On the Internet* page that lists pertinent Internet resources. At the back of the book, a listing of the *contributors to this volume* provides information on the authors whose views are debated in this volume.

Given the format of the book, it can be used for many purposes: combined with the *introduction* it can provide an excellent foundation for the study of issues in secondary education; it can serve as a text for educational leadership and philosophy courses; it can be used in administrator preparation and continuing development programs; it can provide the basis for school faculty professional growth and in-service activities; and it can be used by PTA and other parent organizations in their educational programs.

A word to the instructor　An *Instructor's Manual With Test Questions* (multiple-choice and essay) is available through the publisher for the instructor using *Taking Sides* in the classroom. A general guidebook, *Using Taking Sides in the Classroom*, which discusses methods and techniques for integrating the pro-con approach into any classroom setting, is also available. An online version of *Using Taking Sides in the Classroom* and a correspondence service for *Taking Sides* adopters can be found at http://www.dushkin.com/usingts/.

Taking Sides: Clashing Views on Controversial Issues in Secondary Education is only one title in the Taking Sides series. If you are interested in seeing the table of contents for any of the other titles, please visit the Taking Sides Web site at http://www.dushkin.com/takingsides/.

Acknowledgments　My sincere appreciation goes to Theodore Knight, list manager, and Juliana Gribbins, developmental editor, of McGraw-Hill/Dushkin, who shepherded me through this entire project. I am also grateful to the many individuals who provided me with contacts regarding possible sources.

Dennis L. Evans
University of California–Irvine

Contents In Brief

Contents

what one studies is less important than that it sparks legitimate interest in each learner.

Molefi Kete Asante, professor of African American studies at Temple University, argues that Eurocentricity presents the particular historical reality of Europeans as the sum total of the human experience. Diane Ravitch, senior fellow of the Brookings Institution, states that the mission of public schools should be to instill in children our shared, not our separate, cultures.

The Secretary's Commission on Achieving Necessary Skills (SCANS) report, issued during the George H. W. Bush administration, states that a fundamental purpose of education is to create an entire people trained to think and equipped with the know-how to make their knowledge productive. John I. Goodlad, codirector of the Center of Educational Renewal at the University of Washington, cautions that "to make the dozen or more years of schooling instrumental to the future needs of the workplace, however carefully predicted, is immoral and dangerous."

PART 2   POLICIES   79

Michael W. McConnell, professor in the School of Law at the University of Utah, argues that many parents have come to believe that the First Amendment is "stacked against them" with respect to their desire to see more religion in the schools. Annie Laurie Gaylor, editor of *Freethought Today,* states that public schools exist to educate, not to proselytize.

The United States Department of Education endorses school uniform policies, presenting suggestions for implementation and examples of successful programs. David L. Brunsma and Kerry A. Rockquemore, professors at the University of Alabama and the University of Connecticut, respectively, report the results of their research, which has caused them to reject the idea that school uniforms improve student performance in areas such as attendance, academic achievement, behavioral issues, and substance abuse.

Issue 8.   Are Zero Tolerance Policies Necessary and Effective?   116

The National Association of Secondary School Principals (NASSP) argues that zero tolerance policies, clearly stated and fairly administered, meet parental and societal expectations and protect the physical well-being of students and staff. Russ Skiba, associate professor at Indiana University, and Reece Peterson, associate professor at the University of Nebraska, state that virtually no data suggest that zero tolerance policies reduce school violence.

Issue 9.   Is Achievement Level Tracking of Students a Defensible Educational Practice?   136

Tom Loveless, director of the Brown Center on Education Policy at Brookings Institution, suggests that many of the charges against tracking are more political than educational and are not supported by research. Jeannie S. Oakes, professor in the Graduate School of Education at the University of California–Los Angeles, indicts the results of tracking, especially tracking's damaging impact on the education of minority students.

Issue 10.   Is High-Stakes Standardized Testing Defensible?   154

Journalist Richard P. Phelps suggests that the criticisms directed at high-stakes standardized testing are misguided and do not hold up upon careful scrutiny. Peter Sacks, a journalist and essayist on education and American culture, argues that the penchant for high-stakes testing is counterproductive to meaningful teaching and learning and thus harmful to students.

Lewis C. Solmon, senior vice president of the Milken Family Foundation, and Michael Podgursky, a professor of economics at the University of Missouri–Columbia, state that new compensation methods are not only feasible but necessary in order to attract the best and the brightest into the teaching profession, keep the most effective of these in teaching, and motivate all teachers. Wellford W. Wilms, professor of education at the University of California–Los Angeles, and Richard R. Chapleau, 1995 winner of the California Milken Teacher of the Year Award, posit that shifting the focus of education from the student to the pocketbook erodes teachers' professional judgment and demeans the process of education.

Ann Weaver Hart, provost and vice president for academic affairs at Claremont Graduate School, and Paul V. Bredeson, professor of educational administration at the University of Wisconsin–Madison, assert that principals' instructional leadership forges the efforts of others into successes for students. Donal Sacken, professor of education at Texas Christian University, states that school principals distort the operations of schools because of their managerial ethic.

Joseph M. Carroll, a former school superintendent and a senior associate at Copernican Associates, contends that the traditional ("Carnegie unit") high school schedule is a system under which teachers cannot teach effectively and students cannot learn effectively. Reginald D. Wild, a professor in the Department of Curriculum Studies at the University of British Columbia, asserts that all-year students outperform semester/block students in science and mathematics.

Issue 14. Is Homework Beneficial to Students? 234

Harris Cooper, chair of the Department of Psychological Sciences at the University of Missouri–Columbus, argues that research supports the contention that for high school students more homework results in higher achievement levels. Etta Kralovec, vice president for learning at Training and Development Corporation, and John Buell, a freelance journalist, present three "myths" supporting homework that they maintain insulate that traditional practice from careful study and criticism.

Issue 15. Does the Practice of Grading Students Serve Useful Purposes? 250

Robert J. Marzano, a senior fellow of Mid-continent Research for Education and Learning (McREL), argues that grading is useful for feedback purposes, which in turn enhance student learning. Alfie Kohn, an author and educational commentator, takes the position that grades reduce students' interest in learning, their willingness to choose challenging work, and the quality of their thinking.

Issue 16. Can Technology Transform Education? 272

Author Don Tapscott posits that the "Net Generation" (N-Gen) requires and will demand an approach to teaching and learning built upon educational technology. Todd Oppenheimer, a freelance writer with a special interest in interactive media, presents a caveat with regard to the unexamined proliferation of electronic learning tools in America's classrooms.

Sheldon Berman, superintendent of schools in Hudson, Massachusetts, posits that both the academic content of the school curriculum and the ethics of young people can be positively impacted by student engagement in community service learning (CSL). Educational and social commentators Chester E. Finn, Jr. and Gregg Vanourek argue that "service learning," a euphemism for mandatory volunteerism, is not only an oxymoron but also fosters a left-of-center approach to political activism.

The National Center for History in the Schools advocates courses that are "genuinely global in scope." Gilbert T. Sewall, director of the American Textbook Council, warns that a world history that slights the achievements of the West and concocts a "pseudohistory calculated to please contemporary multiculturalists" seems destined to become the rule in U.S. classrooms.

Carol Jago, a high school English teacher and director of the California Reading and Literature Project at the University of California–Los Angeles, states that a critical reading of classical literature results in a deep literacy that she believes is an essential skill for anyone who wants to attempt to make sense of the world. Donald R. Gallo, a former professor of English who writes and edits books for teachers and teenagers, posits that the United States is a nation that teaches its children how to read in the early grades, then forces them during their teenage years to read literary works that most of them dislike so much that they have no desire whatsoever to continue those experiences into adulthood.

The Arkansas Activities Association, which serves as the rule-making body for Arkansas high school athletic programs, points to criteria such as grades, discipline referrals, drop-out rates, attendance, and graduation rates wherein high school athletes outperform nonathletes. Jay J. Coakley, professor at the University of Colorado, contends that students who choose to participate in activities, including athletics, are different to begin with, and thus differences on simple statistics between participants and nonparticipants do not establish cause for concluding that participation in sports is the reason for increased academic success.

Introduction

Sources of Controversy in Secondary Education

Dennis L. Evans

Origins and Governance

With over 15 million, or 95 percent, of current 13–17 year olds in the United States involved in some form of public or private schooling, it is important to note that, from a historical perspective, universal secondary education is a relatively recent development. The emergence of the concept as an important feature of schooling in America coincided with the Progressive Era of 1890–1920, which was also period of enormous increases in immigration into the United States. At the beginning of that dynamic sociopolitical period, the number of adolescents of high school age who were in school was approximately 200,000, or slightly less than 7 percent of the age group. Thirty years later in 1920 the numbers had increased to 2 million, which was approximately 32 percent of the age group. Obviously, the rate of individuals who completed at least a high school education also grew with the increase in enrollment. In 1890 only 6 percent of adults 25 years and older held a high school diploma; that figure grew to 16 percent by 1920 and has continued to increase up to today's figure of approximately 83 percent.

The history of secondary education in the United States is a history of controversy. Indeed, disagreements regarding the very appropriateness of such "advanced" education arose early in colonial America. In 1647 the "Old Deluder Satan Act" was enacted in Massachusetts with the accompanying language supportive of education:

> It being one chief object of that old deluder, Satan, to keep men from the knowledge of the scriptures,... It is therefore ordered, that every township... after the lord hath increased them to the number of fifty householders... shall... appoint one within their town to teach all children as shall resort to him to read and write. It is further ordered, that where any town shall increase to the number of one hundred families... they shall set up a grammar school, the master thereof being able to instruct youth so far as they may be fitted for the university.

> — As cited in *History of Education in America* by John Pulliam and James Van Patten (Prentice Hall, 1994)

In 1671 Sir William Berkeley, the Colonial Governor of Virginia, expressed his disdain for the idea of widespread and advanced education with this statement:

> I thank God that there are no free schools nor printing, and I hope we shall not have them these hundred years, for learning has brought disobedience, and heresy, and sects into the world, and printing has divulged them, and libels against the best government.

> — Also cited in *History of Education in America*

Controversy also arose over what the purposes of any education beyond reading and writing should entail. As can be seen in The Old Deluder Satan Act and later in 1749 in Ben Franklin's treatise, *On the Need for an Academy*, schooling that went much beyond the rudimentary subjects was considered to be only important for those "fitted for the university." From colonial days until the end of the nineteenth century, secondary education was fundamentally only for the wealthy elite, only for those who would benefit from such an education and who would then attend a university in order to move into the "learned professions" of law, medicine, and the clergy.

Even as late as 1893 the tradition of the high school existing only for the purposes of university preparation was articulated by the National Education Association's (NEA) Committee of Ten, chaired by President Charles W. Eliot of Harvard University, which prescribed that high schools offer only a college preparatory curriculum obviously aimed at the needs of the small proportion of students who could benefit from it and whose parents could afford to send them on to the university. However, by 1911, consistent with the radical shift in thinking about secondary schooling that was occurring at that time, the NEA issued a new report highly critical of the Committee of Ten's recommendation. This report, issued by the Committee of Nine, stated that high schools had responsibilities much broader than mere pre-college work, especially since so few students matriculated to the university. (In 1910 only slightly more that 2 percent of the U.S. population 25 and older had graduated from college.) Such responsibilities included preparing students for participation as citizens and as contributors to the workplace and the economy.

This clash over purposes led to a compromise document, which was to become the guidepost for secondary education in the United States. That document, issued in 1918 by the NEA's Commission on the Reorganization of Secondary Education, charged high schools with the responsibility to provide a *comprehensive* curriculum that could accomplish both college preparation and preparation for life and thereby meet the needs of the entire high school age population. The document described the mission of secondary education as involving Seven Cardinal Principles. Those principles were:

- Health
- Command of fundamental processes
- Worthy home membership
- Vocational preparation
- Citizenship

- Worthy use of leisure time
- Ethical character

These cardinal principles reflected the notion of educating the "whole child" and led directly to the notion of the *comprehensive secondary school,* which continues to be the prevailing model of secondary education in the United States.

In spite of the democratization of the American high school, which occurred during the Progressive Era, secondary education continued to lag far behind elementary education in terms of the public's perception of its importance and thus the public's willingness to support it. While all of the then 48 states had enacted compulsory attendance laws by 1920 (pushed by Horace Mann, Massachusetts was first in 1852; Mississippi was last in 1918), as noted earlier only slightly over 16 percent of the population aged 25 and older had completed high school by that year, but 78 percent of that same group had at least five years of elementary schooling. For many years compulsory attendance requirements for secondary school-aged children were generally not viewed by the public as worthy of obeying, and it was not until well after World War II that high school graduates finally exceeded dropouts among adults over the age of 25. It took the combination of societal forces such as massive immigration, urbanization, industrialization and unionization, child protection laws, court decisions, and increased access to college to finally provide the momentum to cause secondary education to become truly compulsory.

The historical reluctance to embrace secondary schooling as an integral part of public education is exemplified by the fact that although taxation for the support of elementary education had its origins and public acceptance in colonial days and fueled the Common School Era for several decades beginning in 1830; the issue of tax support for public secondary schools was not resolved until the U.S. Supreme Court decision in 1874 in the case of *Stuart v. School District No. 1 of the Village of Kalamazoo.* In the *Kalamazoo* case the Court ruled in favor of the right of state legislatures to enact legislation allowing local communities to levy taxes for the support of public secondary schools. This belated lack of resolution regarding tax support combined with general public apathy, if not antipathy, toward public secondary schooling (there were many private academies for college preparatory work) resulted in the very slow growth of the number of public high schools in existence in the United States during the early nineteenth century. The first public high school, the Boston English Classical School, was established in 1821 (renamed the English High School in 1824) to serve the needs of noncollege-bound boys. By 1860 only an additional 300 had appeared nationally, one-third of those in Massachusetts. The *Kalamazoo* decision along with other societal forces dramatically increased those numbers so that by 1900 nearly 6000 high schools existed. The number stands at approximately 17,000 today. (Sources for this statistical information are The National Center for Educational Statistics and infoplease.com.)

Another source of controversy regarding public schooling emanates from the type of structure by which we govern our schools. Flowing from our revolutionary heritage and a concomitant antipathy toward a strong, central government, the Founding Fathers initially designed in 1783, by way of the Articles of Confederation, a national government so bereft of power that the newly formed nation quickly teetered on the brink of chaos and collapse. It became apparent that some concession had to be made with respect to granting greater power to the central government. That realization led to the Constitutional Convention of 1787 and the eventual drafting and ratification of the U.S. Constitution.

But in spite of the crisis mentality which had motivated the Founding Fathers to scuttle the Articles of Confederation and create a new federal system, there was still great resistance to any suggestion that the national government should have substantive power over the daily lives of the people. That fear of centralized power, which was entirely reasonable given the colonists' recently concluded struggles with Great Britain and King George III, resulted in demands that a Bill of Rights be added to the new Constitution. Indeed, for many, the only way they would agree to ratify the Constitution was with assurances that the Bill of Rights protecting the civil liberties of the people from governmental encroachment would be enacted.

That enactment, which took place in December of 1791, curtailed central government power in areas that were directly related to the daily lives of citizens. In their wisdom the Founding Fathers not only enumerated some of these areas such as speech, religion, the press, and due process, but also, through the 10th Amendment, protected other unspecified areas from the power of the central government. The 10th Amendment states that, "The powers not delegated to the United States by the Constitution, nor prohibited by it to the States, are reserved to the States respectively, or to the people." With this one sentence the power to control public education, since it is not mentioned in the Constitution, devolved to the individual states and to the people. Thus it is that in the United States there is no national control over public education. Certainly the federal government is involved in many aspects of education (some would suggest too many), but the constitutional authority is held by each of the 50 states. It is accurate to say that public education is a national interest, a state power, and a local responsibility. Obviously such a decentralized governance structure defies tight organization, consistency of operation, and agreement regarding the purposes of schooling. Advocates of our approach to the governance of public schooling might say that it fits the description of democracy attributed to Winston Churchill: "It has been said that Democracy is the worst form of government except all those other forms that have been tried from time to time." Critics of the approach suggest that many of the problems facing public education are attributable to the "messiness" of the governance structure.

As noted earlier, constitutional authority over the public schools is vested in each individual state. Each state has created local school districts and delegated authority to the local governmental entities such as school boards to govern those districts (the only exception to this approach is Hawaii, which governs its schools as one state-wide district). A fundamental feature of this governance structure is the local lay school board. The origin of citizen control over the schools predates nationhood and goes back to the colonial era when town elders would periodically check on the local school marm or master to make sure that the particular religious orthodoxy of the township was being duly recognized and respected.

The National School Boards Association makes the following statement regarding the role of school boards in governing American public education:

> The National School Boards Association believes local school boards are the nation's preeminent expression of grass roots democracy and that this form of governance of the public schools is fundamental to the continued success of public education.

Critics would suggest that the lay local school board is an anachronism that has outlived its purpose and that its role in governing the schools undermines the professionalism of educators and thwarts reform.

The concept of *grass roots democracy* means that school board members are in close proximity to the people they represent and thus are more subject to public opinion and pressures than are other public officials who serve from more distant venues. This can be both a vice and a virtue. Local school board members know their public and their public knows them. They can be quickly responsive to local issues, but they can also be susceptible to local emotions and orthodoxies. Citizen governance of local schools means that school board members may be elected (or not) because of their stance on certain issues facing local schools. They are also likely to be subject to recall elections more than any other type of public official. Certainly the concept of local school board governance is very consistent with the American heritage of distrusting distant government.

Philosophical Differences

The myriad controversies regarding purposes, policies, and practices in secondary education and the emotions that those controversies engender are testimony to the importance afforded to that level of education by today's public, pundits, and politicians. That was not always the case, and thus we should view such controversies as a healthy sign that secondary education is considered a vital issue on the nation's agenda.

As noted earlier, both the history and the governance of public secondary education make their own contributions to controversy, but beyond those contributions many of the issues dealt with in this book reflect the profound differences that good and honest people can and do have regarding fundamental questions about the nature of and the interrelationship among humankind, society, and education. These are philosophical and value issues and thus can be the source of conflicts and disagreements that are very difficult to resolve. Some of the major philosophical systems that impact secondary education include the following:

Idealism

This is better thought of as "idea-ism."

Essence   Ideas are the only true reality; man must search for knowledge and truth; man is capable through thought and revelation of attaining philosophic wisdom.

Educational goals and characteristics   Self-realization of each individual attained by developing reverence for ideas and the ability to think holistically. Education should focus on heritage and culture, reading and writing, intelligence and morality.

Key thinkers and works   Plato (427–347 B.C.) and Socrates (469–399 B.C.), *The Republic;* Augustine (354–430), *Confessions;* Rene Descartes (1596–1650), *Discourse on Method and Mediations on the First Philosophy;* George Berkeley (1685–1753), *Principles of Human Knowledge;* Immanuel Kant (1724–1804), *Critique of Pure Reason;* Friedrich Hegel (1770–1831), *Philosophy of Right.*

Realism

Essence   Reality, knowledge, and value exist independent of the human mind. The forms of things, the universal properties of objects, remain constant and never change.

Educational goals and characteristics   Providing students with basic and essential knowledge; true understanding requires the ordering and classifying of knowledge; rigorous inquiry based upon observation and experimentation are crucial. Science and scientific principles are pre-eminent.

Key thinkers and works   Aristotle (384–322 B.C.), *Politics and Ethics;* Thomas Aquinas (1225–1274), *Summa Theologica;* Francis Bacon (1561–1626), *Novum Organum;* John Locke (1632–1704), *Some Thoughts Concerning Education;* Alfred North Whitehead (1861–1947), *Science and the Modern World;* Bertrand Russell (1872–1970), *Principia Mathematica* (coauthored with Alfred North Whitehead).

Perennialism/Essentialism

These are later manifestations of Idealism/Realism.

Pragmatism (Progressivism)

Essence   Seek out processes and do things that work best to achieve desirable ends. Inductive thinking, importance of human experience, humanism, and relationship between science and culture are important elements.

Educational goals and characteristics   Education is, like growth, a necessity of life. It provides people with renewal of knowledge and skills to face problems encountered through interaction with the environment. Education is not preparation for life, but life itself. Individuals are social beings and education should help people direct, control, and guide personal and social experience. Motivation, interests, and prior experiences, including knowledge of consequences, are crucial to learning. School as a "laboratory."

Key thinkers and works Jean-Jacques Rousseau (1712–1778), *Emile;* Charles Darwin (1809–1882), *On the Origin of Species;* Charles Peirce (1839–1914), *How to Make Our Ideas Clear;* William James (1842–1910), *Talks to Teachers on Psychology;* John Dewey (1859–1952), *Experience and Education.*

Behaviorism

Essence Behavior is caused by environmental conditions. What is real is external, factual, and observable and is thus capable of being known. A "technology" of behavior is possible through conditioning. Humans are part of, not above, nature. A "good" culture can be designed and created.

Educational goals and characteristics Children's behavior is "programmed" long before they come to school. Primary aim of education is to change behavior and point it in more desirable directions. Change is brought about by reinforcement (aversive or positive) of specified behaviors. Immediate feedback is important. Small, incremental steps are helpful in learning a new task. Machine learning is utilized.

Key thinkers and works Thomas Hobbes (1588–1679), *Leviathan;* Ivan Pavlov (1849–1936), *Conditioned Reflexes;* John Watson (1878–1958), *Behaviorism;* B. F. Skinner (1904–1990), *Beyond Freedom and Dignity.*

Existentialism

Essence Man, alone, estranged and alienated, is caught up in a meaningless and absurd world. Human existence is characterized by anxiety and a lack of certainty. Individuals are confronted with life choices that only they can make and for which they must accept total responsibility. The individual's freedom to choose is daunting. Through thoughtful choice and action the individual can bring about change.

Educational goals and characteristics Each student is an individual and must be allowed to take the major role in his/her education. Schools should be places of freedom where students do the things they want to do. Schools should provide many options and choices. Every teacher is a student and every student is a teacher. The humanities and the arts are significant in the existentialist curriculum. Individual "sensemaking" is a basic goal of schooling. Differences are to be celebrated.

Key thinkers and works Soren Kierkegaard (1813–1855), *Attack on Christendom;* Martin Buber (1878–1965), *I and Thou;* Martin Heidegger (1889–1976), *Being and Time;* Jean Paul Sartre (1905–1980), *Being and Nothingness;* Maxine Greene, *Landscapes of Learning.*

Postmodernism

Essence   Not really a belief system, but rather an iconoclastic challenge to claims of universality; a rejection of objective certainty. Traditions of knowledge (canons), scientific laws, or first principles are challenged as forms of domination. Traditional knowledge is not to be ignored but to be studied or "deconstructed" to see how it elevates some segments of society to power and affluence at the expense of others.

Educational goals and characteristics   Postmodernism in education or critical pedagogy has as its common objective the empowerment of the powerless to overcome inequities and injustices. It challenges the way schools support dominant power and maintain inequities. It envisions schools as places where self and social empowerment can be enhanced. Curriculum is successful when it empowers people and transforms society. Students should explore their own individual histories, including self-reflection on race, gender, and class issues. Teachers are both scholars and practitioners and their role is to help students see the ideological and political interests that curricular knowledge may serve.

Key thinkers and works   Michel Foucalt (1926–1984), *The Order of Things;* Jacques Derrida, *Of Grammatology;* Henry Giroux, *Border Crossings;* Peter Mc-Claren, *Life in Schools;* Cleo Cherryholmes, *Power and Criticism;* Paolo Freire, *Pedagogy of the Oppressed.*

Other Systems

The previous selections are presented to provide an overview of various ideas, influences, and competing complexities that have impacted and continue to impact schooling in our country.

The selections obviously do not represent all of the various philosophical or belief systems that deal with education. Other systems such Marxism, empiricism, phenomenology, reconstructionism, analytic philosophy, Eastern religions, etc., have also influenced educational thought. Also, the views and actions of historical/political figures such as Benjamin Franklin, Thomas Jefferson, and Horace Mann; sectarian religious considerations; socio/economic realities; and other circumstances and individuals associated with the American experience have combined to create the unique character of our educational system.

Note: The source of much of the above material is Howard A. Ozman and Samuel Craver, *Philosophical Foundations of Education,* 5th ed. (Prentice Hall, 1995). As they point out, the various labels or titles given to the philosophies are arbitrary and not universally agreed upon, thus you may find that other descriptors are used in other works.

Given the profound differences that exist between and among these different belief systems, it should not be surprising that conflicts and controversies abound in secondary education. One way that secondary education has survived these "philosophical wars" has been through the creation of the *comprehensive* high school, which has allowed elements of several of the philosophies to become a part of the high school curriculum and program. Manifestations of different philosophies can be seen in such secondary school features as the study of history and the literary canon, science laboratories, electives, service learning, student government, programmed learning, multiculturalism, and the provision of counseling services.

Criticism of the Schools

With so many contrasting viewpoints vying for primacy in terms of what occurs in the schools, it is inevitable that much criticism will be directed at school purposes, polices, and practices when they are perceived to run counter to a given philosophical position. Criticism is also leveled at the schools when outcome measures such as Scholastic Achievement Test (SAT) scores, international test comparisons, and readiness for college do not measure up to expectations. Schools are also criticized for what some see as a breakdown in citizenship, morality, and respect for the law.

Much of the contemporary criticism of schools can be traced from the launching of the Soviet space satellite, Sputnik I, in 1957. This event led to stinging criticism from eminent Americans such as former president of Harvard James B. Conant and Admiral Hyman Rickover, both who bemoaned what they perceived as a lack of intellectual rigor and excellence in the nation's high schools. The turmoil and trauma of the 1960s brought criticism to the schools from both sides of the political fence. Many suggested that the protest movements on college campuses signaled how poorly high schools were doing with respect to instilling patriotism, loyalty, and traditional values in the nation's youth; while others such as Paul Goodman in *Growing Up Absurd: Problems of Youth in the Organized Society* (Vintage Books, 1960), John Holt in *How Children Fail* (Dell 1964), and Neil Postman and Charles Weingartner in *Teaching as a Subversive Activity* (Delacorte Press, 1969) asserted that the school curriculum was no longer relevant, failed to provide for individual needs, and thereby alienated students.

The 1970s continued that theme with a spate of searing indictments of the condition of secondary schooling in America, stating particularly that schooling failed to address the realities of modern life as experienced by many students. Writer/critics of this genre included Charles E. Silberman, *Crisis in the Classroom* (Vintage Books, 1970); Ivan Ilich, *Deschooling Society* (Harper Collins, 1971); John Holt, *Freedom and Beyond* (Dell, 1972); and Jonathan Kozol *Free Schools* (Houghton Mifflin, 1972).

The publication of *A Nation at Risk* in 1983 by the National Commission on Excellence in Education signaled the shift of criticism of the schools from the sociological perspectives of the 1970s to concerns regarding the quality of American secondary schooling vis-à-vis the nation's ability to remain competitive on the world scene. Much of the reform literature of the 1980s and early

1990s focused on shortcomings of secondary school curriculum and organization. Influential works from this era include Mortimer J. Adler's *The Paideia Proposal* (Macmillan, 1982); John I. Goodlad's *A Place Called School: Prospects for the Future* (McGraw-Hill, 1983); Ernest Boyer's *High School: A Report on Secondary Education in America* (Harper Trade, 1984); Theodore Sizer's *A Study of High Schools* (1984) and also from Sizer, *Horace's Compromise: The Dilemma of the American High School* (Houghton Mifflin, 1984); Jeannie Oakes's *Keeping Track: How Schools Structure Inequality* (Yale University Press, 1985); a report from the Carnegie Task Force, *A Nation Prepared: Teachers for the 21st Century* (Carnegie Forum, 1986), E. D. Hirsch's *Cultural Literacy: What Every American Needs to Know* (Houghton Mifflin, 1987), and John Goodlad's *Teachers for Our Nation's School* (Jossey-Bass, 1990). Several of the above references and others can be found in an excellent summary of recent education critics in John Pulliam and James Van Patten's *History of Education in America*, 6th ed. (Prentice Hall, 1994).

These insistent calls for educational change and reform combined with continuing concerns regarding the performance of American students on measures of academic performance especially with respect to international comparisons (Gerald Bracey, in his 1993 report on *The Condition of Public Education*, was one of the few voices suggesting that evaluative data regarding student performance was being misinterpreted and that American schools were not failing) created a political momentum that resulted in the 1990s becoming the decade of standards, accountability, and high-stakes testing. With presidential candidates and other political leaders stressing the importance of education, proposals such as school choice, vouchers, and the charter school movement have become part of the educational lexicon. Their future impact remains to be seen.

The Challenge

Given the irreconcilable and irreducible differences that arise over questions regarding the fundamental purposes and processes of schooling, it becomes obvious that while there are many answers to such questions there is no exclusively "right" answer. What emerges from that realization is the irony that great value can accrue from asking questions even if there is no "right" answer to them. It is important for those involved with the educational enterprise to realize that important questions need to be continually asked and that the divergent and even the diametrically opposite positions that well-meaning and thoughtful individuals will take in attempting to provide answers can become valuable stimuli for reflection and progress. Faced with questions that have many answers but no single correct one, the contemporary educator needs to possess or to develop a tremendous tolerance for ambiguity. To go beyond reactive survival and engage in proactive effectiveness educators must be prepared to face a myriad of questions, none of which have "a right answer." It will be through processes such as the development and articulation of a professional philosophy, self-reflection, and the analysis of the views and values of others that the thoughtful educator will best address such questions.

Some may believe that the various controversial issues that seem to characterize education are symptomatic of the contentious nature of contemporary society. But that is simply not the case. Here is one educator's response to a controversy over the relative merits of home versus public schooling:

> But even if great [large enrollment] schools are to be avoided (a position to which I cannot assent, if numbers flock to a master on account of his merit), the rule is not to be carried so far that schools be avoided altogether. It is one thing to shun schools entirely, another to choose from them.

This response is from "On the Early Education of the Citizen Orator," Book I of *The Institutes of Oratory,* by Quintilian (ca. 95 A.D.). Since we who are engaged in education cannot avoid controversy, we should find ways to learn, and thus benefit, from it.

On the Internet ...

Infoplease.com

The Infoplease Web site has numerous data and information regarding compulsory education laws.

http://www.infoplease.com/ipa/A0112617.html

The National Council for the Social Studies

One of the position statements of the National Council for the Social Studies promotes a common unified civic culture while respecting the cultural values and experiences of the many individuals who are making their new homes in the United States. Explore this site for more information.

http://www.ncss.org

Center for Democracy and Citizenship, Humphrey Institute of Public Affairs

The Humphrey Institute of Public Affairs at the University of Minnesota is dedicated to examining public issues and shaping public policy at the local, state, national, and international levels. This site includes a history of the Humphrey Institute of Public Affairs as well as research materials.

http://www.publicwork.org

Civic Practices Network

The Civic Practices Network describes itself as a collaborative and nonpartisan project dedicated to bringing practical tools for public problem solving into community and institutional settings across America.

http://www.cpn.org

Africana.com

The Africana.com Web site features comments and links related to rationales for an Afrocentric curriculum and other issues.

http://www.africana.com

PART 1

Purposes

*T*he very act of designing, implementing, and maintaining the institution of public education signals the intent that such a system be purposeful; that it contributes to the attainment of certain fundamental goals deemed vital to our nation and its citizenry. Given the diversity that characterizes the views and values of our society, it follows that if public education is expected to serve basic purposes, then controversy will be the rule rather than the exception. This will be especially true at the secondary level where such purposes go well beyond primary considerations such as reading, writing, and arithmetic.

Is our nation well served by compulsory education of all adolescents? What is the best approach to the preparation of future citizens? Should schools focus on our commonalities or our differences? Do public schools exist to serve the workplace? These are core questions that have been discussed and debated from the inception of public education by those who helped to shape it. These questions remain as sources of contention today. Reflecting on these basic purposes of education reveals the philosophical differences that lead to controversy.

- Should School Attendance Be Voluntary?

- Is Citizenship Education Working in the Public Schools?

- Should All Secondary School Students Experience the Same Curriculum?

- Is Ethnocentric Education a Good Idea?

- Should Secondary Schools Emphasize Education for the Workplace?

1

ISSUE 1

Should School Attendance Be Voluntary?

YES: John Holt, from *Escape From Childhood* (E. P. Dutton, 1974)

NO: Horace Mann, from *Tenth Annual Report* and *Twelfth Annual Report* (1846 and 1848)

ISSUE SUMMARY

YES: Educational critic John Holt contends that schools are "corrupt" places because of the power to judge that they hold over children.

NO: Horace Mann, a primary architect of the common school movement and advocate for compulsory education, argues that education is the great equalizer of the conditions of men.

T he development of universal free public education in America does not reflect a purely philosophical commitment to the virtues of learning or to the betterment of the individual child. Rather it was the sense of early advocates such as Benjamin Franklin, Thomas Jefferson, and later Horace Mann that it was in the best interest of a stable society—and most certainly a stable, democratic society—to have an educated citizenry. Contrary to the notion of a spirit of progressive altruism driving the growth of free public education, much of the motivation for the common school movement of the 1930s came from conservatives and persons of wealth who were fearful that the forces of immigration, urbanization, and industrialization if coupled with rigid class distinctions based on restricted access to education could lead to discontent and the eventual disruption of society. The vision of demagoguery and an ignorant and angry "mob" rising against established order was not considered far-fetched. Universal public education was seen as working at several different levels to ensure stability: a common education would include citizenship training for all and thus promote national unity; by reducing ignorance it would also reduce the appeal of demagogues; and by allowing the common man to improve his station in life it would give everyone a stake in maintaining society.

With universal education emerging as a compelling interest of society, it was only logical that such an education would eventually be made mandatory.

Beginning with Massachusetts in 1852, the notion of state-mandated compulsory education for all children spread across the nation, and by 1918 all U.S. states had enacted such legislation. While these compulsory education laws have been consistently upheld by the courts because of the compelling interest that society has in an educated citizenry, the United States Supreme Court in 1925 (*Pierce v. Society of Sisters*) did turn back an attempt in Oregon that would have required attendance at public schools. Thus while all school-age children must attend some form of schooling it does not necessarily need to be in a public school.

Since the 1950s the concept of compulsory education has come under increasing attack especially with respect to concerns regarding the quality of public schools. Movements to give parents greater control over the nature and the location of their child's education are manifested in school choice initiatives, vouchers, charter schools, and home schooling.

At its core this issue is one of conflicting philosophies. John Holt's position goes beyond that of merely increasing parent rights and addresses instead the violation of the rights of children wrought by compulsory education. Mann, while stating the importance of education for the individual, expands that into an exposition with regard to society's compelling interest in having an educated populace and thus presents the rationale for mandatory schooling.

John Holt  **YES**

Escape From Childhood

Young people should have the right to control and direct their own learning, that is, to decide what they want to learn, and when, where, how, how much, how fast, and with what help they want to learn it. To be still more specific, I want them to have the right to decide if, when, how much, and by whom they want to be *taught* and the right to decide whether they want to learn in a school and if so which one and for how much of the time.

No human right, except the right to life itself, is more fundamental than this. A person's freedom of learning is part of his freedom of thought, even more basic than his freedom of speech. If we take from someone his right to decide what he will be curious about, we destroy his freedom of thought. We say, in effect, you must think not about what interests and concerns *you*, but about what interests and concerns *us*.

We might call this the right of curiosity, the right to ask whatever questions are most important to us. As adults, we assume that we have the right to decide what does or does not interest us, what we will look into and what we will leave alone. We take this right for granted, cannot imagine that it might be taken away from us. Indeed, as far as I know, it has never been written into any body of law. Even the writers of our Constitution did not mention it. They thought it was enough to guarantee citizens the freedom of speech and the freedom to spread their ideas as widely as they wished and could. It did not occur to them that even the most tyrannical government would try to control people's minds, what they thought and knew. That idea was to come later, under the benevolent guise of compulsory universal education.

This right to each of us to control our own learning is now in danger. When we put into our laws the highly authoritarian notion that someone should and could decide what all young people were to learn and, beyond that, could do whatever might seem necessary (which now includes dosing them with drugs) to compel them to learn it, we took a long step down a very steep and dangerous path. The requirement that a child go to school, for about six hours a day, 180 days a year, for about ten years, whether or not he learns anything there, whether or not he already knows it or could learn it faster or better somewhere else, is such gross violation of civil liberties that few adults would

stand for it. But the child who resists is treated as a criminal. With this requirement we created an industry, an army of people whose whole work was to tell
young people what they had to learn and to try to make them learn it. Some
of these people, wanting to exercise even more power over others, to be even
more "helpful," or simply because the industry is not growing fast enough to
hold all the people who want to get into it, are now beginning to say, "If it is
good for children for us to decide what they shall learn and to make them learn
it, why wouldn't it be good for everyone? If compulsory education is a good
thing, how can there be too much of it? Why should we allow anyone, of any
age, to decide that he has had enough of it? Why should we allow older people,
any more than young, not to know what we know when their ignorance may
have bad consequences for all of us? Why should we not *make* them know what
they *ought* to know?"

They are beginning to talk, as one man did on a nationwide TV show,
about "womb-to-tomb" schooling. If hours of homework every night are good
for the young, why wouldn't they be good for us all—they would keep us away
from the TV set and other frivolous pursuits. Some group of experts, somewhere, would be glad to decide what we all ought to know and then every so
often check up on us to make sure we knew it—with, of course, appropriate
penalties if we did not.

I am very serious in saying that I think this is coming unless we prepare
against it and take steps to prevent it. The right I ask for the young is a right
that I want to preserve for the rest of us, the right *to decide what goes into our
minds.* This is much more than the right to decide whether or when or how
much to go to school or what school you want to go to. That right is important,
but it is only part of a much larger and more fundamental right, which I might
call the right to Learn, as opposed to being Educated, *i.e.*, made to learn what
someone else thinks would be good for you. It is not just compulsory schooling
but compulsory Education that I oppose and want to do away with.

That children might have the control of their own learning, including the
right to decide if, when, how much, and where they wanted to go to school,
frightens and angers many people. They ask me, "Are you saying that if the
parents wanted the child to go to school, and the child didn't want to go, that
he wouldn't have to go? Are you saying that if the parents wanted the child to
go to one school, and the child wanted to go to another, that the child would
have the right to decide?" Yes, that is what I say. Some people ask, "If school
wasn't compulsory, wouldn't many parents take their children out of school
to exploit their labors in one way or another?" Such questions are often both
snobbish and hypocritical. The questioner assumes and implies (though rarely
says) that these bad parents are people poorer and less schooled than he. Also,
though he appears to be defending the right of children to go to school, what
he really is defending is the right of the state to compel them to go whether they
want to or not. What he wants, in short, is that children should be in school,
not that they should have any choice about going.

But saying that children should have the right to choose to go or not to
go to school does not mean that the ideas and wishes of the parents would
have no weight. Unless he is estranged from his parents and rebelling against

them, a child cares very much about what they think and want. Most of the time, he doesn't want to anger or worry or disappoint them. Right now, in families where the parents feel that they have some choice about their children's schooling, there is much bargaining about schools. Such parents, when their children are little, often ask them whether they want to go to nursery school or kindergarten. Or they may take them to school for a while to try it out. Or, if they have a choice of schools, they may take them to several to see which they think they will like the best. Later, they care whether the child likes his school. If he does not, they try to do something about it, get him out of it, find a school he will like.

I know some parents who for years had a running bargain with their children. "If on a given day you just can't stand the thought of school, you don't feel well, you are afraid of something that may happen, you have something of your own that you very much want to do—well, you can stay home." Needless to say, the schools, with their supporting experts, fight it with all their might—Don't Give in to Your Child, Make Him Go to School, He's Got to Learn. Some parents, when their own plans make it possible for them to take an interesting trip, take their children with them. They don't ask the schools' permission, they just go. If the child doesn't want to make the trip and would rather stay in school, they work out a way for him to do that. Some parents, when their child is frightened, unhappy, and suffering in school, as many children are, just take him out. Hal Bennett, in his excellent book *No More Public School*, talks about ways to do this.

A friend of mine told me that when her boy was in third grade, he had a bad teacher, bullying, contemptuous, sarcastic, cruel. Many of the class switched to another section, but this eight-year-old, being tough, defiant, and stubborn, hung on. One day—his parents did not learn this until about two years later—having had enough of the teacher's meanness, he just got up from his desk and without saying a word, walked out of the room and went home. But for all his toughness and resiliency of spirit, the experience was hard on him. He grew more timid and quarrelsome, less outgoing and confident. He lost his ordinary good humor. Even his handwriting began to go to pieces—it was much worse in the spring of the school year than in the previous fall. One spring day he sat at breakfast, eating his cereal. After a while he stopped eating and sat silently thinking about the day ahead. His eyes filled up with tears, and two big ones slowly rolled down his cheeks. His mother, who ordinarily stays out of the school life of her children, saw this and knew what it was about. "Listen," she said to him, "we don't have to go on with this. If you've had enough of that teacher, if she's making school so bad for you that you don't want to go any more, I'll be perfectly happy just to pull you right out. We can manage it. Just say the word." He was horrified and indignant. "No!" he said, "I couldn't do that." "Okay," she said, "whatever you want is fine. Just let me know." And so they left it. He had decided that he was going to tough it out, and he did. But I am sure knowing that he had the support of his mother and the chance to give it up if it got too much for him gave him the strength he needed to go on.

To say that children should have the right to control and direct their own learning, to go to school or not as they choose, does not mean that the law would forbid the parents to express an opinion or wish or strong desire on the matter. It only means that if their natural authority is not strong enough the parents can't call in the cops to make the child do what they are not able to persuade him to do. And the law may say that there is no limit to the amount of pressure or coercion the parents can apply to the child to deny him a choice that he has a legal right to make.

When I urge that children should control their learning, there is one argument that people bring up so often that I feel I must anticipate and meet it here. It says that schools are a place where children can for a while be protected against the bad influences of the world outside, particularly from its greed, dishonesty, and commercialism. It says that in school children may have a glimpse of a higher way of life, of people acting from other and better motives than greed and fear. People say, "We know that society is bad enough as it is and that if children go out into the larger world as soon as they wanted, they would be tempted and corrupted just that much sooner."

They seem to believe that schools are better, more honorable places than the world outside—what a friend of mine at Harvard once called "museums of virtue." Or that people in school, both children and adults, act from higher and better motives than people outside. In this they are mistaken. There are, of course, some good schools. But on the whole, far from being the opposite of, or an antidote to, the world outside, with all its envy, fear, greed, and obsessive competitiveness, the schools are very much like it. If anything, they are worse, a terrible, abstract, simplified caricature of it. In the world outside the school, some work, at least, is done honestly and well, for its own sake, not just to get ahead of others; people are not everywhere and always being set in competition against each other; people are not (or not yet) in every minute of their lives subject to the arbitrary, irrevocable orders and judgement of others. But in most schools, a student is every minute doing what others tell him, subject to their judgement, in situations in which he can only win at the expense of other students.

This is a harsh judgement. Let me say again, as I have before, that schools are worse than most of the people in them and that many of these people do many harmful things they would rather not do, and a great many other harmful things that they do not even see as harmful. The whole of school is much worse than the sum of its parts. There are very few people in the U.S. today (or perhaps anywhere, any time) in *any* occupation, who could be trusted with the kind of power that schools give most teachers over their students. Schools seem to me among the most anti-democratic, most authoritarian, most destructive, and most dangerous institutions of modern society. No other institution does more harm or more lasting harm to more people or destroys so much of their curiosity, independence, trust, dignity, and sense of identity and worth. Even quite kindly schools are inhibited and corrupted by the knowledge of children and teachers alike that they are *performing* for the judgement and approval of others—the children for the teachers; the teachers for the parents, supervisors, school board, or the state. No one is ever free from feeling that he is being judged all the time, or soon may be. Even after the best class experiences teachers must ask themselves, "Were we right to do that? Can we prove we were right? Will it get us in trouble?"

What corrupts the school, and makes it so much worse than most of the people in it, or than they would like it to be, is its power—just as their powerlessness corrupts the students. The school is corrupted by the endless anxious demand of the parents to know how their child is doing—meaning is he ahead of the other kids—and their demand that he be kept ahead. Schools do not protect children from the badness of the world outside. They are at least as bad as the world outside, and the harm they do to the children in their power creates much of the badness of the world outside. The sickness of the modern world is in many ways a school-induced sickness. It is in school that most people learn to expect and accept that some expert can always place them in some sort of rank or hierarchy. It is in school that we meet, become used to, and learn to believe in the totally controlled society. We do not learn much science, but we learn to worship "scientists" and to believe that anything we might conceivably need or want can only come, and someday will come, from them. The school is the closest we have yet been able to come to Huxley's *Brave New World*, with its alphas and betas, deltas and epsilons—and now it even has its soma. Everyone, including children, should have the right to say "No!" to it.

NO

Horace Mann

The Education of Free Men

I believe in the existence of a great, immutable principle of natural law, or natural ethics,—a principle antecedent to all human institutions and incapable of being abrogated by any ordinances of man,—a principle of divine origin, clearly legible in the ways of Providence as those ways are manifested in the order of nature and in the history of the race,—which proves the *absolute right* of every human being that comes into the world to an education; and which, of course, proves the correlative duty of every government to see that the means of that education are provided for all.

In regard to the application of this principle of natural law,—that is, in regard to the extent of the education to be provided for all, at the public expense, —some differences of opinion may fairly exist, under different political organizations; but under a republican government, it seems clear that the minimum of this education can never be less than such as is sufficient to qualify each citizen for the civil and social duties he will be called to discharge;—such an education as teaches the individual the great laws of bodily health; as qualifies for the fulfillment of parental duties; as is indispensable for the civil functions of a witness or a juror; as is necessary for the voter in municipal affairs; and finally, for the faithful and conscientious discharge of all those duties which devolve upon the inheritor of a portion of the sovereignty of this great republic....

In obedience to the laws of God and to the laws of all civilized communities, society is bound to protect the natural life; and the natural life cannot be protected without the appropriation and use of a portion of the property which society possesses. We prohibit infanticide under penalty of death. We practise a refinement in this particular. The life of an infant is inviolable even before he is born; and he who feloniously takes it, even before birth, is as subject to the extreme penalty of the law, as though he had struck down manhood in its vigor, or taken away a mother by violence from the sanctuary of home, where she blesses her offspring. But why preserve the natural life of a child, why preserve unborn embryos of life, if we do not intend to watch over and to protect them, and to expand their subsequent existence into usefulness and happiness? As individuals, or as an organized community, we have no natural right; we can derive no authority or countenance from reason; we can cite no attribute or purpose of the divine nature, for giving birth to any human being,

From Horace Mann, *Tenth Annual Report* and *Twelfth Annual Report* (1846, 1848).

and then inflicting upon that being the curse of ignorance, of poverty and of vice, with all their attendant calamities. We are brought then to this startling but inevitable alternative. The natural life of an infant should be extinguished as soon as it is born, or the means should be provided to save that life from being a curse to its possessor; and therefore every State is bound to enact a code of laws legalizing and enforcing Infanticide, or a code of laws establishing Free Schools! . . .

—◦◉◦—

Under the Providence of God, our means of education are the grand machinery by which the "raw material" of human nature can be worked up into inventors and discoverers, into skilled artisans and scientific farmers, into scholars and jurists, into the founders of benevolent institutions, and the great expounders of ethical and theological science. By means of early education, those embryos of talent may be quickened, which will solve the difficult problems of political and economical law; and by them, too, the genius may be kindled which will blaze forth in the Poets of Humanity. Our schools, far more than they have done, may supply the Presidents and Professors of Colleges, and Superintendents of Public Instruction, all over the land; and send, not only into our sister states, but across the Atlantic, the men of practical science, to superintend the construction of the great works of art. Here, too, may those judicial powers be developed and invigorated, which will make legal principles so clear and convincing as to prevent appeals to force; and, should the clouds of war ever lower over our country, some hero may be found,—the nursling of our schools, and ready to become the leader of our armies,—that best of all heroes, who will secure the glories of a peace, unstained by the magnificent murders of the battle-field. . . .

Without undervaluing any other human agency, it may be safely affirmed that the Common School, improved and energized, as it can easily be, may become the most effective and benignant of all the forces of civilization. Two reasons sustain this position. In the first place, there is a universality in its operation, which can be affirmed of no other institution whatever. If administered in the spirit of justice and conciliation, all the rising generation may be brought within the circle of its reformatory and elevating influences. And, in the second place, the materials upon which it operates are so pliant and ductile as to be susceptible of assuming a greater variety of forms than any other earthly work of the Creator. The inflexibility and ruggedness of the oak, when compared with the lithe sapling or the tender germ, are but feeble emblems to typify the docility of childhood, when contrasted with the obduracy and intractableness of man. It is these inherent advantages of the Common School, which, in our own State, have produced results so striking, from a system so imperfect, and an administration so feeble. In teaching the blind, and the deaf and dumb, in kindling the latent spark of intelligence that lurks in an idiot's mind, and in the more holy work of reforming abandoned and outcast children, education has proved what it can do, by glorious experiments. These wonders, it has done in its infancy, and with the lights of a limited experience; but, when its faculties shall be fully developed, when it shall be trained to wield its mighty energies for the protection of society against the giant vices which now invade and torment it;—against intemperance, avarice, war, slavery, bigotry, the woes of want and the wickedness of waste,—then, there will not be a height to which these enemies of the race can escape, which it will not scale, nor a Titan among them all, whom it will not slay....

Now, surely, nothing but Universal Education can counter-work this tendency to the domination of capital and the servility of labor. If one class possesses all the wealth and the education, while the residue of society is ignorant and poor, it matters not by what name the relation between them may be called; the latter, in fact and in truth, will be the servile dependants and subjects of the former. But if education be equably diffused, it will draw property after it, by the strongest of all attractions; for such a thing never did happen, and never can happen, as that an intelligent and practical body of men should be permanently poor. Property and labor, in different classes, are essentially antagonistic; but property and labor, in the same class, are essentially fraternal. The people of Massachusetts have, in some degree, appreciated the truth, that the unexampled prosperity of the State,—its comfort, its competence, its general intelligence and virtue,—is attributable to the education, more or less perfect, which all its people have received; but are they sensible of a fact equally important?—namely, that it is to this same education that two thirds of the people are indebted for not being, to-day, the vassals of as severe a tyranny, in the form of capital, as the lower classes of Europe are bound to in the form of brute force.

Education, then, beyond all other devices of human origin, is the great equalizer of the conditions of men—the balance-wheel of the social machinery. I do not here mean that it so elevates the moral nature as to make men disdain and abhor the oppression of their fellow-men. This idea pertains to another of its attributes. But I mean that it gives each man the independence and the means, by which he can resist the selfishness of other men. It does better than to disarm the poor of their hostility towards the rich; it prevents being poor. Agrarianism is the revenge of poverty against wealth. The wanton destruction of the property of others,—the burning of hay-ricks and corn-ricks, the demolition of machinery, because it supersedes hand-labor, the sprinkling of vitriol on rich dresses,—is only agrarianism run mad. Education prevents both the revenge and the madness. On the other hand, a fellow-feeling for one's class or caste is the common instinct of hearts not wholly sunk in selfish regards for person, or for family. The spread of education, by enlarging the cultivated class or caste, will open a wider area over which the social feelings will expand; and, if this education should be universal and complete, it would do more than all things else to obliterate factitious distinctions in society....

But to all doubters, disbelievers, or despairers, in human progress, it may still be said, there is one experiment which has never yet been tried. It is an experiment which, even before its inception, offers the highest authority for its ultimate success. Its formula is intelligible to all; and it is as legible as though written in starry letters on an azure sky. It is expressed in these few and simple words:—"*Train up a child in the way he should go, and when he is old he will not depart from it.*" This declaration is positive. If the conditions are complied with, it makes no provision for a failure. Though pertaining to morals, yet, if the terms of the direction are observed, there is no more reason to doubt the result, than there would be in an optical or a chemical experiment.

But this experiment has never yet been tried. Education has never yet been brought to bear with one hundredth part of its potential force, upon the natures of children, and, through them, upon the character of men, and of the race. In all the attempts to reform mankind which have hitherto been made, whether by changing the frame of government, by aggravating or softening the severity of the penal code, or by substituting a government-created, for a God-created religion;—in all these attempts, the infantile and youthful mind, its amenability to influences, and the enduring and self-operating character of the influences it receives, have been almost wholly unrecognized. Here, then, is a new agency, whose powers are but just beginning to be understood, and whose mighty energies, hitherto, have been but feebly invoked; and yet, from our experience, limited and imperfect as it is, we do know that, far beyond any other earthly instrumentality, it is comprehensive and decisive. . . .

If, then, a government would recognize and protect the rights of religious freedom, it must abstain from subjugating the capacities of its children to any legal standard of religious faith, with as great fidelity as it abstains from con-trolling the opinions of men. It must meet the unquestionable fact, that the old spirit of religious domination is adopting new measures to accomplish its work, —measures, which, if successful, will be as fatal to the liberties of mankind, as those which were practised in by-gone days of violence and terror. These new measures are aimed at children instead of men. They propose to supersede the necessity of subduing free thought, *in the mind of the adult,* by forestalling the development of any capacity of free thought, *in the mind of the child.* They ex-pect to find it easier to subdue the free agency of children, by binding them in fetters of bigotry, than to subdue the free agency of men, by binding them in fetters of iron. For this purpose, some are attempting to deprive children of their right to labor, and, of course, of their daily bread, unless they will attend a government school, and receive its sectarian instruction. Some are attempting to withhold all means, even of secular education, from the poor, and thus pun-ish them with ignorance, unless, with the secular knowledge which they desire, they will accept theological knowledge which they condemn. Others, still, are striving to break down all free Public School systems, where they exist, and to prevent their establishment, where they do not exist, in the hope, that on the downfall of these, their system will succeed. The sovereign antidote against these machinations, is, Free Schools for all, and the right of every parent to determine the religious education of his children.

POSTSCRIPT

Should School Attendance Be Voluntary?

There are few arguments with making a free public education available to all children. But the value-laded question of whether or not education should be mandatory is another matter entirely. While it is true that public school attendance is not mandated for all children (U.S. Department of Education statistics indicate that private and parochial school enrollment now accounts for approximately 12 percent of the total K–12 enrollment of over 54,000,000), as a practical matter most children have the opportunity to attend public school only.

Although for some like Holt it is simply wrong to compel any form of school attendance, for others the issue involves the reality that American public schools are, in essence, government schools. By virtue of the Tenth Amendment of the United States Constitution and supported by historical practice and court decisions, each state has the legal authority and responsibility to establish and run a public school system. That the individual states (Hawaii is the lone exception) delegate operational responsibility for public schools to local authorities does not change the fact that those schools are legal extensions of the government.

Motivated by concerns regarding governmental authority, some of the most eloquent denunciations of compulsory education have been sociopolitical works, such as Paul Goodman's *Compulsory Mis-Education* (Horizon Press, 1964); Paulo Frier's *Pedagogy of the Oppressed* (Herder & Herder, 1970); Ivan Illich's *Deschooling Society* (Harper & Row, 1971); and John Taylor Gatto's *Dumbing Us Down: The Hidden Curriculum of Compulsory Schooling* (New Society Publishers, 1992).

Other critics of compulsory education are more concerned with what they see as the illogic of "trying to force someone to learn." They suggest that compulsory attendance, especially in high schools, only results in alienating those who do not want to attend, which in turn creates unnecessary problems for teachers, administrators, and the students who do wish to learn. Articles with this theme include Dennis L. Evans, "Treating Schools Like Police Holding Tanks," *Education Week* (February 9, 1994); Barry McGhan, "Compulsory School Attendance; An Idea Past Its Prime," *Forum* (Winter 1997) and "Choice and Compulsion," *Phi Delta Kappan* (April 1998); and Lynn Schnaiberg, "Staying Home From School," *Education Week* (June 12, 1996).

Works that support the public and societal purposes of universal schooling for all children as envisioned by Mann include John Goodlad, *In Praise of Education* (Teacher's College Press, 1997) and "Education and Democracy: Advancing the Agenda," *Phi Delta Kappan* (September 2000); and E. D. Hirsch, *The Schools We Need and Why We Don't Have Them* (Doubleday, 1996).

ISSUE 2

Is Citizenship Education Working in the Public Schools?

YES: Diane Stark Rentner, from "Public Schools and Citizenship," Paper of the Center on Education Policy (July 1998)

NO: Rosemary C. Salomone, from "Education for Democratic Citizenship," *Education Week* (March 22, 2000)

ISSUE SUMMARY

YES: Diane Stark Rentner, associate director for the Center on Educational Policy, argues that the American public school system is the only institution dedicated to educating "all of the children of all of the people" and as such it brings a sense of commonality and unity to a diverse society.

NO: Rosemary C. Salomone, a professor of law at St. John's University School of Law in Jamaica, New York, suggests that schools are failing to develop citizens of character and that the school itself must exist as a morally coherent community and as a microcosm of democracy.

From America's very origins as a nation, one of the fundamental purposes of its schools has been the inculcation in students of those attitudes and values held to be compatible with good citizenship. Benjamin Franklin (1674) in his treatise *On the Need for an Academy* stated, "The good Education of Youth has been esteemed by wise Men in all Ages, as the surest Foundation of both private Families and Commonwealths." There is little argument that education for citizenship is a legitimate function of the schools. John Dewey (cited in "Democracy, Chaos, and the New School Order," by Spencer Maxcy [Corwin Press, 1995]) posited that schools are social institutions and that their moral responsibility is to society. Concomitantly with the widely held agreement that schools should be involved in the socialization and citizenship training of students, there is an equally wide disagreement regarding what is entailed in being a "good citizen" in a democracy. Historically, such disagreement has led to competing and conflicting views regarding curriculum content and instructional approaches involved with preparation for citizenship. In today's schools, those historical disagreements are exacerbated by the increasing racial and ethnic diversity of the school-age population. No longer is there an unquestioning acceptance of the "melting pot" role of the school vis à vis cultural differences, and that fact alone makes the school's role in citizenship training more challenging.

But beyond challenges related to demographics, some critics of the public schools assert that the very nature of today's schools, and most especially secondary schools, is a breeding ground for attitudes that do not support active and effective participation as a citizen. Some critics, such as Michael Apple, Paolo Freire, and Cornel West (cited in "Race, Identity, and Representation in Education," by Cameron McCarthy and Warren Crichlow, [Routledge, 1993]) contend that schools find their purpose in helping to maintain the status quo between the empowered and the disempowered in U.S. society. This leads to strategies and practices aimed at producing docility and subservience among students and future citizens. In the following selection, Rosemary C. Salomone acknowledges the legitimacy of the public schools' role in the "preparation for democratic citizenship" but asserts that the development of character and citizenship cannot be done merely through history and social studies courses. Furthermore, schools are failing in this role because they do not embrace "the concept of the school as a democratizing institution."

In contrast to those like Salomone who believe that public schools are failing to help young people develop the characteristics of citizens who will contribute to a democratic society, there are others who contend that the opposite is true, that U.S. schools are indeed successful in this area. The following selection by Diane Stark Rentner is representative of arguments made by many advocates of public education. Her position regarding the development of citizenship is that the potential for divisiveness created by increasing diversity and ethnocentric insularity can only be successfully dealt with by public schools. Advocates of this position hold that it is only in the public schools where all children come together, and it is only the public schools that have a legally mandated responsibility to address citizenship issues. With citizenship development as well as with other areas of schooling, they argue that wide-scale successes can only be achieved by public schools. Capturing that sentiment is this statement from another Center on Education Policy essay (December 1998): "During earlier waves of immigration, public schools were the primary institutions responsible for building a common culture and teaching democratic values.... Whether our children and grandchildren will live in harmony or discord will be influenced in large part by their educational experiences."

 **YES**

Public Schools and Citizenship

[For] two years, the Center on Education Policy, the National PTA, and Phi Delta Kappa sponsored forums to discuss public schools in more than 60 local communities. At these meetings, participants often cited two essential purposes of public education. First, people want public schools to prepare students adequately for jobs or for postsecondary education. Second, people want schools to teach children to be good citizens.

Little attention has been given to that second purpose in the *national* debate about the effectiveness of public schools. Participants in our *local* forums have reminded us to look at both purposes of schooling—preparation for further education and employment and preparation for citizenship.

In the national debate, assertions have often been made that private schools can do a better job of educating children than public schools. Private schools can indeed offer a good education to some children, but public schools by their nature are better able both to educate most children and help them become good citizens. In fact, American democracy depends on public education achieving both purposes.

Historically, schools have prepared students to be good citizens in four ways:

1. teaching students about the role of government in the United States;
2. upholding civic values by teaching students to be good citizens and good neighbors;
3. equipping students with the civic skills they need to be effective participants in a representative democracy; and
4. promoting tolerance and respect for diverse peoples and different points of view.

Civic Education

The first facet of preparing good citizens is to teach students how American government functions. Through the courses they take, students learn the history of the United States, the concepts and operation of our political system, and the fundamental principles and values upon which our system of government is based. Students also learn how our government and political system compare with those of other nations. Through their course-work, and by the examples of teachers, principals, and other school officials, students learn what it takes to be good citizens.

Civic Character

Historically, one of the missions of American public schools has been to instill moral virtues in students that would help to make them good neighbors and good citizens. The early public schools (or "common schools" as they were known in the mid-1800's) used great literature—including religious writings, hero tales, and fables to instruct youth in moral behavior. While private religious schools have maintained their commitment to moral instruction, character education became less prominent in public schools during the 1960's and 1970's. But today, public schools are returning to promoting civic values among students by using stories that illustrate good character and encouraging teachers, principals, and other adults to interact with each other and with students in ways that reflect good civic character. Many public schools are also establishing rules for student conduct that promote such virtues as civility, individual responsibility, respect for the rights of others, respect for the law, open-mindedness, and tolerance—behavior that all citizens should possess in a democratic society.

Skills for Democracy

The survival of a representative democracy like the United States ultimately depends on having a large group of well-educated citizens who will participate responsibly in political and public life. Thus, a third facet of creating good citizens is to prepare students for their role in a democracy. Educated citizens have many important responsibilities in a representative democracy. They select able leaders, understand the issues upon which they will vote, act as a check on the potential excesses of the government, recognize corruption in leaders and take appropriate action, and are not swayed by those who would undermine our democracy. Representative government also demands well-educated citizens who are willing to serve as civic and political leaders of their community, city, state, or nation.

In this process, public schools have a particularly vital role which is not equaled by private education. Public schools are mandated in all state constitutions and are required to educate all children—rich, poor, middle income, immigrant, native-born, those with disabilities. Furthermore, all children are required to attend school. Nearly 90% of all children in America are educated in public schools (U.S. Department of Education, National Center for Education Statistic, *Digest of Education Statistics 1997*). Moreover, because public schools must educate "all who come," they offer all young people the opportunity to build their citizenship skills and thereby they help to ensure that our voters and leaders will come from all walks of life.

Students also learn about the functioning of a representative democracy through the schools themselves. Students can hone their participatory skills by serving on student councils or by running for class and student-body offices. Teachers often teach students about participatory democracy by allowing students to vote on issues that affect the classroom, work in teams, or lead class discussions. The nature of public schools gives students a unique opportunity to observe and participate in the democratic process first hand by following school board elections, or attending public meetings. Parents and other adults who volunteer in the schools or serve on school committees are other common examples of how the community is involved in making decisions about public schools.

Harmony and a More Perfect Union

A fourth, and often overlooked, facet of the citizenship role of public schools is to create harmony among a nation of diverse peoples. Attending public schools is one of the few experiences that people of different backgrounds share. In public schools, students are taught tolerance and respect for other races, ethnic groups, and religions, as well as for children with disabilities who usually receive their education in the regular classroom. In public schools with diverse student populations, students have the opportunity to learn and respect different points of view, to disagree amicably, and to reach livable compromises. In other words, public schools are the places where we all learn to get along with one another. Admittedly, not all public schools are meeting this ideal. Some schools are racially segregated. In other more integrated schools, students may self-segregate into like peer groups. But, in general, students in public schools have more exposure to different kinds of students than do students in private schools. For example, in school year 1993–94, nearly a third of children enrolled in public schools were racial or ethnic or ethnic minorities, but only about a fifth of private school students were minorities. (U.S. Department of Education, National Center for Education Statistics, *Schools and Staffing in the United States: A Statistical Profile 1993–94*)

This role of public schools in creating social harmony is becoming more essential as the nation becomes more heterogeneous, particularly due to recent immigration. In 1997, 73% of the U.S. population was White, 11% Hispanic, 12% Black, and 4% Asian. By 2050, the population is projected to be 53% White, 25% Hispanic, 14% Black, and 8% Asian. (*The Washington Post*, "One Nation Indivisible: Is It History," William Booth, February 22, 1998.) The United States was faced with similar major social challenges in the past, most notably the massive waves of immigration during the early decades of the 20th century. These immigrants had to be assimilated into American society, and public schools were a critical means of creating a common culture and teaching democratic virtues. We ignore this history at our peril.

Without public schools, children would most likely today attend schools that reflected their own racial, ethnic, religious, or economic background, much as in churches, social organizations, and other groups people join voluntarily. Without a common institution like the public schools that bring people together and promote tolerance and understanding, the nation would become more divided and people more fearful of those different from themselves. For example, some of the charter schools now being created are geared toward educating a particular ethnic group. In Michigan, one African-centered charter school starts the day with a pledge to "my African nation," while another charter school that was formerly an Armenian church school continues to enroll mostly children of Armenian descent. (*U.S. News and World Report,* April 27, 1998). While such schools can make positive contributions by focusing on cultures that may be overlooked in mainstream America, where do we draw the line? How many groups will seek their own schools, promoting their own cultures, and isolating their children from those with different backgrounds?

Conclusion

It is natural for parents, policymakers, business leaders, and other adults to care whether public schools are doing a good job of preparing students for work or college. But in the process, all of us must also remember that public schools play a key role in maintaining our democracy. Public schools are uniquely positioned to provide an education to all children, to equip students with the skills they need to participate in a democracy, and to be an instrument of harmony in our society.

Public schools have been and continue to be one of the most important institutions for maintaining our freedoms and democracy. The vast majority of Americans—both leaders and ordinary citizens—are products of the public schools. The country's economic success, the nation's military prowess, and our influence throughout the world have been forged mainly by graduates of public schools. Without public schools, our nation would become more divided and less devoted to the democratic process, and the nation's leaders would be less representative of all segments of the U.S. population.

It would be the ultimate irony of modern history if America should dissolve the unifying glue of public education and splinter along ethnic and religious lines just at the time that many of the world's emerging democracies are looking to the United States and its institutions as role models for building their nations.

Rosemary C. Salomone  **NO**

Education for Democratic Citizenship

O ver the past decade, pollsters and pundits have raised warning flags of moral decay and declining political understanding and commitment among Americans. Scandals from Washington to Wall Street, voter apathy and cynicism, and the regeneration of the "me generation" in a climate of unprecedented prosperity have raised increasing concerns in the media over the moral state of the country. The most alarming evidence has emerged from education, validating and documenting the anxieties that Americans share over the failure of schools to create citizens of character. By the mid-1990s, half of the nation's high school students reported that drugs and violence were a serious problem in their schools, while seven in 10 unabashedly noted that cheating on tests and assignments was commonplace. In fact, two-thirds of high school students admitted that they had cheated on an exam the previous year, while only 33 percent strongly agreed that "honesty is the best policy." More than six in 10 adults deplored the failure of young people to learn such values as honesty, respect, and responsibility. In communities across the country, Americans ranked character development second only to basic skills in a listing of educational purposes.

More current findings sound an equally troubling note. Not only do the nation's young people lack a moral compass but also, according to the recently published results of the 1998 congressionally mandated National Assessment of Educational Progress [NAEP] civics exam, they only vaguely comprehend the underlying principles of democracy and constitutional government. In the first such assessment in 10 years, slightly more than 20 percent of students in the 4th, 8th, and 12th grades scored at the "proficient" level, a strikingly poor performance that must give educators and the general public pause. Add to this a rash of school violence nationwide, and what emerges is a grim picture of a society unable to produce informed and ethical citizens. In recent years, in response to the perceived crisis in public and private morality, educators across the nation have worked their way through the political and pedagogical minefields that surround values education to create programs that affect character. Judging from media reports, the NAEP results undoubtedly will generate a similar flurry of activity surrounding civics education. Both approaches are bound together by a basic belief that schools have an obligation to instill in students

From Rosemary C. Salomone, "Education for Democratic Citizenship," *Education Week*, vol. 19, no. 28 (March 22, 2000). Copyright © 2000 by Rosemary C. Salomone. Reprinted by permission of *Education Week* and the author.

a core of common values and shared understandings that define us as a nation. Both approaches are clearly well-intentioned and important. However, despite the efforts of some educational leaders to underscore the importance of institutional process, the conventional discussion focuses on curricular substance, consequently missing a critical point about the nature of schooling and learning. I suggest that, instead of merely talking about developing character as if it were akin to teaching math skills or fluency in a foreign language or a list of vocabulary words, and instead of concentrating solely on the content of the social studies and history curriculum, we should broaden the discussion to include the concept of the school as a democratizing institution and the notion of education for democratic citizenship. What I mean here is an education that instills in students those core political beliefs and values drawn from liberal principles of individual rights and the republican ideal of civic virtue.

⋙⊙⋘

This is not a novel idea. The indissoluble link between education and a good society dates back to ancient Greece. The Greek *paideia,* or concept of education, joined citizenship and learning around a shared set of norms and values under the legal and moral authority of the *politeia,* or prevailing culture.

In modern times, Thomas Jefferson fervently promoted government-supported schooling as an instrument for creating citizens of virtue and intelligence who could realize republican and democratic ideals. Early school reformers from Horace Mann to John Dewey espoused the belief that education should develop in students a common faith, albeit through markedly different processes, one tied to the values of mainstream Protestantism imposed by the school and the other secular in orientation and based in rational thought.

More recently, the U.S. Supreme Court repeatedly has affirmed that preparation for democratic citizenship is the primary end of state-supported education. In case after case, the justices have noted that schools are the mechanism through which society "inculcate[s] the habits and manners of civility as ... indispensable to the practice of self-government," that they are "vitally important for inculcating fundamental values necessary to the maintenance of a democratic political system," and that they are "the most pervasive means for promoting our common destiny." Whether we agree or disagree with the court's changing perspective on schooling over the past three decades—from a rights-based to a governance-based ideology—the truth remains that schooling is an inherently indoctrinative process that conveys explicit and implicit messages. If schools are to promote the ends of democracy, they must direct these messages toward developing in students the values and understandings they need to participate effectively in democratic government.

⋙⊙⋘

Discussion of values inevitably evokes the question, "Whose values?" Needless to say, schools have been battered in the "culture wars" of recent years by conflicting worldviews and visions of the good life. Most of these disputes have centered on controversial social norms—from teenage sexuality to alternative lifestyles, gender roles, and religious expression in the schools. Despite differences at the margins, however, most Americans would agree that there exists a set of core democratic values that bind us together as a nation.

Such a list, while not meant to be exhaustive, might include such incontestable moral virtues or character traits as honesty, integrity, responsibility, perseverance, and self-discipline, combined with social values such as concern for those less fortunate and more fundamental political principles generally imparted through what we commonly call "civics education." Included among these principles are justice and fairness, freedom of conscience and belief, freedom of expression, political and religious tolerance, and equality in the sense of equal dignity for all. While not immune from attack by the political extremes, these shared commitments draw from several sources, including our common history and folklore, and most significantly from legal norms reflected in the U.S. Constitution, federal statutes, and court interpretations.

Having established the fact that schools, as socializing agents, should convey democratic values, then how should they go about the task? Some character education advocates would suggest that schools adopt a packaged curriculum or teach specified virtues through purposeful moralistic instruction. While such a didactic approach might be appropriate for conveying factual knowledge about government and history, it belies the fact that values and political commitment cannot be partitioned off into a discrete part of the curriculum. To the contrary, ethical or value considerations and civic understandings permeate the entire educational process.

First of all, schools already possess myriad resources and opportunities for developing values throughout the existing educational program, from science to literature and history. But more importantly, for values to be meaningful, they must infuse the entire school experience, including not just the overt but also the "hidden" curriculum. The governance structure of the school (hierarchical or democratic); the grading system (numbers, letters, or anecdotal reports); the range and perspective of extracurricular activities (karate, chess, hockey, or photography); the role models that teachers provide, including their mode of dress and affect; the importance and substance of exams; the student dress code, if any; the layout of the classrooms (lecture- or seminar-style); instructional styles (individual or cooperative)—all of these factors are value-laden and send subtle but powerful messages to students.

This is not to deny that students need to consciously learn the ideals and history of a free society. They need to develop an understanding and appreciation of the processes of self-government by carefully examining and deliberating over the functioning of a democratic community. But in a more real sense, students can best internalize democratic values by living them and not merely by talking about them. As Aristotle tells us, we need to practice virtue in order to become virtuous. The same can be said for the broader range of democratic understandings. In fact, the NAEP data reveal that students with real-world experiences, such as 12th graders who had engaged in community service, actually outperformed those who had not. Of course, one can question whether these results indicate a causative effect or merely a correlation between interest in community service and political concerns.

The issue, however, is larger than the individual class or subject matter. The school itself must exist as a morally coherent community and as a microcosm of democracy, creating a cohesive institutional ethos that persistently reinforces notions of democratic rights and responsibilities at all levels.

For example, schools should reconsider the concept of the "disciplinary" code and replace it with an overarching "behavior" code, developed through a democratic process involving the various constituents, that incorporates behavioral standards for both staff and students and that reflects core democratic values of justice and fairness. If teachers fail to interact with students in a respectful manner, or neglect to clearly inform students of the standards on which their academic performance will be assessed, or close their eyes to cheating or plagiarism, they convey values antithetical to democratic principles. If the sports program suggests, explicitly or implicitly, that winning is paramount and that the rules of good sportsmanship are to be broken whenever possible, school officials are fostering and legitimizing unethical attitudes that students will carry into adult life. If schools engage in "social promotion," they negate the value of diligence and competition, not to mention the negative impact on students' self-esteem and self-worth, although the intent might be opposite. On the other hand, retaining students without having earnestly afforded them the tools to succeed violates fundamental precepts of fair process. No amount of classroom instruction can erase the lessons of these experiences, lessons that harm the individual and ultimately society.

Rather than mandate community service for secondary students—a practice that some students rail against as intrusive and unfair, while others at the opposite extreme embrace in self-interest as a means of enhancing college applications— schools should develop in the youngest students an ethic of care that naturally induces them as adolescents to voluntarily serve their community. And rather than present community service as a self-standing requirement for graduation, schools could create a more meaningful experience by tying it to the instructional program through organized service learning. Here students should have the opportunity to study a social problem (for example, the homeless), to engage in action that addresses the problem (working in a shelter), and to reflect on their particular experience and more general issues of social justice and civic responsibility through writing and group discussion.

Perhaps public schools should adopt the practice, common in the private school sector, of expressly articulating a "mission" or statement of purposes from which all policies, practices, behavior, and instruction consciously flow. An advertisement recently appearing in a local New York City newspaper, juxtaposed with the NAEP results, brought this notion to mind. Clearly intended as a recruitment device for a private, independent K–8 school, the ad explicitly touted the school's emphasis on providing students with "the tools to make the right choices that will create responsible citizens." It talked about the need for children to "hear the same message" regarding the values shared by the home and the school, including honesty, fairness, giving of oneself and sharing, truth-telling, respect for oneself and for others, appreciation of differences, good citizenship, and civility.

I cannot attest to the fact that the school actually delivers on these commitments. What struck me, however, was the fact that this school had a clearly defined mission to educate for citizenship, and it conveyed to parents the clear message that they are partners in that process.

I fully realize the vast distinctions between public schools that serve all and the selectivity of private schools, as well as the levels of parent participation each realistically can garner. Nevertheless, schools serving students at the lowest economic extreme bear an even greater responsibility for creating a community of meaning within the school itself, particularly where the surrounding community provides scarce social capital from which to draw. On the other hand, while privileged children may come to school with a broad understanding of history and government from repeated exposure in the home, teaching them to be ethical and caring individuals in a culture of hyped consumerism and competitive individualism presents its own challenges.

For schools across the economic spectrum, both public and private, a clear statement of purposes focused on democratic values, civil behavior, and community responsibility presents a first step toward creating a democratically infused school climate.

Next to the family, education is the most powerful socializing agent in society. Any project that aims to address the current crisis in democratic values and knowledge among young people must seriously consider institutional process—that is, the way schools are organized and governed and the way teaching and learning take place—and not merely the substance of the formal curriculum as we conventionally know it.

POSTSCRIPT

Is Citizenship Education Working in the Public Schools?

While *"e pluribus unum"* ("one out of many") provides a wonderful vision for America, it also poses monumental challenges for those who try to operationalize it in schools. The concomitant responsibilities of schools to respect and preserve ethnic, racial, and cultural diversity while at the same time promoting citizenship training and unity provide a daunting example of such challenges. While the very essence of a democracy includes qualities such as pluralism and respect for diversity, such qualities are not always seen as being compatible with citizenship. This incompatibility is obvious at a semantic level: pluralism and diversity denote differences whereas citizenship stresses similarities; pluralism and diversity invite separatism whereas citizenship connotes unity; pluralism and diversity honor individuality whereas citizenship speaks to community. But regardless of the difficulty in combining the two concepts it is evident that the American public wants it done. In the 1999 Phi Delta Kappa/Gallup Poll of the Public's Attitudes Toward the Public Schools, 93 percent of respondents thought that "democracy" should be taught in the schools, 93 percent thought that "acceptance of people of different races and ethnic backgrounds" should be taught, and 90 percent thought that "patriotism and love of country" should be taught.

Works that deal with particular aspects of this topic include *American Education,* 9th ed., by Joel Spring (McGraw-Hill, 1998); *School and Society,* by Steven Tozer, Paul Violas, and Guy Senese (McGraw-Hill, 1998); *Cultural Foundations of Education,* 3rd ed. by Young Pai and Susan Adler (Prentice Hall, 2000); *Educating for Diversity: An Anthology of Multicultural Voices,* Carl Grant, ed. (Allyn & Bacon, 1995); and *The Disuniting of America,* by Arthur Schlesinger (Whittle Communications, 1991).

Additionally, professional organizations, such as the National Council for the Social Studies, have position statements on citizenship education, as do individual state curriculum guides. Other sources of commentary on the topic can be found in widely circulated professional journals and periodicals, such as the February 1997 issue of *Educational Leadership,* which focuses on "Education for Democratic Life"; the June 1991 issue of *Phi Delta Kappan,* which includes Henry Boyte's "Community Service and Civil Education"; and the September 1999 issue of *American School Board Journal,* which includes Alfie Kohn's "Constant Frustration and Occasional Violence: The Legacy of American High Schools."

ISSUE 3

Should All Secondary School Students Experience the Same Curriculum?

YES: Robert M. Hutchins, from *The Conflict in Education in a Democratic Society* (Harper & Row, 1953)

NO: Theodore R. Sizer, from "No Two Are Quite Alike," *Educational Leadership* (September 1999)

ISSUE SUMMARY

YES: Robert M. Hutchins, former chancellor at the University of Chicago and a proponent of the Great Books curriculum, argues for a liberal education and states that "if all men are to be free, all men must have this education."

NO: Theodore R. Sizer, University Professor Emeritus at Brown University and chairman of the Coalition of Essential Schools, states that what one studies is less important than that it sparks legitimate interest in each learner.

Certainly the debate over this issue represents an ongoing collision of philosophies and values at a very core level. It represents the essentialist position on education versus that of existentialist; it is the classicist's viewpoint versus that of the progressive. Since the issue does address strongly held beliefs regarding the purposes of education, it goes without saying that it also engenders strong political responses. Indeed the politicized slogan of "back to the basics," as manifested in legislative mandates for a "standards based curriculum," seems to signal the ascendancy of the common curriculum advocates. The goal of individualization and personalization of curriculum and instruction may still be articulated in educational journals, but policymakers do not currently hold it in high regard.

Even where efforts are being made to reduce class and/or school size the rationale is more often than not tied to enabling teachers to deal with fewer students and thus improve achievement and bring up test scores rather than providing greater opportunities to individualize and personalize.

This argument started to generate heat early in the twentieth century when secondary education was coming to be recognized as important for all adolescents and not just for the college bound. With that recognition came the commonsense understanding that secondary education would be the terminal educational experience for many or, as stated by Ernest Boyer in his book *High School* (Harper & Row, 1983), "The high school had, in fact, become the people's college." Concomitant with those realizations it was deemed necessary that secondary education should become an end unto itself rather than simply a college preparatory experience. In 1918, the Commission on the Reorganization of Secondary Education issued its report on *The Cardinal Principles of Secondary Education,* which expanded the role of the high school beyond the "command of fundamental processes" into areas of "health, worthy home membership, and the use of leisure time." These principles reflected the views of John Dewey and began to be translated into curricular practices aimed at educating the "whole child." With this "progressive philosophy" came various elective courses aimed at different aspects of "life adjustment."

But as it is with many educational movements, say many, the "progressive" ideas of Dewey were eventually transmogrified by overzealous advocates whose programs then became easy targets for criticism, such as that leveled in 1953 by University of Illinois history professor Arthur E. Bestor, who charged that schools, in attempting to provide "something for everyone, had in reality provided little for anyone." That this argument continues unabated can be seen in the most recent secondary education reform document in California (*Second to None* [California Dept. of Education, 1992]), in which the phrase "shopping mall high school" was used pejoratively to describe the alleged weaknesses of the secondary curriculum in that state.

The Basis of Education

The obvious failures of the doctrines of adaptation, immediate needs, social reform, and of the doctrine that we need no doctrine at all may suggest to us that we require a better definition of education. Let us concede that every society must have some system that attempts to adapt the young to their social and political environment. If the society is bad, in the sense, for example, in which the Nazi state was bad, the system will aim at the same bad ends. To the extent that it makes men bad in order that they may be tractable subjects of a bad state, the system may help to achieve the social ideals of the society. It may be what the society wants; it may even be what the society needs, if it is to perpetuate its form and accomplish its aims. In pragmatic terms, in terms of success in the society, it may be a "good" system.

But it seems to me clearer to say that, though it may be a system of training, or instruction, or adaptation, or meeting immediate needs, it is not a system of education. It seems clearer to say that the purpose of education is to improve men. Any system that tries to make them bad is not education, but something else. If, for example, democracy is the best form of society, a system that adapts the young to it will be an educational system. If despotism is a bad form of society, a system that adapts the young to it will not be an educational system, and the better it succeeds in adapting them the less educational it will be.

Every man has a function as a man. The function of a citizen or a subject may vary from society to society, and the system of training, or adaptation, or instruction, or meeting immediate needs may vary with it. But the function of a man as man is the same in every age and in every society, since it results from his nature as a man. The aim of an educational system is the same in every age and in every society where such a system can exist: it is to improve man as man.

If we are going to talk about improving men and societies, we have to believe that there is some difference between good and bad. This difference must not be, as the positivists think it is, merely conventional. We cannot tell this difference by any examination of the effectiveness of a given program as the pragmatists propose; the time required to estimate these effects is usually too long and the complexity of society is always too great for us to say that the consequences of a given program are altogether clear. We cannot discover the difference between good and bad by going to the laboratory, for men and societies are not laboratory animals. If we believe that there is no truth, there is no knowledge, and there are no values except those which are validated by laboratory experiment, we cannot talk about the improvement of men and societies, for we can have no standard of judging anything that takes place among men or in societies.

Society is to be improved, not by forcing a program of social reform down its throat, through the schools, or otherwise, but by the improvement of the individuals who compose it. As Plato said, "Governments reflect human nature. States are not made out of stone or wood, but out of the characters of their citizens: these turn the scale and draw everything after them." The individual is the heart of society....

Man is by nature free, and he is by nature social. To use his freedom rightly he needs discipline. To live in society he needs the moral virtues. Good moral and intellectual habits are required for the fullest development of the nature of man.

To develop fully as a social, political animal man needs participation in his own government. A benevolent despotism will not do. You cannot expect the slave to show the virtues of the free man unless you first set him free. Only democracy, in which all men rule and are ruled in turn for the good life of the whole community, can be an absolutely good form of government....

Education deals with the development of the intellectual powers of men. Their moral and spiritual powers are the sphere of the family and the church. All three agencies must work in harmony; for, though a man has three aspects, he is still one man. But the schools cannot take over the role of the family and the church without promoting the atrophy of those institutions and failing in the task that is proper to the schools.

We cannot talk about the intellectual powers of men, though we can talk about training them, or amusing them, or adapting them, and meeting their immediate needs, unless our philosophy in general tells us that there is knowledge and that there is a difference between true and false. We must believe, too, that there are other means of obtaining knowledge than scientific experimentation. If knowledge can be sought only in the laboratory, many fields in which we thought we had knowledge will offer us nothing but opinion or superstition, and we shall be forced to conclude that we cannot know anything about the most important aspects of man and society. If we are to set about developing the intellectual powers of man through having them acquire knowledge of the most important subjects, we have to begin with the proposition that experimentation and empirical data will be of only limited use to us, contrary to the convictions of many American social scientists, and that philosophy, history, literature, and art give us knowledge, and significant knowledge, on the most significant issues.

If the object of education is the improvement of men, then any system of education that is without values is a contradiction in terms. A system that seeks bad values is bad. A system that denies the existence of values denies the possibility of education. Relativism, scientism, skepticism, and anti-intellectualism, the four horsemen of the philosophical apocalypse, have produced that chaos in education which will end in the disintegration of the West.

The prime object of education is to know what is good for man. It is to know the goods in their order. There is a hierarchy of values. The task of education is to help us understand it, establish it, and live by it. This Aristotle had in mind when he said: "It is not the possessions but the desires of men that must be equalized, and this is impossible unless they have a sufficient education according to the nature of things."

Such an education is far removed from the triviality of that produced by the doctrines of adaptation, of immediate needs, of social reform, or of the doctrine of no doctrine at all. Such an education will not adapt the young to a bad environment, but it will encourage them to make it good. It will not overlook immediate needs, but it will place these needs in their proper relationship to more distant, less tangible, and more important goods. It will be the only effective means of reforming society.

This is the education appropriate to free men. It is liberal education. If all men are to be free, all men must have this education. It makes no difference how they are to earn their living or what their special interests or aptitudes may be. They can learn to make a living, and they can develop their special interests and aptitudes, after they have laid the foundation of free and responsible manhood through liberal education. It will not do to say that they are incapable of such education. This claim is made by those who are too indolent or unconvinced to make the effort to give such education to the masses.

Nor will it do to say that there is not enough time to give everybody a liberal education before he becomes a specialist. In America, at least, the waste and frivolity of the educational system are so great that it would be possible through getting rid of them to give every citizen a liberal education and make him a qualified specialist, too, in less time than is now consumed in turning out uneducated specialists.

A liberal education aims to develop the powers of understanding and judgment. It is impossible that too many people can be educated in this sense, because there cannot be too many people with understanding and judgment. We hear a great deal today about the dangers that will come upon us through the frustration of educated people who have got educated in the expectation that education will get them a better job, and who then fail to get it. But surely this depends on the representations that are made to the young about what education is. If we allow them to believe that education will get them better jobs and encourage them to get educated with this end in view, they are entitled to a sense of frustration if, when they have got the education, they do not get the jobs. But, if we say that they should be educated in order to be men, and that everybody, whether he is ditch-digger or a bank president, should have this education because he is a man, then the ditch-digger may still feel frustrated, but not because of his education.

Nor is it possible for a person to have too much liberal education, because it is impossible to have too much understanding and judgment. But it is possible to undertake too much in the name of liberal education in youth. The object of liberal education in youth is not to teach the young all they will ever need to know. It is to give them the habits, ideas, and techniques that they need to continue to educate themselves. Thus the object of formal institutional liberal education in youth is to prepare the young to educate themselves throughout their lives.

I would remind you of the impossibility of learning to understand and judge many of the most important things in youth. The judgment and understanding of practical affairs can amount to little in the absence of experience with practical affairs. Subjects that cannot be understood without experience should not be taught to those who are without experience. Or, if these subjects are taught to those who are without experience, it should be clear that these subjects can be taught only by way of introduction and that their value to the student depends on his continuing to study them as he acquires experience. The tragedy in America is that economics, ethics, politics, history, and literature are studied in youth, and seldom studied again. Therefore the graduates of American universities seldom understand them.

This pedagogical principle, that subjects requiring experience can be learned only by the experienced, leads to the conclusion that the most important branch of education is the education of adults. We sometimes seem to think of education as something like the mumps, measles, whooping cough, or chicken pox. If a person has had education in childhood, he need not, in fact he cannot, have it again. But the pedagogical principle that the most important things can be learned only in mature life is supported by a sound philosophy in general. Men are rational animals. They achieve their terrestrial felicity by the use of reason. And this means that they have to use it for their entire lives. To say that they should learn only in childhood would mean that they were human only in childhood.

And it would mean that they were unfit to be citizens of a republic. A republic, a true *res publica*, can maintain justice, peace, freedom, and order only by the exercise of intelligence. When we speak of the consent of the governed, we mean, since men are not angels who seek the truth intuitively and do not have to learn it, that every act of assent on the part of the governed is a product of learning. A republic is really a common educational life in process. So Montesquieu said that, whereas the principle of a monarchy was honor, and the principle of a tyranny was fear, the principle of a republic was education.

Hence the ideal republic is the republic of learning. It is the utopia by which all actual political republics are measured. The goal toward which we started with the Athenians twenty-five centuries ago is an unlimited republic of learning and a worldwide political republic mutually supporting each other.

All men are capable of learning. Learning does not stop as long as a man lives, unless his learning power atrophies because he does not use it. Political freedom cannot endure unless it is accompanied by provision for the unlimited acquisition of knowledge. Truth is not long retained in human affairs without continual learning and relearning. Peace is unlikely unless there are continuous, unlimited opportunities for learning and unless men continuously avail themselves of them. The world of law and justice for which we yearn, the worldwide political republic, cannot be realized without the worldwide republic of learning. The civilization we seek will be achieved when all men are citizens of the world republic of law and justice and of the republic of learning all their lives long.

NO

Theodore R. Sizer

No Two Are Quite Alike

People differ. Thank goodness they do. How boring the world would be if we were all the same—clones, predictable in our progression through life. Much of the progress of humankind has come because of the restlessness of persons who have stepped beyond the predictable mold. The differences among us have provided the pepper upon which modern society depends.

Those of us who have made our careers in secondary education are daily confronted with a cacophony of difference. Yesterday's little, dutiful William is today's sprawling, sloppy Billy Boy. The noisy kid over there used to be a quiet cherub. The shy, intense girl over here used to be fascinated with science but today seems fascinated with nothing at all. The distracted, tough-talking kid in the corner used to be a bouncy little boy endlessly looking for attention. Hormones cause sprouting of all sorts, the sprouts changing not only how an adolescent looks, but also how that adolescent perceives himself or herself. The dutiful in October become the rude in April. The gigglers of September become the sirens of May.

So has it always been. The load is heavy on each young person to decide which mask to wear for which audience, which ideals to care about, what to believe in and whom to believe, what to aspire for, or even whether to "aspire" at all. No one wants to be a clone. We have our role models, but each of us wants to be someone special. We insist upon our difference, and it is right that we do so. Without difference, our culture and our economy would shrivel. Without citizens who feel that each has something special to offer, we would have a culture without vitality.

A Rigid System

Ironically, for a century, secondary schools in the United States have been built on the assumption that all children should, save those at the carefully defined "special" margins, be treated more or less alike.

Students are categorized by their ages. You were born in June 1985, you are 14 now, so you are a 9th grader. If you were born in December, you are an 8th grader, still in middle school. That is, unless you are in a school district with different cut-off dates.

From Theodore R. Sizer, "No Two Are Quite Alike," *Educational Leadership* (September 1999). Copyright © 1999 by The Association for Supervision and Curriculum Development. Reprinted by permission of *Educational Leadership* and the author; permission conveyed through Copyright Clearance Center.

Grade level counts, socially and academically. There is 9th grade social studies and 10th grade history. There is honors history, but you have to be a 10th grader to get into it. Yes, a few 10th graders take AP classes along with 11th and 12th graders, exceptions that prove the rule. Age relentlessly counts. Anything special beyond that is a matter of exceptional negotiation.

If you are a 10th grader in Massachusetts, you take the MCAS (Massachusetts Comprehensive Assessment System) tests. If you had been born but a few months earlier, you took that test last year. The MCAS is administered in a rigorously consistent way to all students of a certain grade, this in the name of fairness. Of course, one student may feel ill on examination day. Another might be intellectually adept but less able to express that power in a timed, carefully channeled testing routine than in another sort of setting. Yet another glories in the orchestrated, hushed pressure that the testing site reflects, a seriousness often lacking in class discussions. However, such differences make no dent in the testing "instrument." One size fits all; one score makes or breaks one's reputation.

The hold of age grading on the consciousness of the education system is ferocious. The metaphor of steps on a ladder dominates: Learning is always to be a sequential act, block building on block. One must travel up those stairs. There must be no "social promotion."

There is, of course, logic in some of this. You cannot do well at calculus without algebra. It is unlikely that you will create a persuasive 10-page essay unless you can craft a persuasive paragraph. However, such sequencing does not always hold in every field, most obviously in the arts. And sometimes people leapfrog, seemingly serendipitously—a student "gets" a connection among characters in a play, a proof in mathematics, a sophisticated legal argument arising from a historical incident. Such a student doesn't fit in.

The traditional high school confines itself in other ways, including pigeonholing the members of its staff. All of us have specialties. I am a teacher of mathematics. I am a counselor. I am a Dean of Students. I teach physical education and coach lacrosse. I teach art. No one of us, save the students and the librarian, is to express and be held accountable for a general education—even as a "general education" is the ultimate goal for the students. As a science teacher, I do not have to show any interest, much less competence, in the arts; indeed, I can be audibly contemptuous of them.

The school routines through which the student passes reflect this confinement. Little has much to do with anything else. Success at high school is measured by an accretion of scores in subjects taught largely in isolation from one another. A student can have a personal style or a consuming interest as long as it fits the prescribed pattern, but there is precious little room for the student who might harbor interests not reflected by a particular school's division of faculty labor. Again, in many schools, exceptions are made. They remain exceptions, however. Unless an aggressive student or his or her parents or an influential teacher pushes for an exception, nothing happens. There is little incentive for intellectual idiosyncrasy or social idiosyncrasy.

Authentic Options

Does this sound familiar? There are explanations for each piece of the enormously complicated comprehensive high school. Ironically, one reason for the complexity is to accommodate "individual differences"—to make various curricular paths (however age graded and compartmentalized) available for students to match with their likely destinations in life. The school decides the worthy options to be available for all students and then counsels each one (usually advisors who carry loads of 100 to 300 students do this) to take what appears to be the most sensible path. Each path is carefully demarcated and usually age graded (Powell, Farrar, & Cohen, 1985).

Something for everybody is the ideal of the U.S. high school. But options are different from personalization, from taking each young person where he or she is and imaginatively using that understanding. Personalization requires knowing each young person well. If we can achieve that goal, then flexible options among programs make sense. However, options offered without knowing the students well are not authentic options at all.

We all understand this poignantly when we fall ill. If our physician does not know our condition well, how can he or she prescribe a proper treatment? By the same token, if our counselor does not know our minds and dispositions well, how can he or she prescribe a likely regimen?

Facing up to the rigidities of high school is fiercely difficult work. It is not that most educators do not know that "whole school change," especially at the secondary level, is compellingly needed. It is because everything important in a school affects everything else that may be important. When one tries to refashion one part of a school, most other parts unravel. As a result, most reform efforts avoid that prospect and settle for tinkering, often very imaginatively, at the margins—a revised course here, an alternative program there, great gobs of professional development.

However, such tinkering never gets to the heart of the matter, especially if the goal is to know each student well and to use that knowledge in shaping and directioning that young person's education.

Realistic Student Loads

I cannot teach students well if I do not know them well. Each of my adolescent students is in the midst of a growth spurt and the struggle for independence that characterizes every person's route from childhood to adulthood. Each is a complex and evolving human being. Each learns in a somewhat different way; there are discrete "styles" and "intelligences," Robert Sternberg (1997; 1999), Howard Gardner (1983; 1999), and others tell us; their research squares with out experience in classrooms.

How many young people can I know and serve well at once? Assume that I meet with my students in groups each day, this absorbing the majority of my school-time hours. How many minutes a week, either sandwiched amid regular obligations into the school day or spent after school and at home, do I need to read and comment on each student's work and, periodically, to meet with him or her one-on-one? What would happen if I, on average, set aside 10 minutes a week for each student for this personal attention? That works out to an hour a week for every six students. If I have 120 students, that's 20 hours. Impossible.

If I have 50 students, that's a bit more than eight hours a week. Let's say that I, on average, see each student and his or her work every other week. That brings the load down to between four and five hours a week, assigning an hour (in snippets of time, at school or at home) each day to "personalization." Given my other obligations, that is a stretch, but, if I am reasonably experienced, an acceptable one.

But, I think, that is impossible! I then look at the number of students in my (typical) high school for each full-time equivalent professional staff person. It is 14:1. Given that ratio, I conclude, 50:1 for each teacher is possible, at least arithmetically. However, everyone at school is now working flat out. Something has to give. The only recourse is to simplify the school; to narrow its options; streamline its routines; and increase the number, authority, and responsibility of classroom teachers. But won't these narrowed options decrease the possibility of "personalization"? They will only if we do not define "personalization" as access to a set of free-standing separate programs.

A choice clearly emerges. "Personalization" can be a student's choice among a variety of special programs, but that forces most teachers to carry loads in excess of 100 students. Or "personalization" can start with loads half that size in a school where we can accommodate adaptations to individual needs within a simple, common program.

A Hobson's choice [the choice of taking either that which is offered or nothing]? Not necessarily. Paradoxically, simple, focused schools can provide more opportunities for individual students than can the more typical comprehensive high school.

Time and Scale

So I have my 50 students. I see them daily in groups, usually in classes of 15 to 25. My homeroom is largely drawn from this same group. I *know* these young people. They are not quick studies before me, two-dimensional characters. I hope to know their minds and dispositions well, so well that I can sense a change in mood, from engaged to disengaged, or from loneliness to joining in with friends—or whatever—when such appears to emerge.

"Knowing" young people this well results (perhaps paradoxically) in the realization that I never know them well enough: They are too complicated and changeable for that. To help me get the fuller picture, I need, at the least, the counsel of teachers who share these same kids. That means time to talk with those teachers and time to coordinate approaches to help each of the students and their families.

Impossible? It is possible if the design of the school is simple—and thus flexible—and common to all. Time for "talk about out kids" needs to be part of the schedule. If it is not, such talk will rarely happen.

The Authority to Act

All this "personalization" will come to naught if I and my colleagues who share students do not have the authority to act upon our conclusions about an individual or a group of students. Within the basic course of study (one kept sufficiently flexible to allow individual variations), we have to control our time and that of the students. Our decisions have to stick.

If we must always ask for permission or refer every change to higher authorities, there is no "personalization." The people providing the permission are those who, in fact, know the affected students the least. Higher authorities can monitor us (that is, surely, part of their job), and they can help us when we need help (also a part of their job). However, if we cannot control our own piece of turf within our school, we cannot readily act upon judgments arising from "personalization."

Complexity Within Simplicity

Few Americans would disagree with the proposition that each child should be exposed to the worlds of language, science, mathematics, the arts, and history. Within each discipline are a plethora of topics to study. A number of equally engaging topics cut across the disciplines. There is much to learn, far more than time to learn it. Further, we forget most of what we "cover" in school, retaining only that which we use or fragments that appeal to us. The important residue is an understanding of how a discipline works and habits in its use.

Understanding something—and being able to use it in unfamiliar situations—takes time. Engendering the habit of its use requires enough engagement with a discipline, on one's own terms, to be so persuaded of its efficacy that its use becomes almost second nature. Beyond the rudiments, what, in particular, one studies is less important than that it sparks legitimate interest in each learner. Without such interest, most adolescent students will not engage (and do not deeply engage, even as they may appear dutiful and as they may churn out "work" that gives evidence of immediate, limited engagement but not understanding).

My task as a teacher is to cajole each learner into an essential discipline both on the terms of that discipline and on the student's terms. I must interest the student in something that the society deeply believes is important and that the individual adolescent also senses—or can be persuaded to sense—is important. I must ram what is essential down the kid's throat and at the same time pander to his or her immediate interests.

To be successful at this, I must settle on some crucial common knowledge —reading *Romeo and Juliet,* watching *West Side Story,* and studying mid-20th century south Asia and the late 20th century Balkans, for example—as a way of addressing human conflict. Concurrently, I must find any and all means to gather into each student's consciousness and conscience a conflict that may deeply move that child, asking him or her to write about it, argue about it, understand it. If such a ploy works, it is an easy step, for example, to the reasons for and the design of democratic governments, including bills of rights. There are crucial connections here within history and the humanities. With different material, there are analogous ones in every domain. From the connections that I the teacher push forth and those that may energize a student can come serious learning.

Such activity takes time, more time than allotted in most high schools, where coverage is king. Grotesque coverage—Cleopatra to Clinton by April 1, three Shakespeare plays in six weeks, evolution as one of 36 chapters in an eight-pound biology textbook—is a recipe for teacher frustration, academic trivialization, and student detachment. Yes, we all "covered the material." We passed the test at the end. But, if such were ever given, we could not pass that test 18 months from now, and we could not explain what the purpose of the time we had earlier spent together might be. For most—all save those engaged by the standardized lesson—the time would have been largely wasted.

Give me the smallest defensible number of the absolutely most critical matters, disciplines, and skills that I should teach. Give me time, autonomy, supportive colleagues, and few enough students so that I can understand each one well enough to tailor some of my teaching to him or her—and I will show you students who perform well, today and tomorrow.

A simple program allows complex learning. A simple program makes possible the adaptations in teaching that arise from authentic personalization.

It is inconvenient that students learn in different ways and that they are attached to differing enthusiasms. But, unless we face up to that inconvenience, we will not teach well.

Progress by Performance

If strict age grading flies in the face of the commonsense experience of teachers and researchers, what is to replace grade levels? The only alternative is progress by performance. It means an individual educational plan for each student, not just the "handicapped" or the "precocious."

This approach is as difficult to accomplish as it is easy to embrace. Its practice demands that the school be clear on the shape, standards, and character of the "performance" and on the basis upon which such performance will be judged. Being clear on this is very hard and very unfamiliar work for teachers. We are more used to "U.S. History up to the Civil War" in the 10th grade or "Physics" in the 12th grade. The state frameworks or district curriculums are usually an amalgamation of "content" and "skills" to cover over a defined period of time. They rarely address—beyond necessarily constricted standardized paper-and-pencil tests—how the student expresses mastery or uses that mastery over time.

Further, few schools insist on the regular "cross grading" of papers by staff. In most schools, each teacher is assessment king in his or her classroom. "Cross grading"—the collective assessment of pieces of work by a variety of teachers, students, and parents—is very rare. So if a B does not mean the same to Ms. Schmidt as it does to Mr. Saginaw, what does a B at their school really mean? If Ms. Schmidt and Mr. Saginaw don't take the time to tune their standards, inequitable fuzziness will be the rule.

There must be agreement on what a student puts forth for consideration of the quality of his or her "performance," agreement that participants and outsiders constantly monitor. For obvious reasons, the students and their guardians must also understand the criteria for this performance. When "What is good enough?" is a question on the table, all sorts of issues emerge. Is what is appropriately good enough for Jose precisely the same as what is good enough for William? If not, how can the same ultimate standard be applied to different expressions of that standard (for example, Jose depending heavily on written work and William using oral and artistic devices)?

Personalization—meaning fundamental fairness arising from the differences among students—requires the expression of common, general "standards" in a variety of forms. Creating such standards is difficult work, far more difficult than saying that "high standards" are to be assessed by one "instrument" in one way and at one time. Time has to be made for it—the same sort of time that each of us prays happens among our physicians when they caucus to decide on a treatment for our disease.

Leadership to Personalize Learning

A school or school system that resolutely accepts the lively but annoying diversity among its students must break away from many deeply ingrained notions about the keeping of school, from One Best Curriculum to One Best Test to One Best Schedule. Something far more complex and more fluid must take their places. Schools must adapt to the legitimate differences among students; these adaptations will themselves be in constant flux.

Idiosyncrasy is an obvious fact: Those of us who are parents of at least two children and who thereby see daily the variety of energies and enthusiasms emerging from the same gene pool and kitchen table are keenly aware of that. But accommodating those realities within a school system designed to be universal in its routines is intellectually very demanding and politically very dangerous work.

Some will find the implications of "personalization" so unsettling as to be far-fetched. Nothing can come of it, they will say. But today something is coming of it, most usually in small schools at the edges of big systems or in autonomous small-schools-within-big-buildings. Nothing that I have suggested is not being tried somewhere. And where the trying has gone on long enough, the results are beginning to show where it counts—on what is happening to the graduates of schools that have "personalized" (Meier, 1995).

Those of us who are struggling with personalization will be the first to say that the work is as difficult as it is unfamiliar and that the trade-offs necessary to get the time to do the job well are nerve-racking. At its heart, "personalization" implies a profoundly different way of defining formal education. What is here is not the delivery of standard instructional services. Rather, it is the insistent coaxing out of each child on his or her best terms of profoundly important intellectual habits and tools for enriching a democratic society, habits and tools that provide each individual with the substance and skills to survive well in a rapidly changing culture and economy.

It can be done. It is being done, however against the traditional grain.

References

Gardner, H. (1983). *Frames of mind: The theory behind multiple intelligences.* New York: Basic Books.

Gardner, H. (1999). *The disciplined mind: What all students should understand.* New York: Simon & Schuster.

Meier, D. (1995). *The power of their ideas: Lessons for America from a small school in Harlem.* Boston: Beacon Press.

Powell, A. G., Farrar, E., & Cohen, D. K. (1985). *The shopping mall high school: Winners and losers in the educational marketplace.* Boston: Houghton Mifflin.

Sternberg, R. J. (1997, 1999). *Thinking styles.* Cambridge, England: Cambridge University Press.

POSTSCRIPT

Should All Secondary School Students Experience the Same Curriculum?

When one speaks of "personalizing and individualizing" the curriculum there is often an uncritical acceptance of the worthiness of that goal accompanied by an implicit deprecation of a broad liberal arts education for all students as being tradition bound or "elitist." With that in mind, it is important to take a closer look at some of the implications on both sides of this issue. While it is difficult to argue with "personalizing and individualizing the curriculum" in its idealized sense, caution must be exercised when the ideal is operationalized. Arthur Bestor, in his 1953 book *Educational Wastelands: The Retreat From Learning in Our Public Schools,* expressed the need for such caution when he stated that differentiated curricular paths can become "the epitome of a class structured educational philosophy." If personalizing and individualizing the high school curriculum is translated into curricular paths wherein some students are pursuing vocational education, some college preparation, and still others a general noncollege program, then ability or achievement level tracking is very likely. Obviously individuals such as Sizer would argue that tracking can be avoided while still affording individual students with opportunities to pursue individual interests. The caveat remains, however, that the logistical realities of high school scheduling can cause certain patterns to develop that separate students into different groupings.

On the other side of the issue are those who advocate a rigorous liberal arts education for all students. In an idealized sense they appear to be taking the high ground in terms of arguing for equality of opportunity and setting high academic expectations for all students. Again, while it is difficult to argue with such lofty ideals a cautionary note must be sounded with respect to the reality of the vast differences that high school students bring to school with respect to motivational levels, interests, aptitude for certain types of study, prior academic experiences and achievements, and personal goals and expectations. It is one thing to argue for rigor and common academic experiences, but it is quite another to operationalize that argument in the real world of the classroom.

Other major works relevant to this issue include John Dewey's *School and Society* (University of Chicago Press, 1899) and *Experience and Education* (Macmillan, 1938); Mortimer J. Adler's *The Paideia Proposal* (Macmillan, 1982); John Holt's *Escape From Childhood* (E. P. Dutton, 1974); David B. Tyack's *Turning Points in American Educational History* (Blaisdell, 1967); and Richard Hofstader's *Anti-Intellectualism in American Life* (Knopf, 1963). Additionally there are several related articles in the September 1999 issue of *Educational Leadership* and the December 1996 issue of *Phi Delta Kappan.*

ISSUE 4

Is Ethnocentric Education a Good Idea?

YES: Molefi Kete Asante, from "The Afrocentric Idea in Education," *Journal of Negro Education* (Spring 1991)

NO: Diane Ravitch, from "A Culture in Common," *Educational Leadership* (December 1991/January 1992)

ISSUE SUMMARY

YES: Molefi Kete Asante, professor of African American studies at Temple University, argues that eurocentricity presents the particular historical reality of Europeans as the sum total of the human experience.

NO: Diane Ravitch, senior fellow of the Brookings Institution states that the mission of public schools should be to instill in children our shared, not our separate, cultures.

Melting pot or mosaic, each metaphor is proffered to our schools as being the better descriptor of our society and thus the better approach to the education of our children. Neither side argues that the school should not play a major role in the socialization of children, but they vehemently disagree on what form that role should take and the curricular content that should operationalize it.

In terms of American history this disagreement is relatively new. The "melting pot" conceptualization, however flawed and illusory, has held sway for most of America's first two centuries. Original colonization and the subsequent initial surges of immigration were primarily European in nature. This meant that even while the arriving immigrants did settle into colonies, regions, and neighborhoods where their specific cultural and ethnic characteristics were predominant, there was nevertheless a sense of commonality with others who were coming to America for similar reasons; escape from persecution, the chance for a new and better life, the overarching idealization of America as the promised land, and the fact that most citizens were Caucasian. A significant exception to this original sense of melting-pot commonality was found among those who came here against their will as part of the slave trade and other onerous practices, such as indentured servitude and the displacement of Native Americans. Indeed the case can be made that such tragic practices are evidence that the "melting pot" never truly existed and that it is the descendants of those who suffered most from such coercion who will never accept it as an accurate or a desirable descriptor or the American experience.

But for most of the early immigrants the notion of being "Americanized," in terms of learning a common language and acquiring citizenship, was seen as a first step toward capitalizing on new opportunities and thus was welcomed or at least accepted by most. In turn, this widespread desire to learn the common language and become a citizen contributed to the unquestioning acceptance of school as the place where "Americanization" took place. And since those who wished to could still hold onto the substance and artifacts of their individual cultures in their homes and neighborhoods, there was little sense of alienation or loss.

But as generations passed and sources of immigration expanded to include non-European areas, the sense and the image of commonality became more difficult to sustain. Perhaps simply the passage of time and the incredible growth of the nation caused the label of "American" to lose some of its novelty and romance. Certainly it is not the same now as it was for the early generations. Schooling has expanded beyond being merely a preparation for work and citizenship into an end unto itself, concomitantly bringing with it a more critical look at what occurs in the schoolhouse and whose values are being served. And the ever-increasing size and demographic diversity of the U.S. population also means that attaining a sense of commonality becomes ever more challenging. Understandably for African Americans, Native Americans, and other minorities, certain events and periods in American history resonate more as sources of anger rather than unity. The diminution of the American label and the societal tensions and pressures attendant to diversity have caused many individuals and groups to look inward in terms of finding their identity. In many ways that is a very healthy thing; to take pride in one's cultural, ethnic, and linguistic heritage can be a source of strength and stability for individuals and groups. In other less healthy ways it can lead to intolerance and insularity. And, as it is with so many tension-provoking issues, the resolution is often seen as the responsibility of schools.

Molefi Kete Asante

 **YES**

The Afrocentric Idea in Education

Introduction

Many of the principles that govern the development of the Afrocentric idea in education were first established by Carter G. Woodson in *The Mis-education of the Negro* (1933). Indeed, Woodson's classic reveals the fundamental problems pertaining to the education of the African person in America. As Woodson contends, African Americans have been educated away from their own culture and traditions and attached to the fringes of European culture; thus dislocated from themselves, Woodson asserts that African Americans often valorize European culture to the detriment of their own heritage (p. 7). Although Woodson does not advocate rejection of American citizenship or nationality, he believed that assuming African Americans hold the same position as European Americans vis-à-vis the realities of America would lead to the psychological and cultural death of the African American population. Furthermore, if education is ever to be substantive and meaningful within the context of American society, Woodson argues, it must first address the African's historical experiences, both in Africa and America (p. 7). That is why he places on education, and particularly on the traditionally African American colleges, the burden of teaching the African American to be responsive to the long traditions and history of Africa as well as America. Woodson's alert recognition, more than 50 years ago, that something is severely wrong with the way African Americans are educated provides the principal impetus for the Afrocentric approach to American education.

In this article I will examine the nature and scope of this approach, establish its necessity, and suggest ways to develop and disseminate it throughout all levels of education. Two propositions stand in the background of the theoretical and philosophical issues I will present. These ideas represent the core presuppositions on which I have based most of my work in the field of education, and they suggest the direction of my own thinking about what education is capable

From Molefi Kete Asante, "The Afrocentric Idea in Education," *Journal of Negro Education,* vol. 60, no. 2 (Spring 1991). Copyright © 1991 by Howard University. Reprinted by permission of Howard University and the author.

of doing to and for an already politically and economically marginalized people
—African Americans:

1. Education is fundamentally a social phenomenon whose ultimate purpose is to socialize the learner; to send a child to school is to prepare
   that child to become part of a social group.
2. Schools are reflective of the societies that develop them (i.e., a White
   supremacist-dominated society will develop a White supremacist educational system).

Definitions

An alternative framework suggests that other definitional assumptions can provide a new paradigm for the examination of education within the American
society. For example, in education, *centricity* refers to a perspective that involves locating students within the context of their own cultural references so
that they can relate socially and psychologically to other cultural perspectives.
Centricity is a concept that can be applied to any culture. The centrist paradigm
is supported by research showing that the most productive method of teaching
any student is to place his or her group within the center of the context of
knowledge (Asante, 1990). For White students in America this is easy because
almost all the experiences discussed in American classrooms are approached
from the standpoint of White perspectives and history. American education,
however, is not centric; it is Eurocentric. Consequently, non-White students are
also made to see themselves and their groups as the "acted upon." Only rarely
do they read or hear of non-White people as active participants in history. This
is as true for a discussion of the American Revolution as it is for a discussion of
Dante's *Inferno;* for instance, most classroom discussions of the European slave
trade concentrate on the activities of Whites rather than on the resistance efforts of Africans. A person educated in a truly centric fashion comes to view all
groups' contributions as significant and useful. Even a White person educated
in such a system does not assume superiority based upon racist notions. Thus,
a truly centric education is different from a Eurocentric, racist (that is, White
supremacist) education.

Afrocentricity is a frame of reference wherein phenomena are viewed from
the perspective of the African person. The Afrocentric approach seeks in every
situation the appropriate centrality of the African person (Asante, 1987). In education this means that teachers provide students the opportunity to study the
world and its people, concepts, and history from an African world view. In most
classrooms, whatever the subject, Whites are located in the center perspective
position. How alien the African American child must feel, how like an outsider!
The little African American child who sits in a classroom and is taught to accept as heroes and heroines individuals who defamed African people is being
actively de-centered, dislocated, and made into a nonperson, one whose aim in
life might be to one day shed that "badge of inferiority": his or her Blackness. In
Afrocentric educational settings, however, teachers do not marginalize African
American children by causing them to question their own self-worth because

their people's story is seldom told. By seeing themselves as the subjects rather than the objects of education—be the discipline biology, medicine, literature, or social studies—African American students come to see themselves not merely as seekers of knowledge but as integral participants in it. Because all content areas are adaptable to an Afrocentric approach, African American students can be made to see themselves as centered in the reality of any discipline.

It must be emphasized that Afrocentricity is *not* a Black version of Eurocentricity (Asante, 1987). Eurocentricity is based on White supremacist notions whose purposes are to protect White privilege and advantage in education, economics, politics, and so forth. Unlike Eurocentricity, Afrocentricity does not condone ethnocentric valorization at the expense of degrading other groups' perspectives. Moreover, Eurocentricity presents the particular historical reality of Europeans as the sum total of the human experience (Asante, 1987). It imposes Eurocentric realities as "universal"; i.e., that which is White is presented as applying to the human condition in general, while that which is non-White is viewed as group-specific and therefore not "human." This explains why some scholars and artists of African descent rush to deny their Blackness; they believe that to exist as a Black person is not to exist as a universal human being. They are the individuals Woodson identified as preferring European art, language, and culture over African art, language, and culture; they believe that anything of European origin is inherently better than anything produced by or issuing from their own people. Naturally, the person of African descent should be centered in his or her historical experiences as an African, but Eurocentric curricula produce such aberrations of perspective among persons of color.

Multiculturalism in education is a nonhierarchical approach that respects and celebrates a variety of cultural perspectives on world phenomena (Asante, 1991). The multicultural approach holds that although European culture is the majority culture in the United States, that is not sufficient reason for it to be imposed on diverse student populations as "universal." Multiculturalists assert that education, to have integrity, must begin with the proposition that all humans have contributed to world development and the flow of knowledge and information, and that most human achievements are the result of mutually interactive, international effort. Without a multicultural education, students remain essentially ignorant of the contributions of a major portion of the world's people. A multicultural education is thus a fundamental necessity for anyone who wishes to achieve competency in almost any subject.

The Afrocentric idea must be the stepping-stone from which the multicultural idea is launched. A truly authentic multicultural education, therefore, must be based upon the Afrocentric initiative. If this step is skipped, multicultural curricula, as they are increasingly being defined by White "resisters" (to be discussed [later]) will evolve without any substantive infusion of African American content, and the African American child will continue to be lost in the Eurocentric framework of education. In other words, the African American child will neither be confirmed nor affirmed in his or her own cultural information. For the mutual benefit of all Americans, this tragedy, which leads to the psychological and cultural dislocation of African American children, can and should be avoided.

The Revolutionary Challenge

Because it centers African American students inside history, culture, science, and so forth rather than outside these subjects, the Afrocentric idea presents the most revolutionary challenge to the ideology of White supremacy in education during the past decade. No other theoretical position stated by African Americans has ever captured the imagination of such a wide range of scholars and students of history, sociology, communications, anthropology, and psychology. The Afrocentric challenge has been posed in three critical ways:

1. It questions the imposition of the White supremacist view as universal and/or classical (Asante, 1990).
2. It demonstrates the indefensibility of racist theories that assault multiculturalism and pluralism.
3. It projects a humanistic and pluralistic viewpoint by articulating Afrocentricity as a valid, nonhegemonic perspective.

Suppression and Distortion: Symbols of Resistance

The forces of resistance to the Afrocentric, multicultural transformation of the curriculum and teaching practices began to assemble their wagons almost as quickly as word got out about the need for equality in education (Ravitch, 1990). Recently, the renowned historian Arthur Schlesinger and others formed a group called the Committee for the Defense of History. This is a paradoxical development because only lies, untruths, and inaccurate information need defending. In their arguments against the Afrocentric perspective, these proponents of Eurocentrism often clothe their arguments in false categories and fake terms (i.e., "pluralistic" and "particularistic" multiculturalism) (Keto, 1990; Asante, 1991). Besides, as the late African scholar Cheikh Anta Diop (1980) maintained: "African history and Africa need no defense." Afrocentric education is not against history. It is *for* history—correct, accurate history—and if it is against anything, it is against the marginalization of African American, Hispanic American, Asian American, Native American, and other non-White children. The Committee for the Defense of History is nothing more than a futile attempt to buttress the crumbling pillars of a White supremacist system that conceals its true motives behind the cloak of American liberalism. It was created in the same spirit that generated Bloom's *The Closing of the American Mind* (1987) and Hirsch's *Cultural Literacy: What Every American Needs to Know* (1987), both of which were placed at the service of the White hegemony in education, particularly its curricular hegemony. This committee and other evidences of White backlash are a predictable challenge to the contemporary thrust for an Afrocentric, multicultural approach to education.

Naturally, different adherents to a theory will have different views on its meaning. While two discourses presently are circulating about multiculturalism, only one is relevant to the liberation of the minds of African and White people in the United States. That discourse is Afrocentricity: the acceptance of

Africa as central to African people. Yet, rather than getting on board with Afro-centrists to fight against White hegemonic education, some Whites (and some Blacks as well) have opted to plead for a return to the educational plantation. Unfortunately for them, however, those days are gone, and such misinformation can never be packaged as accurate, correct education again.

Ravitch (1990), who argues that there are two kinds of multiculturalism —*pluralist multiculturalism* and *particularist multiculturalism*—is the leader of those professors whom I call "resisters" or opponents to Afrocentricity and multiculturalism. Indeed, Ravitch advances the imaginary divisions in multicultural perspectives to conceal her true identity as a defender of White supremacy. Her tactics are the tactics of those who prefer Africans and other non-Whites to remain on the mental and psychological plantation of Western civilization. In their arrogance the resisters accuse Afrocentrists and multiculturalists of creating "fantasy history" and "bizarre theories" of non-White people's contributions to civilization. What they prove, however, is their own ignorance. Additionally, Ravitch and others (Nicholson, 1990) assert that multiculturalism will bring about the "tribalization" of America, but in reality America has always been a nation of ethnic diversity. When one reads their works on multiculturalism, one realizes that they are really advocating the imposition of a White perspective on everybody else's culture. Believing that the Eurocentric position is indisputable, they attempt to resist and impede the progressive transformation of the monoethnic curriculum. Indeed, the closets of bigotry have opened to reveal various attempts by White scholars (joined by some Blacks) to defend White privilege in the curriculum in much the same way as it has been so staunchly defended in the larger society. It was perhaps inevitable that the introduction of the Afrocentric idea would open up the discussion of the American school curriculum in a profound way.

Why has Afrocentricity created so much of a controversy in educational circles? The idea that an African American child is placed in a stronger position to learn if he or she is centered—that is, if the child sees himself or herself within the content of the curriculum rather than at its margins—is not novel (Asante, 1980). What is revolutionary is the movement from the idea (conceptual stage) to its implementation in practice, when we begin to teach teachers how to put African American youth at the center of instruction. In effect, students are shown how to see with new eyes and hear with new ears. African American children learn to interpret and center phenomena in the context of African heritage, while White students are taught to see that their own centers are not threatened by the presence or contributions of African Americans and others.

The Condition of Eurocentric Education

Institutions such as schools are conditioned by the character of the nation in which they are developed. Just as crime and politics are different in different nations, so, too, is education. In the United States a "Whites-only" orientation has predominated in education. This has had a profound impact on the quality of education for children of all races and ethnic groups. The African American child has suffered disproportionately, but White children are also the victims of monoculturally diseased curricula.

The Tragedy of Ignorance

During the past five years many White students and parents have approached me after presentations with tears in their eyes or expressing their anger about the absence of information about African Americans in the schools. A recent comment from a young White man at a major university in the Northeast was especially striking. As he said to me: "My teacher told us that Martin Luther King was a commie and went on with the class." Because this student's teacher made no effort to discuss King's ideas, the student maliciously had been kept ignorant. The vast majority of White Americans are likewise ignorant about the bountiful reservoirs of African and African American history, culture, and contributions. For example, few Americans of any color have heard the names of Cheikh Anta Diop, Anna Julia Cooper, C. L. R. James, or J. A. Rogers. All were historians who contributed greatly to our understanding of the African world. Indeed, very few teachers have ever taken a course in African American Studies; therefore, most are unable to provide systematic information about African Americans.

Afrocentricity and History

Most of America's teaching force are victims of the same system that victimizes today's young. Thus, American children are not taught the names of the African ethnic groups from which the majority of the African American population are derived; few are taught the names of any of the sacred sites in Africa. Few teachers can discuss with their students the significance of the Middle Passage or describe what it meant or means to Africans. Little mention is made in American classrooms of either the brutality of slavery or the ex-slaves' celebration of freedom. American children have little or no understanding of the nature of the capture, transport, and enslavement of Africans. Few have been taught the true horrors of being taken, shipped naked across 25 days of ocean, broken by abuse and indignities of all kinds, and dehumanized into a beast of burden, a thing without a name. If our students only knew the truth, if they were taught the Afrocentric perspective on the Great Enslavement, and if they knew the full story about the events since slavery that have served to constantly dislocate African Americans, their behavior would perhaps be different. Among these events are: the infamous constitutional compromise of 1787, which decreed that African Americans were, by law, the equivalent of but three-fifths of a person (see Franklin, 1974); the 1857 Dred Scott decision in which the Supreme Court avowed that African Americans had no rights Whites were obliged to respect (Howard, 1857); the complete dismissal and nonenforcement of Section 2 of the Fourteenth Amendment to the Constitution (this amendment, passed in 1868, stipulated as one of its provisions a penalty against any state that denied African Americans the right to vote, and called for the reduction of a state's delegates to the House of Representatives in proportion to the number of disenfranchised African American males therein); and the much-mentioned, as-yet-unreceived 40 acres and a mule, reparation for enslavement, promised to each African American family after the Civil War by Union General William T. Sherman and Secretary of War Edwin Stanton (Oubre, 1978, pp. 18–19, 182–183; see also Smith, 1987, pp. 106–107). If the curriculum were enhanced to include readings from the slave narratives; the diaries of slave ship captains; the journals of slaveowners; the abolitionist newspapers; the writings of the freedmen and freedwomen; the accounts of African American civil rights, civic, and social organizations; and numerous others, African American children would be different, White children would be different—indeed, America would be a different nation today.

America's classrooms should resound with the story of the barbaric treatment of the Africans, of how their dignity was stolen and their cultures destroyed. The recorded experiences of escaped slaves provide the substance for such learning units. For example, the narrative of Jacob and Ruth Weldon presents a detailed account of the Middle Passage (Feldstein, 1971). The Weldons noted that Africans, having been captured and brought onto the slave ships, were chained to the deck, made to bend over, and "branded with a red hot iron in the form of letters or signs dipped in an oily preparation and pressed against the naked flesh till it burnt a deep and ineffaceable scar, to show who was the owner" (pp. 33–37). They also recalled that those who screamed were lashed on the face, breast, thighs, and backs with a "cat-o'-nine tails" wielded by White sailors: "Every blow brought the returning lash pieces of grieving flesh" (p. 44). They saw "mothers with babies at their breasts basely branded and lashed, hewed and scarred, till it would seem as if the very heavens must smite the infernal tormentors with the doom they so richly merited" (p. 44). Children and infants were not spared from this terror. The Weldons tell of a nine-month-old baby on board a slave ship being flogged because it would not eat. The ship's captain ordered the child's feet placed in boiling water, which dissolved the skin and nails, then ordered the child whipped again; still the child refused to eat. Eventually the captain killed the baby with his own hands and commanded the child's mother to throw the dead baby overboard. When the mother refused, she, too, was beaten, then forced to the ship's side, where "with her head averted so she might not see it, she dropped the body into the sea" (p. 44). In a similar vein a captain of a ship with 440 Africans on board noted that 132 had to be thrown overboard to save water (Feldstein, 1971, p. 47). As another wrote, the "groans and soffocating [sic] cries for air and water coming from below the deck sickened the soul of humanity" (Feldstein, 1971, p. 44).

Upon landing in America the situation was often worse. The brutality of the slavocracy is unequalled for the psychological and spiritual destruction it wrought upon African Americans. Slave mothers were often forced to leave their children unattended while they worked in the fields. Unable to nurse their children or to properly care for them, they often returned from work at night to find their children dead (Feldstein, 1971, p. 49). The testimony of Henry Bibb also sheds light on the bleakness of the slave experience:

> I was born May 1815, of a slave mother... and was claimed as the property of David White, Esq.... I was flogged up; for where I should have received moral, mental, and religious instructions, I received stripes without number, the object of which was to degrade and keep me in subordination. I can truly say that I drank deeply of the bitter cup of suffering and woe. I have been dragged down to the lowest depths of human degradation and wretchedness, by slaveholders. (Feldstein, 1971, p. 60)

Enslavement was truly a living death. While the ontological onslaught caused some Africans to opt for suicide, the most widespread results were dislocation, disorientation, and misorientation—all of which are the consequences of the African person being actively de-centered. The "Jim Crow" period of second-class citizenship, from 1877 to 1954, saw only slight improvement in the lot of African Americans. This era was characterized by the sharecropper system, disenfranchisement, enforced segregation, internal migration, lynchings, unemployment, poor housing conditions, and separate and unequal educational facilities. Inequitable policies and practices veritably plagued the race.

No wonder many persons of African descent attempt to shed their race and become "raceless." One's basic identity is one's self-identity, which is ultimately one's cultural identity; without a strong cultural identity, one is lost. Black children do not know their people's story and White children do not know the story, but remembrance is a vital requisite for understanding and humility. This is why the Jews have campaigned (and rightly so) to have the story of the European Holocaust taught in schools and colleges. Teaching about such a monstrous human brutality should forever remind the world of the ways in which humans have often violated each other. Teaching about the African Holocaust is just as important for many of the same reasons. Additionally, it underscores the enormity of the effects of physical, psychological, and economic dislocation on the African population in America and throughout the African diaspora. Without an understanding of the historical experiences of African people, American children cannot make any real headway in addressing the problems of the present.

Certainly, if African American children were taught to be fully aware of the struggles of our African forebears they would find a renewed sense of purpose and vision in their own lives. They would cease acting as if they have no past and no future. For instance, if they were taught about the historical relationship of Africans to the cotton industry—how African American men, women, and children were forced to pick cotton from "can't see in the morning 'til can't see at night," until the blood ran from the tips of their fingers where they were pricked by the hard boll; or if they were made to visualize their ancestors in the burning sun, bent double with constant stooping, and dragging rough, heavy croaker sacks behind them—or picture them bringing those sacks trembling to the scale, fearful of a sure flogging if they did not pick enough, perhaps our African American youth would develop a stronger entrepreneurial spirit. If White children were taught the same information rather than that normally fed them about American slavery, they would probably view our society differently and work to transform it into a better place.

Correcting Distorted Information

Hegemonic education can exist only so long as true and accurate information is withheld. Hegemonic Eurocentric education can exist only so long as Whites maintain that Africans and other non-Whites have never contributed to world civilization. It is largely upon such false ideas that invidious distinctions are made. The truth, however, gives one insight into the real reasons behind human actions, whether one chooses to follow the paths of others or not. For example, one cannot remain comfortable teaching that art and philosophy originated in Greece if one learns that the Greeks themselves taught that the study of these subjects originated in Africa, specifically ancient Kemet (Herodotus, 1987). The first philosophers were the Egyptians Kagemni, Khun-anup, Ptahhotep, Kete, and Seti; but Eurocentric education is so disjointed that students have no way of discovering this and other knowledge of the organic relationship of Africa to the rest of human history. Not only did Africa contribute to human history, African civilizations predate all other civilizations. Indeed, the human species originated on the continent of Africa—this is true whether one looks at either archaeological or biological evidence.

Two other notions must be refuted. There are those who say that African American history should begin with the arrival of Africans as slaves in 1619, but it has been shown that Africans visited and inhabited North and South America long before European settlers "discovered" the "New World" (Van Sertima, 1976). Secondly, although America became something of a home for those Africans who survived the horrors of the Middle Passage, their experiences on the slave ships and during slavery resulted in their having an entirely different (and often tainted) perspective about America from that of the Europeans and others who came, for the most part, of their own free will seeking opportunities not available to them in their native lands. Afrocentricity therefore seeks to recognize this divergence in perspective and create centeredness for African American students.

Conclusion

The reigning initiative for total curricular change is the movement that is being proposed and led by Africans, namely, the Afrocentric idea. When I wrote the first book on Afrocentricity (Asante, 1980), now in its fifth printing, I had no idea that in 10 years the idea would both shake up and shape discussions in education, art, fashion, and politics. Since the publication of my subsequent works, *The Afrocentric Idea* (Asante, 1987) and *Kemet, Afrocentricity, and Knowledge* (Asante, 1990), the debate has been joined in earnest. Still, for many White Americans (and some African Americans) the most unsettling aspect of the discussion about Afrocentricity is that its intellectual source lies in the research and writings of African American scholars. Whites are accustomed to being in charge of the major ideas circulating in the American academy. Deconstructionism, Gestalt psychology, Marxism, structuralism, Piagetian theory, and so forth have all been developed, articulated, and elaborated upon at length, generally by White scholars. On the other hand, Afrocentricity is the product of scholars such as Nobles (1986), Hilliard (1978), Karenga (1986), Keto (1990), Richards (1991), and Myers (1989). There are also increasing numbers of young, impressively credentialled African American scholars who have begun to write in the Afrocentric vein (Jean, 1991). They, and even some young White scholars, have emerged with ideas about how to change the curriculum Afrocentrically.

Afrocentricity provides all Americans an opportunity to examine the perspective of the African person in this society and the world. The resisters claim that Afrocentricity is anti-White; yet, if Afrocentricity as a theory is against anything it is against racism, ignorance, and monoethnic hegemony in the curriculum. Afrocentricity is not anti-White; it is, however, pro-human. Further, the aim of the Afrocentric curriculum is not to divide America, it is to make America flourish as it ought to flourish. This nation has long been divided with regard to the educational opportunities afforded to children. By virtue of the protection provided by society and reinforced by the Eurocentric curriculum, the White child is already ahead of the African American child by first grade. Our efforts thus must concentrate on giving the African American child greater opportunities for learning at the kindergarten level. However, the kind of assistance the African American child needs is as much cultural as it is academic. If the proper cultural information is provided, the academic performance will surely follow suit.

When it comes to educating African American children, the American educational system does not need a tune-up, it needs an overhaul. Black children have been maligned by this system. Black teachers have been maligned. Black history has been maligned. Africa has been maligned. Nonetheless, two truisms can be stated about education in America. First, some teachers *can and do* effectively teach African American children; secondly, if some teachers can do it, others can, too. We must learn all we can about what makes these teachers' attitudes and approaches successful, and then work diligently to see that their successes are replicated on a broad scale. By raising the same questions that Woodson posed more than 50 years ago, Afrocentric education, along with a significant reorientation of the American educational enterprise, seeks to respond to the African person's psychological and cultural dislocation. By providing philosophical and theoretical guidelines and criteria that are centered in an African perception of reality and by placing the African American child in his or her proper historical context and setting, Afrocentricity may be just the "escape hatch" African Americans so desperately need to facilitate academic success and "steal away" from the cycle of miseducation and dislocation.

References

Asante, M. K. (1980). *Afrocentricity: The theory of social change*. Buffalo, NY: Amulefi.
Asante, M. K. (1987). *The Afrocentric idea*. Philadelphia: Temple University Press.

Asante, M. K. (1990). *Kemet, Afrocentricity, and knowledge.* Trenton, NJ: Africa World Press.

Bloom, A. (1987). *The closing of the American mind.* New York: Simon & Schuster.

Feldstein, S. (1971). *Once a slave: The slave's view of slavery.* New York: William Morrow.

Franklin, J. H. (1974). *From slavery to freedom.* New York: Knopf.

Herodotus. (1987). *The history.* Chicago: University of Illinois Press.

Hilliard, A. G., III. (1978, June 20). *Anatomy and dynamics of oppression.* Speech delivered at the National Conference on Human Relations in Education, Minneapolis, MN.

Hirsch, E. D. (1987). *Cultural literacy: What every American needs to know.* New York: Houghton Mifflin.

Howard, B. C. (1857). *Report of the decision of the Supreme Court of the United States and the opinions of the justices thereof in the case of Dred Scott versus John F. A. Sandford, December term, 1856.* New York: D. Appleton & Co.

Jean, C. (1991). *Beyond the Eurocentric veils.* Amherst, MA: University of Massachusetts Press.

Karenga, M. R. (1986). *Introduction to Black studies.* Los Angeles: University of Sankore Press.

Keto, C. T. (1990). *Africa-centered perspective of history.* Blackwood, NJ: C. A. Associates.

Nicholson, D. (1990, September 23). Afrocentrism and the tribalization of America. *The Washington Post,* p. B-1.

Nobles, W. (1986). *African psychology.* Oakland, CA: Black Family Institute.

Oubre, C. F. (1978). *Forty acres and a mule: The Freedman's Bureau and Black land ownership.* Baton Rouge, LA: Louisiana State University Press.

Ravitch, D. (1990, Summer). Multiculturalism: E pluribus plures. *The American Scholar,* pp. 337–354.

Richards, D. (1991). *Let the circle be unbroken.* Trenton, NJ: Africa World Press.

Smith, J. O. (1987). *The politics of racial inequality: A systematic comparative macro-analysis from the colonial period to 1970.* New York: Greenwood Press.

Van Sertima, I. (1976). *They came before Columbus.* New York: Random House.

Woodson, C. G. (1915). *The education of the Negro prior to 1861: A history of the education of the colored people of the U.S. from the beginning of slavery.* New York: G. P. Putnam's Sons.

Woodson, C. G. (1933). *The Mis-education of the Negro.* Washington, DC: Associated Publishers.

Woodson, C. G. (1936). *African background outlined.* Washington, DC: Association for the Study of Afro-American Life and History.

NO

Diane Ravitch

A Culture in Common

The classrooms of America today are more racially and ethnically diverse than ever. Now that the children in American schools are the descendants of so many different nationalities, religions, races, and ethnic groups, teachers and curriculum makers are asking "Whose history, literature, and art? Whose ideas and perspectives?"

The answers to such questions are not simple. They will determine not only the curriculum, but the purpose of the public school and the nature of American national identity. Thus it is important to reflect on what we mean by teaching "culture." We want to convey to children the knowledge, skills, language, and habits they will need to participate successfully in their own society, but it is also important for them to learn about other cultures, so they will have a broader understanding of the world.

Both of these goals are important, but priority must be given to teaching about the history and culture of the United States. American history and literature should explain who the American people are and where we came from. What were the turning points, the crises, that shaped and changed our nation? Who are our heroes? What are our ideals? Which poems, novels, essays, orations, and songs best typify the American spirit? What ideas, institutions, and values have held this polyglot people together as a nation for more than 200 years?

Common vs. Separate Identities

Today, there are many people who argue that America has no "we," no national culture at all; our society, they say, is nothing more than a collection of distinctive racial and ethnic cultures. Some of the more vehement partisans in this camp claim that any effort to teach a "common culture" disparages the role and contributions of minority groups. Such critics speak contemptuously of the common culture, as if it were a vehicle of oppression. They claim that public schools must teach children to revere the culture of their parents, grandparents, and ancestors. The goal of the public school, they say, must be to transmit, preserve, and strengthen the separate identities of the nation's many racial and ethnic cultures. By this definition, the culture taught by the school will vary according to the color or language of the children in the school.

The most strident critics of the common culture demand that the curriculum teach contempt for the founders of the nation and for everything European or white. This extremism is simply an inverted form of racism, which should be rejected outright by teachers and curriculum developers everywhere. Race-bashing and nation-bashing should never be permitted.

Several cities have endorsed the trend toward using ethnicity as the organizing principle of the social studies curriculum. This is a dangerous development that may encourage ethnic separatism and cause intergroup tension. It is not the role of public schools to teach children the customs and folkways of their ethnic or racial group; that is, as it has always been, the role of the family, the church, and the local community. Nor is it the role of the public school to encapsulate children in the confines of their family's inherited culture. It *is* the role of the public school to open children's minds to new worlds, new ideas, new possibilities.

The historic mission of the American public schools—the common schools —has been to help forge a national identity that all Americans share. And the increasing diversity of our population makes it even more imperative that our schools teach children what we as Americans have in common. The schools have failed in this mission whenever they excluded any group from equal opportunity for education. Conversely, they have succeeded whenever they taught children the knowledge and skills that are necessary for citizenship, for work, for continued education, and for full participation in American society.

Amalgamated America

The common culture is not an Anglo-Saxon melting pot: it is an amalgam of the contributions of all the different groups that have joined American society and enriched our shared culture. The common culture is the work of whites and blacks, of men and women, of Native Americans and African Americans, of Hispanics and Asians, of immigrants from England, France, Germany, Mexico, Haiti, Ireland, Colombia, Scandinavia, Cuba, Italy, Poland, Russia, Thailand, Korea, India, China, the Philippines, and Ghana; of Protestants, Catholics, Jews, Muslims, Mormons, and millions of other individuals who added their voices to the American chorus.

The sons and daughters of every other nation in the world have made the United States their home. No matter where they came from, they are Americans. With their music, their foods, their sports, their customs, their holidays, their dress, and their dreams, they have made their mark on America. The United Sates has changed them, and they in turn have changed the United States.

The common culture is a Thai deli in San Francisco that sells bratwurst, pizza, espresso, and tropical ice cream. It is the Puerto Rican bakery that makes the best bagels on the upper West Side of Manhattan. It is the Colombian woman in New York who tells a reporter after her naturalization ceremony that she intends to celebrate her new American citizenship by going out for sushi.

The common culture is jazz, the blues, the square-dance, the waltz, salsa, the polka, rock-and-roll, the fox trot, and rap. It is "America the Beautiful," "The Star-Spangled Banner," "America," and "Go Down Moses." It is Shakespeare, Mozart, Bob Dylan, Spike Lee, and Norman Lear.

The common culture is a blend of high technology and bland commercialism. It is Coca-Cola, IBM, Kleenex, Saran Wrap, McDonald's, Levi's, Sesame Street, and bubble gum. It is Oprah, Johnny, Madonna, and the Simpsons. It is Thomas Alva Edison, George Washington Carver, and Henry Ford. It is Superman, Batman, Robin Hood, Dick Tracy, and WonderWoman.

The common culture is Patrick Henry, declaring, "Give me liberty, or give me death!" It is Ralph Waldo Emerson celebrating individualism, and Henry David Thoreau counseling civil disobedience. It is Abraham Lincoln pledging "that this nation, under God, shall have a new birth of freedom—and that government of the people, by the people, for the people, shall not perish from the earth." It is Martin Luther King, Jr., calling on others to share his dream of a nation where people are judged by their character, not by the color of their skin. It is Elizabeth Cady Stanton rewriting the Declaration of Independence as a feminist document.

The common culture is Samuel Gompers fighting for an eight-hour day, and Ida B. Wells crusading against lynching. It is Cesar Chavez organizing migrant workers, and it is Hubert Humphrey battling for civil rights at the 1948 Democratic convention. It is Frederick Douglass demanding an end to slavery, and it is Susan B. Anthony trying to cast a vote for president in 1872, when women did not have the right to vote.

The common culture is Thomas Jefferson, writing "We hold these truths to be self-evident, that all men are created equal, that they are endowed by their Creator with certain unalienable Rights, that among these are Life, Liberty, and the pursuit of Happiness." It is George Washington, gladly handing over the reins of power to his duly elected successor, a remarkable event in world history. It is Bayard Rustin, putting his life on the line time and again for oppressed people of every race, creed, and nationality.

The common culture is Franklin D. Roosevelt, reminding Americans in the depths of the Great Depression that "the only thing we have to fear is fear itself." And it is the eminent jurist Learned Hand, telling his fellow citizens in 1944 that "the spirit of liberty is the spirit which is not too sure that it is right."

The common culture is Langston Hughes and Benjamin Franklin, both of whom spoke directly to the common man and woman. The common culture is the folk songs of Woody Guthrie, the pop songs of Irving Berlin, and Julia Ward Howe's "The Battle Hymn of the Republic." It is the eloquent voices of James Weldon Johnson, Countee Cullen, Chief Seattle, Alice Walker, Harvey Milk, and Abelardo Delgado.

The common culture is the Constitution and the Bill of Rights, which majestically delineate the democratic form of government under which we live and the rights that protect us as equal citizens. The common culture is regular elections, where people choose their leaders. It is the Supreme Court, the Congress, the state legislatures, the local school boards, town meetings, and the debates about their decisions. The common culture may be found at the newsstand, on the radio, and on television, where citizens know that they have a right to express their opinion and to read or hear whatever they choose.

For anyone who lives in a city in the United States today, the common culture offers daily contact with people of every race and many different ethnic origins. Within a mile of where I sit writing, there are communities and city blocks where whites, blacks, Puerto Ricans, Central Americans, Indian-Americans, Korean-Americans, and Arab-Americans live and work in close proximity. The nearest commercial street is a placid yet lively symbol of culinary multiculturalism: it has a Jewish delicatessen, a German butcher, an Irish bar, a Mexican restaurant, a sushi bar, a Thai restaurant, several Arab restaurants, an Italian bakery, and several Korean grocers.

The Crossroads of Multiculturalism

Those ethnocentrists who insist on going to war against the common culture, which they claim is an insidious form of European domination, are like children rejecting one of their parents. What they do not understand is that the common culture *is* multicultural. Take a look at the United States' contingent at the next Olympics. Our team looks like a microcosm of the world. And it is, because it accurately reflects American society.

We lose no part of our multicultural heritage by appreciating the European ideas that created our democratic institutions and honoring the British men who wrote the Declaration of Independence and the Constitution. Indeed, we are at risk of losing our democratic heritage if we fail to study and understand the ideas that established our government and institutions.

Multiculturalism is at a crossroads: Should the public schools encourage racial and ethnic loyalties, or should they remain the agencies of a transformed and enriched common culture? The danger of the former, I believe, is that the public schools will become hopelessly ensnared in ethnic controversies and will lose their central purpose as agencies of social meliorism. The promise of the latter is that it will strengthen the bonds of fellowship that make us one nation and one people—the American people.

A multicultural curriculum can succeed, but to do so it must achieve several goals. It must teach the core democratic values that enable us to work together, to reach decisions, and to live peaceably as citizens of the same society, values such as tolerance, respect for dissenting opinions, a sense of responsibility for the common good, and a readiness to participate in civic life. It must also teach the history of the American people and of the institutions that made it possible to forge a nation from people of many different backgrounds. Then it must teach children about the rest of the world beyond our borders. Finally, it should demonstrate that racial and ethnic diversity may be a source of strength —as they are in the United States—or a cause of conflict and civil war—as they are in many troubled nations.

Teaching the Common Culture

The curriculum in American public schools must reflect both multicultural-ism and the common culture, both the pluribus and the unum. The common American culture was built over generations by people of many different races, religions, ethnic groups, and cultural backgrounds. Children in every grade must learn that American history, like American culture, is constantly being made and remade by those who live it.

Those who teach history and social studies must avoid mindless celebra-tion of our own or anyone else's history. It is important in teaching history to acknowledge honestly the violations of human rights that mar the history of every country, including our own. It is of no less importance to teach children the democratic ideas and institutions that provide the mechanisms to correct injustice. Children must learn that evil is ended not by some invisible benign force, but by human effort, by active and thoughtful participation in the polit-ical process, and by a willingness to make sacrifices to defend democracy and human rights.

If we teach children to identify only with members of their own race or ethnic culture, we run the risk of promoting and sanctioning ethnocentrism and prejudice. Throughout the world, people have a tendency to care only about the members of their own group. Unchecked, this tendency turns into hatred based on race, religion, ethnicity, language, appearance, and customs.

We don't have to look far to see the dire consequences of ethnocentrism. The Soviet Union, India, Lebanon, Canada, Yugoslavia, and South Africa are current examples where competing nationalisms are causing social havoc. No nation—certainly not our own—has been innocent of the brutal excesses of ethnocentrism. Throughout human history, people have demonstrated their readiness to persecute and oppress those who are different from themselves. Under no circumstances should the curriculum be patterned to stir ethnocen-tric pride or to make children feel that their self-worth as human beings is derived from their race or ethnic origin.

The Future of Public Education

It is the job of the schools to teach history, literature, and art in such a way as to diminish and actively combat prejudice. It is the job of the schools to promote a generous appreciation of the common humanity that transcends skin color, religion, language, and other accidents of birth.

If the public schools abandon their historic mission as the common schools of the nation, if they instead foster racial and ethnic separatism, they will forfeit their claim to public support. If the public schools relinquish their responsibility for teaching children an awareness of their American identity, then they will lose their privileged status as public schools. Such a trend would inevitably encourage a flight from public education by those who are repelled by relentless ethnic struggles for control of the curriculum.

If they remain true to their historic role, the public schools will fulfill their obligation to serve as a bulwark against ethnic chauvinism and counter the forces of social fragmentation. And they will exercise their responsibility to teach democratic values and the civic ethics that promote respect for other human beings, without regard to their race or social origins. What is at stake, then, in the current debate about multiculturalism, is nothing less than the future of public education.

POSTSCRIPT

Is Ethnocentric Education a Good Idea?

There is some irony in the fact that while "culture" is not really a course in the secondary school curriculum, it nevertheless is a dominant consideration in any policy discussion or decision related to curriculum standards, instructional materials, and assessment practices in the public schools. From issues such as the content of history books to the appropriateness of certain speech patterns such as "Ebonics" in the school setting, contention and conflict are widespread regarding how such issues impact the different "publics" represented in public schools. No longer is there quiet acquiescence to the schools' unilateral right to make decisions reflecting the "traditional" perspective regarding what is to be taught.

Spokespersons for different racial and ethnic groups, especially minorities, argue against what they see as the overemphasis or primacy of the artifacts of the majority white culture in school curricular and organizational decisions to the detriment of children from other backgrounds. Such views are passionately articulated by authors and critics such as James A. Banks in *Multiethnic Education: Theory and Practice* (Allyn & Bacon, 1981); Cameron McCarthy in "After the Canon: Knowledge and Ideological Representation in the Multicultural Discourse on Curriculum Reform," in Cameron McCarthy and Warren Crichlow, eds., *Race, Identity and Representation in Education* (Routledge, 1993); and Cornel West in *The New Cultural Policies of Difference* (1990).

Equally passionate are those who believe that attempts in the schools to provide equal "coverage" to all cultural and ethnic groups are at best unrealistic and at worst divisively destructive. Authors with that perspective include Arthur M. Schlesinger, Jr. in *The Disuniting of America* (Whittle Direct Books, 1991); Irving Howe in "The Value of the Canon," *New Republic* (February 18, 1991); and J. Jarolimek in *Born Again Ethnics* (Macmillan, 1988).

Further complicating this very complex issue is the fact that the vast majority of teachers in the public schools are white. Some see this as an almost insurmountable obstacle to improving race relations. Christine Sleeter in "How White Teachers Construct Race" in *Race and Representation in Education,* Cameron McCarthy and Warren Crichlow, eds. (Routledge, 1993) states, "I . . . argue that a predominantly white teaching force in a racist and multicultural society is not good for anyone, if we wish to have schools reverse rather than reproduce racism." While many would argue that such pessimistic, postmodern polemics do little to solve problems, there nevertheless is a strong case to be made that we need to redouble our efforts to bring more minorities into the teaching profession while at the same time making certain that teacher education programs continue to seriously address issues of race, diversity, and cultural sensitivity.

ISSUE 5

Should Secondary Schools Emphasize Education for the Workplace?

YES: The Secretary's Commission on Achieving Necessary Skills, from "What Work Requires of Schools," a SCANS Report for America 2000 (June 1991)

NO: John I. Goodlad, from "Education and Democracy: Advancing the Agenda," *Phi Delta Kappan* (September 2000)

ISSUE SUMMARY

YES: The Secretary's Commission on Achieving Necessary Skills (SCANS) report, issued during the George H. W. Bush administration, states that a fundamental purpose of education is to create an entire people trained to think and equipped with the know-how to make their knowledge productive.

NO: John I. Goodlad, codirector of the Center of Educational Renewal at the University of Washington, cautions that "to make the dozen or more years of schooling instrumental to the future needs of the workplace, however carefully predicted, is immoral and dangerous."

The phrase *education for the workplace* speaks of a concept that is certainly not new. When, in 1749, Benjamin Franklin wrote *On the Need for an Academy*, he envisioned two fundamental goals for colonial education. He saw schooling as a means to promote social and civic harmony and secondly as a source to enhance performance in the world of work and thus benefit society. He wrote, "Thus instructed, Youth will come out of the School fitted for learning any Business, Calling or Profession."

Franklin's goals to prepare a trained and efficient workforce and a law-abiding citizenry capture the essence of the utilitarian vision of the purposes of education. Given the conditions of the times, Franklin's motives and plans were both appropriate and necessary. But critics of a utilitarian approach to education will point out that colonial America in 1749 was a highly elitist society and that Franklin, while extolling the value of teaching English and other practical subjects to the working/merchant class, knew full well that the elite members of society would continue to be distinguished by their knowledge of the classical languages ("All intended for the Divinity should be taught the Latin and Greek; for Physick, the Latin, Greek and French; for Law, the Latin and French").

To John I. Goodlad and others, education for the workplace represents a capitulation to an economic agenda for schooling and concomitant diminution of liberal education. They are concerned that an overemphasis on the "workplace education" may result in a divided curriculum with a "workforce" track for some and a college preparatory program for others—a return to elitism and a social structure based on different forms of education.

Advocates of education for the workplace point to the increased globalization and technological basis of America's economy and argue that current approaches to secondary education are not preparing students with the skills and knowledge that will allow them to compete in that future economy. And they caution that if we do not have a well-prepared and competitive workforce, all of society will suffer. This sentiment was expressed by a brochure for a recent conference in California called "The Education of the New California Workforce" wherein it was stated, "[E]ducation, in partnership with business can and must take the lead in re-directing the education of the workforce, teaching them to become better citizens, more effective leaders, and world-competitive workers, literate in the basics of spoken, written, and computer communication.... [This is] a conference dedicated to the role of education in the advancement of workforce excellence and economic development."

 **YES**

What Work Requires of Schools

Executive Summary

The Secretary's Commission on Achieving Necessary Skills (SCANS) was asked to examine the demands of the workplace and whether our young people are capable of meeting those demands.

Specifically, the Commission was directed to advise the Secretary on the level of skills required to enter employment. In carrying out this charge, the Commission was asked to:

- Define the skills needed for employment;
- Propose acceptable levels of proficiency;
- Suggest effective ways to assess proficiency; and
- Develop a dissemination strategy for the nation's schools, businesses, and homes.

This report results from our discussions and meetings with business owners, public employers, unions, and workers and supervisors in shops, plants, and stores. It builds on the work of six special panels we established to examine all manner of jobs from manufacturing to government employment. We also commissioned researchers to conduct lengthy interviews with workers in a wide range of jobs.

The message to us was universal: good jobs will increasingly depend on people who can put knowledge to work. What we found was disturbing: more than half our young people leave school without the knowledge or foundation required to find and hold a good job. These people will pay a very high price. They face the bleak prospects of dead-end work interrupted only by periods of unemployment.

Two conditions that arose in the last quarter of the 20th Century have changed the terms of our young people's entry into the world of work: the globalization of commerce and industry and the explosive growth of technology on the job. These developments have barely been reflected in how we prepare young people for work or in how many of our workplaces are organized. Schools need to do a better job and so do employers. Students and workers

From The Secretary's Commission on Achieving Necessary Skills, "What Work Requires of Schools," a SCANS Report for America 2000 (U.S. Department of Labor, June 1991). Washington, DC: U.S. Government Printing Office, 1991.

must work smarter. Unless they do, neither our schools, our students, nor our businesses can prosper.

SCANS research verifies that what we call workplace know-how defines effective job performance today. This know-how has two elements: competencies and a foundation. This report identifies five competencies and a three-part foundation of skills and personal qualities that lie at the heart of job-performance. These eight requirements are essential preparation for all students, both those going directly to work and those planning further education. Thus, the competencies and the foundation should be taught and understood in an integrated fashion that reflects the workplace contexts in which they are applied.

We believe, after examining the findings of cognitive science, that the most effective way of learning skills is "in context," placing learning objectives within a real environment rather than insisting that students first learn in the abstract what they will be expected to apply.

The five SCANS competencies span the chasm between school and the workplace. Because they are needed in workplaces dedicated to excellence, they are hallmarks of today's expert worker. And they lie behind the quality of every product and service offered on today's market.

The competencies differ from a person's technical knowledge. For example, both accountants and engineers manage resources, information, systems, and technology. They require competence in these areas even though building a bridge has little to do with balancing a set of books. But in each profession, the competencies are at least as important as the technical expertise. The members of the Commission believe these competencies are applicable from the shop floor to the executive suite. In the broadest sense, the competencies represent the attributes that today's high-performance employer seeks in tomorrow's employee.

To describe how this know-how is used on the job, our report provides a series of five scenarios that portray work requirements in the context of the real world. The scenarios show that work involves a complex interplay among the five competencies we have identified and the three elements of the foundation — the basic skills, higher order thinking skills, and diligent application of personal qualities.

The scenarios make clear that tomorrow's career ladders require even the basic skills — the old 3 Rs — to take on a new meaning. First, all employees will have to read well enough to understand and interpret diagrams, directories, correspondence, manuals, records, charts, graphs, tables, and specifications. Without the ability to read a diverse set of materials, workers cannot locate the descriptive and quantitative information needed to make decisions or to recommend courses of action. What do these reading requirements mean on the job? They might involve:

- interpreting blueprints and materials catalogues;
- dealing with letters and written policy on complaints;
- reading patients' medical records and medication instructions; and
- reading the text of technical manuals from equipment vendors.

At the same time, most jobs will call for writing skills to prepare correspondence, instructions, charts, graphs, and proposals, in order to make requests, explain, illustrate, and convince. On the job this might require:

- writing memoranda to justify resources or explain plans;
- preparing instructions for operating simple machines;
- developing a narrative to explain graphs or tables; and
- drafting suggested modifications in company procedures.

Mathematics and computational skills will also be essential. Virtually all employees will be required to maintain records, estimate results, use spreadsheets, or apply statistical process controls as they negotiate, identify trends, or suggest new courses of action. Most of us will not leave our mathematics behind us in school. Instead, we will find ourselves using it on the job, for example, to:

- reconcile differences between inventory and financial records;
- estimate discounts on the spot while negotiating sales;
- use spreadsheet programs to monitor expenditures;
- employ statistical process control;
- project resource needs over the next planning period.

Finally, very few of us will work totally by ourselves. More and more, work involves listening carefully to clients and co-workers and clearly articulating one's own point of view. Today's worker has to listen and speak well enough to explain schedules and procedures, communicate with customers, work in teams, understand customer concerns, describe complex systems and procedures, probe for hidden meanings, teach others, and solve problems. On the job, these skills may translate readily into:

- training new workers or explaining new schedules to a work team;
- describing plans to supervisors or clients;
- questioning customers to diagnose malfunctions; and
- answering questions from customers about post-sales service.

SCANS estimates that less than half of all young adults have achieved these reading and writing minimums; even fewer can handle the mathematics; and, schools today only indirectly address listening and speaking skills.

Defining the minimum levels of proficiency in the SCANS competencies is also a crucial part of the Commission's task. It requires judgments about the learning possible in yet-to-be designed schools. It also requires imagining what the workplaces of the year 2000 could and should look like.

... For over 200 years Americans have worked to make education part of their national vision, indispensable to democracy and to individual freedom. For at least the last 40 years, we have worked to further the ideal of equity—for minority Americans, for the disabled, and for immigrants. With that work still incomplete, we are called to still another revolution—to create an entire people

Table 1

Five Competencies

Resources: Identifies, organizes, plans, and allocates resources

  A. *Time* — Selects goal-relevant activities, ranks them, allocates time, and prepares and follows schedules
  B. *Money* — Uses or prepares budgets, makes forecasts, keeps records, and makes adjustments to meet objectives
  C. *Material and Facilities* — Acquires, stores, allocates, and uses materials or space efficiently
  D. *Human Resources* — Assesses skills and distributes work accordingly, evaluates performance and provides feedback

Interpersonal: Works with others

  A. *Participates as a Member of a Team* — contributes to group effort
  B. *Teaches Others New Skills*
  C. *Serves Clients/Customers* — works to satisfy customers' expectations
  D. *Exercises Leadership* — communicates ideas to justify position, persuades and convinces others, responsibly challenges existing procedures and policies
  E. *Negotiates* — works toward agreements involving exchange of resources, resolves divergent interests
  F. *Works With Diversity* — works well with men and women from diverse backgrounds

Information: Acquires and uses information

  A. *Acquires and Evaluates Information*
  B. *Organizes and Maintains Information*
  C. *Interprets and Communicates Information*
  D. *Uses Computers to Process Information*

Systems: Understands complex inter-relationships

  A. *Understands Systems* — knows how social, organizational, and technological systems work and operates effectively with them
  B. *Monitors and Corrects Performance* — distinguishes trends, predicts impacts on system operations, diagnoses deviations in systems' performance and corrects malfunctions
  C. *Improves or Designs Systems* — suggests modifications to existing systems and develops new or alternative systems to improve performance

Technology: Works with a variety of technologies

  A. *Selects Technology* — chooses procedures, tools or equipment including computers and related technologies
  B. *Applies Technology to Task* — Understands overall intent and proper procedures for setup and operation of equipment
  C. *Maintains and Troubleshoots Equipment* — Prevents, identifies, or solves problems with equipment, including computers and other technologies

---

trained to think and equipped with the know-how to make their knowledge productive.

This new revolution is no less exciting or challenging than those we have already completed. Nor is its outcome more certain. All that is certain is that we must begin.

Table 2

A Three-Part Foundation

Basic Skills: Reads, writes, performs arithmetic and mathematical operations, listens and speaks

A. *Reading* —locates, understands, and interprets written information in prose and in documents such as manuals, graphs, and schedules

B. *Writing* —communicates thoughts, ideas, information, and messages in writing; and creates documents such as letters, directions, manuals, reports, graphs, and flow charts

C. *Arithmetic/Mathematics* —performs basic computations and approaches practical problems by choosing appropriately from a variety of mathematical techniques

D. *Listening* —receives, attends to, interprets, and responds to verbal messages and other cues

E. *Speaking* —organizes ideas and communicates orally

Thinking Skills: Thinks creatively, makes decisions, solves problems, visualizes, knows how to learn, and reasons

A. *Creative Thinking* —generates new ideas

B. *Decision Making* —specifies goals and constraints, generates alternatives, considers risks, and evaluates and chooses best alternative

C. *Problem Solving* —recognizes problems and devises and implements plan of action

D. *Seeing Things in the Mind's Eye* —organizes, and processes symbols, pictures, graphs, objects, and other information

E. *Knowing How to Learn* —uses efficient learning techniques to acquire and apply new knowledge and skills

F. *Reasoning* —discovers a rule or principle underlying the relationship between two or more objects and applies it when solving a problem

Personal Qualities: Displays responsibility, self-esteem, sociability, self-management, and integrity and honesty

A. *Responsibility* — exerts a high level of effort and perseveres towards goal attainment

B. *Self-Esteem* — believes in own self-worth and maintains a positive view of self

C. *Sociability* — demonstrates understanding, friendliness, adaptability, empathy, and politeness in group settings

D. *Self-Management* — assesses self accurately, sets personal goals, monitors progress, and exhibits self-control

E. *Integrity/Honesty* — chooses ethical courses of action

The World Has Changed

A strong back, the willingness to work, and a high school diploma were once all that was needed to make a start in America. They are no longer. A well-developed mind, a passion to learn, and the ability to put knowledge to work are the new keys to the future of our young people, the success of businesses, and the economic well-being of the nation.

Two events of the last generation serve as metaphors for how radically and irreversibly the economic environment for all work has changed, both for Americans and for the rest of the world. In 1973, the OPEC oil embargo made it unmistakably clear that our nation's economic future was no longer ours alone to decide. Since then, the lessons of globalization and interdependence have been reinforced at every turn. In many ways, 1973 was a boundary line defining new territory.

Two years later, the first plans for an unheard of new product—a personal computer—appeared in a popular scientific magazine. That device has altered both the speed with which work is done and its very nature. It has configured the world of work as have perhaps no other invention since electricity or the assembly line. It has created not only a new industry; it has redefined the way thousands of different kinds of work are now carried out.

Globalization and technology contain both threat and promise. The threat is easily summarized in the economic implications of energy dependence, disappointing productivity growth, and stagnant wages. For example:

- **Productivity.** Productivity growth (output per hour) in the United States slowed significantly after 1973. Labor productivity actually declined in 1989 and 1990. Some estimate that if current international productivity trends continue, nine countries may exceed the U.S. in output per worker-hour by the year 2020.
- **Earnings and Income.** Stagnant productivity has seriously affected workers' earnings. Median family income increased nearly three percent a year between 1947 and 1973. Since 1973, it has scarcely increased at all. Families with heads of households under the age of 34 have watched their real income decline since 1979.
- **Jobs.** Job opportunities in the United States are changing. Twenty years ago, manufacturing accounted for 27 percent of all nonagricultural employment in the U.S.; services and retail trade for 32 percent. By 1990, manufacturing accounted for only 17 percent of these jobs; while services and retail trade made up 44 percent. In 1990, manufacturing jobs paid an average of $10.84 per hour; while service jobs paid $9.86 and jobs in retail trade paid only $6.78.

But the promise of an internationalized economic environment and a workplace grounded in new technologies is equally dramatic. The promise is a healthy economy that improves the standard of living for all by growing—by increasing productivity, creating new jobs, and meeting the challenges placed before it.

Work Is Changing

To paraphrase futurist Alvin Toffler, we are now caught up in a "third wave" of industrialization. Just as the United States powered its early industrial growth with steam and built a manufacturing empire on the assembly line, it can now catch the crest of computer technology to create a high-wage, high-skill future.

That future depends on high-performance work organizations and a highly competent workforce. It will be as different from our present as today's most advanced work and workplace are different from Henry Ford's assembly line. As a corporate member of the commission observed, in reviewing preliminary descriptions is the realization that they are accurate, but ten years ago I could not possibly have imagined them. What will our workplace look like ten years from today?

John I. Goodlad  **NO**

Education and Democracy

The past 15 years have witnessed the emergence of several educational improvement initiatives of national scope that have taken shape largely with the support of private philanthropy. Most have focused on schools; several, on teacher education. Since its inception, ours has assumed the close relationship of the two and has addressed their simultaneous renewal. Our initiative is driven by a research-based agenda referred to by the thousands of school and university people involved in the effort as the Agenda for Education in a Democracy.

Context

Three agencies have been and are engaged with the Agenda for Education in a Democracy: the Center for Educational Renewal (CER) at the University of Washington, founded in 1985; the National Network for Educational Renewal (NNER), assembled in 1986 and reconstructed in 1990–91; and the nonprofit Institute for Educational Inquiry (IEI), created in 1992. The major function of the CER has been research, that of the NNER has been implementation, and IEI has focused on leadership training. The Agenda emerged out of two decades of inquiry on educational change, schooling, and teacher education, conducted first by teams in the research division of the Institute for Development of Educational Activities, located in Los Angeles, and then at the CER in Seattle.

The Agenda is comprehensive in its inclusion of a four-part mission; some five dozen conditions necessary for advancing this mission, which are embedded in 20 propositions referred to as postulates; and a strategy of individual and institutional renewal. (The 20th postulate was added to the original 19 in 2000 and pertains to supporting and sustaining the teaching career.) The whole is grounded in a concept of education as a moral endeavor serving both the individual and the common good through the development of those civil and civic dispositions espoused by the great religions and by lay thinkers in their pursuit of the ideal human condition. In the rhetoric of the Agenda, these attitudes and behaviors are referred to as indicators of "democratic character," both individual and collective, whether social or political.

From John I. Goodlad, "Education and Democracy: Advancing the Agenda," *Phi Delta Kappan*, vol. 82, no. 1 (September 2000). Copyright © 2000 by Phi Delta Kappa International. Reprinted by permission of *Phi Delta Kappan* and the author. Notes omitted.

The Agenda's strategy has focused on the simultaneous renewal of schooling and teacher education for the well-being of children and young people. The mission for schools addresses this end in two parts: 1) the enculturation of the young into the freedoms and responsibilities of a democratic society and 2) their deep and broad introduction into and preparation for participation in the human conversation. For those who teach the young in schools, the mission includes education in and commitment to this conception of what our schools are for and adds two other responsibilities: 1) employing a caring pedagogy and 2) providing moral stewardship of schools.

Whereas successive eras of school improvement have emphasized reform and accountability, the Agenda emphasizes renewal and responsibility. "Reform" and "accountability" connote compliance, a response that ranks low in its appeal to the human spirit. "Renewal" and "responsibility" connote limitless possibilities and disciplined commitment to moral principles. It should come as no surprise that most people who choose to work in education are motivated and challenged by an agenda of renewal but are scarcely moved by still another round of reform. We might well be surprised, however, to discover that renewal has scarcely been tried.

Introspection

As with those other educational improvement ventures of recent years that have challenged educators to take the high ground of responsibility for renewing themselves and their institutions, the Agenda for Education in a Democracy has been funded almost entirely by private philanthropy, supplemented by institutional budgets. Several of the foundations have signed on for the long haul. The goal put forward in the early 1990s to be reached by the end of the decade was to have each major component of the Agenda at an advanced level of implementation somewhere in the settings of the NNER so that a person visiting all sites in the network would see in composite all these components.

Three years prior to the end of the decade, we began a process of comprehensively assessing progress toward this goal and the lessons learned. Four books published in 1999 describe the Agenda and recent engagements of NNER settings with it; our conception of partner "teaching" schools and the progress of settings with them; the emergence of the much-discussed innovation, the center of pedagogy; and an ongoing institutional renewal effort designed to make teacher preparation coherent from admission to completion. These books were a rich resource for the 1,500 educators, journalists, lay citizens, and representatives of 20 other educational improvement initiatives who joined delegates from the NNER settings in demonstrating their accomplishments and discussing issues at a conference titled "In Praise of Education," which was hosted by the IEI in June 1999.

While these books were being written, we began a more formal assessment of the implementation effort, drawing on an array of data gathered over a 10-year period: the field notes of our staff members' visits to NNER settings, participants' evaluations of the leadership program conducted by the IEI each year since 1992, various self-assessments of the settings in response to specific questions, interviews with individuals in positions to observe changes in local teacher education programs over a period of years, the assessments of our senior staff members, and more.

A draft of the report on all these data sets, pulled together by Kenneth Sirotnik of our staff, became a primary resource document for meetings with four groups of thoughtful individuals during the academic year 1999–2000. Each group joined us in Seattle for a couple of days of intense conversation. The whole constituted a kind of Janus-like look into the past and future of the entire educational improvement initiative embraced by the Agenda for Education in Democracy.

The discussions in these sessions ranged by deliberate design over virtually the entire array of programmatic alternatives and activities from which to select and order priorities designed to advance the Agenda. But one major theme seemed to envelop them all and was judged of paramount significance. Indeed, it stimulated from time to time moods of idealistic passion, which were quickly tempered by moods of deep concern. The central issue can be described as the gulf between a prevailing narrative or world view that perceives economic advancement as the nation's educational imperative and the virtually marginalized alternative represented by our Agenda. The national political debate over schooling is so focused on the former that it is commonly viewed as *the* debate. Not to be part of it—or at least not to voice support for it—leads to accusations not just of opposition but of irrelevance or of being anti-improvement. For the education of the young to be channeled in this fashion endangers the future of the work in progress referred to as democracy.

The discussions frequently probed deeper than just the conceptual differences between these two views of what our schools are for. The deeper stratum we explored has to do with what childhood is for: whether valued for its own sake, like the rest of the life span, or for its instrumental worth in service to some other end. The latter view has prevailed for centuries. Indeed, in the Western world there was no recognition of childhood until relatively recently; one was a young adult learning by observation and participation how to be a mature adult. The positive moralization of society that took place in Europe in the 17th century aroused in some parents a sense of their role as spiritual guardians charged with ensuring the training of their children as preparation for later life. This special training would be provided by a school—"an instrument of strict discipline, protected by the law-courts and the police-courts." In a sense, school created childhood, not as a period of maximum cultivation of the self but as preparation for responsible adulthood. This concept of a formal system of "civilizing" the young carried over into the New World, where it has prevailed and narrowed into the idea of ensuring workers for sustaining the nation's economy —what Neil Postman refers to as the narrative of economic utility.

An alternative narrative that values no phase of the life cycle above another and values education as a civic right for the enhancement of each phase has made onstage cameo appearances throughout the 20th century. But it has often been given short shrift and dismissed as soft and tender, not suited for the tough rigors of adulthood. Although childhood has achieved an identity as a market of consumers and an investment in future economic productivity, it has not yet been accorded existential human value equal to that of adulthood. So long as schooling continues to be perceived primarily as instrumental to the future economy, the scope of the education provided will continue to narrow, to the detriment of childhood.

The Agenda for Education in a Democracy is *not* an alternative in the sense of replacing or rejecting the prevailing economic agenda. Rather, it encompasses much more and rearranges educational priorities. The well-educated individual is not a certified product, but a self engaged in acquiring wisdom, with each step along the journey important in its own right. The desired habits of the workplace are also the habits of civil and civic associational living in the family, on the playground, in the classroom, and at the shopping mall. The well-educated individual easily acquires the skills of a specific workplace when these become necessary. But to make the dozen or more years of schooling instrumental to the future needs of the workplace, however carefully predicted, is immoral and dangerous.

To educate for the future is to educate for the long view of many possible scenarios, no one of which is predictable or all-encompassing. Hence, to educate for the future is to educate broadly and deeply in the here and now and not let ourselves be blindsided by confidence in 20-year forecasts. "What happens fast is illusion, what happens slow is reality. The job of the long view is to penetrate illusion." Penetrating the illusion, oft-repeated in school reform, that "it's all for the children" constitutes a long-term undertaking.

The introspection we have engaged in for the past two or three years has strengthened our belief in the Agenda. It has not been challenged. Rather, part of the Agenda has been described as challenging the teacher education community to fill teacher education's "empty suit" through teaching a core of ethical values. David Imig, arguably our best-informed analyst of trends in teacher education, sees the Agenda as increasingly filling a very large void in the field.

Our initial ambition for the Agenda was that it would guide teacher-preparing institutions and collaborating schools in a process of jointly renewing their respective institutions and programs. We were hopeful but cautiously optimistic that the dependence of teacher education on the arts and sciences would serve to draw the general education components into the renewing process. This is occurring, but slowly, as expected. One gratifying development is the degree to which raising questions about the adequacy of general education for teachers is raising corresponding questions about the adequacy of general education for all students.

We are less than satisfied with our attention to the school side of simultaneous renewal. Substantial immersion of groups of future teachers in partner schools is becoming commonplace. But this immersion is taking place less than we would wish in schools that are busily renewing their practices in line with the Agenda's mission. There are teachers in the partner schools who are every bit as knowledgeable about and committed to the Agenda as are their university colleagues. But they often see the focus of our work as more on renewing teacher education than on renewing schools—even though the two are companion pieces in the change process. Clearly, we have much yet to do toward making the Agenda more compelling and relevant to principals and teachers in elementary and secondary schools.

It became increasingly clear in the discussions of this past year that the success of any agenda addressed to schooling and teacher education on the inside must have considerable understanding and support on the outside. Our seminar program conducted for journalists on the West Coast was strongly endorsed by discussants. But clearly we must do more: with journalists nationwide and, perhaps, with school board members, policy makers, business leaders, and others. Since we cannot reach all groups directly, a promising alternative is to develop a print and electronic media program for selected segments of the general public as a supplement to, not a substitute for, the materials we produce for professional educators.

The challenge, it appears, is to operationalize an agenda now rather widely perceived by teacher educators as relevant and useful so as to make it more widely appealing to both school-based educators and the general public. The centerpiece is the place called school. Teacher education is in the service of the school's mission.

Could it be, then, that the renewal of teacher education as a moral imperative has catalytic power for motivating educational renewal beyond? We think so, and the process of ordering priorities for our future work reflects this assumption.

There is a period of at least a dozen years (from age 4 through age 16) when children and young people play no significant role in the work force and when we must provide them with responsible custodial care. This is a top priority for the majority of parents, most of whom—because of the demands of their employment or other reasons—trust others with this care. Reformers commonly forget this traditional function of our schools, which a technological future for education will not soon, if ever, replace.

The legal protection of the young from the marketplace and, in turn, the prolonging of adolescence to protect adults' participation in the work force gave "going to school" an occupational identity but no clear and highly valued social identity in the 19th and 20th centuries. Neither schools nor their teacher custodians counted for much in the marketplace; indeed, they became a financial burden on communities.

Our recent research into schooling and teacher education revealed a near vacuum with respect to mission, with much of the once-robust debate among educators languishing. It should come as no surprise that the entrepreneurial eyes of the marketplace were opened to schooling when the 1983 report *A Nation at Risk* charged the schools with responsibility for fueling the nation's leadership in the global economy. Our schools and the fifth of the human life span they encompass have acquired, in part by default, a pervasive economic mission.

For want of a clearly articulated alternative that includes attention to the workplace and to both individual and collective well-being, we are on the verge of losing a unique opportunity to create out of a period of necessary custodial care a richly educative phase of life that is geared to a mission not addressed anywhere else: developing the essence of each individual self in the context of justice, fairness, responsibility, and mutual caring to which the Declaration of Independence and the Constitution speak so eloquently.

But the cause is far from lost. Scholarly books and papers on the need for such learning abound, and the message is entering the more popular press. The Agenda for Education in a Democracy is an ongoing response with an encouraging track record that cries out for expansion.

Future Priorities

This intensive period of introspection did not produce a map of new terrain to be explored. Rather, the message emerging was repetitive and clear: the Agenda for Education in a Democracy must be unpeeled like an onion to reveal its wide-ranging implications for schooling, teacher education, the educative environment, and the human conversation. The challenge is to spell out and implement the role of education, particularly during what we call schooling, in developing civil, civic, and ecological democratic character as our guiding narrative. We envision a long-term, five-part schedule of inquiry and implementation. First, whereas the past decade of advancing the Agenda that emerged from the preceding two decades of inquiry on educational change, schooling, and teacher education focused somewhat more heavily on teacher education, that imbalance will be corrected by bringing more attention to schools in our efforts to renew both institutions. Before, the appeal was for the universities to reach out to the schools by attending to the education of educators; now, we will endeavor to help the schools reach out to the universities to seek their involvement in school renewal. There are tough questions to be answered and acted upon.

POSTSCRIPT

Should Secondary Schools Emphasize Education for the Workplace?

The history of secondary education in the United States provides an excellent example of the truth of I. L. Kandel's statement in *Conflicting Theories of Education* (MacMillan, 1938), "Education does not take place in a vacuum. The school is an agency established by society to achieve certain ends. These ends will differ according to the form of each society." And while the basic "form" of society, in terms of America's commitment to a democratic form of government, may not have changed dramatically over the years, the historical, social, and economic forces impacting America's citizens certainly have. And consistent with Kandel's statement, each significant or "sea" change in society has brought new expectations regarding what the curricular priorities of the schools should be. One aspect of this reality is the historical proliferation of different courses and subjects taught in U.S. public schools as new expectations have emerged. This has resulted in what some critics have labeled as "the shopping mall curriculum."

If, as many pundits and politicians suggest, we are now engaged in a sea change from an industrial age to an information age, there will be concomitant demands that the school curriculum respond/react to that change accompanied by criticisms that the response/reaction is not rapid enough. That is precisely the message in the SCANS report: "These developments (globalization of the economy and the 'explosive growth of technology') have barely been reflected in how we prepare young people for work.... Schools need to do a better job."

But there are others, such as Goodlad, who suggest that the education of American children is not well served if the school curriculum is forced to reflect a prevailing narrative or worldview that perceives economic advancement as the nation's educational imperative. Robert Hutchins in *The Conflict in Education in a Democratic Society* (Harper, 1953), states this perspective: "If we allow them [young people] to believe that education will get them better jobs and encourage them to get educated with this end in view, they are entitled to a sense of frustration if, when they have got the education, they do not get the jobs. But if we say that they should be educated in order to be men, and that everybody, whether he is ditch-digger or a bank president, should have this education because he is a man, the ditch-digger may still feel frustrated, but not because of his education."

Other literature regarding this issue includes Carol M. Baker, *Liberal Arts Education for a Global Society* (Carnegie Corporation, 2000); "Making the Grade? What American Workers Think Should Be Done to Improve Education," *A Report by a Joint Project of the John J. Heldrich Center for Workforce Development*

76

at Rutgers University and the Center for Research Analysis at the University of Connecticut (June 2000); Dennis L. Evans, "Education for the Workplace: Another Form of Elitism," *Education Week* (November 8, 1995); Rod Beaumont, "Tech Prep and School to Work: Working Together to Foster Educational Reform," *Horizon* (2000); and Arthur G. Wirth, *Education and Work for the Year 2000: Choices We Face* (Jossey-Bass, 1992).

On the Internet . . .

Ask ERIC Database

The federally funded Educational Resources Information Center (ERIC) is a national information system that provides, through its 16 subject-specific clearinghouses, associated adjunct clearinghouses and support components. A variety of services and products on a broad range of education-related issues can be found at this site.

http://ericir.syr.edu

Americans United for Separation of Church and State

Americans United for Separation of Church and State is a national advocacy group that describes its mission as working to protect the constitutional principle of church-state separation, a vital cornerstone of religious liberty.

http://www.au.org

National Organization for Fair and Open Testing (FairTest)

The National Center for Fair and Open Testing (FairTest) is an advocacy organization that states that it is working to end the abuses, misuses, and flaws of standardized testing and to ensure that evaluation of students and workers is fair, open, and educationally sound.

http://www.fairtest.org

The Thomas Fordham Foundation

The Thomas B. Fordham Foundation supports research, publications, and action projects of national significance in elementary/secondary education reform, including the examination of issues such as standardized testing.

http://www.edexcellence.net

The American Federation of Teachers

The American Federation of Teachers has policy positions on many educational issues, including merit pay for teachers. Explore this site for articles on the subject.

http://www.aft.org/issues/meritpay/

PART 2

Policies

*E*ducational policies are an amalgam of precedent, politics, and philosophy. Policies are usually enacted as responses to perceived problems
and/or reactions to public pressure. Given the unique nature of our approach to the governance of public schools, which has been aptly described as a "national interest, a state power, and a local responsibility,"
it should come as no surprise that controversy abounds regarding educational policies. Such controversy can take the form of support or
opposition to an existing policy or support or opposition to a proposed
policy. Some policies such as those dealing with religion in the schools,
zero tolerance, and mandatory school uniforms can become embroiled
with legal and constitutional issues; others such as high-stakes standardized testing and merit pay for teachers represent accountability issues;
while still others such as achievement level tracking of students and the
role of the principalship represent long-standing policies that have only
recently become reform issues. Some educational policies are formally
legislated while others have developed informally over time and have
become institutionalized. However, no matter what their origin, educational policies can be the source of emotional and volatile disagreements
among the public and within the education profession.

- Should Religious Content and Concepts Be More Evident in Our Schools?

- Do School Uniforms Cause Improvements?

- Are Zero Tolerance Policies Necessary and Effective?

- Is Achievement Level Tracking of Students a Defensible Educational Practice?

- Is High-Stakes Standardized Testing Defensible?

- Should Teacher Pay Be Tied to Measures of Student Learning?

- Is the School Principal Indispensable?

ISSUE 6

Should Religious Content and Concepts Be More Evident in Our Schools?

YES: Michael W. McConnell, from Testimony Before the Subcommittee on the Constitution, Committee on the Judiciary (June 8, 1995)

NO: Annie Laurie Gaylor, from "The Case Against School Prayer," A Brochure of the Freedom From Religion Foundation (1995)

ISSUE SUMMARY

YES: Michael W. McConnell, professor in the School of Law at the University of Utah, argues that many parents have come to believe that the First Amendment is "stacked against them" with respect to their desire to see more religion in the schools.

NO: Annie Laurie Gaylor, editor of *Freethought Today*, states that public schools exist to educate, not to proselytize.

There is perhaps no educational issue that generates as much emotion and disagreement as that which deals with the appropriateness of allowing religious practices and beliefs into public schools. Public school authorities often find themselves in the middle of highly contentious and volatile arguments, with one side asserting the absolute imperative of bringing religious perspectives and practices such as prayer into the schools in order to imbue young people with a sense of morality, while the other side is equally adamant about the fundamental need to maintain a strict separation between church- and state-controlled public schools.

Each side asserts that America's history supports their views. Advocates of increasing the role of religion in schools can point to the origins of schooling in America, which were directly tied to the purposes and promulgations of church and religion. Indeed, the 1647 enactment in colonial Massachusetts of the Old Deluder Satan Act, which is generally accepted as the first legislative mandate for the creation and public support of schools and schooling, found its fundamental purpose in "It being one chief object of that Old Deluder, Satan, to keep men from the knowledge of the scriptures, ... it is therefore ordered, ... that every township, ... shall appoint one within their town to teach all children as shall resort to him to read and write."

Opponents of religious involvement in public schools find their mantra in the First Amendment of the U.S. Constitution, which establishes that the "Congress shall make no law respecting an establishment of religion, or prohibiting the free exercise thereof..." Thomas Jefferson is credited with creating the phrase most often invoked in discussions of that part of the amendment when he wrote of "building a wall of separation between Church and State."

These arguments go beyond school prayer and include issues such as the teaching of evolution versus creationism, the posting of the Ten Commandments in classrooms, and Christmas decorations and displays in the schools. The school choice and voucher movements are also impacted by this controversy. Advocates of choice and vouchers argue that by supporting those concepts we will enable more students to benefit from religious instruction and values and thus improve society. Opponents assert that choice and vouchers are merely not-so-subtle attempts to circumvent the strictures against state support of religion and religious schooling.

The selections that follow summarize many of the arguments with regard to this issue. Michael W. McConnell stresses that bans on religion in the schools go far beyond what true government neutrality on religious issues mandates, while Annie Laurie Gaylor takes the position that mixing public schools and church issues is counterproductive to preserving and promoting freedom of religion, and this invariably persecutes some children.

Michael W. McConnell  **YES**

Testimony of Michael W. McConnell

Causes of the Present Discontent

By any realist standard of comparison, religious liberty in the United States is in excellent shape. There is no official state religion, Americans are free to practice their faith, for the most part, without fear or hindrance, with a diversity and freedom that does not exist anywhere else in the world.

But for many Americans, especially those in public schools and other parts of the government-controlled sector, religious liberty is not all it should be, or all that our Constitution promises. All too often, religious Americans, young and old, are finding that their viewpoints and speech are curtailed because of its religious character. In the past few decades, there has been an extraordinary secularization of American public life, especially in the schools. Religious and traditionalist parents are finding that their viewpoints and concerns are ruled out-of-order, while at the same time the schools can be used to promote ideas and values that are sometimes offensive and hostile to their own.

Tolerance and diversity, it often seems, are one-way streets. There is scrupulous concern lest any child (and increasingly, any adult) be exposed to unwanted religious influence, but little or no concern for the religious or traditionalist child (or adult) who objects to the far-more-prevalent proselytizing that is carried on under the banner of various progressive causes. To object to foul language, relativistic values education, or inappropriate sex education is to risk being branded as a censor. To object to a moment of silence at the beginning of the classroom day, or to the singing of the Hallelujah Chorus, makes one a champion of civil liberty. Students who circulate scurrilous underground newspapers or who interrupt the school day with political causes receive the full protection of the First Amendment; but students who circulate Bible verses or try to meet with their friends for prayer or Bible study are often silenced. In reported cases in state and federal court..., valedictory speeches have been censored, student research topics have been selectively curtailed, distribution of leaflets has been limited on the basis of religious content, and public employees have been forced to hide their Bibles. All too often, the freedom of religion protected by the First Amendment has been twisted into a one-sided freedom religion....

U.S. House of Representatives. Committee on the Judiciary. Subcommittee on the Constitution. *Religious Liberty and the Bill of Rights.* Testimony, June 8, 1995. Washington, DC: U.S. Government Printing Office, 1995.

In the decades preceding World War II, the dominant Protestant majority in this country not infrequently ran roughshod over the rights of others: Catholics, Jews, and other non-Christians alike. Public schools were the vehicle for transmission of majority values, which were heavily imbued with a Protestant orientation. Aid to non-public schools was opposed because such schools were generally Roman Catholic. Prayer, Bible reading, and the celebration of holidays was often conducted without regard to the coercive impact on children of other faiths. Much of the Religion Clause jurisprudence of the past 40 years has been a response to this. And properly so. I cannot read accounts by those who grew up in the era of Protestant hegemony without a keen appreciation for the injustice and casual cruelty of the system.

But—largely under the prodding of courts with little understanding or appreciation for the place of religion in the lives of ordinary Americans—we adopted the wrong solution to this very real problem. We should have opened up the government sector to a wider range of voices, promoted diversity and choice in education, sought pluralistic approaches to public activities with a cultural and religious aspect, and reduced the ability of those with power over public institutions to monopolize channels of education and influence. Instead, we preserved the structures by which Protestant Christians had dominated the public culture, and only changed the content. Secular ideologies came into a position of cultural dominance. The tables were turned. The winners and losers changed places. But the basic injustice—the use of government authority, over education and elsewhere, to favor and promote the values and ideals of one segment of the community—continued unabated.

Some have responded with a call to cultural warfare: if one worldview or another is to be in the ascendancy, let it be ours. Hence the persistent calls for return to a "Christian America." I think there is a better way. The solution is to insist, in a rigorous and principled way, on the rights of all Americans, without regard to faith and ideology, to participate in public life on an equal basis. No more double standard. When speech reflecting a secular viewpoint is permitted, then speech reflecting a religious viewpoint should be permitted, on the same basis. And vice versa. When the government provides benefits to private activities—be it charitable endeavor, health care, education, or art—there should be no discrimination or exclusion on the basis of religious expression, character, or motivation. Religious citizens should not be required to engage in self-censorship as a precondition to participation in public programs. Public programs should be open to all who satisfy the objective purposes of the program. This is already the rule for controversial secular ideas and viewpoints; it should be the rule for religious ideas and viewpoints as well.

The beginning of wisdom in this contentious area of law is to recognize that neutrality and secularism are not the same thing. In the marketplace of ideas, secular viewpoints and ideologies are in competition with religious viewpoints and ideologies. It is no more neutral to favor the secular over the religious than it is to favor the religious over the secular. It is time for a reorientation of constitutional law [and move] from the false neutrality of the secular state, toward a genuine equality of rights.

This will require a great deal of forebearance, for toleration of the expression of others does not come easily. But toleration must be even-handed. I am hard pressed to understand why traditionalist citizens should be expected to tolerate the use of their tax dollars for lewd and sacreligious art, while others go to court to ban nativity scenes from public property at Christmas. The proper task of the Establishment Clause of the First Amendment is to ensure that no religion is given a privileged status in American public life—indeed, that religion in general is not given a privileged status. There is no basis in the history or purpose of the Establishment Clause for the secularization of society, or for discriminating against religious voices in the public sphere. As Justice William J. Brennan, Jr., wrote in *McDaniel v. Paty*, 435 U.S. 618, 641 (1978), "Religionists no less than members of any other group enjoy the full measure of protection afforded speech, association, and political activity generally. The Establishment Clause . . . may not be used as a sword to justify repression of religion or its adherents from any aspect of public life." . . .

Why Not School Prayer?

. . .The great problem is not that public officials are failing to sponsor prayers, but that—in a well-meaning but mistaken commitment to what they think is a constitutional ideal of a secular public sphere—teachers, principals, school boards, and other public officials often engage in discrimination against religious expression. . . .

Some of this anti-religious discrimination is blatantly unconstitutional; some of it has been upheld under current constitutional doctrine; all of it thrives on the uncertainty and confusion of Supreme Court decisions over the past 40 years. And however problematic Supreme Court decisions have been, the effect "in the trenches" has been much, much worse. Among lower courts and governmental administrators, the nuance and confusion of Supreme Court rulings tends to be resolved by a wooden application of the three part test of *Lemon v. Kurtzman*, 403 U.S. 602, 612-13 (1971), and a reflexive invalidation of anything that might be thought to "advance" religion or "entangle" religion and government—no matter how neutral, voluntary, or fair that religious participation might be.

Interpretation of the Establishment Clause of the First Amendment during the past 40 years has wavered between two fundamentally inconsistent visions of the relation between religion and government. Under one vision, which has gone under the rubric of the "no aid" view or the "strict separation" view, there is a high and impregnable wall of separation between goverment and religion. Religion is permitted—indeed it is constitutionally protected—as long as it is confined to the private sphere of home, family, church, and synagogue. But the public sphere must be strictly secular. Laws must be based on strictly secular premises, public education must be strictly secular, public programs must be administered in a strictly secular manner, and public monies must be channeled only to strictly secular activities. This vision is reflected in the lemon test, which states that all law must have a "secular purpose"; that governmental action may not "advance" religion; and that religion and government must not become excessively entangled." ...

Under the separationist view, the various parts of the First Amendment are at war with one another. The Free Exercise Clause forbids the government from inflicting penalties for the practice of religion. As the Court stated in *Sherbert v. Verner*, 374 U.S. 398, 404 (1963), "the liberties of religion and expression may be infringed by the denial of or placing of conditions upon a beneift or privilege," just as they may by the imposition of a "fine" for the exercise of religion. But the Establishment Clause (under the separationist interpretation) requires the government to withhold otherwise available benefits if the beneficiaries would use it for a religious activity. ...

When different parts of the same constitutional amendment are in conflict, the results inevitably will be confusing, inconsistent, and unpredictable. ... Worse yet, in the hands of school administrators, local officials, and lower courts, the effect is all too often to deny religious citizens benefits to which they would otherwise be entitled. In the public schools in particular, this means that religious references in the curriculum have been comprehensively eliminated and religious students forced to shed their constitutional rights at the schoolhouse gate—all the while advocates of various "progressive" ideologies are free to use the schools to advance their ideas of public morality, even when it means running roughshod over the desires and convictions of religious and traditionalist parents. It is no wonder that many parents have come to believe that the First Amendment is stacked against them. ...

Denial of Benefits on Account of Religion

...[N]o discussion of problems in this area would be complete without reference to the Supreme Court's disgraceful record with regard to educational choice. Much of the problematic precedent in this area arose in the context of state efforts to provide some assistance to parents who choose to educate their children under religious auspices. The Supreme Court, in a series of decisions beginning with *Lemon v. Kurtzman,* has made these efforts virtually impossible. The most egregious decision, in my opinion, was *Aquilar v. Felton*, 473 U.S. 402 (1985), in which the Court struck down those portions of the Elementary and Secondary Education Act that provided remedial English and math training by public school teachers to educationally and economically disadvantaged students on the premises of their schools, both public and private. The effect has been to deny less affluent parents the practical ability to exercise choice in education, as is their constitutional right, and to deny to urban school districts the more practicable way to provide remedial services to some of their neediest children. This makes no sense, either pedagogically or constitutionally. In a pluralistic nation, the parents—not the voting majority—should determine the content of their children's education, and they should not be penalized for it. Diversity and choice are far more consistent with the purposes of the First Amendment than the present system.

Even today, when most expert observers believe the Supreme Court would uphold a well-drafted, genuinely neutral educational choice plan, the lower courts continue to rule to the contrary. A recent example is *Miller v. Benson,* 878 F. Supp. 1209 (E.D.Wis.), in which the federal district court ruled that the State of Wisconsin may not extend its private school choice plan to so-called sectarian schools. In Milwaukee, a student qualifying for the program can attend the private school of his choice, including progressive schools, Afrocentric schools, or other schools reflecting the philosophical orientation of the parents, teachers, and administration. But he cannot attend a school where the philosophical orientation is religious. This obviously excludes a large number of the schools parents would like to choose in Milwaukee, and which deliver an excellent education where the public schools have failed. . . .

Is Congressional Action Appropriate?

. . . I agree with those who say that the First Amendment does not require improvement. But it is plain that the interpretation of the First Amendment by the courts does require improvement. This could come about in one of three ways. First, we could hope that the courts will correct their ways. This is always possible, but the record of inconsistent interpretations of the Establishment Clause for the past 40 years does not give much ground for optimism that the Court will adopt a clear position and stick to it. Second, Congress could pass a statute, modelled after the Equal Access Act or the Religious Freedom Restoration Act. This could well be an effective strategy. But since much of the problem here is caused by an exaggerated and distorted interpretation of the Establishment Clause, it is far from obvious that such a statute would be enforceable. Where the problem is constitutional in nature, a constitutional solution may be required. Third, Congress could propose a constitutional amendment, embodying the fundamental principle of religious equality. Although it is to be expected that some separationist groups would fight such an effort with great vigor, the principle of religious equality will no doubt strike a chord with the American public as reflecting a fair and workable approach to church-state problems. If adopted, it would guarantee that religious expression is given equal treatment in public forums and that religious activities are given equal access to public benefits, without giving religion in general (or any specific religion) an advantage. It would thus contribute to religious liberty while guaranteeing to all Americans, secular as well as religious, an equal liberty. Unlike separationist and secularist interpretations of the First Amendment, it would stand for neutrality.

Even if not ultimately adopted, public deliberation over such a proposal would bring these important questions to the forefront, and—like the proposed Child Labor Amendment and Equal Rights Amendments in the past—might well be a stimulus for reform that would make ultimate ratification unnecessary. Because of a lack of interest among the press and the often arcane language of legal decisions, the public has not been made aware of the extent to which our constitutional freedom of religion has been transformed into a freedom from religion. Public discussion of these issues would in itself be a positive development. Much of the problem has occurred because religious discrimination has been cloaked in language of "the separation between church and state" and other legal formulas that disguise what really is going on. It is time to bring these issues out into the open.

Annie Laurie Gaylor

NO

The Case Against School Prayer

"I pledge allegiance to the flag of the United States of America, and to the republic for which it stands, one nation indivisible, with liberty and justice for all."

— The "godless" Pledge of Allegiance, as it was recited by generations of school children, before Congress inserted a religious phrase, "under God," in 1954.

Keep the Church and State Forever Separate

Should Students Pray in Public Schools?

Public schools exist to educate, not to proselytize. Children in public schools are a captive audience. Making prayer an official part of the school day is coercive and invasive. What 5, 8, or 10-year-old could view prayers recited as part of class routine as "voluntary"? Religion is private, and schools are public, so it is appropriate that the two should not mix. To introduce religion in our public schools builds walls between children who may not have been aware of religious differences before.

Why Should Schools Be Neutral?

Our public schools are for *all* children, whether Catholic, Baptist, Quaker, atheist, Buddhist, Jewish, agnostic. The schools are supported by *all* taxpayers, and therefore should be free of religious observances and coercion. It is the sacred duty of parents and churches to instill religious beliefs, free from government dictation. Institutionalizing prayers in public schools usurps the rights of parents.

School prayer proponents mistake government *neutrality* toward religion as *hostility*. The record shows that religious beliefs have flourished in this country not in spite of but because of the constitutional separation of church and state.

From Annie Laurie Gaylor, "The Case Against School Prayer," A Brochure of the Freedom From Religion Foundation (1995). Copyright © 1995 by The Freedom From Religious Education, Inc. Reprinted by permission.

What Happens When Worship Enters Public Schools?

When religion has invaded our public school system, it has singled out the lone Jewish student, the class Unitarian or agnostic, the children in the minority. Families who protest state/ church violations in our public schools invariably experience persecution. It was commonplace prior to the court decision against school prayer to put non-religious or nonorthodox children in places of detention during bible-reading or prayer recitation. The children of Supreme Court plaintiffs against religion in schools, such as Vashti McCollum, Ed Schempp and Ishmael Jaffree, were beaten up on the way to and from school, their families subjected to community harassment and death threats for speaking out in defense of a constitutional principle. We know from history how harmful and destructive religion is in our public schools. In those school districts that do not abide by the law, school children continue to be persecuted today.

Can't Students Pray in Public Schools Now?

Individual, silent, personal prayer never has and never could be outlawed in public schools. The courts have declared *government-fostered* prayers unconstitutional—those led, required, sanctioned, scheduled or suggested by officials.

It is dishonest to call any prayer "voluntary" that is encouraged or required by a public official or legislature. By definition, if the government suggests that students pray, whether by penning the prayer, asking them to vote whether to pray or setting aside time to pray, it is endorsing and promoting that prayer. It is coercive for schools to schedule worship as an official part of the school day, school sports or activities, or to use prayer to formalize graduation ceremonies. Such prayers are more "mandatory" than "voluntary."

What's Wrong With a "Voluntary" Prayer Amendment?

Proponents of so-called "voluntary" school prayer amendment (such as the one proposed in 1995) are admitting that our secular Constitution prohibits organized prayers in public schools. Otherwise, why would an amendment to our U.S. Constitution be required? The nation must ask whether politically motivated Newt Gingrich & Co. are wiser than James Madison, principal author of the Constitution, and the other founders who engineered the world's oldest and most successful constitution!

The radical school prayer amendment would negate the First Amendment's guarantee against government establishment of religion. Most distressing, it would be at the expense of the civil rights of children, America's most vulnerable class. It would attack the heart of the Bill of Rights, which safeguards the rights of the individual from the tyranny of the majority.

What Would the Prayer Amendment Permit?

The text of the proposed federal amendment (as of January, 1995) reads:

> "Nothing in this Constitution shall be construed to prohibit individual or group prayer in public schools or other public institutions. No person shall be required by the United States or by any State to participate in prayer. Neither the United States or any State shall compose the words of any prayer to be said in public schools."

Since the right to "individual prayer" already exists, the real motive is to instill "group prayer."

No wording in this amendment would prevent the government from *selecting* the prayer, or the particular version of the bible it should be taken from. Nothing restricts prayers to "nondenominational" or "nonsectarian" (not that such a restriction would make it acceptable). Nothing would prevent a school from selecting the Lord's Prayer or other prayers to Jesus, and blasting it over the intercom. For that matter, nothing would prevent the school from sponsoring prayers to Allah or Zoroaster. Nothing would prevent principals, teachers or clergy from leading the students. Nothing would prevent nonparticipating students from being singled out. The proposal also seeks to institutionalize group prayer in other public settings, presumably public-supported senior centers, courthouses, etc.

School prayer supporters envision organized, vocal, group recitations of prayer, daily classroom displays of belief in a deity or religion, dictated by the majority. Those in the minority would be compelled to conform to a religion or ritual in which they disbelieve, to suffer the humiliation and imposition of submitting to a daily religious exercise against their will, or be singled out by orthodox classmates and teachers as "heretics" or "sinners" for not participating.

Haven't Public Schools Always Had Prayer?

At the time the U.S. Supreme Court issued its 1962 and 1963 decrees against school-sponsored prayers and bible-reading, it is estimated religious observances were unknown in about half of the nation's public schools.

Horace Mann, the father of our public school system, championed the elimination of sectarianism from American schools, largely accomplished by the 1840's. Bible reading, prayers or hymns in public schools were absent from most public schools by the end of the 19th century, after Catholic or minority-religion immigrants objected to Protestant bias in public schools.

Until the 20th century, only Massachusetts required bible-reading in the schools, in a statute passed by the virulently anti-Catholic Know Nothing Party in the 1850's. Only after 1913 did eleven other states make prayers or bible-reading compulsory. A number of other states outlawed such practices by judicial or administrative decree, and half a dozen state supreme courts overruled devotionals in public schools.

As early as the 1850's, the Superintendent of Schools of New York State ordered that prayers could no longer be required as part of public school activities. The Cincinnati Board of Education resolved in 1869 that "religious instruction and the reading of religious books, including the Holy Bible, was prohibited in the common schools of Cincinnati."

Presidents Ulysses S. Grant and Theodore Roosevelt spoke up for what Roosevelt called "absolutely nonsectarian public schools." Roosevelt added that it is "not our business to have the Protestant Bible or the Catholic Vulgate or the Talmud read in these schools."

For nearly half a century, the United States Supreme Court, consistent with this nation's history of secular schools, has ruled against religious indoctrination through schools (*McCollum v. Board of Education,* 1948), prayers and devotionals in public schools (*Engel v. Vitale,* 1962) and prayers and bible-reading (*Abington School District v. Schempp,* 1963), right up through the 1992 *Weisman* decision against prayers at public school commencements.

How Can Prayer Be Harmful?

Contrary to right-wing claims, piety is not synonymous with virtue. People should be judged by their actions, not by what religion they believe in or how publicly or loudly they pray.

Some Americans believe in the power of prayer; others believe nothing fails like prayer. Some citizens say prayer makes them feel better, but others contend that prayer is counterproductive to personal responsibility. Such a diversity of views is constitutionally protected; our secular government simply is not permitted to pick a side in religious debates.

"The hands that help are better far than lips that pray," wrote Robert G. Ingersoll. Who could disagree?

Should Government Become "Prayer Police"?

How ironic that those campaigning on an anti-Big Government theme, who contend that government should get out of our private lives, would seek to tell our children who to pray to in our public schools! As many editorials across the country have pointed out, the school prayer debate seems calculated to deflect attention away from the more pressing economic questions facing our nation. As one conservative governor put it: "If we don't deal with the economic issues, we'll need more than prayer to solve our problems."

Can't Moral Decline Be Traced to the Prayer Decisions?

Some politicans like to blame everything bad in America upon the absence of school prayer. Get real! Entire generations of Americans have grown up to be law-abiding citizens without ever once reciting a prayer in school! If prayer is the answer, why are our jails and prisons bulging with born-agains! Japan, where no one prays at school, has the lowest crime rate of any developed nation.

Institutionalizing school prayer can not raise the SAT scores (only more studying and less praying can do that). It is irrational to charge that the complicated sociological problems facing our everchanging population stem from a lack of prayer in schools.

One might just as well credit the lack of prayer with the great advances that have taken place since the 1962 and 1963 decisions on prayer. Look at the leap in civil liberties, equality, environmental awareness, women's rights, science, technology and medicine! The polio scare is over. Fountains, buses, schools are no longer segregated by law. We've made great strides in medical treatment. We have VCRs and the computer chip. The Cold War has ended! Who would turn the clock back?

What About the Rights of the Majority?

Our political system is a democratic republic in which we use majority vote to elect certain officials or pass referenda. But we do not use majority vote to decide what religion, if any, our neighbors must observe! The "majority" is free to worship at home, at tax-exempt churches, on the way to and from school, or privately in school. There are 16 school-less hours a day when children can pray, not to mention weekends.

Many in the "majority" do not support school prayers. And if the majority religion gets to choose which prayers are said in schools, that would mean a lot of Protestant kids will be reciting Catholic prayers! The Roman Catholic Church is the single largest denomination in our country. Should Protestant minorities be excused so the classroom can pray in unison to the Virgin Mary? In a few school districts, Muslims outnumber other religions. Should Christian minorities march into the hall with their ears covered while the principal prays to Allah over the intercom?

What's Wrong With a Moment of Silence?

Given the regimentation of school children, it would make more sense to have a "moment of bedlam" than a "moment of silence"! Obviously, the impetus for "moments of silence or meditation" is to circumvent the rulings against religion in schools. The legislative history of such state laws reveals the religious motives behind the legislation, as in the Alabama law struck down by the U.S. Supreme Court in 1985 calling for a "moment of silence for meditation or prayer."

When a "moment of silence" law was enacted in Arkansas at the suggestion of then-Gov. Bill Clinton, the law mandating this meaningless ritual was later repealed following popular indifference. We know from experience that many teachers and principals would regard a "moment of silence" mandate as a green light to introduce prayers, causing more legal challenges at the expense of taxpayers.

Should Commencements Start With Prayers?

In 1992, the Court ruled in *Lee v. Weisman* that prayers at public school commencements are an impermissible establishment of religion: "The lessons of the First Amendment are as urgent in the modern world as the 18th Century when it was written. One timeless lesson is that if citizens are subjected to state-sponsored religious exercises, the State disavows its own duty to guard and respect that sphere of inviolable conscience and belief which is the mark of a free people," wrote Justice Kennedy for the majority. He dismissed as unacceptable the cruel idea that a student should forfeit her own graduation in order to be free from such an establishment of religion.

What About "Student-Initiated" Prayer?

This is a ruse proposed by extremist Christian legal groups such as the Rutherford Institute, and the American Center for Law and Justice run by televangelist Pat Robertson. Religious coercion is even worse at the hands of another student, subjecting students to peer pressure, pitting students in the majority against students in the minority, treating them as outsiders with school complicity.

Imposing prayer-by-majority-vote is flagrant and insensitive abuse of school authority. Such schools should be teaching students about the purpose of the Bill of Rights, instead of teaching them to be religious bullies. Some principals or school boards have even made seniors hold open class votes on whether to pray at graduation, leading to hostility and reprisal against those students brave enough to stand up for the First Amendment.

"The notion that a person's constitutional rights may be subject to a majority vote is itself anathema," wrote Judge Albert V. Bryan, Jr. in a 1993 ruling in Virginia, one of several similar district court rulings around the nation banning any prayer, whether student- or clergy-led.

We cannot put liberties protected by our Bill of Rights up to a vote of school children! Should kindergartners be forced about whether to pray before their milk and cookies? Under such reasoning, what would make it wrong for students to vote to segregate schools or otherwise violate the civil liberties of minorities?

Keep the State and Church Forever Separate

Our founders wisely adopted a secular, godless constitution, the first to derive its powers from "We, the People" and the consent of the governed, rather than claiming divine authority. They knew from the experience of religious persecution, witchhunts and religious discrimination in the Thirteen Colonies, and from the bloody history left behind in Europe, that the surest path to tyranny was to entangle church and state. That is why they adopted a secular constitution whose only references to religion are exclusionary, such as that there shall be no religious test for public office (Art. VI). There were no prayers offered at the Constitutional Convention, which shows their intent to separate religion from secular affairs.

Prayers in schools and religion in government are no panacea for social ills— they are an invitation to divisiveness. More people have been killed in the name of religion than for any other cause. As Thomas Paine pointed out, "Persecution is not an original feature in any religion; but it is always the strongly marked feature of all religions established by law."

Even Jesus Was Against School Prayer

> *"Thou shalt not be as the hypocrites are: for they love to pray standing in the synagogues and in the corners of the streets, that they may be seen of men...*
>
> *"But thou, when thou prayest, enter into thy closet, and when thou hast shut thy door, pray to thy Father which is in secret."*

— Matt. 6:5-6

> *"There is no such source and cause of strife, quarrel, fights, malignant opposition, persecution, and war, and all evil in the state, as religion. Let it once enter our civil affairs, our government would soon be destroyed. Let it once enter our common schools, they would be destroyed."*

— Supreme Court of Wisconsin, Weiss v. District Board
March 18, 1890

> *"Leave the matter of religion to the family altar, the church, and the private school, supported entirely by private contributions. Keep the church and state forever separate."*

— Ulysses S. Grant
"The President's Speech at Des Moines" (1875)

> *"Congress shall make no law respecting an establishment of religion, or prohibiting the free exercise thereof."*

— First Amendment, Bill of Rights, U.S. Constitution

Thomas Jefferson, author of the sweeping Virginia Statute of Religious Freedom, stating that no citizen "shall be compelled to frequent or support any religious worship, place, or ministry whatsoever..." and that to "compel a man to furnish contributions of money for the propagation of [religious] opinions which he disbelieves is sinful and tyrannical."

> *"I contemplate with sovereign reverence that act of the whole American people which declared that their legislature should make no law 'respecting an establishment of religion, or prohibiting the free exercise thereof,' thus building a wall of separation between church and state."*

— President Thomas Jefferson
1802 letter to the Baptists of Danbury, Connecticut

Supreme Court Cases Opposing Religious Worship in Schools

- *McCollum v. Board of Education*, 333 U.S. 203, 212 (1948). Struck down religious instruction in public schools. The case involved school-sponsored religious instruction in which the sole nonreligious student, Jim McCollum, was placed in detention and persecuted by schoolmates in Champaign, Illinois.

- *Tudor v. Board of Education of Rutherford,* 14 J.N. 31 (1953), cert. denied 348 U.S. 816 (1954). Let stand a lower court ruling that the practice of allowing volunteers to distribute Gideon Bibles at public school was unconstitutional.
- *Engel v. Vitale,* 370 U.S. 421 (1962). Declared prayers in public school unconstitutional.
- *Abington Township School District v. Schempp,* 374. U.S. 203 (1963). Declared unconstitutional devotional Bible reading and recitation of the Lord's Prayer in public schools.
- *Epperson v. Arkansas,* 393 U.S., 97, 104 (1968). Struck down state law forbidding schools to teach the science of evolution.
- *Stone v. Graham,* 449 U.S. 39 (1980). Declared unconstitutional the posting of the Ten Commandments in classrooms.
- *Wallace v. Jaffree,* 472 U.S. 38, 72 (1985). Overturned law requiring daily "period of silence not to exceed one minute . . . for meditation or daily prayer."
- *Jager v. Douglas County School District,* 862 F.2d 824 (11th Cir.), Cert. den. 490 U.S. 1090 (1989). Let stand a lower court ruling in Georgia that pre-game invocations at high school football games are unconstitutional.
- *Lee v. Weisman,* 120 L.E. 2d 467/ 112 S.C.T. 2649 (1992). Ruled prayers at public school graduations an impermissible establishment of religion.
- *Berger v. Rensselaer,* 982 F.2d, 1160 (7th Cir.) Cert. denied. 124 L.E. 2d 254 (1993). Let stand ruling barring access to Gideons to pass out bibles in Indiana schools.

POSTSCRIPT

Should Religious Content and Concepts Be More Evident in Our Schools?

It is understandable that where there is a coming together of competing or conflicting core values there is a potential for conflict. Thus it should come as no surprise that when America's historic and constitutional commitment to the right of free exercise of religious belief and the equally fundamental tradition of separating government from establishing or supporting religious practices meet at the public schoolhouse door, we do indeed have controversy.

Many parents want their children to be educated in public schools, but they also want such education to include values and ideas drawn from religious beliefs and practices. Other parents, equally adamant about public education for their children, see real dangers to the diversity of religious beliefs (or the lack thereof) if religion is brought into public schools.

It is a well-established point of constitutional law that state-sponsored public schools and public school teachers, administrators, and school board members are considered extensions of state government and as such are subject to the provisions of the Constitution (the proscriptions and limitations of governmental power contained in the Bill of Rights originally applied only to the national government, but with the adoption of the Fourteenth Amendment in 1868 and subsequent court decisions, those proscriptions and limitations have been extended to include state and local governments as well). Over the past 50 years the Supreme Court has made numerous rulings on the relationship between religion and state-sponsored public schools. A cursory review of a few such cases shows the wide-ranging topics involved in this controversy:

- *West Virginia Board of Education v. Barnette* (1943). The Court ruled that the state could not require Jehovah's Witnesses to salute the flag.
- *McCollum v. Board of Education* (1948). The Court struck down a program that allowed religious educators to provide instruction in public schools.
- *Zorach v. Clausen* (1952). The Court allowed released time, off-campus religious instruction to public school children.
- *Engle v. Vitale* (1962). The Court struck down a nondenominational prayer in New York schools.
- *Abington Township v. Schempp* (1963). The Court prohibited the required reading of the Bible and recitation of the Lord's Prayer.
- *Stone v. Graham* (1983). The Court overturned a Kentucky statute that required the posting of the Ten Commandments in every public school classroom.

- *Lee v. Welsman* (1992). The Court ruled that public schools may not sponsor invocations at graduation ceremonies.
- *Santa Fe Independent School District v. Doe* (2000). The Court ruled that student-initiated public address invocations at high school football games violate the First Amendment.

Obviously this issue and the controversies surrounding it will continue to be of great interest and importance and will necessitate future decisions by the Court. In the near term it is predictable that the Court will be called upon to rule on the constitutionality of using public monies by way of vouchers and/or tax credits to assist parents in sending their children to parochial schools.

ISSUE 7

Do School Uniforms Cause Improvements?

YES: U.S. Department of Education, from *Manual on School Uniforms* (February 1996)

NO: David L. Brunsma and Kerry A. Rockquemore, from "The Effects of Student Uniforms on Attendance, Behavior Problems, Substance Use, and Academic Achievement," *Journal of Educational Research* (September–October 1998)

ISSUE SUMMARY

YES: The United States Department of Education endorses school uniform policies, presenting suggestions for implementation and examples of successful programs.

NO: David L. Brunsma and Kerry A. Rockquemore, professors at the University of Alabama and the University of Connecticut, respectively, report the results of their research, which has caused them to reject the idea that school uniforms improve student performance in areas such as attendance, academic achievement, behavioral issues, and substance abuse.

$\mathbf{R}$eceiving a strong "bully pulpit" endorsement from former President Bill Clinton, the notion that school uniform policies can be an important force in promoting improved conditions in the nation's schools has gained many advocates over the past five to six years. Perhaps the most widely publicized school uniform policy in terms of assertions of major positive impact has been that of the Long Beach Unified School District in California. In 1996 President Clinton chose the Long Beach district as the setting where he announced the publication of a *Manual on School Uniforms,* by the United States Department of Education (USDE) (February 1996). During his speech in Long Beach the President stated, "I want to say the entire United States of America is in your debt because you took the first step to show elementary and middle school students that wearing uniforms in class reduces violence, reduces truancy, reduces disorder, increases learning and ... gives a bed of unity and purpose and teamwork of students and the schools that are in this school district."

With such a ringing presidential endorsement of school uniforms it is not surprising that a number of other schools and school districts across the nation took steps to implement their own policies. The *Manual on School Uniforms* listed U.S. schools in several large cities, including Seattle, Richmond, Kansas City, Memphis, Baltimore, Norfolk, and Phoenix as having school uniform policies in 1996. Since then the phenomenon has proliferated, with over 3,000 schools reporting the adoption of such policies in a survey conducted by the National Association of Elementary School Principals (NAESP) in 1998.

The NAESP survey indicates that most school uniform policies are found in elementary and middle schools. However, the enthusiastic support and the testimony of positive and dramatic results from those levels bring pressure on secondary schools to implement similar plans. Responding to such pressure, some secondary schools either have or are moving toward adoption of school uniform policies.

It is to the assertions of positive impact of school uniform policies, such as those outlined by the United States Department of Education, that David L. Brunsma and Kerry A. Rockquemore direct their attention. Using data derived from the National Educational Longitudinal Study of 1988 and three follow-up studies, these researchers analyze differences between "uniformed" and "nonuniformed" students on measures of absenteeism, behavioral problems, reduced substance abuse, and improved standardized test scores. They state that their findings provide no support for the idea that school uniform policies cause improvement on the measures studied. They also analyze the statement of the Long Beach school district regarding the positive impact that school uniforms had on student behavior and find no substantiation. Similar findings were reported by researchers studying the impact of school uniforms in the Miami–Dade County public schools in Florida.

Manual on School Uniforms

School Uniforms: Where They Are and Why They Work

A safe and disciplined learning environment is the first requirement of a good school. Young people who are safe and secure, who learn basic American values and the essentials of good citizenship, are better students. In response to growing levels of violence in our schools, many parents, teachers, and school officials have come to see school uniforms as one positive and creative way to reduce discipline problems and increase school safety.

They observed that the adoption of school uniform policies can promote school safety, improve discipline, and enhance the learning environment. The potential benefits of school uniforms include:

- decreasing violence and theft—even life-threatening situations—among students over designer clothing or expensive sneakers;
- helping prevent gang members from wearing gang colors and insignia at school;
- instilling students with discipline;
- helping parents and students resist peer pressure;
- helping students concentrate on their school work; and
- helping school officials recognize intruders who come to the school.

As a result, many local communities are deciding to adopt school uniform policies as part of an overall program to improve school safety and discipline. California, Florida, Georgia, Indiana, Louisiana, Maryland, New York, Tennessee, Utah and Virginia have enacted school uniform regulations. Many large public school systems—including Baltimore, Cincinnati, Dayton, Detroit, Los Angeles, Long Beach, Miami, Memphis, Milwaukee, Nashville, New Orleans, Phoenix, Seattle and St. Louis—have schools with either voluntary or mandatory uniform policies, mostly in elementary and middle schools. In addition, many private and parochial schools have required uniforms for a number of

From U.S. Department of Education, *Manual on School Uniforms* (February 1996). Washington, DC: U.S. Government Printing Office, 1996.

years. Still other schools have implemented dress codes to encourage a safe environment by, for example, prohibiting clothes with certain language or gang colors.

Users' Guide to Adopting a School Uniform Policy

The decision whether to adopt a uniform policy is made by states, local school districts, and schools. For uniforms to be a success, as with all other school initiatives, parents must be involved. The following information is provided to assist parents, teachers, and school leaders in determining whether to adopt a school uniform policy.

1. Get Parents Involved From the Beginning

Parental support of a uniform policy is critical for success. Indeed, the strongest push for school uniforms in recent years has come from parent groups who want better discipline in their children's schools. Parent groups have actively lobbied schools to create uniform policies and have often led school task forces that have drawn up uniform guidelines. Many schools that have successfully created a uniform policy survey parents first to gauge support for school uniform requirements and then seek parental input in designing the uniform. Parent support is also essential in encouraging students to wear the uniform.

2. Protect Students' Religious Expression

A school uniform policy must accommodate students whose religious beliefs are substantially burdened by a uniform requirement. As U.S. Secretary of Education Richard W. Riley stated in *Religious Expression in Public Schools,* a guide he sent to superintendents throughout the nation on August 10, 1995:

> Students may display religious messages on items of clothing to the same extent that they are permitted to display other comparable messages. Religious messages may not be singled out for suppression, but rather are subject to the same rules as generally apply to comparable messages. When wearing particular attire, such as yarmulkes and head scarves, during the school day is part of students' religious practice, under the Religious Freedom Restoration Act schools generally may not prohibit the wearing of such items.

3. Protect Students' Other Rights of Expression

A uniform policy may not prohibit students from wearing or displaying expressive items—for example, a button that supports a political candidate—so long as such items do not independently contribute to disruption by substantially interfering with discipline or with the rights of others. Thus, for example, a uniform policy may prohibit students from wearing a button bearing a gang insignia. A uniform policy may also prohibit items that undermine the integrity of the uniform, notwithstanding their expressive nature, such as a sweatshirt that bears a political message but also covers or replaces the type of shirt required by the uniform policy.

4. Determine Whether to Have a Voluntary or Mandatory School Uniform Policy

Some schools have adopted wholly voluntary school uniform policies which permit students freely to choose whether and under what circumstances they will wear the school uniform. Alternatively, some schools have determined that it is both warranted and more effective to adopt a mandatory uniform policy.

5. When a Mandatory School Uniform Policy Is Adopted, Determine Whether to Have an "Opt Out" Provision

In most cases, school districts with mandatory policies allow students, normally with parental consent, to "opt out" of the school uniform requirements.

Some schools have determined, however, that a mandatory policy with no "opt out" provision is necessary to address a disruptive atmosphere. A Phoenix, Arizona school, for example, adopted a mandatory policy requiring students to wear school uniforms, or in the alternative attend another public school. That Phoenix school uniform policy was recently upheld by a state trial court in Arizona. Note that in the absence of a finding that disruption of the learning environment has reached a point that other lesser measures have been or would be ineffective, a mandatory school uniform policy without an "opt out" provision could be vulnerable to legal challenge.

6. Do Not Require Students to Wear a Message

Schools should not impose a form of expression on students by requiring them to wear uniforms bearing a substantive message, such as a political message.

7. Assist Families That Need Financial Help

In many cases, school uniforms are less expensive than the clothing that students typically wear to school. Nonetheless, the cost of purchasing a uniform may be a burden on some families. School districts with uniform polices should make provisions for students whose families are unable to afford uniforms. Many have done so. Examples of the types of assistance include: (a) the school district provides uniforms to students who cannot afford to purchase them; (b) community and business leaders provide uniforms or contribute financial support for uniforms; (c) school parents work together to make uniforms available for economically disadvantaged students; and (d) used uniforms from graduates are made available to incoming students.

8. Treat School Uniforms as Part of an Overall Safety Program

Uniforms by themselves cannot solve all of the problems of school discipline, but they can be one positive contributing factor to discipline and safety. Other initiatives that many schools have used in conjunction with uniforms to address specific problems in their community include aggressive truancy reduction initiatives, drug prevention efforts, student-athlete drug testing, community efforts to limit gangs, a zero tolerance policy for weapons, character education classes, and conflict resolution programs. Working with parents, teachers, students, and principals can make a uniform policy part of a strong overall safety program, one that is broadly supported in the community.

Model School Uniform Policies

States and local school districts must decide how they will ensure a safe and disciplined learning environment. Below are some examples of school districts that have adopted school uniforms as part of their strategy.

Long Beach, California

Type: Uniforms are mandatory in all elementary and middle schools. Each school in the district determines the uniform its students will wear.

Opt-out: Yes, with parental consent

Size of program: 58,500 elementary and middle school students

Implementation date: 1994

Support for disadvantaged students: Each school must develop an assistance plan for families that cannot afford to buy uniforms. In most cases, graduating students either donate or sell used uniforms to needy families.

Results: District officials found that in the year following implementation of the school uniform policy, overall school crime decreased 36 percent, fights decreased 51 percent, sex offenses decreased 74 percent, weapons offenses decreased 50 percent, assault and battery offenses decreased 34 percent, and vandalism decreased 18 percent. Fewer than one percent of the students have elected to opt out of the uniform policy.

Dick Van Der Laan of the Long Beach Unified School District explained, "We can't attribute the improvement exclusively to school uniforms, but we think it's more than coincidental." According to Long Beach police chief William Ellis, "Schools have fewer reasons to call the police. There's less conflict among students. Students concentrate more on education, not on who's wearing $100 shoes or gang attire."

Seattle, Washington

Type: Mandatory uniform policy at South Shore Middle School

Opt-out: Yes, with parental consent. Students who opt out must attend another middle school in the district.

Size of program: 900 middle school students

Implementation: 1995

Support for disadvantaged students: South Shore works with local businesses that contribute financial support to the uniform program. In addition, the administration at South Shore found that the average cost of clothing a child in a school with a prescribed wardrobe is less than in schools without such a program, sometimes 80 percent less. School officials believe that durability, reusability and year-to-year consistency also increase the economy of the school's plan.

Results: The principal of South Shore, Dr. John German, reports that "this year the demeanor in the school has improved 98 percent, truancy and tardies are down, and we have not had one reported incident of theft." Dr. German explains that he began the uniform program because his students were "draggin', saggin' and laggin'. I needed to keep them on an academic focus. My kids were really into what others were wearing." Only five students have elected to attend another public school.

Richmond, Virginia

Type: Voluntary uniform policy at Maymont Elementary School for the Arts and Humanities

Opt-out: Uniforms are voluntary.

Size of program: 262 elementary school students

Implementation date: 1994

Support for disadvantaged students: Responding to parent concerns about the cost of uniforms, the school sought community financial support for the uniform program. Largely as a result of financial donations from businesses and other community leaders, the percentage of students wearing uniforms rose from 30 percent in 1994–95, the first year of the program, to 85 percent during the current year.

Results: Maymont principal Sylvia Richardson identifies many benefits of the uniform program, including improved behavior, an increase in attendance rates and higher student achievement. . . .

Memphis, Tennessee

Type: Voluntary uniform policy at Douglas Elementary School

Opt-out: Uniforms are voluntary.

Size of program: 532 elementary school students

Implementation date: 1993

Support for disadvantaged students: Douglas has business partners in Memphis that have contributed financial support to purchase uniforms for needy families.

Results: According to Guidance Counselor Sharon Carter, "The tone of the school is different. There's not the competitiveness, especially in grades, 4, 5, and 6, about who's wearing what." Ninety percent of the students have elected to wear uniforms on school uniform days, Monday through Thursday. Fridays are "casual" days during which none of the students wear uniforms.…

Norfolk, Virginia

Type: Mandatory uniform policy at Ruffner Middle School

Opt-out: None. Students who come to school without a uniform are subject to in-school detention.

Size of program: 977 middle school students

Implementation date: 1995

Support for disadvantaged students: The school provides uniforms for students who cannot afford them.

Results: Using U.S. Department of Education software to track discipline data, Ruffner has noted improvements in students' behavior. Leaving class without permission is down 47 percent, throwing objects is down 68 percent and fighting has decreased by 38 percent. Staff attribute these changes in part to the uniform code.

Phoenix, Arizona

Type: Mandatory uniform policy at Phoenix Preparatory Academy

Opt-out: Yes, with parental consent. Students who opt out must attend another middle school in the district.

Size of program: 1,174 middle school students

Implementation date: 1995

Support for disadvantaged students: A grant from a local foundation covers the $25 to $30 cost of uniforms for families that cannot afford to buy them.

Results: According to the principal, Ramon Leyba, "The main result is an overall improvement in the school climate and a greater focus on positive behavior. A big portion of that is from uniforms."

**David L. Brunsma and
Kerry A. Rockquemore**

The Effects of Student Uniforms on Attendance, Behavior Problems, Substance Use, and Academic Achievement

Recent discourse on public school reform has focused on mandatory uniform policies. Proponents of such reform measures emphasize the benefits of student uniforms on specific behavioral and academic outcomes. This research empirically tests the claims made by uniform advocates using 10th grade data from The National Educational Longitudinal Study of 1988. Our findings indicate that student uniforms have no direct effect on substance use, behavioral problems or attendance. A negative effect of uniforms on student academic achievement was found. These findings are contrary to current discourse on student uniforms. We conclude that uniform policies may indirectly affect school environment and student outcomes by providing a visible and public symbol of commitment to school improvement and reform.

Introduction

Public discourse surrounding educational reform has recently focused on the importance of uniform policies in public schools. School uniform policies have historically been restricted to the private sector and have only recently begun to be discussed as a viable policy option in public school districts. A decade of research showing the effectiveness of private schools has led some school reformers to consider various policies which are linked to private and Catholic school success. Within the Catholic school literature, school uniforms have never been asserted as a primary factor in producing the Catholic school effect. Nevertheless, public school administrators are beginning to consider uniform policies as a way to improve the overall school environment and student achievement. Due to the controversial nature of mandatory school uniform policies, educators are speaking out, both advocating and condemning the proposed reform efforts.

Uniform advocates propose several different arguments. First, uniforms are argued to positively effect student safety by: lowering student victimization (Scherer 1991), decreasing gang activity and fights (Kennedy, 1995; Loesch, 1995), and differentiating strangers from students in the school building (Department of Justice, 1996; Gursky, 1996). Second, uniforms are asserted to increase student learning and attitudes towards school through: enhancing the learning environment (Stover, 1990), raising school pride (Jarchow, 1992), increasing student achievement (Thomas, 1994), raising levels of preparedness (Thomas, 1994), and promoting conformity to organizational goals (LaPointe, Holloman, and Alleyne, 1992; Workman & Johnson, 1994). Additionally, uniforms are attributed to decreasing behavior problems by: increasing attendance rates, lowering suspension rates, and decreasing substance use among the student body (Gursky, 1996). Finally, various psychological outcomes are attributed to wearing uniforms including: increased self-esteem (Thomas, 1994), increased spirit (Jarchow, 1992), and increased feelings of "oneness" among students (LaPointe, Holoman, & Alleyne, 1992).

Opponents of adopting uniform policies stress the legal, financial, and questionable effectiveness of such policies. The legal concerns focus on the supposition that requiring a uniform violates children's individual rights (Thomas, 1994; Virginia State Department of Education, 1992). This argument is extended by opponents who argue that mandatory uniform policies are being considered largely for urban school districts, and hence are being forced upon a predominately minority and poor student population (Thomas, 1994). Financially, groups such as the American Civil Liberties Union have voiced concerns about the cost of uniforms, specifically that purchasing one is a mandatory cost which some disadvantaged parents are unable to afford (Gursky, 1996). Finally, the strongest opponents to uniform policies charge that there currently exists no empirical evidence to support the numerous and varied claims of uniform proponents (LaPointe, Holoman, & Alleyne, 1992).

The case study most often cited in the political rhetoric surrounding the uniform debate is that of the Long Beach Unified School District (LBUSD). LBUSD was one of the first large urban school districts within the United States to adopt a mandatory school uniform policy. This case provides some context for the discussion in that it serves as a prime example of a system which has recently instituted a school uniform requirement, has received national attention for its efforts, and attributes students' behavioral changes to the mandatory uniform policy. In a press release, the Board President of LBUSD had the following to say about the uniform policy:

> These schools are becoming educational workplaces. Students arrive dressed for success, ready to learn. They're getting along with one another better and experiencing significant gains. Principals and teachers tell us that students' success is taking many forms—fewer absences, fewer tardies, fewer truancies, fewer referrals to the office for behavior problems, fewer suspensions and expulsions, better grades and, in some cases, significantly higher achievement.

> — (Polacheck, 1996)

In this district, school uniforms are currently required from kindergarten through eighth grade in 70 schools, including approximately 60,000 students. School District press releases indicate that there is widespread parental support for the mandatory uniform policy. . . .

It is typically assumed, as exemplified by the Long Beach case, that uniforms are the sole factor causing direct change in numerous behavioral and academic outcomes. It is these pronouncements by uniform proponents that have raised strident objections and created a political climate in which public school uniform policies have become highly contested. This ongoing public discourse is not only entrenched in controversy, but largely fueled by conjecture and anecdotal evidence. Hence, it seems critical at this point in time, for empirical analyses to be conducted to inform the school uniform debate. This paper examines the relationship between uniforms and several outcomes which represent the core elements of uniform proponents' claims. Specifically, we will examine the effect of wearing a uniform on attendance, disciplinary behavior problems, substance abuse, and academic achievement. It is the intention of the authors that a thorough analysis of the arguments proposed by uniform advocates will add critical insight to the ongoing debate on the effects of school uniform policies.

Theoretical Framework

Nathan Joseph (1986) has formulated an analysis of clothing as communication which provides a framework within which uniform proponents claims can be better understood. He asserts that clothing can be considered a sign, which he defines as "anything that stands for something else." Clothing, as a sign, conveys information about values, beliefs and emotions. If the clothing that adolescents wear can be considered a sign, then that which they freely choose as individuals can be seen as conveying an expression of their personal identity. School uniforms, by contrast, are clothing which is selected by school officials and mandated to students. It is simple in style and color and it is intended to convey the institutional values of the school.

Joseph suggests that for clothing to be considered a 'uniform' it must fulfill the following criteria: 1) it must serve as a group emblem, 2) it must certify the institution's legitimacy by revealing an actor's status position, and 3) it must suppress individuality (1986). Within the context of an educational institution, school uniforms clearly function as a symbol of membership to the school community. The presence of a uniform in schools automatically implies a two-tiered hierarchical structure, those that wear uniforms (subordinates) and those that do not wear uniforms (superiors). School uniforms serve as a clear sign of this status distinction between students and faculty and therefore, certify the legitimacy of that distinction by all members. School uniforms act as suppressers of students' individuality by mandating standardization of appearance and removing student expression through clothing. . . .

If uniforms are considered a sign which facilitates social control of student behavior, then it can be expected that students in uniforms will display behaviors which are consistent with the institutional goals of the school. Inconsistent attendance, disciplinary behavior problems, and substance abuse represent student behaviors which are non-representative of the values of public high schools. By contrast, high levels of academic achievement are consistent with the goals of educational institutions. The following hypotheses are provided to test the validity of the uniform advocates' statements.

- H1: Student uniforms will decrease substance use
- H2: Student uniforms will decrease behavioral problems
- H3: Student uniforms will increase attendance
- H4: Student uniforms will increase academic achievement

Within the context of the public debate on mandatory uniform policies, the mechanisms through which uniforms effect the above stated outcomes are subtly implied. They include pro-school attitudes, peer pro-school orientation, and academic preparedness. In testing each of the above stated relationships, it is expected that the direct effect of uniforms on the four outcomes will disappear when these moderating variables are added to the equation. If this is in fact the case, arguments stating uniform policies' direct effect on a given outcome should be abandoned and more attention given to the actual mechanisms which produce the sought after effects. Finally, it should be emphasized that the purpose of this paper is to test the claims made in the context of the school uniform debate using a nationally representative sample of students.

Data and Methods

The National Educational Longitudinal Study of 1988 (NELS:88) is used to test the relationships outlined above. NELS:88 is a national stratified random sample of schools and students which began with eighth grade students (in 1988). It has since gone through three follow-ups with the most current one (1994) collecting data on the original eighth graders in their second year of postsecondary education. The data used for this analysis comes from the first follow-up of NELS:88 when students were in tenth grade. NELS:88 oversampled certain minority groups, private sector schools, and high performance schools. Thus, standardized weights and design effects will be applied in order to make statements about the population of tenth grade students in the United States and the effects of uniforms on them. The student component as well as the school-administrator component were used to provide data on uniform policies and the student background, peer group, achievement and behavioral characteristics needed for this analysis.

Variables

... A variable from the School Component of NELS:88 was used to ascertain whether or not a student was, due to school policy, required to wear a uniform. Some 5% of the students in the entire sample were required by policy to wear a school uniform. This can be further broken down into: 65.4% of Catholic, 16.6% of Private Non-Religious, 5.4% of Private Other-Religious, .8% of Public, and 0% of Private Non-Ascertained students are required to wear a uniform at their high school. Student uniform use is the focal independent variable of this research project.

Three scales were created to represent school preparedness, student pro-school attitudes, and the peer group's pro-school attitudes. These scales represent variables which are hypothesized to be the critical moderating variables explaining why uniforms might affect the dependent variables as opposed to uniform use having direct effects....

Dependent Variables

The debate over school uniforms suggests using several outcomes to test the effectiveness of adopting a uniform policy on how students fare on these consequences. The dependent variables chosen were student absenteeism, student behavior problems, student substance use, and student achievement. A variable was used to assess how often a student was absent from school. A behavioral scale was created from a number of variables to assess the degree to which a student has been involved in behaviorally problematic conduct in relation to school. Some of the variables in the behavior scale included whether the student: got into physical fights, got put on in-school suspension, skipped or cut classes, was suspended from school, and in general got in trouble. To assess the degree of substance usage among students, a scale was computed to reflect student use of cigarettes, alcohol, and marijuana. To assess student achievement a composite standardized achievement test (composite of reading and math tests) was used.

Regressions were also conducted on pro-school attitudes, peer pro-school attitudes and academic preparedness to observe the effect of uniforms on these characteristics. By testing the logic of claims made by advocates of school reform, several interesting findings result that have implications for the ongoing debate. The authors remain specifically interested in the relationships and the predictive power of student uniform policies on the outcomes of interest....

Results and Findings

.... Catholic schools and uniforms go together in most people's minds, and in fact, they are the sector which utilizes uniform policies the most (65.4%). Thus, one would expect the relationship to hold here as well–uniformed Catholic students should have the desired outcomes to a greater extent then non-uniformed Catholic students (if uniforms are indeed a force behind what occurs there).... Only the results for absenteeism and achievement are significant and it is important to note that these relationships reverse. Uniformed Catholic students are absent more often ($p < .05$) and, on average, score some 3 points less ($p < .01$) on an achievement test than non-uniformed Catholic students. This fails to support the thesis that uniforms are related to these outcomes....

Student Uniforms as Predictors

So far this paper has presented somewhat weaker, though interesting, tests of the relationship between student uniforms and the various outcomes. The debate tends to imply stronger claims than simple correlations and mean comparisons: there is an implicit charge that uniforms "cause" or "impact" the outcomes with which educators and policymakers are concerned. A number of weighted regression analyses were run in order to test the predictive impact of student uniforms on absenteeism, behavior problems, substance use, and achievement....

Do uniforms have an impact on absenteeism? Model I presents the unstandardized coefficients for the impact of the control variables on absenteeism. These explain 3% of the variance in the dependent variable. In Model II, the variable for student uniforms is added. The uniform coefficient is not significantly different from zero and no statements can be made. No extra variance is explained in Model II. An interesting finding is that once the variation for uniform use is taken into account the Catholic effect actually gets stronger in decreasing absenteeism. This implies that the Catholic effect, often cited in the literature as effecting these sorts of outcomes, remains supported. However, the effect is not associated with whether the students wear uniforms or not; it is more likely due to the social relations fostered in Catholic schools. Finally, the variables added in Model III explain an extra 8% of the variance in absenteeism and are all significant predictors of decreased absenteeism indicating that academic preparedness, pro-school attitudes and peer norms significantly affect attendance at school in the desired direction. Hypothesis One, which stated that student uniforms would decrease absenteeism, is not supported by these results.

Do student uniforms significantly decrease behavioral problems? Again, Model I shows the results for the control variables alone on the dependent variable. These variables alone explain 8% of the variance in behavior problems. The student uniform variable is added in Model II and the insignificant effect is similar to that for absenteeism. No extra variance is explained. When the mediating variables are added in Model III, an extra 33% of the variance in behavioral problems is explained. Academic preparedness, pro-school attitudes and peer norms effectively lessen behavioral problems on average. Hypothesis Two, which stated that student uniforms will decrease behavior problems, is not supported by this analysis.

A final question of uniform's relationship to school commitment can be posed: Do student uniforms significantly decrease substance use among high school students?... The uniform variable is non-significant and it adds no extra explanatory power. Finally, academic preparedness, pro-school attitudes, and peer norms which are pro-school again effectively decrease substance use among high school students.... Thus, Hypothesis Three, which stated that student uniforms will decrease substance use, is unsupported, implying that implementing uniform policies at the high school level will not effectively create the desired outcomes.

... [C]ontrary to the expected, student uniform use actually decreases, on average, the standardized test score of these tenth graders who wear them due to mandatory school policy. It is, in fact, almost a 3-point decrease.... [T]he coefficient for uniforms is statistically significant ($p < .01$) and negative.... Finally, Hypothesis Four, stating that student uniforms will increase student achievement, is not supported by these data. In fact, all four of the original hypotheses, derived from the public discourse surrounding the uniform debate, are not supported. Most striking is uniform's significant negative effects on achievement—an outcome of much concern to educators and policy makers.

Uniforms and Pro-School Attitudes: Is There a Relationship?

Though the hypotheses were not borne out, the authors decided to examine whether uniforms directly impact the development of academic preparedness, pro-school attitudes, or peer structures with pro-school norms. Since these variables consistently produce the desired outcomes it is important to assess uniform's effects on these as well.... [I]n fact, uniforms do not have any effect on the moderating variables in the analysis. Though academic preparedness, pro-school attitudes, and peer norms significantly effect the outcomes studied, uniforms have no effect on the moderating attitudinal variables either.

Interactions of student uniforms and each of the following variables of interest were computed...: academic preparedness, pro-school attitudes, peer pro-school attitudes, urbanicity, socioeconomic status, and Catholic sector. The following questions apply, respectively, to the tests of interactions: Do uniformed kids with high academic preparedness significantly differ in the desired direction from their counterparts on the dependent measures? Do uniformed kids with high pro-school attitudes significantly differ in the desired direction from their counterparts on the dependent measures? Do uniformed kids with strong pro-school peer groups significantly differ in the desired direction from their counterparts on the dependent measures? Do uniformed kids in urban areas significantly differ in the desired direction from their counterparts on the dependent measures? Do uniformed kids with high socio-economic status significantly differ in the desired direction from their counterparts on the dependent measures? Finally, do uniformed Catholic kids significantly differ in the desired direction from their counterparts on the dependent measures?

.... [O]nly one significant coefficient is found: uniformed kids with high pro-school attitudes actually have worse behavior problems than their counterparts. This is contrary to the expected. Uniforms seemingly have no impact in tandem with those things which are proven effective.

Implications and Discussion

The Discourse/Rhetoric Re-Examined

Our failure to find a direct effect of uniforms on behavioral outcomes or academic achievement provide cause for a closer examination of the uniform debate. It seems that reformers have seriously considered the educational research showing outcome differentials between public and Catholic school students. However, it is equally apparent that the most superficial policies are those that have been extracted for possible reform efforts. A closer reading of the public versus private school literature would suggest that uniforms are merely symbolic of the communal organization of Catholic schools which, researchers have proposed (Bryk, Lee, & Holland, 1993; Bryk & Driscoll, 1988; Coleman & Hoffer, 1987), is the fundamental cause of the Catholic school advantage.

A reconsideration of the Long Beach case sheds light on the flawed logic of uniform proponents' assertions. The descriptive information provided by LBUSD suggested that school crime was significantly reduced between the 1994–1995 and 1995–1996 school years. Between these periods a mandatory uniform policy was established district wide. Seemingly, the correlation between these two events is reason enough for Long Beach administrators to state that a causal relationship exists. While in fact, these two events may be empirically verifiable, the argument that uniforms have caused the decrease in school crime is simply not substantiated. Taking into consideration both the findings provided in this paper and the additional materials from the Long Beach public school system, we would propose an alternative interpretation. What is omitted from the discourse on school uniforms is the possibility that, instead of directly impacting specific outcomes, uniforms work as a catalyst for change and provide a highly visible window of opportunity. It is this window which allows additional programs to be implemented. An examination of the Long Beach case shows that several additional reform efforts were simultaneously implemented with the mandatory uniform policy. These programs include a reassessment of content standards, a $1 million grant from the Edna McConnell Clark Foundation to develop alternative pedagogical strategies, and the Focused Reporting Project (Kahl, 1996). It seems curious that given these substantive reform efforts, administrators continue to insist that uniforms are the sole factor causing a variety of positive educational outcomes.

Requiring students to wear uniforms is a change which not only affects students, but school faculty and parents. Instituting a mandatory uniform policy is a change which is immediate, highly visible, and shifts the environmental landscape of any particular school. This change is one that is superficial, but attracts attention because of its visible nature. Instituting a uniform policy can be viewed as analogous to cleaning and brightly painting a deteriorating building in that on the one hand, it grabs our immediate attention but on the other, is, after all, really only a coat of paint. This type of change serves the purpose of attracting attention to schools, it implies that serious problems are existent and necessitate this sort of drastic change, and it seems entirely possible that this attention renews an interest on the parts of parents and communities, and opens the possibilities for support of additional types of organizational change.

The juxtaposition of these findings and the ongoing rhetoric in the public debate on school uniforms provides a lens for viewing the effects of public opinion on school reform in general. The nature and magnitude of the support behind the mandatory uniform policies of districts such as Long Beach seem to illustrate the "quick fix" nature of school reform policies in the 1990's. A policy which is simplistic, readily understandable, cost-free (to taxpayers) and appealing to common sense is one which is politically pleasing and hence, finds great support. When challenged with broader reforms, those whose results are not immediately identifiable, those that are costly and demand energy and a willingness to change on the part of school faculty and parents are simply unacceptable.

POSTSCRIPT

Do School Uniforms Cause Improvements?

S chool uniform policies are similar to many proposals related to school reform and improvement in that they generate much support and much opposition in spite of little empirical evidence related to their efficacy (or lack thereof). This is perhaps due to the fact that many such proposals emanate from opinions and values rather than from analysis and evidence. Because opinions and values are often fixed and inflexible, contentious issues such as school uniforms can become extremely emotional and divisive.

Obviously such disagreements can evolve into controversy and lawsuits. In an attempt to avoid litigation some school districts have adopted "voluntary school uniform policies." (A "voluntary policy" may strike some as an oxymoron.) Most school uniform policies, following the lead of enabling legislation at the state level, provide "opt-out" provisions by which parents can exempt their child from the wearing of the school uniform. However, even these provisions can be controversial if school districts turn down parental "opt-out" requests. A recent example of this occurred in the Forney Independent School District in Texas wherein several parents have joined in a federal lawsuit challenging the school district's decision to reject their requests for an "opt-out" from the district's school uniform policy.

Articles and reports representing different views on this issue include Alfie Kohn, "The Trouble With School Uniforms," *Boston Globe* (October 2, 1996); Dennis Evans, "School Uniforms: An Unfashionable Dissent," *Phi Delta Kappan* (October 1996); Kathleen Paliokas and Ray Rist, "Do They Reduce Violence —Or Just Make Us Feel Better?" *Education Week* (April 3, 1996); Paul Loesch, "A School Uniform Policy That Works," *Principal* (March 1995); Carl Cohn, "Mandatory School Uniforms," *The School Administrator* (February 1996); and Richard Murray, "The Impact of School Uniforms on School Climate," *NASSP Bulletin* (December 1997).

Given the fact that most school uniform policies have been instituted at the elementary and middle school levels, it is obvious that even greater controversy and related litigation will arise as attempts are made to implement such policies in secondary schools. School boards and school administrators contemplating such policies would be well advised to carefully study the need and rationales for such a move, evaluate alternative approaches to resolving the problems that give rise to the consideration of uniforms, engage all elements of the school community in discussion and review of any proposed policy, and anticipate and prepare for the inevitable dissent that will come from secondary school students.

ISSUE 8

Are Zero Tolerance Policies Necessary and Effective?

YES: The National Association of Secondary School Principals, from Statement Before the United States Commission on Civil Rights (February 18, 2000)

NO: Russ Skiba and Reece Peterson, from "The Dark Side of Zero Tolerance: Can Punishment Lead to Safe Schools?" *Phi Delta Kappan* (January 1999)

ISSUE SUMMARY

YES: The National Association of Secondary School Principals (NASSP) argues that zero tolerance policies, clearly stated and fairly administered, meet parental and societal expectations and protect the physical well-being of students and staff.

NO: Russ Skiba, associate professor at Indiana University, and Reece Peterson, associate professor at the University of Nebraska, state that virtually no data suggest that zero tolerance policies reduce school violence.

O f the myriad responsibilities held by schoolteachers and school administrators, none may be more important than that of maintaining a safe school environment. It risks tautology to state that not much can occur educationally unless students and staff feel safe and secure in the school environment. This imperative is recognized by all states, each of which has legally established provisions related to the rights of students and staff vis à vis safe schools. For example, in California, voters in 1982 added the following provision to the state constitution: "All students and staff of public primary, elementary, junior high and senior high schools have the inalienable right to attend campuses which are safe, secure, and peaceful."

Given the magnitude of this responsibility and the public concern related to it, it follows that educational policymakers and school administrators constantly revisit this issue, especially the disciplinary standards and procedures that operationalize the commitment to school safety. Although this commitment to student safety is not new, the term *zero tolerance* is of more recent vintage. The phrase, which is used to describe disciplinary policies dealing with the most serious breaches of student conduct, first came into national prominence in the mid-1980s as school policymakers responded to increased concerns regarding substance abuse among adolescents by establishing stronger sanctions for students involved in selling or providing drugs. Later, as tragic incidents of school violence made headlines, the term *zero tolerance* and related policy pronouncements were also applied to the possession of weapons and other dangerous items.

Zero tolerance means different things in different school locales. In some school systems it means expulsion, while in other jurisdictions it may mean suspension from school or transfer to another school in the same system. But in all systems the phrase is reserved for those student acts deemed to be the most egregious in terms of their impact on the safety and security of other students and staff. In some ways the phrase is an unfortunate one, since critics of zero tolerance policies can stress the draconian ring of the phrase and point to instances of overzealousness in its administration. Russ Skiba and Reece Peterson reference several such examples. In spite of the publicity given to these examples, public support for zero tolerance polices remains high, with 87 percent of the respondents to the 2000 Phi Delta Kappa/Gallup Poll of the Public's Attitudes Toward the Public Schools favoring such policies.

Statement of The National Association of Secondary School Principals

School climate is an important catalyst for learning, not visible in educational outcomes, but very much affecting the process of teaching and learning that leads to those outcomes.

> *"Youngsters who are intimidated and fearful cannot be at ease; they cannot give education the single-minded attention needed for success. Nor can teachers teach with the required attention and purpose if they are anxious and worried about their own safety and that of their students."*

> — This statement appears in the school reform publication *Breaking Ranks: Changing an American Institution* produced by NASSP [The National Association of Secondary School Principals] and the Carnegie Foundation for the Advancement of Teaching.

One of the key messages provided in this seminal document is that schools must be safe and effective environments conducive to teaching and learning if our students are to prosper. Therefore, safety and order must prevail at all times. Only in such an environment may teaching and learning thrive. To make zero tolerance laws fair, they should:

- Clearly state that weapons, drugs, alcohol, violent acts, discrimination, and harassment will not be tolerated in our schools.
- Be implemented consistently, fairly and responsibly.
- Allow principals and local school boards the discretion to ensure that the punishment fits the act.
- Ensure the continuation of educational services with appropriate funding for all school age children.

From The National Association of Secondary School Principals, "Civil Rights Implications of Zero Tolerance Programs," Statement Before the United States Commission on Civil Rights (February 18, 2000).

Clear Statement That Acts Are Not Tolerated in Our Schools

Every school day, principals struggle to protect students while at the same time work to make sure that these students receive the best education possible. As a society, we cannot tolerate violence against our students and staffs. For many students, the only place that they feel safe is in school. We as a society need to declare unequivocally that weapons, illegal drugs, alcohol, violent acts, discrimination, and harassment have no place in an academic setting.

Policies Must Be Applied Consistently, Fairly and Responsibly

At this time in our nation's history, we are reacting to violence in our communities, in our homes, and in our schools by building more prisons, mandating specific sentences for criminal convictions, and finally mandating specific discipline (expulsion) for certain acts committed in our nation's schools.

The concerns of disparate treatment in sentencing and now discipline created the movement to establish specific sentencing guidelines and zero tolerance policies. In an effort to treat everyone exactly the same, we have created federal, state, and local laws that remove any discretion from the traditional finders of fact (judges, hearing officers, school boards, and principals). Their hands are tied. If a person commits an act covered by a zero tolerance policy, that is the end of inquiry and the stated mandatory discipline is applied. There is no discussion of the age or maturity of the individual, the severity of the violation, or any other factors such as ethnicity, race, or gender.

There are claims that zero tolerance laws are unfair and unequal because there is a higher rate of suspension and expulsion for students of ethnic and racial minorities. Is this reflective of discrimination or ethnic and racial bias? No, it is not an issue of discrimination or bias between ethnic or racial groups, but a socio/economic issue. As we have seen in the area of standards and assessments the greatest predictor of a student's score is not race or ethnicity but the student's socio/economic status. Therefore, a higher incidence of ethnic and racial minority students being affected by zero tolerance policies should not be seen as disparate treatment or discrimination but in terms of an issue of socio/economic status. The solution to overcome this problem is not more restrictive laws but a concerted effort by principals, community leaders, and parents to provide all members of our society with a sense of self-worth and hope for the future. Students need to be invested with the sense that their actions and lives do make a difference.

Discretion Is Needed to Ensure Equal Treatment

Current laws and policies state unequivocally that weapons, drugs, alcohol, violent acts, discrimination, and harassment will not be tolerated in our schools. However, some go beyond the declaration that certain acts will not be tolerated to mandate expulsion for any student that commits any of these acts. These policies remove any professional judgment from the discipline process. Under these policies, a principal has no authority to evaluate the specific circumstances of each incident. The only decision that a principal has is if the act falls within the definition of prohibited acts. Does this create an opportunity for disparate treatment? No, because the only factor is the act itself. The ethnicity, race, and gender of the perpetrator do not even come into question.

Is this equal? It depends upon your definition of equal. If your definition of equal is that everyone is treated the same, then yes. However, if you define equal as the punishment fits the act, then no, because the severity of the act is not taken into account. This causes a student who brings a butter knife to school in their lunch box to be treated the same as a student who brings a gun to school.

In addition, for some equality means that all zero-tolerance policies must be the same for every school in the Nation. To require that all zero tolerance policies be equal means that the federal government would be creating the discipline code for every school in America. The instances over the last year provide evidence against this prescription. Instead it supports a system of policies that clearly define the acts that will not be tolerated in our schools, but leaves to the discretion of school principals and local school boards the discipline that is warranted in each case. We need to trust the principals in our schools and the processes established by the local school boards which fairly, consistently, and responsibly implement and enforce these policies. To do otherwise, would continue to create the situations we see in headlines today claiming the punishment does not fit the act.

Because Federal zero tolerance laws specifically exempt students with disabilities and the Individuals with Disabilities Education Act preempts the application of any state or local zero tolerance policies, zero tolerance policies do not affect disabled students other than creating a greater division between the general and special education students in our schools.

All Children Should Receive Educational Services

Zero tolerance policies address the law and order portion of the equation but not the personal or societal issues related to removing educational opportunities for a child. Even though a student may lose the privilege of receiving an education in a particular local school because of that student's actions, that student should not lose access to educational services. Federal, state, and local governments must come together to ensure that no child is denied the opportunity to receive educational services. To deny any educational services to a child increases that child's chances of ending up in the criminal justice system and ultimately being a burden on society their entire life rather than a productive member of the community. It is not in our country's economic or social interest to deny educational services to any child.

In addition to providing for alternative educational opportunities, schools need to instill students with a core set of values. Principals, teachers, parents, and the community as a whole, need to teach students about such key virtues as honesty, dependability, trust, responsibility, tolerance, and respect. Many schools have become large and impersonal, causing those students who feel disconnected from their peers, their school, and their community to feel further isolated. Proactive programs need to be implemented in order to make the educational environment more personal for each student. NASSP supports: limiting the size of schools to no more than 600 students or creating schools within schools to meet the 600 student limit, the creation of an adult advocate for each student, a personalized educational plan for each student and encouraging students to participate in co-curricular activities.

Conclusion

While we respect the position of those who protest zero-tolerance policies, we ask for unified support for principals, who at the school level and on a daily basis, bear the major responsibility for the safety and well being of students and staff. As a nation, we must take a strong and unified position that weapons, drugs, violent acts, discrimination, and harassment cannot and will not be tolerated in our schools. Students who commit such acts must be prepared to face the consequences of their actions. To back away from a zero tolerance policy places students and staff in harm's way and enhances the probability of future acts of violence.

Students have the right to expect that their lives will not be endangered in a school building and that the climate is free of threats and violence. Zero tolerance policies, clearly stated and fairly administered, meet parental and societal expectations and protect the physical well being of students and staff.

It is our hope that parents, communities, and governments will support school leaders as they make difficult decisions and exert leadership in maintaining a school climate that is safe, orderly, drug-free, and conducive to teaching and learning.

Russ Skiba and Reece Peterson  **NO**

The Dark Side of Zero Tolerance

T he 1997–98 school year was a shocking and frightening one, filled with reports of seemingly random violence in communities heretofore immune to such incidents. In the wake of these tragedies, we can expect to hear renewed calls for increasingly severe penalties for any kind of school disruption, a stance that has led to the widespread adoption of so-called zero tolerance discipline policies.

Already many districts have decreed that making any sort of threat will result in automatic expulsion. Some have gone as far as to suggest that principals be armed in order to deter—or perhaps outshoot—students who bring firearms to school. Such an approach is extreme, to say the least, and is unlikely to be implemented. Yet it is simply the far end of a continuum of responses to what has become the largely unquestioned assumption that school violence is accelerating at an alarming rate and that increasingly draconian disciplinary measures are not only justified but necessary to guarantee school safety.

Before we continue down a path that may well turn school principals into town marshals and cafeterias into free-fire zones, however, we would do well to examine more closely the track record of zero tolerance. What is "zero tolerance"? What is the nature of the school violence that has brought us to this point? How well does the approach address the serious issues of school safety toward which it has been aimed?

The Origins of Zero Tolerance

The term "zero tolerance"—referring to policies that punish all offenses severely, no matter how minor—grew out of state and federal drug enforcement policies in the 1980s. The first use of the term recorded in the Lexis-Nexis national newspaper database was in 1983, when the Navy reassigned 40 submarine crew members for suspected drug abuse. In 1986 zero tolerance was picked up and used by a U.S. attorney in San Diego as the title of a program developed to impound seacraft carrying any amount of drugs. By February 1988 the program had received national attention, and U.S. Attorney General Edwin Meese authorized customs officials to seize the boats, automobiles, and passports of anyone

From Russ Skiba and Reece Peterson, "The Dark Side of Zero Tolerance: Can Punishment Lead to Safe Schools?" *Phi Delta Kappan* (January 1999). Copyright © 1999 by Phi Delta Kappa International. Reprinted by permission.

crossing the border with even trace amounts of drugs and to charge those individuals in federal court. Zero tolerance took hold quickly and within months was being applied to issues as diverse as environmental pollution, trespassing, skateboarding, racial intolerance, homelessness, sexual harassment, and boom boxes.

From the outset, the harsh punishments meted out under zero tolerance drug policies engendered considerable controversy. Private citizens whose cars, boats, and even bicycles were impounded for sometimes minute amounts of drugs complained bitterly, and the American Civil Liberties Union considered filing suit against the program. By 1990 the U.S. Customs Service quietly discontinued its initial zero tolerance program after strict applications of the rule resulted in the seizure of two research vessels on which a small amount of marijuana was found.

Yet just as the early zero tolerance drug programs in the community were being phased out, the concept was beginning to catch on in the public schools. In late 1989 school districts in Orange County, California, and Louisville, Kentucky, promulgated zero tolerance policies that called for expulsion for possession of drugs or participation in gang-related activity. In New York, Donald Batista, superintendent of the Yonkers public schools, proposed a sweeping zero tolerance program as a way of taking action against students who caused school disruption. With its restricted school access, ban on hats, immediate suspension for any school disruption, and increased use of law enforcement, the program contained many of the elements that have come to characterize zero tolerance approaches in the past decade.

By 1993 zero tolerance policies were being adopted by school boards across the country, often broadened to include not only drugs and weapons but also tobacco-related offenses and school disruption. In 1994 the federal government stepped in to mandate the policy nationally when President Clinton signed the Gun-Free Schools Act into law.[1] This law mandates an expulsion of one calendar year for possession of a weapon and referral of students who violate the law to the criminal or juvenile justice system. It also provides that the one-year expulsions may be modified by the "chief administrative officer" of each local school district on a case-by-case basis.

School Violence: Reality and Perception

[The recent] string of school shootings has left all educators shaken and nervous about the potential for violence in their own schools. The fear that drugs and violence are spreading in our nation's schools provided the initial motivation for adopting zero tolerance disciplinary policies and may well motivate still another round of tough disciplinary measures. But what is the reality of school violence and drug use? How bad is it, and is it getting Worse?

It is hard to say that we are overreacting when the incidents we have witnessed on a regular basis are so horrific. Yet some data on the topic suggest that we are doing just that. In a report titled *Violence and Discipline Problems in U.S. Public Schools, 1996–1997,* the National Center for Education Statistics (NCES) surveyed a nationally representative sample of 1,234 school principals or disciplinarians at the elementary, middle, and high school levels.[2] When these principals were asked to list what they considered serious or moderate problems in their schools, the most frequently cited problems at all levels were the less violent behaviors such as tardiness (40%), absenteeism (25%), and physical conflicts between students (21%). The critical incidents that are typically the focus of school safety debates were reported to be at least "a moderate problem" only relatively infrequently: drug use (9%), gangs (5%), possession of weapons (2%), and physical abuse of teachers (2%). The NCES report found that violent crimes occurred at an annual rate of only 53 per 100,000 students.

Table

Table 1: Percentage of Principals Reporting Which Discipline Issues Were Moderate or Serious Issues in Their Schools, 1990–91 and 1996–97

Discipline Issue	1990–91 %	1996–97 %
Student tardiness	34	40
Student absenteeism/class cutting	25	25
Physical conflicts among students	23	21
Student tobacco use	13	14
Verbal abuse of teachers	11	12
Student drug use	6	9
Vandalism of school property	12	8
Student alcohol use	10	7
Robbery or theft of items over $10	7	5
Gangs	*	5
Trespassing	7	4
Racial tensions	5	3
Student possession of weapons	3	2
Physical abuse of teachers	1	2
Sale of drugs on school grounds	1	2

*Item was not included in 1991 survey.

Source: Violence and Discipline Problems in U.S. Public Schools: 1996–1997 (Washington, D.C.: National Center for Education Statistics, NCES12 98-030, 1998).

When we watch the evening news or walk through the edgy and noisy corridors of urban middle schools, it is difficult to believe that school behavior is not worsening. But again, the evidence seems to contradict our gut feelings. Comparisons of the current NCES survey data with results from an earlier survey of public school principals conducted in 1991 show virtually no changes across either minor misbehavior or more serious infractions (see Table 1). Noted school violence researcher Irwin Hyman tracked a number of indicators of school violence over the past 20 years and concluded, "As was the case 20 years ago, despite public perceptions to the contrary, the current data do not support the claim that there has been a dramatic, overall increase in school-based violence in recent years."[3]

It seems almost inconceivable that there are so few incidents of truly dangerous behavior and that things are not necessarily getting worse. Perhaps there are some behaviors that just shake us up, whatever their absolute frequency. School shootings involving multiple victims are still extremely rare from a statistical standpoint. However, statistics are hardly reassuring as long as the possibility exists that it could happen in *our* school, to *our* children. It is probably healthier that a single shooting on school grounds be viewed as one too many than that we become inured to violence.

Yet this fear of random violence is clearly the prime motivator for the adoption of zero tolerance approaches to school discipline. From that first boat's impoundment in San Diego harbor, zero tolerance has cast a broad net, by its very definition treating both minor and major incidents with equal severity in order to "send a message" to potential violators.

Indeed, infractions that fall under the rubric of zero tolerance seem to multiply as the definition of what will not be tolerated expands. Test cases of school district zero tolerance policies reported in the media from 1988 to 1993 did involve difficult judgments about the severity of the punishment, but they were also clearly concerned with weapons and drugs: a high school senior in Chicago was expelled from school when police found marijuana in the trunk of his car during the lunch hour; an honor student in Los Angeles was expelled when he pulled out a knife to scare away peers who had been harassing him because of his Filipino-Mexican heritage.[4]

Over time, however, increasingly broad interpretations of zero tolerance have resulted in a near epidemic of suspensions and expulsions for seemingly trivial events. Table 2 provides a list of some of the events that have received national attention in recent years, we note here that this is just a partial list, including only those incidents that have been reported in detail.

The reaction to these cases has created sharp divisions in schools and communities. In a number of these incidents, parents have filed lawsuits against the school districts, for the most part unsuccessfully.[5] A number of states have amended their zero tolerance policies to allow more flexibility for individual cases,[6] while the Office for Civil Rights in the U.S. Department of Education began advocating a less comprehensive interpretation of sexual harassment after the suspension of 6-year-old Jonathan Prevette for kissing a classmate made national headlines.[7] Yet in many cases school administrators and school boards have not backed down even in the face of public clamor. They claim that their hands are tied by federal or state law (despite language in the federal law that allows local review on a case-by-case basis), or they assert that continued application of zero tolerance is necessary to send a message to disruptive students.

Table

Table 2: Selected School Events Leading to Suspension or Expulsion as Reported in National News

Location and Date	Description of Incident	Outcome
Weapon-Related		
Columbus, Ohio May 1998	Nine-year-old on way to school found a manicure kit with 1" knife.	Suspended for one day for violating school's zero tolerance antiviolence policy.
Chicago May 1998	Seventeen-year-old junior shot a paper clip with a rubber band at classmate, missed, and broke skin of cafeteria worker.	Expelled from school; taken to county jail for seven hours and charged with misdemeanor battery; advised by school officials to drop out of school.
Phoenix October 1997	Sixteen-year-old sophomore pulled skeet shooting gun out of trunk of car after school to lend to a 17-year-old senior.	Both boys expelled for violating zero tolerance weapons policy; charged by local police with misconduct with a firearm.
Woonsocket, R.I. March 1997	Twelve-year-old brought and flashed toy gun in class.	Suspended; principal stated that suspension "sends an unambiguous message to students and protects the school from possible legal action."
Alexandria, La. February 1997	Second-grader brought grandfather's watch for show and tell; had 1" pocketknife attached.	Suspended and sent for one month to local alternative school.
Columbia, S.C. October 1996	Sixth-grader brought steak knife in her lunch box to cut chicken; asked teacher if she could use it.	Police called; girl taken in cruiser; suspended even though never took knife out; threatened with expulsion.
Centralia, Calif. November 1994	Five-year-old found a razor blade at his bus stop and brought it to school to show teacher.	Expelled for violation of district's zero tolerance weapons policy; transferred to another school.
Drug-Related		
Cherry Creek, Colo. May 1998	Fourteen seventh- and eighth-graders sipped a thimbleful of wine as part of a trip to Paris.	Principal suspended and banished to a teaching job in another district for violating school's zero tolerance policy on alcohol.

Mount Airy, Md. April 1998	Twelve-year-old honor student shared her inhaler with student suffering asthma attack on bus.	Student barred from participation in extracurricular activities: violation of district's zero tolerance drug policy noted in her record.
Belle, W. Va. November 1997	Seventh-grader shared zinc cough drop with classmate.	Suspended three days under school anti-drug policy since cough drop was not cleared with the office.
Colorado Springs October 1997	Six-year-old shared organic lemon drops with fellow students on playground.	Suspended for possession of "other chemical substances"; mother complained of administrator use of scare tactics when she was called in.
Manassas, Va. September 1997	Nine-year-old boy handed out Certs Concentrated Mints in class.	One-day suspension for possession and distribution of "look-alike" drugs; interviewed by police officer.
Fairborn, Ohio September 1996	Fourteen-year-old shared two Midol tablets with 13-year-old classmate.	Fourteen-year-old suspended for 10 days with expulsion forgiven; 13-year-old allowed back after nine days of 10-day suspension after agreeing to attend drug awareness classes.

Other

San Diego October 1997	Twelve-year-old scuffled with classmates when they taunted him for being fat.	Expelled for violation of zero tolerance policy toward fighting.
San Diego September 1997	Third-grader engaged in two incidents: twisted finger of girl he said was "saying bad things in line" and got into scuffle with boy on playground during tetherball.	Suspended for five days for each incident; expelled after second suspension; principal stated she had no choice under district's zero tolerance policies.
Newport News, Va. October 1996	Five-year-old brought beeper from home and showed it to classmates on field trip.	Suspended for violation of school rule forbidding students from bringing pagers to school.
Lexington, N.C. September 1996	Six-year-old kissed classmate; said the girl asked him to.	One-day suspension for violation of school rule prohibiting "unwarranted and unwelcome touching."

*Incidents selected were reported after the signing of the Gun-Free Schools Act (October 1994) and were included if media account provided information on date, location, student age or grade, offense, and school response.

Who Gets Suspended and Expelled?

If the NCES data on school violence are correct, it is not surprising that the broad net of zero tolerance will catch a host of minor misbehaviors. Since there are few incidents of serious violence and many incidents of minor disruption, policies that set harsh consequences indiscriminately will capture a few incidents of serious violence and many incidents of minor disruption.

In fact, data on suspension and expulsion suggest that the incidents brought to national attention by the media are not all that inaccurate in describing the types of behavior that lead to exclusion from school. Data on suspension consistently show that, as the NCES has reported, referrals for drugs, weapons, and gang-related behaviors constitute but a small minority of office referrals leading to suspension. Fighting among students is the single most frequent reason for suspension, but the majority of school suspensions occur in response to relatively minor incidents that do not threaten school safety.[8] At the middle school level, disrespect and disobedience are among the most common reasons for suspension, and a significant proportion of suspensions are for tardiness and truancy. In one of the few reported studies of school expulsion in American education, Gale Morrison and Barbara D'Incau reported that the majority of offenses in the sample they investigated were committed by students who would not generally be considered dangerous to the school environment.[9] In their study, as in many that have explored suspension and expulsion, poor academic skill was a strong predictor of school exclusion.

One of the more troubling characteristics of the zero tolerance approach to discipline is that a disproportionate number of those at risk for a range of school punishments are poor and African American. In 1975 the Children's Defense Fund, studying data on school discipline from the Office for Civil Rights (OCR), found high rates of suspension for black students. Of the nearly 3,000 school districts represented in the OCR data, more than two-thirds showed rates of black suspension that exceeded rates for white students.[10]

Since then, researchers have consistently found disproportionate minority representation among students on the receiving end of exclusionary and punitive discipline practices. African American students are overrepresented in the use of corporal punishment and expulsion, and they are underrepresented in the use of milder disciplinary alternatives.[11] This overrepresentation of minorities in the application of harsh discipline appears to be related to the overall use of school exclusion: schools that rely most heavily on suspension and expulsion are also those that show the highest rates of minority overrepresentation in school disciplinary consequences.

Of course, there are hypotheses other than racial bias that might be called upon to explain minority overrepresentation in school discipline. First, the unfortunate correlation of race and poverty in our society suggests that inequitable racial treatment in discipline may be a socioeconomic issue rather than a racial one. Yet multivariate studies have continued to find evidence of black overrepresentation in suspension—even after controlling for socioeconomic background—suggesting that racial disproportionality in suspension involves more than just poverty.[12]

A second hypothesis suggests that racial differences in punishment are the result of differences in school behavior: higher rates of suspension for African American students would not be bias if those students misbehaved more frequently. Yet when rates of behavior for African American and other students are taken into account, the differences are minor at best, and behavior makes a weak contribution to explaining the discrepancy in the suspension rates of blacks and whites.[13] While there are doubtless complex factors involving defiance, fighting, and school authority that determine who is suspended or expelled in any given situation, it is clear that the burden of suspension and expulsion falls most heavily on poor black males.

How Effective Is Zero Tolerance?

It has been almost a decade since school districts first began to adopt zero tolerance policies. And it has been four years since the policy was institutionalized nationally in the Gun-Free Schools Act. How well has it worked?

The short answer is that we don't really know. Unlike the domain of academic achievement, in which constant calls for accountability have led to state and national standards and tests, there has been no concomitant pressure to test the efficacy of interventions that target school behavior. Perhaps as a result, there are almost no studies that evaluate the effectiveness of zero tolerance strategies.

Of course, the media have reported claims by school districts that zero tolerance approaches have curtailed guns, gangs, or fighting in their schools. The most comprehensive and controlled study of zero tolerance policies, however, appears once again to be the NCES study of school violence. The NCES survey asked principals to identify which of a number of possible components of a zero tolerance strategy (e.g., expulsions, locker searches, the use of metal detectors, school uniforms) were employed at their school. Of the responding principals, 79% reported having a zero tolerance policy for violence. Schools with no reported crime were less likely to have a zero tolerance policy (74%) than schools that reported incidents of serious crime (85%). From one perspective, the relationship is unsurprising, since unsafe schools might well be expected to try more extreme measures. Yet after four years of implementation, the NCES found that schools that use zero tolerance policies are still less safe than those without such policies.

As time has allowed all of us to gain some perspective on the [recent] school shootings..., the media have begun to report data showing that the rate of school violence has remained fairly level since the early 1990s. One overlooked implication of these figures is their evaluative significance for the Gun-Free Schools Act. In an era of accountability, is it unfair to expect that a national policy implemented consistently, one might even say aggressively, over a four-year period should demonstrate some measurable effect on its target: school disruption and violence? Virtually no data suggest that zero tolerance policies reduce school violence, and some data suggest that certain strategies, such as strip searches or undercover agents in school, may create emotional harm or encourage students to drop out.[14] When the lives of schoolchildren and staff members continue to be claimed in random shootings after extensive implementation of the most extreme measures in our schools, is it wise to push these strategies harder?

Our concerns about the long-term effects of zero tolerance multiply when we look more closely at one of its central components: school exclusion. In the 1980s, national concern over children termed "at risk" led to extensive investigations of the causes and correlates of dropping out. Consistently, school suspension was found to be a moderate to strong predictor of a student's dropping out of school. More than 30% of sophomores who dropped out of school had been suspended, a rate three times that of peers who stayed in school.[15]

Indeed, the relationship between suspension and dropping out may not be accidental. In ethnographic studies, school disciplinarians report that suspension is sometimes used as a tool to "push out" particular students, to encourage "troublemakers" or those perceived as unlikely to succeed in school to leave.[16]

Recent advances in developmental psychopathology suggest other explanations for the relationship between suspension and dropping out. In the elementary school years, students at risk for developing conduct disorders exhibit disruptive behavior, below-average achievement, and poor social skills. Together, these deficits cause them to become increasingly alienated from teachers and peers.[17] As they reach middle school, these youngsters become less interested in school and seek the company of other antisocial peers, perhaps even gangs. At the same time, their families often fail to monitor their whereabouts, allowing more unsupervised time on the streets. In such a context, it seems unlikely that suspension will positively influence the behavior of the student being suspended. Rather, suspension may simply accelerate the course of delinquency by giving a troubled youth with little parental supervision a few extra days to "hang" with deviant peers. One student interviewed while in detention expresses this aptly.

> When they suspend you, you get in more trouble, 'cause you're out in the street.... And that's what happened to me once. I got into trouble one day 'cause there was a party, and they arrested everybody in that party.... I got in trouble more than I get in trouble at school, because I got arrested and everything.[18]

Whether and how to provide services to students who are suspended and expelled may be our next pressing national discussion. Without such services, school personnel may simply be dumping problem students out on the streets, only to find them later causing increased violence and disruption in the community. In sum, we lack solid evidence to support the effectiveness of harsh policies in improving school safety, and we face serious questions about the long-term negative effects of one of the cornerstones of zero tolerance, school exclusion.

Indeed, the popularity of zero tolerance may have less to do with its actual effects than with the image it portrays. Writing in the *Harvard Educational Review,* Pedro Noguera argues that the primary function of harsh punishment is not to change the behavior of the recipient, but to reassert the power of authority.[19] Seemingly random violence poses a profound threat to schools and to the authority of those who administer those schools. In the face of an apparent inability to influence the course of violence in schools, harsh measures are intended to send a message that the administration is still in charge. Whether the message is effectively received or actually changes student behavior may be less important than the reassurance that sending it provides to administrators, teachers, and parents.

In his recent book, *The Triumph of Meanness,* Nicholas Mills argues that a culture of meanness has come to characterize many aspects of our nation's social policies, from "bum-proof" park benches to sweeping social welfare reform. According to Mills, "Meanness today is a state of mind, the product of a culture of spite and cruelty that has had an enormous impact on us."[20] The zeal with which punitive policies are sometimes implemented suggests that zero tolerance discipline may be yet another example of what Mills is referring to. Whether such policies work or how they affect the lives of students may be less important than providing harsh punishment for offenders as a form of generalized retribution for a generalized evil.

What Else Should We Do?

In any institution, the preservation of order demands that boundaries be set and enforced. Children whose families set no limits for them soon become uncontrolled and uncontrollable. In the same way, schools and classrooms in which aggressive, dangerous, or seriously disruptive behaviors are tolerated will almost inevitably descend into chaos.

Yet the indiscriminate use of force without regard for its effects is the hallmark of authoritarianism, incompatible with the functioning of a democracy, and certainly incompatible with the transmission of democratic values to children. If we rely solely, or even primarily, on zero tolerance strategies to preserve the safety of our schools, we are accepting a model of schooling that implicitly teaches students that the preservation of order demands the suspension of individual rights and liberties. As we exclude ever-higher proportions of children whose behavior does not meet increasingly tough standards, we will inevitably meet many of those disruptive youths on the streets. In choosing control and exclusion as our preferred methods of dealing with school disruption, even as we refrain from positive interventions, we increase the likelihood that the correctional system will become the primary agency responsible for troubled youths. Ultimately, as we commit ourselves to increasingly draconian policies of school discipline, we may also need to resign ourselves to increasingly joyless schools, increasingly unsafe streets, and dramatically increasing expenditures for detention centers and prisons.

Seriousness of purpose in seeking to avert the tragedy of school violence does not necessarily demand rigid adherence to harsh and extreme measures. There *are* alternatives to politically facile get-tough strategies, alternatives that rely on a comprehensive program of prevention and planning. However, prevention is not a politically popular approach to solving problems of crime and violence in America. A recent task force on prevention research, commissioned by the National Institutes of Mental Health, found wide gaps in our knowledge, noting that "virtually no preventive services research of any kind was found under NIMH sponsorship."[21]

Yet if we are to break the cycle of violence in American society, we must begin to look beyond a program of stiffer consequences. We must begin with long-term planning aimed at fostering nonviolent school communities. First, programmatic prevention efforts—such as conflict resolution and schoolwide behavior management—can help establish a climate free of violence. Conflict resolution has been shown to have a moderate effect on the level of student aggression in schools,[22] but more important, it teaches students to consider and use alternatives to violence in solving conflicts. Schoolwide discipline plans and the planning process required to develop and implement them help ensure that school staff members have both the consistent philosophy and the consistent procedures that are so critical to effective behavior management.[23]

Second, screening and early identification of troubled young people appear to be critical in preventing the eruption of violence. In a number of the multiple-victim shooting incidents that occurred [in 1998], the shooter left warning signs, cries for help that went unheeded.[24] There is at least one widely available and well-researched measure designed to screen for troubled students, whether the primary concern is acting-out behavior or social withdrawal.[25] With such screening and with knowledge of the early warning signs listed in the President's guide for preventing violence,[26] we are beginning to have the capability of identifying students with serious problems while they can still be helped.

Finally, schools with effective discipline have plans and procedures in place to deal with the disruptive behaviors that inevitably occur. School safety teams or behavior support teams—composed of regular and special education teachers, personnel from related services, administrators, and parents—ensure a consistent and individualized response to disruptive students.[27] Individual behavior plans and a functional assessment process for developing those plans provide consistent consequences for offenders and teach disruptive youngsters alternatives to aggression.[28] Emergency and crisis planning before serious incidents occur can help ensure that, if violence erupts, its negative short- and long-term effects will be minimized.[29] In short, effective interventions emphasize building positive prosocial behaviors rather than merely punishing inappropriate behaviors. Whether at the level of the school or at the level of the individual, effective intervention requires a wide spectrum of options that extend significantly beyond a narrow focus on punishment and exclusion.

There are doubtless those with little patience for the complex and careful planning that such a program demands, those who prefer the quick fix that zero tolerance purports to be. But the problems that have brought us to the current precarious situation in our nation's schools are highly complex and will not abide simplistic solutions. Zero tolerance strategies have begun to turn our schools into supplemental law enforcement agencies, but they have demonstrated little return despite a decade of hype. In contrast, long-term, comprehensive planning and prevention can build safe and responsive schools over time by emphasizing what American education has always done best: teaching.

Notes

1. The original definition of "firearm" as contained in the Gun-Free Schools Act did not include weapons other than firearms. Later amendments and state policies have since expanded the definition to include any instrument intended to be used as a weapon.

2. *Violence and Discipline Problems in U.S. Public Schools: 1996–1997* (Washington, D.C.: National Center for Education Statistics, NCES 98-030, 1998).

3. Irwin A. Hyman and Donna C. Perone, "The Other Side of School Violence: Educator Policies and Practices That May Contribute to Student Misbehavior," *Journal of School Psychology,* vol. 30, 1998, p. 9.

4. Tom McNamee, "Student's Expulsion Tests Zero Tolerance," *Chicago Sun-Times,* 4 April 1993, p. 5; and Bert Eljera, "Schools Get Dead Serious: No Weapons," *Los Angeles Times,* 7 March 1993, p. B-1.

5. Perry A. Zirkel, "The Right Stuff," *Phi Delta Kappan,* February 1998, pp. 475–76.

6. Chris Pipho, "Living with Zero Tolerance," *Phi Delta Kappan,* June 1998, pp. 725–26.

7. Jessica Portner, "Suspensions Spur Debate over Discipline Codes," *Education Week on the Web,* 23 October 1996 (http//www.edweek.org.ew/vol16/08react.h16).

8. For a more complete review, see Russell J. Skiba, Reece L. Peterson, and Tara Williams, "Office Referrals and Suspension: Disciplinary Intervention in Middle Schools," *Education and Treatment of Children,* vol. 20, 1997, pp. 295–315.

9. Gale M. Morrison, and Barbara D'Incau. "The Web of Zero Tolerance: Characteristics of Students Who Are Recommended for Expulsion from School." *Education and Treatment of Children,* vol. 20, 1997, pp. 316–35.

10. Children's Defense Fund, *School Suspensions: Are They Helping Children?* (Cambridge, Mass.: Washington Research Project, 1975).

11. See Skiba, Peterson, and Williams, op. cit.

12. Shi-Chang C. Wu et al., "Student Suspension: A Critical Reappraisal," *Urban Review,* vol. 14, 1982, pp. 245–303.

13. Ibid.; and John D. McCarthy and Dean R. Hoge, "The Social Construction of School Punishment: Racial Disadvantage out of Universalistic Process," *Social Forces,* vol. 65, 1987, pp. 1101–20.

14. Hyman and Perone, op. cit.

15. Ruth B. Ekstrom et al., "Who Drops Out of High School and Why? Findings from a National Study," *Teachers College Record,* Spring 1986, pp. 356–73.

16. Christine Bowditch, "Getting Rid of Troublemakers: High School Disciplinary Procedures and the Production of Dropouts," *Social Problems,* vol. 40, 1993, pp. 493–507; and Michelle Fine, "Why Urban Adolescents Drop into and out of Public High School," *Teachers College Record,* Spring 1986, pp. 393–409.

17. Gerald R. Patterson, "Developmental Changes in Antisocial Behavior," in Ray D. Peters, Robert J. McMahon, and Vernon L. Quinsey, eds., *Aggression and Violence Throughout the Life Span* (Newbury Park, Calif.: Sage, 1992), pp. 52–82.

18. Sue Thorson, "The Missing Link: Students Discuss School Discipline," *Focus on Exceptional Children,* vol. 29, 1996, p. 9.

19. Pedro A. Noguera, "Preventing and Producing Violence: A Critical Analysis of Responses to School Violence," *Harvard Educational Review,* Summer 1995, pp. 189–212.

20. Nicholas Mills, *The Triumph of Meanness: America's War Against Its Better Self* (Boston: Houghton Mifflin, 1997), p. 2.

21. National Institutes of Mental Health, *Priorities for Prevention Research at NIMH: A Report by the National Advisory Mental Health Council Workshop on Mental Disorders Prevention Research* (Washington, D.C.: National Institutes of Health, 1998).

22. Richard J. Bodine, Donna K. Crawford, and Fred Schrumpf, *Creating the Peaceable School: A Comprehensive Program for Teaching Conflict Resolution* (Champaign, Ill.: Research Press, 1995).

23. Denise C. Gottfredson, Gary D. Gottfredson, and Lois G. Hybl, "Managing Adolescent Behavior: A Multiyear, Multischool Study," *American Educational Research Journal,* vol. 30, 1993, pp. 179–215; J. David Hawkins, Howard J. Doueck, and Denise M. Lishner, "Changing Teaching Practices in Mainstream Classrooms to Improve Bonding and Behavior of Low Achievers," *American Educational Research Journal,* vol. 25, 1988, pp. 31–50; and Geoff Colvin, Edward J. Kameenui, and George Sugai, "Reconceptualizing Behavior Management and Schoolwide Discipline in General Education," *Education and Treatment of Children,* vol. 16, 1993, pp. 361–81.

24. T. Egan, "Where Rampages Begin: A Special Report: From Adolescent Angst to Shooting Up Schools," *New York Times,* 14 June 1998, p. 1.

25. Hill M. Walker and Herbert H. Severson, *Systematic Screening for Behavior Disorders (SSBD): User's Guide and Administration Manual,* 2nd ed. (Longmont, Calif.: Sopris West, 1992).

26. Kevin Dwyer, David Osher, and Cynthia Warger, *Early Warning, Timely Response: A Guide to Safe Schools* (Washington, D.C.: U.S. Department of Education, 1998).

27. Barbara Ries Wager, "No More Suspensions: Creating a Shared Ethical Culture," *Educational Leadership,* December 1992/January 1993, pp. 34–37.

28. Russ Skiba et al., "A Four-Step Model for Functional Behavior Assessment," *NASP* [National Association of School Psychologists] *Communique,* May 1998, pp. 24–25.

29. Gayle D. Pilcher and Scott Poland, *Crisis Intervention in the Schools* (New York: Guilford Press, 1992).

POSTSCRIPT

Are Zero Tolerance Policies Necessary and Effective?

The issue of zero tolerance discipline policies is perhaps best understood by placing it in some sort of historical perspective. In the early years of public education, schoolteachers and school administrators enforced school discipline from the very comfortable legal status of *en loco parentis* (in the place or role of a parent). Corporal punishment, public humiliation, and other forms of control in the schoolhouse went unchallenged. However, as state control over the public schools became more established and as state certification of public school educators became more commonplace, it also became clear that school officials functioned more as representatives of the state than they did as surrogate parents. This trend away from *en loco parentis* was solidified in 1969 when the United States Supreme Court issued its famous *Tinker v. Des Moines* decision, establishing that students do not lose their constitutional rights at "the schoolhouse gate."

While the *Tinker* case signaled the passing of the *en loco parentis* era, it also ushered in a decade or so of legislation and school policymaking aimed at protecting student rights and limiting the discretion of school administrators in the handling of disciplinary cases. Due process considerations became part of suspension and expulsion hearings, and generally the overall approach to student discipline issues became more legalistic. The *Tinker* decision expanding student rights coincided with increased student activism and protests related to the Vietnam War and with what many in the public felt was a deterioration of discipline in the schools. Also contributing to this growing concern about students and the quality of U.S. schools was the release in 1983 of *A Nation at Risk* by the National Commission on Excellence in Education, which detailed a steady pattern of decline in achievement levels of American schoolchildren.

Whether motivated by such concerns or not, the United States Supreme Court in 1985 made the first of three decisions reversing the trend toward increased student rights. While falling short of reestablishing *en loco parentis* for school officials, these decisions did reassert their authority to deal with school disciplinary matters in a reasonable manner without being encumbered by legal standards imposed on law enforcement officials. The three cases were *New Jersey v. T.L.O.* (1985); *Bethel School District v. Fraser* (1986); and *Hazelwood School District v. Kuhlmeier* (1988). The *T.L.O.* case dealt with searches of students by school officials, while the other two cases concerned student speech (*Fraser*) and the student press (*Kuhlmeier*). In each case the Court held that schools are special places—and student rights in school are not coextensive with their rights elsewhere.

ISSUE 9

Is Achievement Level Tracking of Students a Defensible Educational Practice?

YES: Tom Loveless, from "The Tracking and Ability Grouping Debate," *Fordham Report* (August 1998)

NO: Jeannie S. Oakes, from "Limiting Students' School Success and Life Chances: The Impact of Tracking," in Allan C. Ornstein and Linda S. Behar-Horenstein, eds., *Contemporary Issues in Curriculum*, 2d ed. (Allyn and Bacon, 1999)

ISSUE SUMMARY

YES: Tom Loveless, director of the Brown Center on Education Policy at Brookings Institution, suggests that many of the charges against tracking are more political than educational and are not supported by research.

NO: Jeannie S. Oakes, professor in the Graduate School of Education at the University of California–Los Angeles, indicts the results of tracking, especially tracking's damaging impact on the education of minority students.

The practice of ability/achievement-level grouping of students into different classes for instructional purposes, or *tracking* as it is more popularly known, exists in some fashion or another in many if not most of the nation's secondary schools. In spite of the flurry of research and rhetorical attacks against it, especially in the 1970s and 1980s, when issues of equity and equal opportunity dominated the educational agenda, the practice continues to show great resiliency. Given this resiliency and widespread use, it is important to note that tracking, like most prevailing practices of teachers and schools, emanates from good intentions. Speaking of this in an article entitled "The Realities of Un-Tracking a High School," *Educational Leadership* (May 1991), Dennis Evans states,

After 20 years as a high school principal, I never cease to be amazed by the naiveté and arrogance of many of those who propose changes in educational practice. The reason that most of their proposals are never enacted is that they so often fail to take into account two fundamental realities about schools: (1) teachers are professionals who are predisposed to do what is best for their clients, and (2) teachers have made an investment of time, energy, and personal and professional pride in their current practices. Because they stand to lose so much in the process of change, they will not change merely for the sake of change.

Tracking of students for the avowed purposes of facilitating instruction and enhancing learning is not a new practice, and its origins can be traced to defensible goals of improved efficiency and meeting targeted student needs. Those supporting such goals argue that separating students into different groups or classes based upon student achievement or ability levels enables teachers to tailor instructional materials and teaching approaches to fit the particular characteristics of the grouped students. Indeed one might make the case that the very notion of evaluating and grading students, which has been an accepted function of secondary schools, as well as the related practice of sorting students for postsecondary education or for the world of work are themselves examples of grouping and tracking.

But as it is with any controversial issue, the arguments supporting tracking are challenged by compelling arguments against it. Many of these arguments contend that while there is little evidence that tracking improves the achievement of any group of students, there is strong evidence that it can harm students, especially those relegated to the lower tracks.

In the following selection, Tom Loveless makes the case that many of the arguments against tracking are ideologically motivated, overstated, and generally unsupported by research. Jeannie S. Oakes presents her analysis of tracking practices in two urban school districts and highlights the disproportionate numbers of minority students who are placed in the lower tracks and the concomitant negative impact on their achievement rates.

Tom Loveless

 **YES**

The Tracking and Ability Grouping Debate

Section One: What Is Tracking?

Thirty years ago, the terms "ability grouping" and "tracking" were used to identify two distinct approaches to grouping students.

Ability grouping referred to the formation of small, homogeneous groups within elementary school classrooms, usually for reading instruction. Children of approximately the same level of reading proficiency would be grouped for reading instruction, perhaps into "redbirds" and "bluebirds."

Tracking referred to a practice in which high schools tested students, typically with both achievement and IQ tests, and used these scores to place their students into separate curricular tracks, or "streams," as they are called in Europe....

Writers now use the terms "tracking" and "ability grouping" interchangeably. One hears, for example, that "tracking begins in kindergarten." In this report, I adhere to the conventional definitions employed by researchers, using "ability grouping" to refer to the grouping of students by ability within classes, which is primarily an elementary school practice, and "tracking" to refer to the grouping of students by ability between classes, a strategy common in middle and high schools. I will refer to untracked or mixed ability classes as "heterogeneously grouped." ...

Tracking in High Schools

High school systems have changed significantly from the college-general-vocational tracks of yore. They are still distinguished by a hierarchy of coursework, especially in mathematics and English, but two and three track systems and mixed systems with both tracked and heterogeneous classes are prevalent. Typically, students are grouped independently from subject to subject. A student who is a poor reader but strong in mathematics and science, for example, can progress to advanced placement (AP) courses in calculus or

From Tom Loveless, "The Tracking and Ability Grouping Debate," *Fordham Report* (August 1998). Copyright © 1998 by The Thomas B. Fordham Foundation. Reprinted by permission. Notes omitted.

physics. The independence of subjects is not pure, however. The vagaries of scheduling may still allow a student's placement in one subject to influence placement in another, and the mere existence of prerequisites can't help but link a student's present and past track levels. Nevertheless, it is more accurate to think of today's tracks as multiple pathways through different disciplines than as a single road winding through the full high school curriculum.

These tracks have diminished their preoccupation with students' destinations, most notably with deciding who will be prepared for college and who will be prepared for work. The honors track remains focused on college preparation, to be sure, but, invariably, middle and low tracks also declare preparation for college as goals. With enrollment in vocational courses in steep decline, the focus of low tracks has shifted toward academic remediation.... Classroom studies indicate that low tracks continue to dwell on basic skills, featuring a dull curriculum and inordinate amounts of drill and practice. But such curricular banality may be caused by the lack of interesting materials or good instructional strategies for addressing stubborn learning problems, especially problems persisting into the high school years. Despite remedial students' academic deficiencies, counselors frequently point low track students toward community colleges. The bottom line is that all high school tracks may lead to colleges, albeit to dramatically different types of institutions.

Another change is that the high track has become more accessible. When principals are asked how they assign students to tracks, they report that completion of prerequisite courses, course grades, and teacher recommendations are the chief criteria, not scores on standardized tests. Parent and student requests are also factored into track placement. More than 80% of schools allow students to elect their course level provided prerequisites have been met, and many schools offer a waiver option for parents who insist, despite the school's recommendation, that their child enroll in a high track class. A degree of self-tracking exists today that was unheard of decades ago....

Not Your Mother's Tracking System

To summarize, today's tracking systems differ from the severely deterministic systems that many people conjure up when they hear the term "tracking." Placement by IQ tests is a thing of the past. The rigidity of tracks has softened, with track assignments usually made on a subject-by-subject basis. Curricular differences still exist, but they have narrowed. Middle and lower level courses join honors classes in focusing on academic work and preparation for college. Some of the barriers to entering high tracks have fallen. Academic performance, as measured by grades and teachers' recommendations, dictates most placements, not scores on standardized tests. And tracking decisions are frequently negotiable. Parents and students who are willing to risk lower grades for a more rigorous education routinely gain access to the courses that they want....

Ability grouping is one way of bringing students and curriculum together to produce learning. Making judgments about what students can and can't do and the curriculum from which they will and will not benefit carries real consequences for students. How to best do this hangs over the high school's institutional history.

Section Two: The History of Tracking

Tracking at the Turn of the Century

... The 20th century's comprehensive high school emerged from [a] cauldron of political, social, economic, and intellectual upheaval, housing within it distinct curricular tracks but promising a common set of educational experiences and a single diploma for all graduates. Entrance exams tottered and fell, and high schools gradually accepted all comers. The lines of stratification for students had shifted: from distinctions drawn by the highest grade level one attained, or by whether one even attended high school, to distinctions emanating from the track one belonged to within high school.

This structure guided the high school's evolution into a mass institution over the next several decades. It was not without faults. Social Darwinists and racial segregationists twisted to their own ends the idea that schools should tailor activities more closely to the characteristics of students, insisting that children of different races and economic classes needed vastly different forms of education to prepare them for their rightful stations in life. Tracking was used as a tool of discrimination, especially during the Depression years, when students who might otherwise have been working poured into high schools by the thousands. Tests measuring IQ and academic achievement lent legitimacy to the task of placing students in tracks—and were used with both humane and pernicious intentions....

Sputnik and The Great Society

A flurry of criticism and the Russian launch of Sputnik [the first artificial Earth satellite] forced a reconsideration. Suddenly, Americans fretted that students weren't working hard enough, weren't learning enough, and weren't keeping pace with pupils abroad. In the 1960s, programs for gifted youngsters flourished, especially in math and science. The Great Society heightened concern about racial discrimination, poverty, and social inequality, spotlighting students who were badly served by the school system and giving birth to a multitude of programs that offered a helping hand. All of these programs—gifted education, special education, compensatory education, bilingual programs—targeted specific categories of students. Categorical programs institutionalized the conviction that any standardized education would shortchange youngsters with extraordinary needs. As categorical programs gained legal backing, their own administrative structures, and their own funding streams, the comprehensive high school grew more internally differentiated.

The Pendulum Swings Again

In the latter half of the 20th century, differentiation in the form of tracking came under fire. In books such as James Rosenbaum's (1976) *Making Inequality,*

Samuel Bowles and Herbert Gintis's (1976) *Schooling in Capitalist America,* John Goodlad's (1984) *A Place Called School,* and Jeanne Oakes's (1985) *Keeping Track,* critics assailed tracking for reproducing and exacerbating social inequalities.

They pointed out that poor, non-English speaking, and minority young-sters were disproportionately assigned to low tracks and wealthier, white stu-dents to high tracks—and concluded that this was not a coincidence. Oakes's book helped ignite a firestorm of anti-tracking activity. Tracking was blamed for unfairly categorizing students, stigmatizing struggling learners, and consigning them to a fate over which neither they nor their parents had control.

To sum up, the school system's historical search for the best way of orga-nizing students and curriculum has never produced a method immune from criticism. The contemporary indictment of tracking boils down to the con-tention that ability grouping systems are inefficient and unfair, that they hinder learning and distribute learning inequitably. These complaints command center stage in the research on tracking and ability grouping.

Section Three: The Research

The research on tracking and ability grouping is frequently summarized in one word: inconclusive. This pronouncement is accurate in that nearly a cen-tury's worth of study has failed to quantify the impact of tracking and ability grouping on children's education. It doesn't necessarily mean, however, that the gallons of ink spilled on these issues have been much ado about nothing. A non-effect in educational research is quite common. It can mean that the prac-tice under study is truly neutral vis-à-vis a particular outcome. But it can also mean that the practice has off-setting negative and positive effects, that positive effects are produced under some conditions and negative effects under others, or that effects occur that researchers either don't measure, because they're mea-suring something else, or can't measure, because of inadequate methods or expertise....

I will review the research on tracking and ability grouping by first survey-ing what is known about its effect on academic achievement and then examin-ing the evidence on ... the most serious charges leveled against tracking....

National Data

In the last two decades, researchers have ... analyzed large national surveys to evaluate tracking. High School and Beyond (HSB) is a study that began with tenth graders in 1980. The National Education Longitudinal Study (NELS) started with eighth graders in 1988. These two studies followed tens of thou-sands of students through school, recording their academic achievement, courses taken, and attitudes toward school. The students' transcripts were analyzed, and their teachers and parents were interviewed. The two massive databases have sustained a steady stream of research on tracking.

Three findings stand out. High track students in HSB learn more than low track students, even with prior achievement and other pertinent influences on achievement statistically controlled. Not surprising, perhaps, but what's staggering is the magnitude of the difference. On average, the high track advantage outweighs even the achievement difference between the student who stays in school until the senior year and the student who drops out.

The second major finding is that race and tracking are only weakly related. Once test scores are taken into account in NELS, a student's race has no bearing on track assignment. In fact, African-American students enjoy a 10% advantage over white students in being assigned to the high track. This contradicts the charge that tracking is racist. Considered in tandem with the high track advantage just described, it also suggests that abolishing high tracks would disproportionately penalize African-American students, especially high achieving African-American students. Moreover, NELS shows that achievement differences between African-American and white students are fully formed by the end of eighth grade. The race gap reaches its widest point right after elmentary and middle school, when students have experienced ability grouping in its mildest forms. The gap remains unchanged in high school, when tracking between classes is most pronounced.

Third, NELS identifies apparent risks in detracking. Low-achieving students seem to learn more in heterogeneous math classes, while high and average achieving students suffer achievement losses—and their combined losses outweigh the low achievers' gains. In terms of specific courses, eighth graders of all ability levels learn more when they take algebra in tracked classes rather than heterogeneously grouped classes. For survey courses in eighth grade math, heterogeneous classes are better for low achieving students than tracked classes.

These last findings are important because we don't know very much about academic achievement in heterogeneous classes. When the campaign against tracking picked up steam in the late 1980s, tracking was essentially universal. Untracked schools didn't exist in sufficient numbers to evaluate whether abandoning tracking for a full regimen of mixed ability classes actually works. The NELS studies that attempt to evaluate detracked classes, which thus far have been restricted to mathematics, point toward a possible gain for low achieving students and a possible loss for average and above average students, but these findings should be regarded as tentative.

To summarize what we know about ability grouping, tracking, and achievement: The elementary school practices of both within-class and cross-grade ability grouping are supported by research. The tracking research is more ambiguous but not without a few concrete findings. Assigning students to separate classes by ability and providing them with the same curriculum has no effect on achievement, positive or negative, and the neutral effect holds for high, middle, and low achievers. When the curriculum is altered, tracking appears to benefit high ability students. Heterogeneous classes appear to benefit low ability students but may depress the achievement of average and high achieving students.

Fosters Race and Class Segregation?

Critics charge that tracking perpetuates race and class segregation by disproportionately assigning minority and poor children to low tracks and white, wealthy
children to high tracks. When it comes to race, the disparities are real, but, as
just noted, they vanish when students' prior achievement is considered. A small
class effect remains, however. Students from poor families are more likely to
be assigned to low tracks than wealthier students with identical achievement
scores. This could be due to class discrimination, different amounts of parental
influence on track assignments, or other unmeasured factors.

The issue ultimately goes back to whether tracking is educationally sound.
Those who complain of tracking's segregative impact do not usually attack
bilingual or Title I programs for promoting ethnic and class segregation, no
doubt because they see these programs as benefiting students. If low tracks
remedied educational problems, the charge of segregation would probably dissipate. Does tracking harm black students? A telling answer is found in African-
American parents' attitude toward tracking. A study conducted by the Public
Agenda Foundation found that "opposition to heterogeneous grouping is as
strong among African-American parents as among white parents, and support
for it is generally weak." If tracking harmed African-American students, one
would not expect these sentiments.

Harms Self-Esteem?

Little research indicates that tracking harms students' self-esteem. In fact, the
evidence tilts slightly toward the conclusion that low ability students' self-
concept is strengthened from ability grouping and tracking, although the effect
is insignificant. The public labeling of low track students may cause embarrass-
ment, but the public display of academic deficiencies undoubtedly has a similar
effect in heterogeneous classrooms. There, a low ability student's performance
is compared daily to that of high-achieving classmates.

Locks Students In?

It would be reprehensible if students were denied the opportunity to move up
in track or denied, in the tracking critics' phrase, "access to knowledge," the
learning that gets students into college and ultimately betters their lives. Data
on this issue are difficult to interpret. Mobility rates tell us how much movement occurs, but they don't answer the key question of whether that movement
is warranted. For some students, keeping them in the same group year after year
may be wise, while for others, moving them up or down in group may be the
educationally prudent decision.

Even where the opportunity to move up and out of low tracks exists, the
qualities that one must have to seize this opportunity—strong achievement motivation, independence, and drive—may be lacking in many low track students.
Without a push, a lot of students remain in low tracks who are capable of
moving up.

High Track Privilege?

Critics of tracking charge that high tracks get more resources than low tracks. Detailed data on school budgets are sparse, and inconsistent expense categories render them almost impossible to compare across schools. It appears that high tracks are taught by better qualified teachers, however, in the sense of having teachers more schooled in content knowledge. High school principals are inclined to assign teachers who know advanced subject matter to teach advanced subjects. As pointed out by high track defenders, the alternative is unattractive. Does it advance the cause of equity to have teachers with advanced degrees in mathematics teach basic arithmetic while teachers without a single college math course teach calculus? A better solution is to insist that all students take more challenging classes and to staff these classes with well-qualified teachers.

Section Four: Principles for Future Policy

Serious charges have been made about tracking and ability grouping, especially tracking. Several states and districts have pushed schools to abolish tracking, and a storm of controversy has ensued. In recent years, tracking and ability grouping have come under increased fire for (1) being inefficient, that is, for not promoting academic achievement, and for (2) being inequitable, i.e., for condemning low group and low track students, and especially poor students and students of color, to impoverished educational settings.

These charges are mostly unsubstantiated by research. The evidence does not support the charge that tracking is inherently harmful, and there is no clear evidence that abandoning tracking for heterogeneously grouped classes would provide a better education for any student. This being said, tracking's ardent defenders cannot call on a wealth of research to support their position either. The evidence does not support the claim that tracking benefits most students or that heterogeneous grouping significantly depresses achievement. High achieving students are the exception. For them, tracked classes with an accelerated or enriched curriculum are superior to heterogeneously grouped classes.

Based on the foregoing analysis, I offer three principles to guide future policy making on tracking and ability grouping. I also furnish some suggestions derived from these principles. The suggestions are admittedly speculative, as they must be, given the limitations of the evidence.

1. Schools Should Decide Policy

Individual schools must have the latitude to make decisions about the best way to educate students, including whether tracking, ability grouping, or heterogeneous grouping works best for their pupils. In classrooms, learning depends upon a multitude of factors, some within educators' control, and many not. Teachers and principals are in the best position to structure the learning environment so that it works well because they know their students better than policymakers sitting many miles away. Managing instruction by remote control rarely succeeds.

Tracking's critics see school governance differently. Robert Slavin states, "Given the antidemocratic and antiegalitarian nature of ability grouping, the burden of proof should be on those who would group rather than on those who favor heterogeneous grouping, and in the absence of evidence that grouping is beneficial, it is hard to justify continuation of the practice." Jeannie Oakes urges federal and state mandates and court orders to force reluctant schools to detrack. "The reality in many school districts," she writes, "is that much needed equity-minded reforms will not come about if the decision is left to local policymakers. State and federal level policymakers (as well as the courts) have an obligation to step in and protect underserved (generally poor and minority) students." ...

Non-effects in research should not invite policymakers (or researchers) to impose a particular ideology or educational philosophy on local schools. No evidence indicates that abruptly and universally abolishing tracking would help anyone. It may even harm the students it is intended to benefit. Proclamations that tracking is undemocratic, inequitable, or educationally unsound cannot be reconciled with the non-effects found by research. Polls indicate that parents, teachers, and students support tracking. That part of democracy that premises governmental action on the preferences of the governed stands in favor of tracking's use. Moreover, the intervention advocated by Jeannie Oakes, attempting to dictate schools' operations and procedures from courtrooms and legislative arenas, is rapidly going the way of the dinosaur. Results are now assuming a dominant role in public policy. In this spirit, states and districts should establish clear expectations for achievement, judge schools by whether they attain them, and leave decisions about tracking and ability grouping to teachers, parents, and principals. Some schools will track, others will untrack.

2. Improve Tracked Schools

What's important are schools' accomplishments in teaching young people. It is the tracked school's responsibility to make tracking work well and to work well for all students. The low track is the aspect of tracking that draws the most criticism, and that's where schools should focus their energies for improvement. Low tracks should be small, well-managed by teachers who are competent in their subjects, monitored closely by administrators, and relentlessly focused on academics. The success of low tracks in Catholic schools needs to be investigated further and replicated. To promote mobility upward in tracks, schools should clearly communicate prerequisites for high tracks to their feeder schools, provide bridge courses (perhaps in summer school) that allow students to move up in track level, and offer challenge exams for track entry, where students can demonstrate sufficient preparation for more difficult coursework. Low functioning students should be scheduled into double periods of the subjects in which they need intensive help.

Many urban schools offer no IB [International Baccalaureate] or advanced placement courses. Every school's highest track in English, math, history, and science should end with a senior—year AP class. If some schools have insufficient numbers of qualified AP students, districts should pool several schools' students, offer AP at a central location, schedule the course at the beginning or end of the school day, and provide transportation so that qualified students may attend. A high track in an inferior school benefits no one.

3. Learn More About Untracked Schools and Improve Them

To make their case more persuasively, advocates of tracking's abolition need a substantial number of untracked schools that they can point to as successes. They also need a reliable body of research showing that the evils attributed to tracking don't also plague heterogeneously grouped classrooms. With untracked schools now in greater abundance, well-designed studies should be conducted to assess whether they can deliver on the promise of both equity and high achievement.... We need to learn much more about untracked schools, and having more of them now should allow us to do that....

A final point. The politics of tracking have generated intense debate for over seventy years. More than 700 studies have not succeeded in quelling the controversy. The simple question of whether ability grouping and tracking are better or worse than heterogeneous grouping remains unanswered. More research should be conducted on this question, of course. We have much to learn. But we also need to realize that another 700 studies and seven decades of debate may not resolve the issue.

We shouldn't permit the tracking debate to sidetrack the national effort to raise the quality of education for all students. American education now includes both tracked and untracked schools. The principles for policy outlined here recognize that fact. We should allow schools to decide their own practices, strive to improve tracked schools, and find out more about untracked schools so they too may be improved. The next generation of research and policy should concentrate on providing a better education in both tracked and untracked settings.

NO

Jeannie S. Oakes

Limiting Students' School Success and Life Chances: The Impact of Tracking

Since the 1920s, most elementary and secondary schools have tracked their students into separate "ability" groups designed for bright, average, and slow learners and into separate programs for students who are expected to follow different career routes after high school graduation. Tracking has seemed appropriate and fair, given the way psychologists have defined differences in students' intellectual abilities, motivation, and aspirations. Tracking has seemed logical because it supports a nearly century old belief that a crucial job of schools is to ready students for an economy that requires workers with quite different knowledge and skills. According to this logic, demanding academic classes would prepare bright, motivated students heading for jobs that require college degrees, while more rudimentary academic classes and vocational programs would ready less able and less motivated students for less-skilled jobs or for post–high school technical training. With the development early in the century of standardized tests for placement, most people viewed a tracked curriculum with its ability-grouped academic classes as functional, scientific, and democratic—an educationally sound way to accomplish two important tasks: (1) providing students with the education that best suits their abilities and (2) providing the nation with the array of workers it needs.

Despite its widespread legitimacy, there is no question that tracking, the assessment practices that support it, and the differences in educational opportunity that result from it limit many students' schooling opportunities and life chances. Those limits affect schoolchildren from all racial, ethnic, and socioeconomic groups. However, schools far more often judge African-American and Latino students to have learning deficits and limited potential. Not surprisingly, then, schools place these students disproportionately in low-track, remedial programs.

Educators justify these placements by pointing out that African-American and Latino children typically perform less well on commonly accepted assessments of ability and achievement. Moreover, conventional school wisdom holds that low-track, remedial, and special education classes help these students, since they permit teachers to target instruction to the particular learning deficiencies of low-ability students. However, considerable research demonstrates that students do not profit from enrollment in low-track classes; they do not learn as much as comparably skilled students in heterogeneous classes; they have less access than other students to knowledge, engaging learning experiences, and resources. Thus, school tracking practices create racially separate programs that provide minority children with restricted educational opportunities and outcomes.

In what follows, I will illustrate these points with evidence from two school systems whose ability grouping and tracking systems have been subject to scrutiny in the past year in conjunction with school desegregation cases. The first system, Rockford Public Schools, in Rockford, Illinois.... was the target of a liability suit brought by a community group, The People Who Care. Among other complaints, the group charged the school system with within-school segregation through ability grouping and discrimination against the district's nearly 30 percent African-American and Latino students. The second system, [was the] San Jose Unified School District, in San Jose, California.... The plaintiffs in the San Jose case argued, among other things, that the district had used its ability-grouping system to create within-school segregation and, thereby, circumvented the intent of the court order with regard to approximately 30 percent Latino student population. I analyzed data about the grouping practices in both these cities, prepared reports for the court, and testified....

To shed light on the grouping practices in these two systems, I conducted analyses and reported my conclusions about tracking and ability-grouping practices around several questions:

1. Does the school system employ tracking and/or ability grouping? If so, what is the specific nature of these practices?
2. Does the system's use of tracking and/or ability grouping create racially imbalanced classrooms?
3. Does the system's use of these grouping practices reflect sound, consistent, and educationally valid considerations?
4. Are the racial disproportionalities created by the system's ability grouping practices explained by valid educational considerations?
5. What are the consequences of the system's grouping and tracking practices for the classroom instructional opportunities of Latino children?
6. What are the consequences of the system's grouping and tracking practices for the educational outcomes of Latino children?
7. Does the system have the necessary support and capacity to dismantle racially identifiable tracking and create heterogeneously grouped classrooms?

I addressed these questions with analyses using data specific to the two school systems. These data were gathered from a variety of sources; district and individual school curriculum documents (e.g., curriculum guides, course catalogs, course descriptions, etc.); school plans; computerized student enrollment and achievement data; prior reports prepared by court monitors; and depositions taken from school district employees in the course of the discovery process.

Several analytic methods were applied to these data, all of which had been used in prior published research on tracking and ability grouping. In both systems, I used statistical methods to calculate the achievement range within each track, the distribution of students from various ethnic groups into various tracks, and the probability of placement of students from each ethnic group whose prior achievement "qualified" them for various tracks. In San Jose, but not in Rockford, I was also able to calculate rather precisely the impact of track placement on achievement gains of students with comparable prior achievement....

Proliferation of Tracking

Grouping practices and their effects on minority children were remarkably similar in both systems. Both systems used tracking extensively. At most grade levels and in most academic subject areas at nearly all schools, educators assigned students to classes based on judgments about students' academic abilities. The schools then tailored the curriculum and instruction within classes to the students' perceived ability levels. The districts' tracking systems were not only very comprehensive (in terms of the subject areas and grade levels that are tracked), but they were also very rigid and stable. That is, the districts tended to place students at the same ability level for classes in a variety of subject areas and to lock students into the same or a lower ability-level placement from year to year.

Racially Disproportionate Track Enrollments

In both school systems, tracking had created racially imbalanced classes at all three levels—elementary, middle, and senior high. This imbalance took two forms: (1) white (and Asian, in San Jose) students are consistently overrepresented and African-American and Latino students are consistently underrepresented in high-ability classes in all subjects; (2) in contrast, African-American or Latino students were consistently overrepresented, while white and Asian students were consistently underrepresented, in low-ability tracks in all subjects.

Inconsistent Application of Placement Criteria

The criteria used to assign students to particular tracks were neither clearly specified nor consistently applied. Accordingly, neither district's tracking policies and practices could be construed as the enactment of valid educational purposes; neither did either district present an educational justification for the racial imbalance that results from tracking.... To the contrary, neither district had enacted ability grouping and tracking in ways that narrow the range of measured student ability and achievement in classrooms sufficiently so that these classrooms can be considered bona fide ability groups....

Additionally, teacher and counselor recommendations at the critical transitions between elementary and middle school and between middle and high school included a formal mechanism to take into account highly subjective judgments about students' personalities, behavior, and motivation. For example, the screening process for gifted programs usually began with a subjective teacher identification of potentially gifted children, who were then referred for formal testing. Such referrals were often based on subjective judgments about behavior, personality, and attitudes.

Tracks Actually Heterogeneous Groups

The theory of tracking argues that, to facilitate learning, children should be separated into groups so that they may be taught together with peers of similar ability and apart from those with higher or lower abilities. But in both school systems, classes that were supposed to be designated for students at a *particular* ability level actually enrolled students who spanned *a very wide range* of measured ability. These ranges demonstrate dramatically that in both Rockford and San Jose racially imbalanced tracked classes have borne little resemblance to homogeneous ability groups—even though they have been labeled and treated as such by schools. While the mean scores in each of the tracks followed expected patterns—with average achievement score for students in the low track less than average score for students in the standard or accelerated tracks—the extraordinarily broad range of achievement in each of the three tracks makes clear how far these classes are from being homogeneous ability groups. In sum, the district's practices do not represent what tracking advocates would claim is a trustworthy enactment of a "theory" of tracking and ability grouping....

Placements Racially Skewed Beyond the Effects of Achievement

As a group, African-American and Latino students scored lower on achievement tests than whites and Asians in Rockford and San Jose. However, African-American and Latino students were much less likely than white or Asian students *with the same test scores* to be placed in accelerated courses. For example, in San Jose, Latino eighth graders with average scores in mathematics were three times less likely than whites with the same scores to be placed in an accelerated math course. Among ninth graders, the results were similar.... The discrimination is even more striking among the highest scoring students. While only 56 percent of Latinos scoring between 90 and 99 NCEs [Normal Curve Equivalents] were placed in accelerated classes, 93 percent of whites and 97 percent of Asians gained admission to these classes....

In both San Jose and Rockford, placement practices skewed enrollments in favor of whites over and above that which can be explained by measured achievement.

Low Tracks Providing Less Opportunity

In both school systems, African-American and Latino students in lower-track classes had fewer learning opportunities. Teachers expected less of them and gave them less exposure to curriculum and instruction in essential knowledge and skills. Lower-track classes also provided African-American and Latino students with less access to a whole range of resources and opportunities; to highly qualified teachers, to classroom environments conducive to learning, to opportunities to earn extra grade points that can bolster their grade-point averages, and to courses that would qualify them for college entrance and a wide variety of careers as adults.

Low Tracks and Lower Achievement

Not only did African-American and Latino students receive a lower-quality education as a result of tracking in San Jose and Rockford; their academic achievement suffered as well. In Rockford the initial average achievement gap (i.e., the difference in group mean achievement scores) between white and African-American and/or white and Latino students (i.e., that found on district-administered achievement tests in first grade) did not diminish in higher grades. To the contrary, eleventh graders exhibited gaps somewhat larger than first graders. For example, on the 1992 Stanford Achievement Test in reading comprehension, the gap between African-American and white first graders was 25 percent; that between African-American and white eleventh graders was 30 percent. Undoubtedly more telling, at the time of the seventh-grade test—probably the last point before considerable numbers of lower-achieving minority students drop out of school—the achievement gap between African Americans and whites had grown considerably wider, to 36 percent.... Clearly, the district's tracked programs failed to close the minority–white gap between average group scores....

Rockford's grouping practices that created racially identifiable classrooms and provided unequal opportunities to learn (with fewer such opportunities provided to minority students) *did not serve a remedial function for minority students*. To the contrary, these practices did not even enable minority students to sustain their position, relative to white students, in the district's achievement hierarchy.

In San Jose, better data permitted me to analyze the impact of track placement on individual students over time. Students who were placed in lower-level courses—disproportionately Latino students—consistently demonstrate lesser gains in achievement over time than their peers placed in high level courses....

These results are consistent across achievement levels: Whether students began with relatively high or relatively low achievement, those who were placed in lower-level courses showed lesser gains over time than similarly situated students who were placed in higher-level courses.

In Sum, Considerable Harm

The findings from my analyses of San Jose and Rockford support disturbing conclusions about tracking and within-school segregation and discrimination. The districts' tracking systems pervade their schools. The harm that accrues to African Americans and Latinos takes at least three demonstrable forms: (1) unjustifiable, disproportionate, and segregative assignment to low-track classes and exclusion from accelerated classes; (2) inferior opportunities to learn; and (3) lower achievement. In both systems, grouping practices have created a cycle of restricted opportunities and diminished outcomes and have exacerbated differences between African-American and Latino and white students.

POSTSCRIPT

Is Achievement Level Tracking of Students a Defensible Educational Practice?

The case can be made that issues related to equity of educational opportunity, which were especially prominent in the 1970s and up through the early 1990s, are now receiving less emphasis as the quest for higher educational standards and accountability takes center stage. If that is true, then the practice of achievement-level grouping, or tracking, which has remained widespread in spite of the negative press it received vis à vis equity issues, may gain even greater acceptability as an efficient way to target the specific instructional needs of students at different ability levels, and thereby raise collective student test scores at the school and state levels.

Supporters of providing targeted instruction of selected groups of students argue that such practices are not only effective but are consistent with legitimate educational goals related to improving the achievement of all students. Further, they point out that tracking and grouping are not the same. As stated by Joseph S. Renzulli and Sally M. Reis, in their article "The Reform Movement and the Quiet Crisis in Gifted Education," *Gifted Child Quarterly* (vol. 35, no. 1, 1991), "Tracking is the general, and usually permanent, assignment of students to classes that are taught at a certain level and with whole-group instruction. Grouping is a more flexible, less permanent arrangement of students that takes into account factors in addition to ability, such as motivation, interests, instructional levels, and student efforts."

Detractors of "detrackers" of achievement-level grouping continue to attack it in terms of not only the harm they believe it does to the educational opportunities of students assigned to the lower tracks and the disproportionate numbers of minority students in those tracks, but also that it does not deliver greater achievement for anyone. Perhaps the most influential of such arguments comes from researcher Robert Slavin, who conducted a meta-analysis of 29 studies of tracking at the secondary level and concluded that the effect of tracking on the achievement of students of any ability was "essentially zero" (from Laura Argys, Daniel I. Rees, and Dominic J. Brewer, "Detracking America's Schools: The Reform Without Cost?" *Phi Delta Kappan* [November 1995]). Slavin also argues that studies that show that gifted students in accelerated classes do show appreciable gains when compared to similar students in regular classes are tainted by the selection process, which often places the more motivated and engaged students in the accelerated classes.

ISSUE 10

Is High-Stakes Standardized Testing Defensible?

YES: Richard P. Phelps, from "Why Testing Experts Hate Testing,"
Fordham Report (January 1999)

NO: Peter Sacks, from "Standardized Testing: Meritocracy's Crooked
Yardstick," *Change* (March/April 1997)

ISSUE SUMMARY

YES: Journalist Richard P. Phelps suggests that the criticisms directed
at high-stakes standardized testing are misguided and do not hold up
upon careful scrutiny.

NO: Peter Sacks, a journalist and essayist on education and American
culture, argues that the penchant for high-stakes testing is counterproductive to meaningful teaching and learning and thus harmful
to students.

T he growing stridency of advocates and adversaries of high-stakes testing, especially the type of testing exemplified by the Scholastic Aptitude Test (SAT),
by high school exit examinations, and by state-level measures of school performance, ultimately speaks to the divisions that exist among educators and the
public regarding the purposes of schooling. Certainly the prevailing public and
political support for standards-based objective measures of accountability can
be seen as being consistent with the views of those who subscribe to a competitive marketplace approach to school improvement. Other mechanisms within
this approach include school vouchers and merit pay for teachers.

On the other side are those who value the antibehaviorism tenet, which
posits that "most important things cannot be measured." They see schooling
as a more qualitative and personal experience, one wherein the most important outcomes may not be directly observable and/or compatible with testing.
The proponents of this view hold that if we are compelled to measure student
growth and learning then we should at least be "authentic" in what we measure
and how we do the measuring. They deplore what they see as the inadequacies
of objective standardized testing and instead opt for learner portfolios and "real
world" performances as the bases for assessment.

Both sides in this increasingly heated debate can find data that support their respective positions in the 32nd Annual Phi Delta Kappa/Gallup Poll of the Public's Attitudes Toward the Public Schools (September 2000). In responding to a question that asked about the current emphasis on testing, a plurality of 43 percent of the respondents indicated that it was "about the right amount." This would indicate that the American public is not greatly concerned with overemphasis on testing. But when asked what is the best way to measure student academic achievement, a plurality of 44 percent of the public chose "portfolios of students' work" while only 13 percent opted for a single standardized test. This seems to indicate that the public is not solidly behind the standardized testing movement.

In his selection, Richard P. Phelps presents the major criticism aimed at high-stakes standardized testing and then analyzes and rebuts each point of criticism. Phelps believes that many testing experts "share an ideological orientation that makes any type of standardized test impossible to swallow." He states that the education philosophy driving many of these criticisms of testing is constructivism. In particular, Phelps indicts education professors for their preferences for "process over content," "facilitating learning" rather than teaching, and "partnership and collaboration" over imparting knowledge.

Peter Sacks takes to task the standardized testing industry as exemplified by the Educational Testing Service (ETS) and its best-known examination, the SAT. He contends that much of what is measured by such testing, especially in terms of predictive value, is exaggerated and/or redundant. Sacks also explores why the American public continues to support standardized testing in spite of the many criticisms against it; his conclusion is that "America is hooked. We are a nation of standardized-testing junkies."

Richard P. Phelps  **YES**

Why Testing Experts Hate Testing

Appraising the Criticisms

The basic argument made by testing critics is that the use of high-stakes standardized tests is counterproductive. Instead of leading to stronger academic achievement, it actually interferes with good teaching and learning. Testing experts embrace a sort of domino theory. Pressure to produce higher scores leads teachers to focus on material that will be covered by the tests and to exclude everything else. The curriculum is thereby narrowed, which means that some subjects are ignored. Within those that are taught, lower-order thinking skills are emphasized since these are what the tests tap. As a result of teachers teaching to the tests, subsequent test scores are inflated while real learning suffers.

In addition to the alleged harms of 1) test score inflation, 2) curriculum narrowing, 3) emphasis on lower-order thinking, and 4) declining achievement, testing experts add a quartet of other arguments against testing—that: 5) standardized tests hurt minorities and women, 6) tests are too costly, 7) other countries don't test nearly as much as we do, and 8) parents, teachers, and students in this country are all opposed to testing. These eight claims will be examined in detail in the section that follows, and a rebuttal will be offered to each.

What testing experts particularly do not like are high-stakes, multiple-choice, external tests. They excoriate these tests with bad-sounding words (e.g., "lower-order thinking," "factory model of education," "uncreative," "rote recall," and so on), but the terms are seldom well explained. The root of most of the objections can be traced to the dominant worldview of testing experts (and many other educators).

The education philosophy driving many of these criticisms is constructivism, the view that every student and teacher constructs his or her own meanings from classroom activities, books, etc. Hence no construction is wrong or bad. We all know that there is often more than one way to get to a right answer. We all think differently, using different combinations of several different kinds of intelligence. Moreover, we all know that a student can process much of a problem well but still get the "wrong" answer in the end because of a fairly minor error, such as misplacing a decimal point.

As test critic (and constructivist) Mary Lee Smith of CRESST [Center for Research on Education Standards and Student Testing] and Arizona State University describes it:

> Constructivist theory assumes that students construct their own knowledge (rather than passively receiving knowledge transmitted by school) out of intentional transactions with materials, teachers, and other pupils. Learning is more likely to happen when students can choose and become actively engaged in the tasks and materials, and when they can make their own connections across subject matter on tasks that are authentic and organized around themes. According to this theory, literacy is whole, embodying reading authentic texts and writing as a way of unifying all the subjects. For example, to be literate is to be able to explain the reasoning one uses to discover and solve math problems. Explicit in constructivist theory is the rejection of the pedagogy of worksheets and the exclusive reliance on phonics, spelling out of context, computation, isolated subject matter and the like.

Constructivists oppose school practices that they think "fix" behavior. They see standardizing curricula and instructional practice as restricting teacher behavior and multiple-choice standardized tests as shackling student responses to problems.

For constructivists, the more open-ended the assessment the better, and portfolios are the most open-ended of all. They involve no standardized, mandated, pre-set responses and not necessarily even a standardized question to impede any student's unique understanding of the problem, creative solution, and personal construction of the work. This constructivist worldview will be seen to underlie most of the arguments marshaled by testing experts against testing.

1) Test Score Inflation

An initial set of harms ascribed to standardized testing falls under the rubric of "teaching to the test." A CRESST paper entitled "The Effects of High-Stakes Testing on Achievement," by Daniel Koretz, Lorrie Shepard, and others, purports to demonstrate that high-stakes tests in fact cause teaching to the test. The researchers compared student performance in math and reading from one commercial test given under high-stakes conditions in one school district to student performance on a different commercial test with no stakes. Student performance on the high-stakes test improved over time, according to the researchers, as the teachers adapted their instruction to the curriculum implicit in the test. Student performance on the other test, administered solely for the purpose of the study, did not improve over time. The difference in student performance between the two tests is offered by the CRESST researchers as proof that high-stakes tests "narrow the curriculum" and induce "teaching to the test." Test critics would describe the second set of scores on the high-stakes test as artificially inflated, "polluted," or "corrupted."

The idea behind score inflation is that, as teachers become more familiar with test content, they spend more time teaching that test content and less time teaching other material. So, over time, as familiarity grows, scores climb on the test while real learning suffers.

In the early 1980s, a West Virginia physician named John J. Cannell investigated a statistical anomaly that he had discovered: statewide average scores for students on some widely used test batteries were above the national average in every state in which they were given. It was dubbed the "Lake Wobegon Effect" after the fictional community where "all the children are above average."

Response:

The Lake Wobegon anomaly might have been caused—observed Cannell and a group of test experts—by a number of factors, including schools reusing old tests year after year and growing familiar with their specific content, and test publishers waiting years before "renorming" the reference scales. Other factors could have included the "nonrepresentativeness" of the norming samples; the choice by school districts of the one test, from among various test versions, that most closely aligned with their curriculum and on which their pupils would likely perform best; and the fact that student achievement really was improving throughout the 1980s, as verified by independent testing, such as that for SAT [Scholastic Assessment Test], ACT [American College Test], and NAEP [National Assessment for Educational Progress] exams. There may also have been some statistical anomalies in Dr. Cannell's calculations.

The Lake Wobegon controversy led to calls for more state government control over test content and administration and less local discretion. In most states, those calls were answered. Today most school districts are aware of the problem of test score inflation, and do not use tests with the exact same questions year after year. Many jurisdictions now either use tests that are custom-built to their state standards and curricula or that are adapted from commercial publishers' test item banks. A simple way to prevent score inflation is to use different tests or test forms from year to year without announcing in advance which one will be used. Indeed, most of the likeliest sources of the Lake Wobegon effect are fairly easily avoided.

The larger argument about teaching to the test has several components, which will now be addressed.

2) Curriculum Narrowing

We might suppose that preparing youngsters to do well on tests would find favor with testing experts, yet many of them condemn all forms of "teaching to the test." These arguments tend to come in several forms. One is that valuable subjects that are not tested (e.g., art and music, maybe even social studies or science) will be ignored or slighted by test-obsessed teachers and school systems. Lorrie Shepard of CRESST and the University of Colorado has asserted:

> Although critics may originally have feared that testing would take instructional time away from "frills," such as art and citizenship, the evidence now shows that social studies and science are neglected because of the importance of raising test scores in the basic skills.

A variation on this theme holds that, even within a subject that *is* taught, content coverage will be narrowed (or curricular depth made shallow) in order to conform to the content or style of the test.

Response:

There is only so much instructional time available, and choices must be made as to how it is used. (Of course, some new school designs also extend the school day or year to ameliorate this problem.) If non-tested subjects are being dropped, either they, too, should be tested or, perhaps, educators and policymakers are signalling that, in a world of tough choices among competing priorities, some subjects must in fact take a backseat to others. A state or school system could easily add high-stakes tests in art, music, language, and civics, or any other subjects. Attaching high-stakes to tests in some subjects and not others would be interpreted by most as a signal that the former subjects are considered to be more important. Perhaps that's actually true. Especially where students are sorely deficient in basic skills and need extra instruction in them, it is likely that few parents would object to such priorities. Survey results show clearly that the public wants students to master the basics skills first, before they go on to explore the rest of the possible curriculum. If that means spending more time on "the basics," so be it. As for subject content being narrowed or made shallow in anticipation of a test, a better response than eliminating the test might be to replace it with one that probes deeper or more broadly.

3a) Emphasis on Lower-Order Thinking (in Instruction)

Lorrie Shepard has also asserted:

> High-stakes testing misdirects instruction even for the basic skills. Under pressure, classroom instruction is increasingly dominated by tasks that resemble tests.... Even in the early grades, students practice finding mistakes rather than do real writing, and they learn to guess by eliminating wrong answers....

In an extensive 18-month observational study, for example, Mary Lee Smith and her colleagues found that, because of external tests, elementary teachers had given up on reading real books, writing, and undertaking long-term projects and were filling all available time with word recognition; recognition of errors in spelling, language usage, and punctuation; and arithmetic operations...

Response:

Critics like Smith and Shepard say that intensive instruction in basic skills denies the slow students instruction in the "the neat stuff" in favor of "lower-order thinking." They argue that time for preparing students for high-stakes tests reduces "ordinary instruction." They cannot abide the notion that preparing students for a standardized test could be considered instruction, because it is not the kind of instruction that they favor.

Instruction to which teachers may resort to help students improve their scores on standardized tests tends not to be constructivist. It is the type of instruction, however, that teachers feel works best for knowledge and skill acquisition. Teachers in high-stakes testing situations do not deliberately use instructional practices that impede learning: they use those that they find to be most successful.

These testing critics idealize the concept of teachers as individual craftspersons, responding to the unique needs of their unique pupils in unique ways with "creative and innovative" curriculum and instruction. But the most difficult jobs in the world are those that must be created anew every day without any consistent structure, and performed in isolation without collaboration or advice. In Public Agenda's research, "teachers routinely complained that teaching is an isolated and isolating experience."

By contrast, teachers in other countries are commonly held to more narrowly prescribed curricula and teaching methods. Furthermore, because their curricula and instructional methods are standardized, they can more easily and productively work together and learn from each other. They seem not to suffer from a loss of "creativity and innovation"; indeed, when adjusted for a country's wealth, teachers in other nations are commonly paid more, and usually have greater prestige.

Critics like Shepard and Smith cannot accept that some teachers may *want* to conform to systemwide standards for curriculum, instruction, and testing. Standardization brings the security, convenience, camaraderie, and common professional development that accompany a shared work experience.

3b) Emphasis on Lower-Order Thinking (in Test Content)

One CSTEEP [Center for the Study of Testing, Education, and Educational Policy] study, funded by the National Science Foundation, analyzed whether several widely used commercial (and mostly multiple-choice) tests required "higher-" or "lower-order" thinking. A press account boasted, "In the most comprehensive study of its kind yet conducted, researchers from Boston College have found evidence to confirm the widespread view that standardized and textbook tests emphasize low-level thinking and knowledge and that they exert a profound, mostly negative effect on classroom interaction."

Researcher Maryellen Harmon told a reporter, "None of [the test content] calls for high-order thinking that requires that they go in-depth into the concept, that they use math skills in nonconventional contexts, or pull together concepts from geometry and algebra." Project Director George Madaus was quoted as saying that the findings present a "depressing picture.... If this doesn't change, an inordinate amount of time, attention, and preparation will be given to the wrong domains in math and science, domains that are not reflecting the outcomes we want."

Response:

Many readers would be astonished, as I still am, by the vehemence of some critics' ire toward something as seemingly dull and innocuous as item response format. Yet many of the accusations leveled at multiple-choice items have little substance. For example, you can often find in CSTEEP and FairTest [organization devoted to protecting the interests of consumers of standardized tests] publications assertions that multiple-choice items demand only factual recall and "lower-order" thinking, while "performance-based" tests do neither. Both claims are without merit. It is the structure of the *question,* not the response format, that determines the character of the cognitive processing necessary to reach a correct answer.

Test items can be banal and simplistic or intricately complex and, either way, their response format can be multiple-choice or open-ended. There is no necessary correlation between the difficulty of a problem and its response format. Even huge, integrative tasks that require fifty minutes to classify, assemble, organize, calculate, and analyze can, in the end, present the test-taker with a multiple-choice response format. Just because the answer to the question is among those provided, it is not necessarily easy or obvious how to get from the question to the answer.

... [I]s "higher-order thinking" always a superior form of thinking, as testing critics imply? Consider the type of thinking surgeons do. They are highly paid and well-respected professionals. Their study, however, consists of a considerable amount of rote memorization, and their work entails a considerable amount of routine and factual recall (all "lower-order thinking"). Moreover, the medical college admissions test is largely multiple-choice, and tests administered during medical training largely elicit the recall of discrete facts.

If you were about to go under the knife, which kind of surgeon would you want? Perhaps one who used only "higher-order thinking," only "creative and innovative" techniques, and "constructed her own meaning" from every operation she performed?

Or, would you prefer a surgeon who had passed her "lower-order thinking" exams—on the difference, say, between a spleen and a kidney—and used tried-and-true methods with a history of success: methods that other surgeons had used successfully? ...

The surgery analogy also addresses another of the testing critics' arguments. They say that multiple-choice tests limit students to the "one correct answer" when there may really be more than one valid answer and more than one way to get to each. Moreover, they say, students should not get an entire exercise counted wrong if they analyze most of the problem correctly, but make one careless error.

Most of us would sympathize with this sentiment, but we should remember that there are countless examples in real life where there is just one right answer or where one careless error can have devastating consequences—in brain surgery, for example.

4) Declining Achievement

Testing experts claim that high-stakes tests actually interfere with learning and student achievement in states that use them. In "High Stakes Tests Do Not Improve Student Learning," FairTest asserted that states with high-stakes graduation exams tend to score lower on NAEP [National Assessment of Educational

Progress]. According to FairTest, this "contradicts the... common assumption of standards and tests-based school reform... that high-stakes testing... will produce improved learning outcomes."

The FairTest solution is to restrict testing to occasional no-stakes monitoring with samples of students using the types of response formats that FairTest favors (no multiple-choice!). Scores on "portfolios" of each student's best work would track individual student progress. Indeed, the only state testing program to garner the highest rating from FairTest was Vermont, which has a statewide portfolio program and no high-stakes or multiple-choice standardized testing.

Response:

The claim that high-stakes tests inhibit learning is a weak argument supported by dubious research. The FairTest report provides a good example of just how simplistic that research can be. FairTest argues that states with high-stakes minimum-competency test graduation requirements tend to have lower average test scores on NAEP. They make no effort, however, to control for other factors that influence test performance, and the relationship between cause and effect is just assumed to run in the direction FairTest wants. Most honest observers would assume the direction of cause and effect to be just the opposite —poorly performing states initiate high-stakes testing programs in an effort to improve academic performance while high performing states do not feel the need to.

The work of the Cornell labor economist John Bishop does not get the press attention bestowed on FairTest. Yet in a series of solid studies conducted over a decade, Bishop has shown that, when other factors that influence academic achievement are controlled for, students from states, provinces, or countries with medium- or high-stakes testing programs score better on neutral, common tests and earn higher salaries after graduation than do their counterparts from states, provinces, or countries with no- or low-stakes tests....

5) Testing Hurts Women and Minorities

... [T]he NAACP [National Association for the Advancedment of Colored People] and the Mexican-American Legal Defense Fund [have] both argued that the Texas Assessment of Academic Skills [TAAS] was biased against minorities.

The brunt of FairTest's attack on the SAT involves alleged bias as well. The argument is straightforward: on average, girls score worse on the SAT than boys, despite getting better grades in school. Therefore the SAT is gender-biased. Blacks and Hispanics score lower than whites. Therefore the SAT is race-biased. FairTest argues that this bias against minorities depresses minority college admissions.

Response:

After investigating why girls score worse on the SAT than boys, despite getting better grades in school, the Educational Testing Service (ETS), the SAT's developer, concluded that the gender difference in SAT scores was almost entirely explained by high school course selection (e.g., girls took fewer math and science courses than boys, and so got lower SAT math scores). FairTest called the ETS explanation a "smokescreen." Yet similar evidence is available for blacks and Hispanics: almost all the SAT math score differences between them and their white counterparts disappear when they take as much algebra and geometry in high school as white students do.

The charge that the use of SATs in college admissions artificially depresses minority admissions is also misguided. As David W. Murray writes in "The War on Testing":

> Nor is it even clear that relying more exclusively on grades would bump up the enrollment numbers of blacks and Hispanics, as many seem to think. While it is true that more minority students would thereby become eligible for admission, so would other students whose grade point averages (GPAs) outstripped their test scores. A state commission in California, considering the adoption of such a scheme, discovered that in order to pick students from this larger pool for the limited number of places in the state university system, the schools would have to raise their GPA cut-off point. As a result, the percentage of eligible Hispanics would have remained the same, and black eligibility actually would have dropped.

There is a double sadness to the focus of some minority spokespersons on the messenger instead of the message. Black and Hispanic students in the United States generally receive an education inferior to that received by white students. This is a shame and a disgrace. By blaming standardized tests instead of the schools that are responsible for their students' poor achievement, however, these advocacy groups waste efforts that would be better expended reforming bad schools....

6) Excessive Cost

Some experts have criticized standardized tests, particularly those which include performance-based items, as too costly. Daniel Koretz, of CRESST, appeared before a congressional committee to argue against a national testing proposal, and stressed cost as a major negative. He claimed that the costs of performance-based national tests would be well over $100 per student, perhaps as high as $325 per student.

Another study of the extent and cost of testing by Walter Haney and George Madaus of CSTEEP calculated a "high" estimate of $22.7 billion spent on standardized testing in a year. U.S. schools, the CSTEEP report claimed, suffered from "too much standardized testing" that amounted to "a complete and utter waste of resources." Their estimate breaks down to about $575 per student per year for standardized testing.

A recent CRESST report by Larry Picus which counted cost components in much the same way as the CSTEEP study estimated costs of a certain state test at between $848 and $1,792 per student tested.

Response:
Several years ago, the U.S. General Accounting Office (GAO) surveyed a national sample of state and local testing directors and administrators to appraise the

costs of then-current statewide and districtwide tests, many of which contained some performance-based items. GAO found that eleven state tests ranging from 20% to 100% performance-based cost an average of $33 per student, including the salary time of teachers and other staff engaged in test-related activity, as well as the purchase of test materials and services. GAO estimated that slightly over $500 million was spent by U.S. school systems on systemwide testing in a year, or about 0.2% of all spending on elementary and secondary schools.

The GAO estimate of $33 per student contrasts with CRESST and CSTEEP estimates of $575 to $1792. The GAO estimate of about $500 million for the total national cost of systemwide testing contrasts with a CSTEEP estimate 45 times higher.

Testing critics estimate standardized tests' costs so much higher because they count the costs of any activities "related to" a test as costs *of* a test. In the CRESST study of Kentucky's performance-based testing program, for example, teachers were asked to count the number of hours they spent "preparing materials related to the assessment program for classroom use." In an instructional program with the intention of unifying all instruction and assessment into a "seamless" web, where the curriculum and the test mutually determine each other, *all* instruction throughout the entire school year will be "related to" the assessment. . . .

7) Other Countries Don't Test as Much

CSTEEP's Madaus has claimed that "American students [were] already the most heavily tested in the world." He has also asserted that the trend in other developed countries is toward less standardized testing. He reasoned that other countries are dropping large-scale external tests because they no longer need them as selection devices since places in upper secondary programs are being made available to everyone and access to higher education programs has widened. Thus, he argued, a worldwide trend toward less external testing could be found at all levels of education "even at the postsecondary level" and it was unidirectional— large-scale, external tests were being "abolished."

Response:
Are U.S. students the "most heavily tested in the world"? No. U.S. students actually spend less time taking high-stakes standardized tests than do students in other developed countries. A 1991 survey for the Organisation for Economic Co-operation and Development (OECD) revealed that "U.S. students face fewer hours and fewer numbers of high-stakes standardized tests than their counterparts in every one of the 13 other countries and states participating in the survey and fewer hours of state-mandated tests than their counterparts in 12 of the 13 other countries and states."

What of Madaus's assertion of a trend toward less standardized testing in other countries?

The primary trend appears to be toward more testing, with a variety of new test types used for a variety of purposes. In a study I conducted, I found twenty-seven countries and provinces had increased or planned to increase testing over the period 1974–1999, while only two decreased it. Altogether, fifty-three tests were added and only three dropped.

8) All Those Who Really Care About Children Oppose Testing

Testing experts who hate testing imply that they speak on behalf of teachers and students, defending them against politicians, mean-spirited conservatives, and the greedy testing industry. The critics claim that those who care about teachers and students see testing for what it really is, and oppose it.

Regarding teachers, for example, Robert Stake, who was chosen by the AERA [American Educational Research Association] to speak at their press conference on testing, said "[teachers] have essentially no confidence in testing as the basis of the reform of schooling in America."

The laundry list of costs attributed to *students* from the use of standardized tests ranged from a change in instruction away from the "neat stuff" in the curriculum toward "lower-order thinking," to an increase in grade retention and dropout rates from the use of standardized tests in high-stakes situations. A CRESST study by Mary Lee Smith, referred to at the conference on the "unintended consequences of external testing," claimed to find "stress, frustration, burnout, fatigue, physical illness, misbehavior and fighting, and psychological distress" among the effects of testing on young students.

Response:

To learn the true attitudes toward testing among teachers, students, parents, and the public, I attempted to gather all relevant U.S. poll and survey items on student testing by collecting many surveys myself and searching the Roper Center archives. I discovered 200 items from seventy-five surveys over three decades.

The results are fairly decisive. Majorities of the general public favor more testing and higher stakes in testing. The majorities have been large, often very large, and fairly consistent over the years, across polls and surveys, and even across respondent groups. Parents, students, employers, state education administrators, and even teachers (who exhibit more guarded opinions and sometimes fear being blamed if their students score badly on tests) consistently favor more student testing and higher stakes.

Twenty-seven polls taken between 1970 and the present asked specific respondents whether they thought education would improve if there were higher (student) stakes in school testing. In twenty-six of the twenty-seven polls the answer was yes, in most cases by huge margins.

... The National Association of State Boards of Education has come out strongly in favor of a greater use of high-stakes standardized testing. So have state superintendents and governors. The American Federation of Teachers (AFT) has been the nation's most forceful and vocal advocate for greater use of high-stakes standardized student testing. The other large teachers' union, the National Education Association [NEA], has recently moved closer to the AFT position.

Nationwide polls of teachers conducted over three decades by the Carnegie Foundation for the Advancement of Teaching, the Metropolitan Life Insurance Co., the American Federation of Teachers, the *Phi Delta Kappan* magazine, and Public Agenda show strong teacher support for high-stakes standardized tests. . . .

Testing in Perspective

The fact that tests and test results can be misused is beyond dispute. Human beings are responsible for administering them and interpreting their results, and humans are imperfect creatures. There is also no denying that tests are imperfect measurement devices. If the items in the anti-testing canon were also beyond dispute, one might well be disposed to give up on high-stakes standardized testing. But that would be an enormous mistake.

The critics would have us believe that all problems with high-stakes and standardized testing must always be with us, i.e., that nothing can be changed or improved. They're wrong. Some of the alleged problems—that they hurt learning and are expensive, for instance—are really not problems at all, as shown above. Other problems apply equally to the alternatives to testing. Still others are solvable and are being or have been solved by state, local, or national testing directors.

Probably the single most important recent innovation in relation to the quality and fairness of testing in the United States has been the addition of managerial and technical expertise in state education agencies. At that level, it is possible to retain an adequate group of technically proficient testing experts, adept at screening, evaluating, administering, and interpreting tests, who are not "controlled by commercial publishers" or naïve about test results. They, along with governors and legislatures, are currently calling the shots in standardized testing. Some of the most important decisions affecting the design and content of the tests, the character of the testing industry, and the nature of its work, are today being made by state testing directors.

They can, for example, deploy a number of relatively simple solutions to the problems of score inflation, curricular compression and teaching to the test, including not revealing the contents of tests beforehand; not using the same test twice; adding items on the test that sample broadly from the whole domain of the curriculum tested; requiring that non-tested subjects also get taught (or testing them, too); and maintaining strict precautions against cheating during test administrations. . . .

The critics unfairly compare high-stakes standardized testing to their own notion of perfection. Administration of high-stakes tests will never be perfect. There will always be some teachers and pupils who cheat. There will always be some students who are better prepared to take a test than others, and so on.

Perfection, however, is not a reasonable standard of comparison for standardized testing. Too often, the alternative is a system of social promotion with many levels of (nominally) the same subject matter being taught, ranging from classes for self-motivated kids to those for youngsters who quit trying years before, and whom the system has ignored ever since. Too often, the result is a system that graduates functional illiterates.

If *none* of the curriculum is tested, we cannot know if any of it has been learned. Without standardized tests, no one outside the classroom can reliably gauge student progress. No district or state superintendent. No governor. No taxpayer. No parent. No student. Each has to accept whatever the teacher says and, without standardized tests, no teacher has any point of comparison, either.

While it is unfair to test what has not been taught, no such claim can be made about testing what has been taught. And if what is tested is the curriculum, then attacks on "teaching to the test" seem silly, since teachers are teaching what they should be teaching.

Eliminating *high-stakes* standardized testing would necessarily increase our reliance on teacher grading and testing. Are teacher evaluations free from all the complaints of the anti-testing canon? Not exactly. Individual teachers can also narrow the curriculum to that which they prefer. Grades are susceptible to inflation with ordinary teachers, as students get to know a teacher better and learn his idiosyncrasies. A teacher's grades and test scores are far more likely to be idiosyncratic and non-generalizable than any standardized tests'.

Moreover, teacher-made tests are not necessarily any better supplied with "higher-order thinking" than are standardized tests. Yet many test critics would bar all high-stakes standardized tests and have us rely solely on teacher evaluations of student performance. How reliable are those evaluations? Not very. There are a number of problems with teacher evaluations, according to research on the topic. Teachers tend to consider "nearly everything" when assigning marks, including student class participation, perceived effort, progress over the period of the course, and comportment, according to Gregory Cizek. Actual achievement vis-à-vis the subject matter is just one factor. Indeed, many teachers express a clear preference for non-cognitive outcomes such as "group interaction, effort, and participation" as more important than averaging tests and quiz scores. It's not so much what you know, it's how you act in class. Being enthusiastic and group-oriented gets you into the audience for TV game shows and, apparently, also gets you better grades in school.

... Parents of students who assume that their children's grades represent subject matter mastery might well be surprised.

Conclusion: Two Views of Testing and Learning

There is perhaps no more concise exposition of the general philosophy undergirding opposition to standardized testing among education experts than that revealed in the Public Agenda survey of education school professors, *Different Drummers*. Among the reasons most dislike standardized tests are their preferences for "process over content"; "facilitating learning" rather than teaching; and "partnership and collaboration" over imparting knowledge.

A large majority of education school professors surveyed felt that it was more important that "kids struggle with the process of trying to find the right answers" (86 percent) than that "kids end up knowing the right answers to the questions or problems" (12 percent): "It is the process, not the content, of learning that most engages the passion and energy of teacher educators. If students learn how to learn, the content will naturally follow."

The role of teachers, then, in this education worldview, should be that of "facilitator," not "sage on the stage." When asked which statement was "closer to their own philosophy of the role of teachers," 92 percent of the education professors agreed that "Teachers should see themselves as facilitators of learning who enable their students to learn on their own." Only 7 percent felt that "Teachers should see themselves as conveyors of knowledge who enlighten their students with what they know."

The constructivist criticism of any teaching or testing that fixes the manner of solving a problem and penalizes students for careless or "minor" errors is not shared by the public or even by students. In *Getting By*, Public Agenda reported that 79 percent of teens say "most students would learn more if their schools routinely assured that kids were on time and completed their homework.... [Sixty-one percent said] having their class work checked regularly and being forced to redo it until it was correct would get them to learn a lot more. When interviewed in focus groups, teens often remembered "tough" teachers with fondness: "I had a math teacher [who] was like a drill sergeant. She was nice but she was really strict. Now I don't have her this year, and looking back, I learned so much."

In the real world, testing will continue. Testing experts have much to contribute to efforts to ensure that testing is done well. Unfortunately many of them share an ideological orientation that makes any type of standardized test impossible to swallow. Until these experts reexamine their most fundamental beliefs about teaching and learning, all the hard work of improving standardized tests will have to be done without them.

NO

Peter Sacks

Standardized Testing

Most Americans have taken standardized mental tests from the day they entered kindergarten. Test scores have told the gatekeepers of America's meritocracy—educators, academic institutions, and employers—that one student is bright, the other is not bright, that one is worthy academically, the other less so. Some, with luck, are able to overcome the stigma of poor performance on mental tests. But others will not.

... [W]hile the anti-testing bandwagon has gathered many adherents since the peak of the revolt around 1980, the wagon itself has crashed head-on into an entrenched system, one obsessed with the testing of American minds. With roots in intelligence testing that go back generations, the mental measurement establishment continues to define merit largely in terms of test-taking and potential rather than actual performance. The case against standardized mental testing may be as intellectually and ethically rigorous as any argument made about social policy in the past 20 years, but such testing continues to dominate the education system, carving further inroads into the employment arena as well, having been bolstered in recent years by a conservative backlash advocating advancement by "merit."

How has the standardized-testing paradigm managed to remain entrenched, despite the many criticisms leveled against it? Like a drug addict who knows he should quit, America is hooked. We are a nation of standardized-testing junkies.

The Anti-Testing Movement

Granted, there has been a withering, sustained attack against standardized testing in American education that came on the heels of an explosive growth in such testing during the 1960s. Baby boomers were funneled through the school system and tested to death. After adjusting for inflation, sales of standardized tests to public schools more than doubled between 1960 and 1989, to $100 million a year—even while enrollments were up just 15 percent—according to the U.S. Office of Technology Assessment (OTA). Some estimates of the amount Americans spend on testing—a figure difficult to come by given the fragmented and often private nature of the testing industry—are as high as $500 million annually. Estimates of testing volume are mind-boggling: as many as 127 million tests a year at the K–12 level alone. . . .

The Evidence

A long line of independent academic research bolsters the claims of the anti-testing movement. Much of the research confirms suspicions that such tests thwart rather than help educational reform and that they continue to produce inaccurate—if not biased—assessments of the abilities of many Americans. From this recent work, we know that:

> *Standardized tests generally have questionable ability to predict one's academic success, especially for certain subgroups.*

Take the Graduate Record Exam (GRE), for instance, the multiple-choice test required for admission or financial aid by most of the nation's graduate programs. Graduate departments use the tests in hopes of predicting a candidate's chances of succeeding in their programs. In an April 1995 "meta-analysis" published in the journal *Educational and Psychological Measurement,* Todd Morrison and Melanie Morrison examined two dozen GRE validity studies encompassing more than 5,000 test-takers over the past 30 years. The authors found that GRE scores accounted for just 6 percent of the variation in grades in graduate school. The GRE appears to be "virtually useless from a prediction standpoint," wrote the authors. . . .

What about the validity of the SAT, which is required for admission to a great range of undergraduate colleges and universities? . . . We know that a student's high school record alone is the best predictor of performance in the first year of college. We also know that the SAT, when combined with high school grades, adds only modestly to the predictive power of high school grades alone. . . .

What is more, standardized tests tend especially to penalize women and many minority students. To an even greater extent than other groups, these subgroups, on average, earn better grades in college than their test scores would predict. Researchers consistently find that adding test scores to the admissions equation results in fewer women and minorities being accepted than if their academic records alone are considered.

Researchers have reached similar conclusions about the validity of standardized testing in the public schools. In a 1993 study, Teresa A. Dais of the University of Illinois commented: "Minorities and students with disabilities, in particular, are suffering as a result of traditional assessment practices, which have proven to be inaccurate and inconsistent, yet continue to be used in prediction, decision-making, and inferences about student performance and lifelong success."

But a fundamental point about the relationship of test scores to academic success is often lost in many psychometric validity studies. It's worth remembering that the SAT, for instance, isn't designed to predict one's ability to succeed at four years of college study—or at life beyond college—but merely to predict freshman grades. When researchers have asked the larger question of how test scores correlate to a student's performance beyond the freshman year, or to broader measures of college success, the case for the SAT becomes tenuous indeed.

In a 1985 study, *Success in College,* published by the SAT sponsor, the College Board, Warren W. Willingham writes: "Can a college effectively recruit and enroll students whom it is likely to regard as most successful four years later by evaluating applicants only on the basis of school rank and test scores? If the institution defines success broadly... the answer is no."

When researchers have asked the even more basic question of how well standardized test scores predict one's eventual success in the workplace, the correlations all but disappear. High test scores are pretty good indicators of *participation* in professions such as law, medicine, or university teaching, simply because only high scorers are admitted to a required academic program. But test scores predict little about a person's subsequent real-world capabilities in medicine, law, or teaching. In short, scoring high on standardized tests is a good predictor of one's ability to score high on standardized tests.

Standardized test scores tend to be highly correlated with socioeconomic class.

While standardized tests correlate weakly with success in school and work, they correlate all too well with the income and education of one's parents. Call it the "Volvo Effect." The data are so strong in this regard that one can make a good guess about a child's standardized test scores simply by looking at how many degrees her parents have and at what kind of car they drive. Evidence suggests that this relationship holds even across racial lines.

... In a study of California high school students, parental education alone explained more than 50 percent of the variation in SAT scores, according to a 1991 study by Mark Fetler of the California Community Colleges' chancellor's office. College Board data show that someone taking the SAT can expect to score about 30 test points higher for every $10,000 in his parents' yearly income. And, in 1995, the U.S. Department of Education examined the backgrounds of students who made the SAT cut (a minimum score of 1,100) for highly selective colleges. One-third of these high scorers came from upper income brackets, while just 8 percent were from the lower economic rungs.

Standardized tests can reward superficial learning, drive instruction in undesirable directions, and thwart meaningful educational reform.

Teachers, researchers, and other educators have expressed widespread disenchantment with the results of several decades of standardized testing in the United States. Evidence strongly suggests that standardized testing flies in the face of recent advances in our understanding of how people learn to think and reason. In the research over the past few years, especially at the K–12 level, one repeatedly finds evidence that traditional tests reinforce passive, rote learning of facts and formulas, all quite contrary to the active, critical thinking skills many educators and employers now believe schools should be encouraging. Many suspect that the tests are themselves powerful incentives for compartmentalized and superficial learning....

At the K–12 level especially, teachers testify that standardized tests don't accurately measure their students' abilities and that widespread practices of "teaching to the test" render test scores virtually meaningless. In 1994, *Educational Policy* published a study on teachers' views of standardized tests. Just 3 percent of teachers in one sample agreed that such tests are generally good, "whereas 77 percent felt that tests are bad and not worth the time and money spent on them." According to the study, about eight in 10 teachers believe their colleagues teach to the tests.

Preoccupied with winning the standardized-testing game for the sake of kudos from parents, the press, and state legislators, schools have often neglected reforms that would promote deeper, more active ways of thinking and learning than are typically captured by multiple-choice tests. The OTA concluded in 1992: "It now appears that the use of these tests misled policymakers and the public about the progress of students, and in many places hindered the implementation of genuine school reforms." ...

This widespread tendency of teachers to "teach to the test" might be harmless if the tests were adequate indicators of students' skills, ability, and performance, says educational researcher Bruce C. Bowers. He writes:

> However, the main purpose of standardized testing is to sort large numbers of students in as efficient a manner as possible. This limited goal, quite naturally, gives rise to short-answer, multiple-choice questions. When tests are constructed in this manner, active skills, such as writing, speaking, acting, drawing, constructing, repairing, or any of a number of other skills that can and should be taught in schools are automatically relegated to second-class status.

The Shifting Policy Landscape Since 1980

This rich vein of research into the validity, fairness, and efficacy of standardized testing has unquestionably wrought some changes in the assessment landscape. But anti-testing trends have been counterbalanced by a conservative backlash that promises to reinforce standardized testing's continued domination of the educational system....

The rising popularity of performance-based assessment in schools and colleges has contributed to the anti-testing side of the policy ledger, too. As educators became disenchanted with standardized testing, they've managed to implement different ways to evaluate students and educational progress. These alternatives frequently fall under the rubric of "authentic" assessment, the notion that students ought to be judged on the basis of what they can actually do, not how well they take tests. Performance assessment can mean anything from evaluating portfolios of student work or writing samples to art and science projects.

The OTA reported earlier this decade that almost half the states (21) had launched performance assessment programs. But it would be an overstatement to conclude that states are embracing the new and abandoning traditional tests. Indeed, most states continue to use traditional standardized tests, supplemented by forays into performance assessment....

Entrenched or on the Wane?

What, then, are we to conclude from recent developments? Is standardized testing on the wane? Some observers say so. But it would be naive to underestimate the hold that mental measurement has on the American mind. Recent events running opposite to the anti-testing movement suggest that standardized testing remains entrenched and is ready to dig itself in deeper in coming years.

It's worth noting that the mental measurement culture has withstood similar attacks in the past: Walter Lippman wrote a series of articles in *The New Republic* in the early 1920s, warning that the prevalent use of IQ tests in time "could... lead to an intellectual caste system in which the task of education had given way to the doctrine of predestination and infant damnation."

Some 70 years after Lippman's warning, we got *The Bell Curve*. And tests such as the SAT, the roots of which go back to the very same intelligence tests Lippman condemned, continue to flourish; indeed, they remain the centerpiece, the given, in our "meritocratic" views of who has "merit" and who does not.

This is especially true given the recent assaults on affirmative action in higher education.... Critics of affirmative action argue that people ought to be judged on "merit," not gender or race; to them, the indisputable, "unbiased" criteria for admission are grades and (especially) standardized tests. Abolishing affirmative action means that test scores, regardless of their limits or what educators may think of them, become far more decisive a factor in admissions decisions....

Similarly, under the banner of higher academic standards, recent moves by the NCAA have given new prominence to the already huge role standardized test scores play in determining which athletes get scholarships to attend college. Despite strong opposition from FairTest and other groups, the NCAA recently *raised* the standardized test scores required for athletic eligibility. The NCAA changed its policy contrary to compelling evidence that the real effect of the new rules would be to exclude many minorities from scholarships who nevertheless would have succeeded in college....

Indeed, in the name of "higher academic standards," a conservative backlash in recent years has resulted in several states shelving efforts at alternative forms of assessment in public schools. In California, Governor Pete Wilson vetoed the reauthorization of the California Learning Assessment System, a decision that FairTest called "a tremendous setback to educational progress." Arizona put its alternative learning assessment program on a one-year hold amid controversy over its effectiveness. The Indiana Legislature defeated proposals to replace multiple-choice tests with essays and short-answer questions....

When you add up these shifting, often contradictory trends in policy, the net result doesn't look like a standardized-testing establishment that is withering under the heat of popular revolt. Indeed, in many respects, the standardized testing industry has even greater dominance over American lives than it did at the time of the Nader report in 1980. Indeed, just 26 states in 1980 had mandated testing programs for public schools; in 1990, 46 states did so, according to OTA. . . .

What Are the True Costs of Standardized Testing?

Why, then, has standardized mental testing managed to continue to explode in this fashion? Why does it remain so entrenched in American life, despite what we know about its validity?

For their part, the educational institutions that continue to buy the tests —the costs of which are borne by test-takers or taxpayers—would argue that standardized tests are a cost-effective way to evaluate people. It's obvious; standardized testing is cheap.

But how cheap is it, really? Research findings about the utility of test scores raise profound questions about the social and economic costs of a de facto national policy that has institutionalized the use of standardized tests for college admissions and as the gauge of local and national educational progress. While the tests might be cheap to individual institutions, in many cases these institutions bear neither the direct costs of the tests nor the indirect social costs of testing.

It seems reasonable to question whether the marginal benefits of standardized tests in terms of their predictive validity are worth the hundreds of millions of dollars test-takers and taxpayers spend annually on the exams. . . .

Moreover, a cost-benefit analysis would need to account for the social and economic costs of erroneous decisions about people. What are the true economic costs to a nation of wrong decisions about its people's talents?

These are the sort of questions that public policymakers must address before we can conclude that, indeed, standardized testing is "cheap." But even if one were to conclude that standardized testing is the best policy to maximize social benefits versus costs—an empirical question that hasn't been fully answered—there are deeper causes for the continued entrenchment of standardized mental testing in the United States.

"American Tests"

First, Americans are fascinated with mental measurement to a degree that is rare in other countries. In contrast to what Europeans call "American tests," the examinations for college or university admission in other industrial countries are typically essay tests, in which students demonstrate knowledge of various subjects they've learned in the classroom. These tests are not unlike what American educators are now calling "performance assessment." Compared to other countries, Americans appear to be far more obsessed with IQ, the notion that intelligence—most often defined narrowly as logical-analytical ability—is both inborn and representable as a single numerical score.

Indeed, a stroll through any Barnes & Noble superstore speaks volumes about how our culture views intelligence and testing. For $3.95, one can buy *Self-Scoring IQ Tests* or *Self-Scoring IQ Tests for Children*, both written by an official from Mensa, the so-called "genius" club. Or there is *Puzzles for Pleasure: Test Your Intelligence with 102 Mind-Stretching Exercises in Logic, Mathematics, and Precise Reasoning.* Then, take a look at Barnes & Noble's Study Guides section, with its dozens of titles on preparing for an incredible array of standardized school and employment exams. My personal favorite, *Can You Pass These Tests?* includes practice mental tests for getting jobs as Bible scholars, baseball umpires, and even wine tasters.

Similarly, our culture places an exceedingly high value on the notion of potential to achieve, rather than achievement itself. For most Americans, a "gifted" student is one who scores off the charts on aptitude tests, not one who demonstrates advanced practical knowledge on worthwhile endeavors. "We are one of the few societies that place so much emphasis on intelligence tests," Yale psychologist Robert Sternberg told *Skeptic* magazine. "In most societies there is more emphasis on what people accomplish." . . .

Indeed, the notion that merit and achievement equal high test scores, or that higher "standards" means requiring higher test scores, is repeated constantly in the popular culture. This reinforces the widely accepted legitimacy of standardized tests to rate students, teachers, schools, and colleges.

. . . Test scores have become so politically charged that a few teachers, besides spending huge amounts of time teaching to tests, have resorted to cheating to make their numbers look good. . . .

But perhaps most responsible for the grip that mental testing has on America is that it is a highly effective means of social control, predominantly serving the interests of the nation's elites. Most people would agree that, in a democracy, merit is a good basis for deciding who gets ahead. The rub is how you define merit. We've settled on a system that defines merit in large part as the potential to achieve according to test results. It turns out that the lion's share of the "potential" in our society goes to those with well-to-do, highly educated parents. Aristocracies used to perpetuate themselves on the basis of birth and parentage. But America's elites now perpetuate themselves with gatekeeping rules of their own making, rules legitimated by scientific objectivity.

POSTSCRIPT

Is High-Stakes Standardized Testing Defensible?

In an enterprise as important and as expensive as public education, it is understandable that accountability for results is viewed by the public and by policymakers as a nonnegotiable imperative. But the phrase *for results* leads to obvious questions about what those results should be and how best to assess the attainment of them. In most states the question related to what those results should be has been answered primarily by the adoption of statewide subject area standards that specify the content of what it is that teachers should be teaching and what it is that students should be learning. This standards-based approach to curricular content, instruction, and learning is not without its critics, but for the most part it enjoys public and policymaker support, with controversies being limited to whether or not a given subject matter should be included or excluded as a curriculum standard.

That same level of general agreement, however, does not exist with respect to the question about how best to assess the attainment of the adopted standards. Some, as manifested in the Phelps selection, argue that the simplest —and indeed the most valid and reliable—way of measuring student learning is through standardized, objective testing on the material mandated by the standards. They believe that such testing will provide the evidence necessary to determine issues related to accountability and serve to inform parents, educators, and policymakers alike about student progress, effective practices, and needed improvements. Chester E. Finn, president of the Fordham Foundation, in the introduction to Phelps's selection, asserts that critics of standardized testing, most notably education professors, may thwart the public's desire to have such testing regimens "become more consequential." He states, "The most curious aspect of this debate is the special animus that many testing 'experts' hold for tests. Indeed, I have sometimes thought that the working definition of a testing expert is a 'person with a Ph.D. who has the reputation of knowing something about testing but who has never met any test that he thinks should actually be used for any real purpose.'"

Chief among the critics of high-stakes standardized testing is "The National Center for Fair & Open Testing" (FairTest), which describes itself as "an advocacy organization working to end abuses, misuses, and flaws of standardized testing and ensure that evaluation of students and workers is fair, open, and educationally sound." FairTest in its advocacy role disseminates information regarding alleged abuses of standardized testing and test makers, supports grass-roots movements against standardized testing, and serves as a network for articles and news information about testing. The cover article in the September 2000 issue of *American School Board Journal* is entitled "The Trouble With Standards: Will Our Obsession With Measurement Blight an Otherwise Healthy Reform?" In it author Lawrence Hardy details some of the dilemmas for those who support the standards movement but are bothered by related testing programs.

Two informative and scholarly articles on issues directly related to standardized testing are "Cognition and the Question of Test Item Format," by Michael F. Martinez, *Educational Psychologist* (vol. 34, no. 4, 1999) and "Using Performance Indicators to Hold School Accountable: Implicit Assumptions and Inherent Tensions," by Rodney T. Ogawa and Ed Collum, *Peabody Journal* (in press). In his article Martinez states, "Prudent policy decisions [related to the structure of standardized testing formats] will take into account... some appreciation of key tradeoffs." He continues, "Sometimes the best policy decision will not be a matter of either/or, but of what mixture of item formats [multiple choice or constructed response] will yield the best possible combined effect." Ogawa and Collom caution that accountability systems built upon educational indicators such as those used in California may not deliver what they promise. They state, "On its face, California's Public Schools Accountability Act (PSAA), with its multiple components, seems to provide a relatively straightforward strategy for improving school performance. However the literature... calls into question many of the assumptions on which the PSAA and other educational accountability systems are based. Specifically, existing evidence while limited, suggests that many of the elements and conditions that enable accountability systems to exert market-like pressure on public schools do not, and perhaps, cannot in most instances exist."

ISSUE 11

Should Teacher Pay Be Tied to Measures of Student Learning?

YES: Lewis C. Solmon and Michael Podgursky, from "The Pros and Cons of Performance-Based Compensation," Paper of the Milken Family Foundation (June 27, 2000)

NO: Wellford W. Wilms and Richard R. Chapleau, from "The Illusion of Paying Teachers for Student Performance," *Education Week* (November 3, 1999)

ISSUE SUMMARY

YES: Lewis C. Solmon, senior vice president of the Milken Family Foundation, and Michael Podgursky, a professor of economics at the University of Missouri–Columbia, state that new compensation methods are not only feasible but necessary in order to attract the best and the brightest into the teaching profession, keep the most effective of these in teaching, and motivate all teachers.

NO: Wellford W. Wilms, professor of education at the University of California–Los Angeles, and Richard R. Chapleau, 1995 winner of the California Milken Teacher of the Year Award, posit that shifting the focus of education from the student to the pocketbook erodes teachers' professional judgment and demeans the process of education.

Performance-based compensation for teachers, or "merit pay" as it is more commonly known, is not a new concept but it is obviously receiving considerable attention in this era of standards-based accountability and high-stakes standardized testing. Additionally, merit pay fits nicely with other compensation-oriented, "market-driven" education initiatives, such as vouchers and school choice.

This linkage of merit pay with the standards and accountability movement is explicitly spelled out in a 1997 report submitted to California State Superintendent of Public Education Delaine Eastin by the Rewards and Interventions Advisory Committee, authorized by state school accountability legislation. In a section of the report entitled "A New Vision for Holding Schools Accountable," the committee made the following statement:

> Part of the confusion about the mission of schools has been lack of clarity about what is expected—a gap now being filled by . . . a clearly articulated set of statewide, grade-by-grade, world class academic standards. . . . A second missing piece has been a statewide assessment system. . . . The third missing element has been a comprehensive program of incentives.

Later in the same report the Committee recommended that these rewards should take the form of "cash awards to the staff at a school."

Teacher organizations, such as the American Federation of Teachers (AFT) and the National Education Association (NEA), while accepting the notion of "differentiated pay" in terms of compensation for extra duty, advanced training, and years of experience, have consistently opposed the idea of merit pay. Their opposition has generally been grounded in mistrust with regard to how any merit pay program would be administered, concern about the impact of competition among teachers, and skepticism about the fairness of using student testing as a basis for determining teacher quality. In stating this opposition, the late Albert Shanker, longtime AFT president, stated, "But if you don't get the incentives right, you are likely to make things worse instead of better."

Proponents of merit pay assert that teacher organizations oppose performance-based compensation because it runs counter to the union philosophy of collectivity and equal treatment of union members. Anti-unionist Myron Lieberman, in an article entitled, "Do Teacher Unions Have a Positive Influence on the Educational System? No," *Insight* (October 1996), states, "The teachers' unions have made sure that teachers' salaries are not based on merit or the type of subjects taught."

As noted above, this issue is being addressed not just in educational journals but in legislative chambers as well. Indeed, in states such as California, political agendas and legislative action related to educational standards and accountability have bypassed the discussion stage, and merit pay—or performance-based compensation (a phrase preferred by advocates)—already exists in terms of cash bonuses recently awarded to schools and individual teachers on the basis of student performance on statewide examinations.

Lewis C. Solmon and
Michael Podgursky

 **YES**

The Pros and Cons of Performance-Based Compensation

Introduction

The Milken Family Foundation has proposed a bold new, systemic school improvement strategy. Its goal is to improve the quality of the teaching profession because excellent teachers enhance student learning. This program, known as the Teacher Advancement Program, or TAP, has five components, one of which is performance-based compensation. Salaries depend upon teacher achievements, teacher performance, tasks undertaken, and student achievement. Thus, it is important to understand the pros and cons of performance-based compensation.

The purpose of this paper is to compile and analyze the current and historical criticisms of performance-based compensation in K–12 education. We believe that new compensation methods are not only feasible, but necessary, in order to attract the best and the brightest into the teaching profession, keep the most effective of these in teaching, and motivate all teachers. However, this is not the prevailing view held by the education establishment. Indeed, the passion and emotion of most educators is so strongly negative on this topic that even the most market-oriented of policy analysts have dropped the term "merit pay" from their vocabulary. Thus, that will be the only time you see the term in this paper.

According to a 1998 Gallup Poll, more teachers (40 percent) now favor performance-based compensation than in previous years—31 percent in 1989 and 32 percent in 1984. (Langdon, 1998) The reasons teachers gave for opposing performance-based compensation were:

- it is difficult to evaluate teacher performance;
- teacher morale problems could result; and
- performance-based compensation programs would present political problems in the schools.

The poll notes that the recent trend in the implementation of teacher pay is to link overall school performance to specific reform goals, instead of rewarding individual teachers for the quality of their teaching.

"Differentiated pay" for teachers can have a number of different meanings, some more controversial than others. First, teachers may receive higher salaries for performing additional functions such as mentoring other teachers, designing curricula, providing in-service programs, and so on. This type of salary differentiation has occurred for quite a while and is relatively uncontroversial. Perhaps the greatest dissatisfaction with "functionally differentiated pay" occurs when some teachers are asked to do more than others, and the salary increase does not adequately compensate them for the time required to perform these added tasks.

Next, teacher salaries may differ based upon their own achievements (passing a certain test, obtaining an advanced degree, or receiving National Board Certification). There may be logic in this type of differential pay if it can be demonstrated that the achievements that qualify a teacher for extra pay are related to improving job performance. Many of the "achievements" recognized with higher pay may be quite shallow. In most districts, passing a course or earning a degree can result in a salary increase. . . .

The above methods of paying teachers differentially are based on process, or judgments of teachers' accomplishments or current practices. However, teachers do things for a purpose: to help students learn. The newest form of differentiated pay says, in essence, we do not care how teachers do it, but if their students learn more, they should be paid more. . . .

If the *basis* of differentiated pay is agreed upon, the next step is to determine the process. The first issue is whether differentiation should be by individual teachers or by groups of teachers. . . . Both group and individual pay may be justified, but our sense is that individual rewards must be included as part of an effective performance-based pay plan. . . .

The Pros and Cons of Performance-Based Compensation

We now consider the concerns over "performance-based compensation" that have been raised over the years and attempt to respond to each of them. For years, schools have discussed the issue of compensating teachers for their accomplishments, their performance, and the achievements of their students. Historically, "performance-based compensation" for teachers has been dismissed, in particular by the unions, for myriad reasons. **We have classified the arguments against such pay systems into general categories and responded to each argument. . . .**

1. Performance-based compensation programs encourage competition rather than collaboration among teachers.

. . . In the Teacher Advancement Program (TAP) designed by the Milken Family Foundation, collaboration among teachers is critical. Learning guides work with associate teachers, who work with mentor and master teachers. By design, the TAP model encourages collegiality and interaction among teachers. We need models of professional development that stimulate and encourage collaboration. Our view is that performance-based compensation models can be implemented in systems that encourage collaboration. Collaboration may be one aspect of performance that gets rewarded.

2. The Union Environment and the Collaborative Nature of Teaching

... Since collaboration is important in schools, some fraction of performance-based pay should be tied to group or school-wide performance. On the other hand, a good deal of effort is not collaborative and, as will be argued below, can be measured or assessed. Thus, it does not seem plausible to argue that individual merit should play no role in teacher compensation.

Moreover, just because effort is collaborative, it does not follow that all pay should be distributed across-the-board. In fact, some members of the group may be better "team players" than others, and advance the goals of the team more than others. Compensation of professional athletes provides a good example. Many professional athletes, including highly paid stars, are members of teams, yet this does not mean that pay raises are distributed across the board.... The key issue is not whether production is collaborative or not, but whether individual contributions to the team effort are observable. In general, individual contributions to team effort are readily observable in sports competition.

The absence of performance-based compensation, and the presence of tenure, is one reason why many "school-wide" collaborative education reforms fail. Teachers in a particular school have little incentive to join a school reform team or advance the goals of the team by changing their teaching practice or collaborating in the implementation of reforms. New forms of work or teaching require additional effort on the part of teachers. Yet the conventional salary schedule provides no incentive for teachers to collaborate or exert the required effort.

3. There is no clear definition of what constitutes a "good teacher." In other words, what is merit based upon?

... If we take this notion to its logical conclusion, then we should hire teachers randomly. After all, if we have no clear idea of who is a good teacher, who's to say that applicant A is better than applicant B? This would also apply to tenure decisions as well as promotions to mentor and master teacher. Yet no one seriously believes that these hiring and promotion decisions should be random. Moreover, most would accept the fact that it is possible to make informed decisions in these areas. Why is compensation any different?

Merit or performance-based pay is also commonplace in industries and organizations in which it would seem to be much more difficult to measure or assess individual performance than in public schools.

In fact, private businesses do pay employees based upon merit or performance. Although the assessment mechanisms and the meaning of high performance may be complex, there is much less difficulty in having workers accept being so judged. People enter other careers knowing they are going to be judged. Sometimes the results will seem fair, at other times, less so. But that is just the way it is and it is accepted.

There are a variety of quantitative indicators of performance that might be linked to individual teachers. This would include various student test scores and student attendance data. Since nearly all teachers have contact with the parent consumers, it is also possible to gauge consumer satisfaction with a particular teacher. Private school administrators are acutely aware of how parents assess the performance of individual teachers. Indeed, whether they solicit such information or not, public school administrators are also well aware of which of their teachers are favored, and which are disfavored, by parents. Moreover, it is relatively simple and low cost for an administrator to directly monitor the performance of teachers by sitting in on their classes, reviewing their lesson plans, etc. . . .

4. If student learning is the sole basis of the merit evaluation, relying on test scores can present major problems.

. . . The education community must seriously study assessment and the ability to measure meaningful change in student performance. We agree that student test scores may be too narrow an indicator of how to evaluate a teacher. Further, we agree that as has been seen in California and New York, there are some reliability issues in standardized tests that need to be addressed. However, we also believe that academic standards can and should be set from which we can judge a teacher's performance. Most states have student standards. There is no reason why teacher standards cannot be developed as well. We need measurable characteristics of excellent teachers.

We are not saying that student performance of achievement should be the only measure of teacher excellence. Indeed, we believe that teacher compensation should depend on teacher functions (tasks done and how well), teacher achievements (e.g. awards, relevant degrees), and teacher performance (as judged by experts), as well as on student achievement. Moreover, we do not define student achievement by test scores alone. Schools and teachers should identify multiple measures of student achievement if they wish (e.g. portfolio assessments and attendance). However, TAP does require that student achievement, however measured, be one aspect of teacher assessment.

. . . It is important to get benchmark data on student achievement at the beginning of the academic year. Student progress against these benchmarks should be continually evaluated. At the end of the year, similar data should be collected and compared to these initial benchmarks. To the extent that student test scores are used in the teacher assessment, they should be gains relative to the beginning of the year assessments. These gain scores are one measure of a teacher's "value-added."

It might be objected that there is a good deal of measurement error in individual test scores, hence they are a poor measure of teacher performance. While gain scores for any individual student may be a "noisy" statistical measure, the average of all a given teacher's students will be far less so (statisticians call this "the law of large numbers"). For example, suppose that the margin of error on an individual student's gain score is plus or minus ten percent. If a teacher has thirty students, then the margin of error of the gain score for the class will be just 1.8 percent.

Just as the "law of large numbers" tells us that changes in the mean of a class are measured with less error than changes in the scores of individual students, it also suggests that it is good to use multiple, independent, indicators of a teacher's performance. For example, suppose that test score gains correctly identify superior teachers 80 percent of the time. Suppose that classroom assessments by supervisors correctly identify superior teachers 75 percent of the time, and parent surveys identify superior teaching 70 percent of the time. Then a teacher assessment based on all three indicators would correctly identify a superior teacher over 98 percent of the time. In other words, multiple "noisy" indicators of teacher quality can add up to very accurate overall assessments.

5. When you reward teachers for student achievement, nobody wants to teach certain kids in certain communities.

. . . Focusing on gains rather than levels of academic achievement should take us a long way in alleviating this concern. However, it may be that gains, say, from the 20th to the 40th percentile are in fact harder to achieve than those from the 60th to 80th percentile. As schools become smarter organizations and begin to use classroom gain scores more effectively, it will soon become apparent where it is easier or harder to achieve gains. Also, state education agencies should assist in developing such information as well. This data would allow schools to establish reasonable "norms" for gain scores based on the starting point of the class. . . .

6. Bias and Favoritism

. . . In a good performance-based pay plan, there needs to be some level of control of the quality or standard of the "qualified" and objective adjudicators of educators, candidates for performance-based compensation. If not, it could easily become a political issue of influence and not of merit. In order to address this argument, we propose that a master teacher and the principal are both involved in the evaluation. We must make sure that master teachers who are still in the bargaining unit are allowed to evaluate other teachers. The perception of bias might also be alleviated with the inclusion of an external evaluator whenever a teacher is going from one rank to the next. The criteria for evaluation would be made clear and the process must be uniform.

. . . [T]eacher evaluations should be based on multiple, independent evaluations of teacher performance. Here is where "independent" becomes important. One dimension of independence should be independence from the opinions of a principal or supervisor. Thus, while a classroom evaluation based on observation by a principal or supervisor is potentially affected by subjective bias, other measures such as test score gains, student attendance or parental surveys are not. That is why it is important to have multiple, independent indicators.

Of course, "what's good for the goose is good for the gander." It is very important that principals and supervisors be held accountable for student performance as well. If principals are held accountable for student achievement gains in their building (e.g., through performance-based compensation and the threat of dismissal), they will have a strong incentive to make evaluations objectively. . . .

To the extent that these reforms take hold on a wide scale, good teachers who are underpaid can leave their current schools and go to schools in which their talents will be rewarded. Performance-based compensation will stimulate a market for superior teachers. Under the current system of seniority and credential-based pay, teachers who have accumulated seniority tend to be locked into districts. If pay is determined by performance-based promotions and annual evaluations, there will develop a lateral market for mentor, master and novice teachers. When teachers are able to document a track record of raising student achievement, their services will be valued in the market. Ultimately, one of the best protections against bias is the teacher's ability to "exit" a school with bad management. The best way to do this is to create a competitive market for high quality educators.

7. Performance-based compensation will take from teachers the ability to teach as they wish and as they do best. It just requires teachers to jump through hoops. It will make everyone teach and behave in the same way.

. . . Very few professionals can work "as they wish." All face some sanctions or constraints. Surgeons who become highly creative and stray too far from professional norms face the possibility of malpractice lawsuits and revocation of their licenses. A less severe, but very potent sanction is loss of business. A trial lawyer who enjoys quoting Latin to juries may lose more cases and find himself short of clients. Ultimately, teachers, along with all public employees, are accountable to the taxpayers and cannot work "as they wish."

Merit or performance-based pay does make teachers "jump though hoops," as does any evaluation. The columns of current salary schedules, which reward education credentials (BA+15, MA, MA+15, etc.) also make teachers jump through hoops. The point is to select hoops that are more closely tied to student achievement gains.

Performance-based compensation will not make everyone teach and behave in the same way. An assessment that focuses on student achievement, for example, does not require any particular style of teaching. Teachers may, in fact, gain more freedom to innovate than is the case in many public school districts currently, since the focus would be on outcomes and not process.

8. Performance-based compensation programs reward the top 15–20 percent of performers without making any effort to improve all teachers.

First, if there is a program it must be open to all, not limited to ten percent or some artificial percentage to limit cost. It should not be apportioned throughout the faculty, one for languages, one in social studies, etc. A single department might have all excellent, deserving teachers. It should not depend upon some artificial minimum number of years of experience; there are some great teachers with three years of experience, some take six, etc. to develop their skills. It should not be just a reward for hanging around....

Performance-based compensation need not be limited to a fixed percentage of the workforce.... [S]upervisors may choose to designate a portion of funds available for pay increases as a merit pool. For example, if four percent of payroll is available for raises, then two percent might be distributed across-the-board and two percent held aside for merit. All teachers would receive a merit or performance assessment and this would guide allocation of merit.... Such a merit scheme gives incentives for all teachers to improve.

9. The costs of implementing a performance-based compensation system are very large.

... One of the reasons voters are reluctant to put more money into education is because they have not seen student achievement improve. They see teachers demanding more money as a right. If they saw new money going only to highly productive teachers, they are more likely to be willing to provide more money.

Under current salary schedules, school districts incur major costs from one year to the next simply because teachers are one year older. A very large share of payroll is taken off the table each year simply to reward seniority. Similarly, school districts spend billions of dollars each year to reward the accumulation of academic course credits which may bear little relationship to current performance. For example, many teachers accumulate graduate credits in education administration but never become principals. They are, nonetheless, rewarded with pay increases on salary schedules even though these classes have little benefit for their current teaching assignments.

In order to make funds available for performance-based compensation, school districts could eliminate or "flatten" salary schedules. A merit pool would be created without any increase in total payroll costs....

10. Teachers should want to teach to serve kids, not for money. We want teachers who love teaching, and who are not in it for the money.

... Not many would dispute this. But the real question is who is *not* in the profession because of low pay?...

Loving one's work and making money at it are not mutually exclusive. Many people thoroughly enjoy being lawyers, businesspeople, or Webmasters, yet still make large salaries. Presumably, most doctors like medicine and most airline pilots enjoy flying. Nonetheless, most doctors and pilots would not choose to practice their profession, and certainly not in the numbers required for satisfying consumer demand, in the absence of pay. Also, research has shown that extrinsic rewards (money) do not undermine intrinsic rewards (satisfaction) as a motivator.

Serving mankind and high pay are also not mutually exclusive. Many physicians do great work in preventing and curing illnesses but still earn handsome salaries. Indeed, the opportunity to earn profits is a major incentive for drug companies to push ahead to find new "miracle drugs." Might it be that the opportunity to earn high salaries might provide a similar incentive for teachers to do a better job and for others to enter the field?

We keep talking about giving teachers more status. Like it or not, in our society, there is a correlation—one might debate how strong a one—between earnings and status. When at least some teachers can afford the same homes, automobiles, colleges for their kids, and vacations as doctors and lawyers can, it is likely that teachers will be accorded the same status as members of these other professions receive....

11. Performance-based compensation forces teachers to work harder to get more pay—but the extra pay is not sufficient for the extra work required.

... Some teachers will exert more effort in order to earn performance-based compensation; others will not. Those who work harder have judged the monetary reward worth the effort. However, some educators may simply be gifted teachers and achieve higher gains for their students without any extra effort whatsoever. It is important to reward such individuals as we do gifted practitioners in other occupations. Under the single salary schedule, aside from seniority, the only way a gifted teacher can raise her pay is to accumulate academic credits. In other words, she needs to exert extra effort to earn an MA simply to demonstrate that she is a superior teacher. Of course, teachers who are not gifted teachers can readily earn MA's as well. Therein lies the problem....

True performance-based compensation simply rewards superior teachers for doing a good job....

12. If the names of those who receive performance-based compensation are posted, parents might be upset if they disagree with the choices. Or they may be upset if their kids get teachers who did not receive performance-based compensation.

Parental satisfaction should be only one factor in merit judgments. This would make the former event unlikely. The latter case might present problems. In part, such problems would be ameliorated if merit were distributed in a more continuous fashion, as noted in section number eight above. In this case, no single group would be identified as getting performance-based compensation. . . .

Of course, evidence might become available as to which teachers earned the highest merit scores. However, this would put pressure on school administrators to hire and retain the best teachers. In the long run, both taxpayers and students benefit from empowering parents with this type of information, even if school administrators are inconvenienced as a result. Are we better off if information concerning superior doctors, dentists, and lawyers is suppressed, even if all of us cannot avail ourselves of their services? Should we suppress information about inferior doctors, dentists, and lawyers?

In the TAP model, all students are exposed to master and mentor teachers for some part of their school day. Thus, all kids benefit from having excellent teachers.

13. Risks of comparing the private, corporate, for-profit sector with education.

. . . Performance-based compensation is commonplace in other government and non-profit institutions, as well as in public and private higher education. However, it is worth noting that the private, for-profit sector of education is growing rapidly. Millions of parents are sending their children to for-profit tutoring firms. . . . School districts in many large cities have contracted with [private firms to] provide Title I services to disadvantaged students. Many for-profit firms . . . provide post-secondary vocational training to businesses and individuals. . . . The burgeoning growth of this for-profit educational sector calls into question assertions that business practices in the private sector are incompatible with the provision of education services.

14. Performance-based compensation cannot be imposed from the outside.

. . . The details of how a performance-based plan will work as well as what share of pay will be based on group versus individual performance will need to be worked out by local school administrators. In all likelihood it will vary from school to school. It is appropriate, however, that pressure for accountability be imposed from the outside.

This does not mean that a performance-based pay scheme must bubble up from the ranks of teachers. These systems will have to be implemented by school administrators. It would probably be productive to have discussions with teachers during the planning and implementation stages of a performance-based pay plan (of course, such discussions are required in states with teacher collective bargaining laws). However, ultimately this is a matter of management rights. School administrators must have the authority to implement pay schemes which they see as representing the best interests of taxpayers, whether or not such schemes are popular with current teachers. Ultimately, some teachers may find performance-based compensation distasteful and leave teaching. They will be replaced by other teachers who find performance-based compensation less distasteful, or actually prefer working in an environment where effort and performance are recognized and rewarded.

15. People are too critical of education—it is actually doing fine, so why rock the boat by changing things?

… Actually, international tests of mathematics find American children generally below-average as compared to children in other industrial nations. In addition, the test scores of urban black and Hispanic students are very low as compared to those of other socioeconomic groups. Dropout rates are also much higher. The income gap separating workers with low and high levels of educational attainment is at post–WWII highs. Careful statistical research finds rising labor market returns in relation to increased basic cognitive skills. Students who drop out of school or graduate with weak academic skills are likely to face a low and declining standard of living.

Conclusion

There are a number of serious objections to performance-based compensation for teachers. Many teachers are quite articulate in their arguments against such a system. However, it is the view of the authors that virtually all of the objections can be dealt with. In some cases, assumptions underlying the dislike of performance-based compensation must be challenged—other objections require some changes in the way schools operate.

Although the most vocal opponents are quick to point out failed efforts of the past, there are examples of long-standing cases where teachers are paid according to their tasks, efforts, achievements and performance. We are now beginning to see a few school districts where teacher pay depends, in part, upon what their students learn. We need to continue the experimenting. That will take courage on the part of teachers, administrators, school boards and parents. But the challenge seems worth the risk if the end product is greater student learning.

References

"Teaching as a Profession," Education Week on the Web, Dec. 1, 1999.

"Re: Merit pay… here's my prediction," Administrators Chatboard, Administrators.net, 1999 (www.administrators.net/chatboard/topic799/10.18. 99.09.45.02.html).

Archer, Jeff, "Sanders 101," Education Week on the Web, May 5, 1999.

Carvin, Andy, "Professionalization and Merit Pay," Education Week on the Web, (www.edweb.cnidr.org/edref.prof.html).

Cornett, Lynn M., "Lessons from 10 Years of Teacher Improvement Reforms," Educational Leadership 54, no. 5 (1995): 4-9 (www.enc.org/reform/journals/enc2402/nf2402.htm).

Denver Classroom Teachers Association, "Merit Pay Plan for Teachers Needs More Study, Research," The Denver Post, June 7, 1999.

Elam, Stanley, "The Second Gallup/Phi Delta Kappa Poll of Teachers' Attitudes Toward the Public Schools," 1989 (www.pdkintl.org/edres/tpol189a.htm).

Ellis, Thomas I., "Merit Pay for Teachers," ERIC Clearinghouse on Educational Management: ERIC Digest, Number Ten (www.ed.gov/databases/ERIC_Digests/ed259453.html).

Gallup, Alec, "The Gallup Poll of Teachers' Attitudes Toward the Public Schools," 1984 (www.pdkintl.org/edres/tpoll84a.htm).

Guinta, Andrea, "Pay for Performance Plan Ignores Kids' Outside Influences," The Denver Post, June 27, 1999.

Houtz, Jolayne, "Reformers Should Put Teachers to the Test," The Seattle Times, Oct. 29, 1997.

Langdon, Carol, "The Fifth Phi Delta Kappa Poll of Teachers' Attitudes Toward the Public Schools," 1998 (www.pdkintl.org/kappan/klan9904.htm).

Milken, Lowell, "A Matter of Quality: A Strategy for Assuring the High Caliber of America's Teachers," Milken Family Foundation, 1999.

National Education Association 1999–2000 Resolutions (www.nea.org/resolutions/99/99--2.html).

Shanker, Albert, "Where We Stand: Beyond Merit Pay," American Federation of Teachers, 1995 (www.aft.org/stand/previous/1995/011595.html).

Van Moorlehem, Tracy, "District seeks to link pay to performance," Detroit Free Press, Sept. 3, 1999.

*Wilms, Wellford, W. and Chapleau, Richard R., "The Illusion of Paying Teachers For Student Performance," Education Week on the Web, Nov. 3, 1999, (www.edweek.org/ew/ewstory.cfm?slup\(=\)10wilms.h19).

Note

*Richard Chapleau is a 1995 Milken Educator.

**Wellford W. Wilms and
Richard R. Chapleau**

The Illusion of Paying Teachers for Student Performance

Frustrated by 25 years of failed school reforms, a growing number of districts are adopting "pay for performance" plans. These plans offer cash payments to teachers and administrators for boosting their students' scores on standardized tests. Yet history shows that any pay-for-performance gains are mostly illusions. Not only do they fail to improve student achievement, they are also destructive, encouraging administrators and teachers to cheat by manipulating statistics, or by teaching to the test. Inevitably, children wind up the losers because curricula are narrowed to include subjects that can be taught by drill and repetition and that are easily measured.

For all of the flaws in the idea, a bigger issue is at stake: our inability to resist these "political fixes" that divert efforts to address the root causes of education's failures at the schoolhouse level.

Pay-for-performance was first tried in England around 1710. Teachers' salaries were based on their children's scores on examinations in reading, writing, and arithmetic. This early payment-for-results system had great appeal because it promised to help keep children from poor families in school, where they might learn the basics. It became fixed in the English system of education in 1862 as part of the Revised Education Code, where it remained for more than 30 years.

As historical accounts show, English teachers and administrators became obsessed with the system's financial rewards and punishments. It was dubbed the "cult of the [cash] register." Schools' curricula were narrowed to include just the easily measured basics. Drawing, science, singing, and even school gardening simply disappeared. Teaching became increasingly mechanical, as teachers found that drill and rote repetition produced the "best" results. One schools inspector wrote an account of children reading flawlessly for him while holding their books upside down.

Payment-for-results in the English system degraded teaching as a calling, because teachers now had to pay close attention to the Education Code. It clearly spelled out standards for their students' success or failure (and their own). Grants were given to the schools, and teachers had to haggle with individual school managers for their share. One teacher of the time elaborated: "I do not deny that many teachers do overwork the youngsters in a terrible way, but the poor souls really act under the pressure of the law of self-preservation. They must either meet the requirements of their superiors or become professionally extinct."

The effect was to erode teachers' creativity. An inspector wrote that the Education Code "did all the thinking for the teacher; it told him in precise detail what he was to do each year." Another recalled, "Every teacher in the country takes his orders from the Code, studies the Code, and devotes his energies to satisfy or to circumvent it." The results were not always benign. Some teachers falsified records by including names of good students who had died or who had moved from the district. They poured energy into fooling inspectors by flashing signals to students who were being examined, telling them when to add, subtract, multiply, or divide.

When payment-for-results was finally dropped in the 1890s, the overwhelming judgment was that it was unsound policy. Cynics referred to schools as "grant factories" and children as "grant-earning units." The English experiment with payment-for-results had created almost irresistible incentives that in the end demeaned teachers and sacrificed children's education for financial gain.

Payment-by-results appeared briefly in Canada in 1876, causing conservatives to rejoice because it made teachers and students work harder to avoid failure. The Canadian experience showed that test scores could be increased quickly, so long as the subject matter could be narrowed and measured. But, as in England, the system caused teachers to focus their energies on students who were most likely to succeed, helping them cram for examinations while ignoring the others. In 1883, a public outcry ended the experiment abruptly.

Almost a century later, in 1969, the idea emerged in this country as "performance contracting," not long after big-city schools began to desegregate. Making American schools accountable became a top priority for the efficiency-minded Nixon administration. President Richard M. Nixon, like English politicians a century earlier, expressed concern over the lack of educational achievement among the growing population of urban poor. He stated:

> "The outcome of schooling—what children learn—is profoundly different for different groups of children.... School administrators and school teachers alike are responsible for their performance, and it is in their interest as well as in the interests of their pupils that they be held accountable.... [T]he avoidance of accountability is the single most serious threat to a continued, and even more pluralistic educational system."

So began a huge experiment with performance contracting designed to overhaul the public schools. But, unlike the 19th-century English experiment, American educators now had the advantage of using standardized tests to measure outcomes. School funding could be scientifically tied to students' test scores. The original experiment, housed in the U.S. Department of Health, Education, and Welfare's offices of education and housing and urban development, aimed to increase reading and math scores for 300 high school and junior high school students in the public schools of Texarkana, Ark. The district was under great pressure from HEW to desegregate, and local officials were desperate to close the performance gap between black and white students.

The Arkansas district offered the federal government a money-back guarantee—funds would be returned for students who failed to pass at a specified level. And students would get free transistor radios, green stamps, and free rock music. The experiment provided incentives for everyone—administrators, teachers, and students. The New York Times' education writer, Fred Hechinger, called it as "American as apple pie." Other journalists observed that performance contracting touched the American consciousness with its "you get what you pay for" philosophy, and the belief that "private industry know-how can solve any problem."

A preliminary evaluation indicated astonishing results. Students averaged gains of more than two grade levels in reading and one in math after only 48 hours of instruction. Buoyed by those preliminary results, supporters of the idea hailed the Texarkana experiment as a success, and new performance contracts were announced.

But scandal quickly clouded the growing enthusiasm, with accusations that one of the key contractors was caught teaching to the test. The contractor was fired, but the idea moved forward in 18 cities, where private contractors taught reading and mathematics using a variety of incentive schemes.

The now-expanded initiative ran into trouble. Contractors were disorganized and, despite the public rhetoric, few companies were willing to actually commit themselves to a money-back guarantee. Also, despite hopes that contractors would bring innovative teaching practices to the classroom, most used conventional methods augmented by teaching machines and incentives for students. Finally, education experts warned federal officials against using standardized-test scores as the ultimate benchmark for student achievement because they were unreliable. Scandal and the lack of results ultimately doomed performance contracting, and it was declared a failure. Like the earlier English and Canadian experiments, performance contracting once again showed how financial incentives failed to produce expected gains, while at the same time generating damaging educational effects.

Today, districts around the country—Denver; the District of Columbia; Fairfax County, Va.; Hartford, Conn.; Minneapolis; and Montgomery County, Md., to name just a few—are rushing to embrace the idea. While none has suggested such harsh financial consequences as the earlier experiments, much can be learned from those past efforts to help focus the education reform debate in more productive directions.

Tying changes in student test scores to teachers' or administrators' pay presents powerful incentives for educators to first consider "what's best for me?" instead of "what's best for the child?" Shifting the focus of education from the student to the pocketbook erodes teachers' professional judgment and demeans the process of education.

The record is rife with examples of how payment-for-results schemes have led to dishonest behavior—falsifying records and teaching to the test. No doubt, safeguards would have to be established to catch cheaters, but this would only further diminish teachers' crucial role. There is little doubt that one of the villains is standardized testing. While testing is only a means to making payment-for-results work, it has far-reaching effects. Standardized tests, created by people who have nothing to do with local schools, eclipse educational judgments made by teachers and parents. Just as the English Educational Code served to narrow the curriculum and drain creativity from teaching a century ago, standardized tests have much the same effect today.

Few reforms that are forced on the schools (especially destructive ones like payment-for-results) will ever penetrate the classroom and positively change the teaching and learning processes. Teachers are every bit as adept at deflecting or sabotaging reforms of this kind today as they were at deceiving English school inspectors in the 1800s. Politically driven reforms like pay-for-performance are nothing more than reflections of public frustration. And rather than helping to solve the root causes of failure, they paralyze us and deflect public attention from reforming educational systems at their core.

Policy leaders must redefine their roles, from legislating reforms to supporting changes that emanate from the schoolhouse, if changes are to endure. Politicians, board members, superintendents, and union leaders must clear the way of obstacles to make innovation in the schoolhouse possible, and provide necessary resources. But only teachers, parents, and students working together at the schoolhouse level can improve the systems by which teachers teach and students learn.

POSTSCRIPT

Should Teacher Pay Be Tied to Measures of Student Learning?

One of the forces contributing to interest in the concept of merit pay for teachers is America's heritage of marketplace competition. Paying teachers on the basis of their students' performance seems to many to be entirely consistent with approaches to compensation in the business and corporate world. Additionally, we are all aware of how salaries and earnings of professional athletes and entertainers are directly tied to their performance. Consistent with that theme, it seems simple enough to use student performance on a standardized test from the previous year as a baseline and then use test results at the end of the year to show student growth in learning. Using a valid and reliable test, why can't we measure learner growth both individually and collectively? Many say that the simple answer to that question is that we can; the problem is what do we do with the results?

Critics of merit pay for teachers based on student test performance are quick to argue test results for students are woefully inadequate measures of teacher performance. Here are but a few of the questions that teachers might pose about using pre- and posttest scores of students as the basis for merit pay: What if the five students in my class who have improved the most transfer out and do not take the posttest? What if 20 of the 30 students in my class show expected growth but 10 decline so appreciably that the class collectively shows no growth—or even a decline? What if my three top students are all victims of text anxiety, or do not feel well the day of the test, or decide to sabotage the test results? What if my students' test scores one year bring me a merit reward, and the following year the scores drop off—am I no longer a meritorious teacher?

Psychometrists will explain that some of the problems implicit in such questions and concerns can be dealt with through statistical treatments. Other proponents of merit pay will say that all such complexities notwithstanding, the whole point of teaching is to get students to learn, and success or failure in doing that must form the basis of how teachers are compensated.

Other positions on this issue can be found in articles such as Dennis L. Evans, "No Merit in Merit Pay," *American School Board Journal* (January 2001) and Albert Shanker, "Beyond Merit Pay," *Where We Stand—AFT* (January 15, 1995). See also several articles in *Education Week*, including Carolyn Kelley, "A New Teacher-Pay System Could Better Support Reform" (February 21, 1996); Clifford B. Janey, "Incentive Pay" (November 6, 1996); and Adam Urbanski, "Merit Pay Won't Work in Schools" (January 15, 1997).

ISSUE 12

Is the School Principal Indispensable?

YES: Ann Weaver Hart and Paul V. Bredeson, from *The Principalship: A Theory of Professional Learning and Practice* (McGraw-Hill, 1996)

NO: Donal Sacken, from "No More Principals!" *Phi Delta Kappan* (May 1994)

ISSUE SUMMARY

YES: Ann Weaver Hart, provost and vice president for academic affairs at Claremont Graduate School, and Paul V. Bredeson, professor of educational administration at the University of Wisconsin–Madison, assert that principals' instructional leadership forges the efforts of others into successes for students.

NO: Donal Sacken, professor of education at Texas Christian University, states that school principals distort the operations of schools because of their managerial ethic.

Conventional wisdom and many research studies suggest that the leadership efficacy of the school principal is a crucial variable in the success of a school. The role of the school principal evolved from simpler days when a "principal teacher" in a small grammar school would assume, in addition to his or her teaching responsibilities, some necessary managerial/ministerial functions. As schools grew larger, and especially with the development and proliferation of secondary schools with their greater complexities, the perceived need for full-time specialization in school administration also grew. Special training and licensure of school principals accompanied this trend. Today the full-time principalship is an almost universal feature of K–12 schools. A striking example of this evolution can be seen in the membership figures of the National Association of Secondary School Principals (NASSP). This professional advocacy organization was created in 1916 and had 78 members. The membership now numbers over 40,000 secondary school administrators, and obviously not all secondary school administrators belong to the group.

By any organizational standard the contemporary role of the secondary school principal is a daunting one. The principal is expected to serve both managerial and leadership functions, the dynamics of which are often times in conflict. As criticism of public education has grown more strident over the past three decades, with concomitant demands for higher standards and greater accountability, so has the "lightning rod" role of the school principal. The clamor for higher standards and greater accountability for improvement exemplifies the type of dilemma that principals often face. In this instance, while higher standards and greater accountability might suggest the need for more direct and decisive leadership on the part of principal, he or she still must deal with demands for greater empowerment of the public and more shared leadership with teachers. There is growing evidence that these types of dilemmas and their accompanying pressures are conspiring to decrease the number of qualified individuals who aspire to the role of principal.

In the following selections, Ann Weaver Hart and Paul V. Bredeson articulate the viewpoint that the school principal must play a pivotal role in determining the effectiveness of a given school, while Donal Sacken's position is that the very nature of the principalship mitigates against the educational mission of the school.

**Ann Weaver Hart and
Paul V. Bredeson**

 **YES**

Principals' Influence on Student and School Outcomes

"In schools where achievement was high... invariably the principal
made the difference."

— (Boyer, 1985)

... What do principals do as designers, teachers, and stewards to bring about desired results for students and for school improvement? Do principals in highly
successful schools carry out their leadership roles differently than do principals
in less successful schools?

Our focus... is on what principals do to make a difference in student
achievement in their schools; however, we eschew the idea that specified leadership behaviors cause predictable learning outcomes. Our understanding of the
relationship between principal leadership and desired student and school outcomes acknowledges the complexity of social and symbolic interactions within
dynamic educational settings. Further, principals often exercise instructional
leadership in unstable environments characterized by contextual uniqueness,
uncertainty, and ambiguity. Despite the complexities of instructional leadership and student learning, we also reject arguments from some critics who
say that such conditions render principals powerless to influence teaching and
learning outcomes in their schools....

Principal Influence on Student Learning:
Some Guiding Assumptions

Our discussion of principals' influence on school and student outcomes is
based on a set of guiding assumptions. These assumptions are the products
of professional experience, theoretical propositions, empirical findings, and
reflection.

1. In their roles as leaders and through their daily work activities, effective
    principals positively affect student, classroom, and school outcomes.

2. Principal instructional leadership, student outcomes, and school effects are complex, multidimensional, interactive phenomena that are not easily separable into discrete variables for conceptualization, observation, measurement, analysis, interpretation, and leadership preparation.

3. The influence of principals on student and school outcomes is significant; however, these outcomes are the products of multiple sources of influence and the efforts of many individuals over time, not solely those of principals.

4. The concept of principal effects on student and school outcomes as reported in much of the literature implies causality, although it is examined from distinct philosophical and methodological traditions.

5. Practitioners and scholars generally agree that principals' leadership influences such mediating factors as school governance, school climate, and instructional organization. There is also general agreement that these factors in turn affect student and school outcomes, despite inconclusive empirical findings and some methodological weakness.

6. Any representational rendering of principals' influence on student and school outcomes through narrative description, theoretical modeling, or causal mathematical equations is partial and therefore may underestimate principals' influence on student learning.

7. Any single managerial activity or principal leadership behavior has the potential to ripple across the school, amplifying its effect on teaching and learning processes, and affecting student and organizational outcomes.

8. The instructional leadership behavior of principals affects student outcomes in school and beyond school.

Implicit in this list of assumptions is the belief that principals' instructional leadership behaviors interact with school and student outcomes in highly complex ways. To deal with the complexity of relationships among principals' leadership behaviors and their impact on teaching and learning outcomes, we have developed a two-dimensional framework. The framework serves as an organizer for our discussion of the ways in which effective principals positively influence student outcomes in their schools. The two dimensions are: (1) sources of influence, and (2) type of impact. Although we discuss each dimension separately, we recognize the interaction and interdependence of factors within each....

A Two-Dimensional Perspective of Principals' Instructional Leadership Behaviors and School-Student Outcomes

The linkage between effective administrative leadership and successful school-student outcomes has long been the *raison d'etre* of educational administration preparation programs. School principals occupy a unique leadership role in which they can exercise enormous influence on teaching and learning structures, processes, and outcomes. The literature in educational administration and in organizational theory is rich with accounts of leadership effectiveness (Lipham, 1981; Bossert, 1988; Pitner, 1988).... More recently, some of the most convincing findings have come from outside the field of educational administration. "Much of the best research, for example, did not set out to look at principals at all, but at some particular program or innovation. Researchers discovered along the way that it was the principal who made the difference" (Lipham, 1981, p. vii). These findings, coupled with research findings in school administration and organizational theory, have helped to renew the focus on the importance of the principal's instructional leadership role in schools.

Research on effective schools, in particular, spawned various theories and descriptive typologies about within-school factors correlated with student achievement. As various theories of school effectiveness were formulated, the leadership of the school principal consistently appeared as a critical within-school factor. Educational reform reports, *A Nation at Risk* (1983), *Time for Results* (1986), *Investing in Our Children* (1985), *Teachers for the 21st Century* (1986), *Principals for 21st Century Schools* (1990) added fuel to the fires of inquiry focused on an examination of the relationships among student achievement, school effectiveness, and the leadership behaviors of building principals. Recognizing that many factors contribute to effective schools and successful student outcomes, a general consensus regarding the importance of the school principal's leadership has emerged.

> If a school is a vibrant, innovative, child-centered place; if it has a reputation for excellence in teaching; if students are performing to the best of their ability, one can almost always point to the principal's leadership as the key to success. (U.S. Senate, 1979)

The descriptive model of principals' instructional leadership influence on teaching and learning outcomes... has two primary dimensions. The first is sources of instructional leadership influence. We describe three important sources of leadership influence—principals' behaviors, principals' beliefs, and principals' use of symbols. The second dimension is type of impact. We describe direct and indirect sources of principals' influence on student learning....

Behaviors: What Instructional Leaders Do

As empirical evidence accumulated on the importance of principals' contributions to school improvement and student learning, researchers began to examine the characteristics of principals and their schools with special interest in the differences in within-school factors in high-student-achievement schools and low-student-achievement schools....

A framework for instructional management (Bossert et al., 1982) A group of researchers from the Far West Laboratory for Educational Research sought to better understand the role of the principal as an instructional manager. These researchers conducted a review of the literature and research on the linkages between school-level factors and student learning. They concluded, "The literature on effective leadership has specified a broad range of behaviors that contribute to effective instructional management" (p. 36). Their review indicated that manipulable variables such as time-on task, class size and composition, instructional grouping, curriculum, and evaluation affect student learning. They acknowledged, however, that given the sheer volume of administrative responsibilities, principals are limited in the amount and quality of time they can spend directly assisting and guiding teaching and learning processes with individual teachers.

Bossert and others suggested an alternative approach. They argued that principals could significantly influence two school-level factors—school climate and instructional organization—through routine administrative behaviors. These routine tasks included goal setting and planning, monitoring of student progress, evaluating of instruction and its outcomes, communicating, scheduling, allocating resources for instruction, organizing and coordinating programs and resources, staffing, modeling, governing, and filling in when necessary. The two school-level factors in turn would shape individual classroom instruction and affect student learning.

This approach indicates that principals can directly influence student learning by engaging in systematic instructional leadership behaviors. However, their primary influence on student learning is indirect, that is, mediated through school climate and instructional organization. For example, to build a positive teaching and learning climate, a principal might work with teachers and other staff to create high expectations for students, establish effective discipline policies and procedures, and build supportive work relationships among teachers. In the area of instructional organization, principals need to understand the connections among desired learning objectives, the curriculum, class groupings, scheduling, the use of time, the allocation of resources, and teacher work. . . .

The framework also suggests that routine managerial behaviors of principals are the products of the influence of antecedent factors (community characteristics, principals' beliefs and experiences, and institutional contexts) and are interactive with school climate, instructional organization, and student outcomes. Principals' management behaviors shape classroom and school instructional organization and climate. These same behaviors are in turn affected by climate, school and classroom instructional organization, and various student outcomes. In our discussion of the dimension of type of impact, direct and indirect, we elaborate on the transformation of seemingly mundane managerial activities into effective instructional leadership strategies.

Instructional management behaviors   Based on a review of school effectiveness research, Murphy and Hallinger (1988) set out to develop a research-based definition of the principal's role in instructional management. They constructed the *Principal Instructional Management Rating Scale* and used it to gather data from teachers, principals, and district central office personnel on the instructional management behaviors of 10 elementary school principals in a district serving 8,000 students. From the data collected, they identified eleven spe-

cific behaviors clustered in three dimensions of instructional management behaviors—Defines the Mission, Manages Instructional Program, and Promotes
School Climate.

Defining the Mission includes two major instructional leadership activities. "The principal's role in defining the mission involves framing school-wide
goals and communicating these goals in a persistent fashion to the entire school
community" (p. 221). Bringing clarity and purpose to teaching and learning activities in the school is an important leadership task. Through vision, planning,
and passion, principals help others in the school community coalesce around a
core set of beliefs, values, and hopes for children.

The second dimension, *Manages Instructional Program,* involves the principal's working with teachers in areas specifically related to curriculum and
instruction. In this role, principals supervise and evaluate to see how school
goals are translated into successful classroom practices. This includes formal
and informal supervision and evaluation, classroom visits, curriculum planning, coordination of programs, and working with teachers and other staff to
monitor student learning. . . .

Promoting a Positive School Learning Climate is the third category of instructional management behaviors discussed by Murphy and Hallinger. Principals
protect instructional time by being buffers against intrusions from internal
and external forces that threaten teachers' instructional time with students.
Principals also promote positive learning climates by their physical presence
and visibility throughout the school—in classrooms, at student activities, and
at curriculum meetings. Promoting professional growth and learning among
the staff, providing incentives for teachers and students to develop and grow
continually, and enforcing academic standards are instructional management
behaviors that promote student learning.

A vision of instructional leadership (Duke, 1987)   In his book, *School Leadership and Instructional Improvement,* Daniel L. Duke (1987) asks the reader to
compare the effects of principal leadership on student outcomes to the effects
of physicians' practice on their patients' health.

> Physicians generally are not evaluated in terms of patient performance, ex-
> cept in cases involving gross malpractice. They are held accountable for
> "good medical practice." Is there an equivalent to "good medical practice,"
> to which school leaders may be held accountable? (p. 26)

He then goes on to describe "good instructional leadership practices." Duke believes these are the professional behaviors for which instructional leaders need
to be held accountable. Unfortunately, even the best professionals operate in
real situations of practice, which at times are anything but routine or ideal.
Thus, principals' authority and discretion in instructional leadership practices
need to be viewed within the context of environmental constraints. These include school structures and staffs that are already in place, collective bargaining agreements, state mandates, local district policies and legal guidelines, and
general systems of rewards and sanctions. . . .

We concur with Duke that no one set of behaviors characterizes what all successful instructional leaders do. Situational uniqueness and indeterminacy within the context of professional practice render any prescriptive list of effective instructional leadership behaviors problematic.... However, "Research suggests that instructional leaders must see to it that certain predictable functions or situations are handled appropriately" (p. 81). Duke identifies five areas of work activity for instructional leaders that affect student learning and school outcomes: (1) teacher supervision and development; (2) teacher evaluation; (3) instructional management and support; (4) resource management; and (5) quality control. Coordination and troubleshooting are two leadership processes that cut across the five areas. Duke's integrated vision of instructional leadership provides a framework for thinking about and enacting what principals do in the area of instruction....

A model of validated instructional leadership behaviors In an effort to build upon past research findings and to move to the next level of theory building related to instructional leadership, Heck, Larsen, and Marcoulides (1990) developed a predictive model of principal instructional leadership variables that influence student achievement....

The results of the analysis of Heck and others support assertions that principals exert instructional leadership that affects student performance. Their data indicated that principals in high- and low-achieving schools focused on the same leadership behaviors. However, principals differed in the extent to which they engaged in key instructional leadership behaviors, and in the sources of influence they used to bring about desired student-school outcomes. Principals in high-achieving schools were more engaged in specific instructional leadership behaviors that positively affected school governance, school instructional climate, and instructional organization than were principals in low-achieving schools....

Student and school outcomes are significantly affected by what principals do in their daily work and the priorities they give to particular instructional leadership activities....

We want to make one final point in our discussion of principals' behaviors as a source of influence on student and school outcomes. Principals' instructional leadership behaviors do make a difference in teaching and learning environments and ultimately on student outcomes; however, principals' behaviors alone will not produce high-achieving students. Student successes are the products of the commitment, energy, and efforts of teachers, parents, support staff, and the students themselves. Principals' instructional leadership forges the efforts of others into successes for students....

What Instructional Leaders Believe

Another powerful source of influence that principals use to affect student and school outcomes positively is what they believe about teaching and learning, about the connections between their instructional leader behaviors and teachers' work with students, and about the effect of their leadership behavior on student learning outcomes. Beliefs are expressions of values. They form the basis of educational visions, plans, and professional behavior. The instructional leadership behaviors of principals . . . are expressions of these basic beliefs.

It should not be surprising that principals' beliefs are connected to their instructional behaviors. After all, principals bring their personal values, unique experiences, and beliefs to their leadership roles in schools. Principals' values and beliefs help them shape their role as leaders and their interaction with aspects of the school's culture affects those same values and beliefs. Salancik and Pfeffer (1978) and cognitive psychologists argue that individuals align their beliefs with their actions to minimize any cognitive dissonance between them.

The effective schools literature includes explicit and implicit statements of belief related to leadership and school improvement. Statements of belief include the following:

- All students can learn.
- The work of teachers and principals makes a difference in the lives of children.
- Learning is the most important reason for being in school.
- A clear and commonly accepted mission is important to student and school success.
- High expectations in academic quality must be upheld by everyone in the school.
- Learning time should be maximized; thus student-teacher time needs to be protected from disruption.
- Instructional programs improve over time, based on systematic monitoring and assessment of program and student outcomes.
- Student outcomes are the products of the efforts of many individuals over time—parents, teachers, staff, community members, and others.
- Safe and orderly school environments are necessary for successful teaching and learning. (Synthesis Update 1990, Effective Schooling Research Bibliography)

Principals who hold these beliefs are likely to behave in particular ways. For example, decisions and actions in curriculum and instructional organization; allocation of resources; priorities in daily work routines; attention to school culture; and relationships among teachers, students, parents, and other community members are grounded in these principles of professional practice.

. . . Building on effective schools literature, Heck, Larsen, and Marcoulides (1990) tested causal relationships among latent variables (school governance, school climate, and instructional organization) and student achievement. Their findings provide strong empirical evidence of the influence of principals' beliefs on student and school outcomes. . . .

The beliefs that separated the principals of ineffective schools from those of effective schools included their beliefs about their ability to influence teachers' work in classrooms through governance, school climate, and instructional organization. For example, principals in highly successful schools involved their staffs more in critical instructional decisions, they involved parents more in school programs, and they protected teachers and learners from undue pressures and distractions. These findings provide an empirical linkage to effective schools findings that describe the connections between the work of principals carried out in governance, instructional organization, and school climate, and principals' beliefs and school-student outcomes. Perhaps the most powerful belief that principals can hold is that their routine managerial activities can be transformative in the area of instructional improvement and student outcomes. These beliefs and behaviors do not require heroic acts of leadership, nor do they demand access to unlimited resources. Rather, as Dwyer and others (1983) concluded,

> [P]rincipals are forceful leaders because they successfully carry out common acts of the principalship, not because they accomplish heroic feats. They require no new program, no innovation, no extensive change. The success of these activities for instructional management hinges, instead, on the principal's capacity to connect them to the instructional system. (p. 54)

Principals are symbolic and cultural leaders in schools; their beliefs are also expressed in personal statements of vision, in their communications with key internal and external constituent groups, in public ceremonies and rituals, and in their daily work to create and nurture positive teaching and learning environments.... Tapping the potential of others, personal vision, security in self, and faith in professional decisions are grounded in beliefs, sustained and improved by practice....

What principals believe influences the beliefs and behaviors of others, and thus influences the culture. Firestone and Wilson (1985) reported that principals influence the quality of instruction and student outcomes by working through bureaucratic and cultural linkages that govern teacher behavior and work routines. They concluded that principals, through hundreds of interactions and activities, influence cultures that focus on the primacy of teaching and learning. Principals exert instructional influence in schools by managing the flow of stories and information, by creating and manipulating symbols and rituals, by serving as cultural communicators, and by expending high levels of energy and putting in long hours.

> The principal's task and challenge is to develop a clear vision of the purposes of the school that gives primacy to instruction and to carry it through consistently during those countless interactions. By doing so, the principal uses bureaucratic linkages to create opportunities for teachers to follow that vision and minimizes chances to operate in different ways. At the same time, the principal uses cultural linkages to communicate that vision so that, to a greater or lesser extent, it becomes the teachers' own culture. The initiative for carrying out instructional work then rests with teachers, but they are much more likely to incorporate the principal's perspective. (Firestone & Wilson, 1985, p. 22)

Effective principals do not keep these beliefs to themselves but work to make their vision for learning a shared vision among teachers and students. Effective principals build school cultures that affirm the primacy of high-quality instruction and student learning and that are supported by norms of collegiality (Little, 1982), high expectations and performance standards, and a belief in professional growth, self-renewal, and continuous improvement.

... Principals' beliefs and behaviors are powerful signals to teachers and students. Next we discuss principal influence on instruction through symbols.

Sources of Influence: Symbols

Symbols provide a third source of instructional leadership influence. Who principals are, what they do and say, and how they choose to communicate and shape school culture are powerful symbolic tools for influencing teaching and learning in schools.

The power of symbols reflects the power of convictions. Robert Owens (1987) describes a symbolic leader as one who "[s]tands for something that is important and that gives meaning and purpose to the seemingly mundane and routine work of others in the school" (p. 155). By employing a repertoire of such symbols as high visibility throughout the school, school mottos, public recognition and rewards, and ceremonies and rituals, principals can affect the attitudes and behaviors of co-workers by helping them understand what is valued and rewarded in the organization. These symbolic acts give meaning to the work of individuals and provide cohesiveness to efforts to accomplish shared goals. "Effective leaders may focus on technical change, but their activities are often highly symbolic, as they build the school's culture around their vision for the school" (Peterson, 1989, p. 5)....

Who principals are and what they stand for provides a model for others in the school. Principals can demonstrate for others the difference, for example, between immediate concerns such as meeting with an angry parent or getting a copy machine repaired, and important long-range issues (instructional focus and goals). They can show how teaching and learning have primacy in school planning, decision making, resource allocation, and daily work. As Edgar Schein (1985) reminds us in his text on leadership and culture, if you want to know what's valued and what's most important in your school, watch what the principal does....

Principals influence instruction and its outcomes by what they do, what they believe, and how they use symbols....

Type of Impact: Direct and Indirect

Principals make a difference in student achievement and school outcomes. This assertion is supported by theory, empiricism, and experience. Less clear to researchers and practitioners of educational administration is exactly how or precisely in what ways principals affect student learning. Our review of the literature affirmed that the behaviors, beliefs, and symbolic leadership of principals have both direct and indirect impact on student learning....

What do we mean when we use the terms, *direct impact* and *indirect impact?* Kleine-Kracht's (1993) definition of direct and indirect instructional leadership is among the most concise and useful. She defines direct instructional leadership as hands-on, face-to-face activities such as the "immediate interactions of principals with teachers and others about the classroom, teaching, student performance, and curricula" (p. 188). In contrast, indirect instructional leadership is invisible to others because either they are unaware of what constitutes instructional leadership or they fail to see the connections between various activities and teaching and learning.

> Indirect instructional leadership activities are behaviors that deal with the school's internal and external environment, the physical and cultural context surrounding the classroom, teaching, and curricula, and the meanings that principals' actions have for teachers. (p. 189)

Principals' Direct Impact on Student Outcomes: Empirical Evidence

... Principals ... are ... not full-time teachers and coaches. Their ability to interact with over 1,000 students on any given day is limited. Even though, "[d]irect activity is potentially more effective than indirect activity because it takes into account individual differences among teachers and students" (Murphy & Hallinger, 1988, p. 221), direct influence ... is likely to be a less efficient use of principals' efforts than more indirect methods because of the narrowness of scope and actual number of individual students that a principal can work with on any given day. Thus, principals engage in instructional leadership and supervisory activities that are more likely to have broad and lasting effects in the teaching-learning environment in the school. These include such activities as being visible in classrooms and at school events, providing feedback to students and teachers, working on curriculum with teachers, planning schoolwide events, coordinating teaching-learning activities, troubleshooting and facilitating instructional delivery, participating on multidisciplinary teams to develop individual educational plans for students, working with teachers to use student test data to improve their curriculum and instruction, and helping to select instructional materials....

In conclusion, principals have direct and indirect influence on student learning outcomes in their schools. The issue is one of balance and congruence. The realities of a principal's daily managerial responsibilities limit opportunities for direct influence. Thus, indirect sources of influence promise to complement direct instructional leadership activities. When direct and indirect instructional leadership behaviors are congruent with shared beliefs about student learning and with norms of high expectations for individual learning emphasizing continuous improvement, they combine to create a powerful instructional leadership strategy.

No More Principals!

[L]ast spring, from the National Policy Board for Educational Administration (NPBEA) I received *Principals for Our Changing Schools: Knowledge and Skill Base,* a truly overwhelming vision of the modern principalship. In its hundreds of pages, one finds 21 domains of essential knowledge and skills that stretch from the vagaries of leadership and philosophical and cultural values to interpersonal sensitivity and nonverbal expression—really a soup-to-nuts compendium.

I had two strong reactions. First, if every principal is expected to fit the profile suggested by this book, we need to admit that the principal's job is impossible for all but a few exceptional individuals. Granted, these myriad, sometimes paradoxical images and expectations (authoritatively democratic, visionary but collegial) represent a wish list, but they have also become a rhetorical measuring stick. For years principals have guiltily confessed that ad-ministrivia consumes their working lives and denies them opportunities for instructional supervision or leadership. This has been an almost universal re-frain among principals, yet over and over they have been criticized or exhorted to reconstitute their work lives and do the "right thing." I always assumed that, if they believed they could do that, they long ago would have. Thus, I decided, their inability to shift must mean that *most* principals are deficient, inadequate, and guilty of misplacing their priorities.

However, when the large majority of a work force does not meet basic job definitions, perhaps we should begin to question the definitions, not the workers. Moreover, as James March observed, the best an organization or sector of organizations should hope for in its managers is routine competence. Yet these standards perpetuate a vision, if you will excuse the term, of principals who are omniscient, omnipotent, responsible for all that happens, accountable to all, water-walkers of the highest order! Indeed, these standards codify the all-too-familiar pyramidal structure of modern organizations wherein those at the top possess the most authority, knowledge, influence, discretion, valor, and wisdom. . . . Just lifting the book of standards is evidence supporting those who argue that principals need a doctorate before assuming office—no less lengthy a period of study could possibly cover all these domains.

My second strong reaction to this remarkable document is that a proper solution to the impossibility of recruiting, training, and retaining enough paragons of so many virtues is to abandon the search—our chances of success rival those of Ponce de León.... I believe we should reverse course, abandon the administrative ethos at the site level, and look to another educational institution for the structure our public schools need.

The Costs of Administrative Hegemony

Among the thousand flowers of reform blooming around the country are various experiments with administrator-less schools. For instance, there are teacher-run schools and schools-within-schools where no one assumes the separate professional role of running the show—no certified administrator stands in charge. The results of such efforts are undoubtedly uneven, in part because none of us are used to nonhierarchical organizations. We instinctively look for someone to step in and make the final decision, resolve our differences, and order more toilet paper. Moreover, we justify avoiding certain dilemmas—sometimes in defiance of authority—by protesting that someone else is responsible for them. But what if the kinks in the "system" were, in fact, merely our own fault?

Of course, the most common version of defusing power or "flattening" schools has been site-based decision making. Although reports of ongoing efforts reveal the emergence of many "building czars," various districts are sincerely trying to engage in collective decision making. One conclusion from those who track these efforts is that the adults in schools must first learn to work together, share responsibility, disagree publicly, and deprivatize the core processes of teaching. In other words, they must learn to act like adults in an adult organization.

Moreover, these efforts are not infrequently compromised by administrators' reluctance to allow actual decisions to slip out of their grasp—hence principals' preference for advisory councils. And even when formal authority is dispersed, the fact that one member of the group has the power to reward and punish the others, to hire and fire, certainly gives lie to the egalitarian myth of all members deliberating as equal stakeholders....

What these stories demonstrate is the pervasive sense of vulnerability among teachers and their largely unquestioned acquiescence to the legitimacy of managerial authority....

[T]he NPBEA standards ... embody the image of a powerful, active leader, shaping, directing, and controlling decisions and behavior in every domain of school operation. These are the principals lionized by the effective schools movement and subsequently labeled "charismatic," "transformative," and "visionary." The standards hope to generalize from a small and skewed sample of unusual principals a uniform image of the principal-as-colossus. It reminds me that when the second wave of reform after *A Nation at Risk* seized on teacher empowerment and professionalization as the panacea for a few years, Ted Elsberg, then president of the American Association of School Administrators, wrote impassioned editorials warning that too much transfer of power from principals would injure the schools' efficiency and, of course, hurt "the kids." There was a certain desperation in these pleas to acknowledge the centrality of the powerful principal in effective and efficient schools.

I believe that our cultural biases are inclined toward managerial authority, toward salvational images of leaders, and toward surrendering responsibility for most of the tedious, ambiguous, and often unpleasant tasks in organizational life. Furthermore, I believe that, among teachers, acceptance of the familiar arrangement of substantial classroom autonomy in exchange for subjugation at the building level is overwhelming and deep-structured. Given these conditions, as long as the building has a patriarchal or matriarchal figure, any progress toward collective duties and authority will eventually dissipate....

Another Cost of Administration Ambition

... A result of professionalizing educational administration has been to draw principals away from the technical core of schooling: teaching and learning. Instead of focusing on those central elements, the administrative curriculum has become essentially an ever-expanding catalog of organizational and managerial courses. Despite a knowledge surge in the fields of pedagogy, learning theory, cognitive science, and allied research on teaching domains, educational administration curricula have, if anything, become even more oriented to the technologies of generic managerial practice....

Simplifying the Terrain

Because I believe that professional/career administrators distort the operations of the schools they head, skewing dialogue and decisions with their managerial ethic, I suggest a different approach to staffing a school—one appropriated from the universities. *No educator who works at a school should be permanently removed from teaching children in a classroom.* Administrative tasks should be assumed for a predetermined period; after serving in an administrative capacity, the educator can return to the classroom or leave for a permanently adult-oriented life in the central office. Administrative work should be handled similarly to jury duty: it should be regarded as a service to the school, and everyone who resides at the school for an extended period should be expected to serve. Critical policy decisions should be made either collectively or by a council of teachers chosen by their peers to serve for a fixed term. In no case should someone work at a school for more than three to five years without returning to full-time teaching. This model corresponds to the departmental governance system at most universities.

I can anticipate a host of objections. The "lost expertise" objection appears most obvious. If the principal's job is so complex that one virtually needs a doctorate and expertise in 21 domains of knowledge and skill to qualify for it, how can we throw neophytes into the breach? Are we not courting disaster? Perhaps, but I do not believe that the principal's job is so complex. Moreover, whether there will be more frequent disasters than now occur is not certain.

... In many experimental schools today, lead teachers exist in place of principals and teach each day. In a school close to my university, two lead teachers share the load of administrivia, conflict resolution, and coordination, but both teach for a portion of each day. That school has also enhanced a traditional source of informal administrative activity by replacing the school secretary with an administrative assistant who can, for instance, carry out budgetary processes. . . .

Taking Arms Against a Sea of Troubles

I can understand why people might view my proposal as foolish. As noted previously, we are accustomed to hierarchical organizations with somebody in charge, and some political theorists today speak of our nation as having too much democracy already. Another lesson from restructuring has been that flattening the system and dispersing authority slows down decision making. Certainly, principals would interpret my rhetoric as just another polemic against them, battered as they already are. There are wonderful principals and wonderful people performing as principals; they are no less committed or devoted than teachers or other professional groups. I see the problem as a professionalization effect: they are simply expending their careers in the wrong job in the wrong place.

Teachers, by and large, quickly lose confidence in the ability of most administrators, including principals, to fully comprehend the realities of teaching. The principal then becomes a member of a second group within the building, the nonteachers. Principals experience strong socialization pressures and identify more and more with other administrators, especially as many teachers communicate a clear sense of their otherness. As principals settle into their second career in education, as nonteachers, they increasingly use the administrative jargon, assimilate the administrative gestalt, and polish their administrative identity. After all, they are not returning to teaching.

That this is so at the school level drives a wedge among the people who work there, one that I believe is dysfunctional. It encourage teachers to accept a passive role, to hide their disagreements, to engage in creative disobedience, and to refuse responsibility for such matters as peer accountability. The school, as an adult workplace, becomes isolating, passive, and disingenuous. The structure of authority contributes mightily to these phenomena.

However, even if that assessment is incorrect, on a more basic level educators should not flee, be relieved of, or be rewarded out of teaching—not if they continue to work in a school. It is the wrong message to send, and it confuses the listeners. The mantra of educators is "We do it for the kids." To hear it from teachers—who, after all, spend their lives "among schoolchildren" —is tolerable, even inspiring, but to hear it from those whose lives are taken up with meetings, messages, organizational politics, coordinating, controlling, and other such adult activities is intolerable. People who want to contribute to the well-being and future of children simply must work with them. At the least, they should not be paid more *not* to work with them.

I basically agree with the teachers' argument that, to know teaching and to know students, you must teach. To designate as an evaluator of teaching someone who once taught but has now chosen to avoid it is offensive. Teaching is both complex and contextual enough that nonteachers wandering around with evaluative instruments collecting generic effective behaviors can help no one but the absolute neophyte or the classroom failure. To be an educator, one should be continuously involved in educating students; all others can go by the term *educationist,* implying someone interested in the processes of education.

POSTSCRIPT

Is the School Principal Indispensable?

Notwithstanding the fact that the role of the principal is commonly accepted as a fundamental "given" in nearly all approaches to school organization and governance, there are certain leadership trends and restructuring schemes that have brought new conceptualizations of the role. Recent legislative enactments that have increased empowerment of parents and community members through devices such as school site councils with school-level budgetary and personnel powers may be seen as a diminution of the traditional authority of the principal. Other legislative mandates, such as collective bargaining, have created limitations and restrictions on management prerogatives in the name of employee rights and teacher empowerment. And of course, in most school systems the principalship is viewed as "middle management," which by definition means that the principal's power is subject to oversight and overrule.

Combined with the decreases in power wrought by legislative and organizational means, there are also several theories of organization and leadership that may be seen as mitigating against the influence and importance of the school principal. Concepts such as decentralization and shared decision making, referred to facetiously by organizational theorist Ray Brown as part of the "hide the boss movement," tend to reduce the hierarchical authority of the principal. Conceptualizations such as transformational leadership, the "school as community," and generally negative postmodern critical perspectives regarding leadership all seem to conspire to diminish the principalship.

But other theorists will argue that the very notion that the leader is somehow diminished when organizational power is shared is wrong because it is built on the erroneous perception that power is "finite." These theorists suggest that power is infinite and tends to expand when shared. They suggest that perhaps old, traditional, hierarchical ways of looking at the principalship should indeed be discarded but that there is still a crucial need for leadership—only in a reconstituted, more democratic mode.

Articles and books on the principalship abound. Popular educational periodicals such as the *NASSP Bulletin, Educational Leadership,* and *Phi Delta Kappan* carry articles regarding the principalship on a regular basis. Books that describe different approaches to leadership and thus different constructs for the principalship include Gordon Donaldson, *Learning to Lead* (Greenwood Press, 1991); Roland Barth, *Improving Schools From Within* (Jossey-Bass, 1991); Lynn Beck, *Recapturing Educational Administration as a Caring Profession* (Teachers College Press, 1994); Thomas Sergiovanni, *Leadership for the Schoolhouse* (Jossey-Bass, 1996); and Paula Short and John Greer, *Leadership in Empowered Schools* (Prentice Hall, 1997).

Phi Delta Kappan

One of the most widely circulated educational journals, each monthly issue of *Phi Delta Kappan* contains articles related to contemporary educational practices.

http://pdkintl.org

Association for Supervision and Curriculum Development

The Association for Supervision and Curriculum Development publishes the popular monthly journal *Educational Leadership*, which is similar to *Phi Delta Kappan* in terms of content regarding educational practices.

http://www.ascd.org

National Service-Learning Clearinghouse

The National Service-Learning Clearinghouse (NSLC) is funded by the Department of Service-Learning, Corporation for National Service. This Web site contains an information database and a collection of publications on service learning.

http://www.servicelearning.org

National Federation of State High School Associations

The National Federation of State High School Associations is the national service and administrative organization of high school athletics and fine arts programs in speech, debate, and music. This site contains sections on current events and news, participation surveys, and a discussion forum.

http://www.nfhs.org/citizens.htm

Practices

*E*ducational practices at the school site and at all classroom levels generally flow from purposes and policies as discussed in Parts 1 and 2. Thus, they too can be controversial. It is important to note that school and classroom practices, with rare exceptions, have been developed and implemented by educational practitioners for the best of motives. Each practice that will be discussed in Part 3, even though it represents a controversial issue, nevertheless can trace its origins to attempts by educators to better serve their students. That some practices may prove to be counterproductive in terms of helping students should in no way be construed as a negative reflection on the integrity or motives of educational practitioners.

- Is Block Scheduling Better Than Traditional Scheduling?

- Is Homework Beneficial to Students?

- Does the Practice of Grading Students Serve Useful Purposes?

- Can Technology Transform Education?

- Should Service Learning Be a High School Graduation Requirement?

- Is the Emphasis on Globalization in the Study of World History Appropriate?

- Should Classical Works Be the Emphasis of the High School Literature Curriculum?

- Should We Be Cheering for High School Sports Programs?

ISSUE 13

Is Block Scheduling Better Than Traditional Scheduling?

YES: Joseph M. Carroll, from "Block Scheduling," *The School Administrator Magazine* (March 1994)

NO: Reginald D. Wild, from "Science Achievement and Block Schedules," Paper presented at the annual meeting of the National Association for Research in Science Teaching (April 20, 1998)

ISSUE SUMMARY

YES: Joseph M. Carroll, a former school superintendent and a senior associate at Copernican Associates, contends that the traditional ("Carnegie unit") high school schedule is a system under which teachers cannot teach effectively and students cannot learn effectively.

NO: Reginald D. Wild, a professor in the Department of Curriculum Studies at the University of British Columbia, asserts that all-year students outperform semester/block students in science and mathematics.

The current interest in alternative forms of scheduling, such as block scheduling, in secondary schools is actually a renewal of a flurry of similar plans that emerged in the 1970s and 1980s. Configurations such as flexible-modular scheduling, which was based on a computer-generated model out of Stanford University, focused on providing differing amounts of time to different subject matter areas and different instructional strategies. In its idealized sense this type of flexible-modular scheduling was an attempt to have "form" in terms of the configuration of instructional time follow "function," or the requirements of different instructional strategies. A similar plan, endorsed by Lloyd Trump, former executive director of the National Association of Secondary School Principals (NASSP), was called *pontoon scheduling* and involved blocks of time devoted to direct instruction, seminars, and independent study/research. Those types of plans, which were structurally dependent on plugging varied amounts of nonstructured time into individual student schedules, generally were abandoned because of the inability of some students of high school age to "handle" the responsibilities inherent in nonstructured time. School administrators reported that while some students benefited from such schedules many others did not, and the gap between high achievers and low achievers increased.

The most popular of the current approaches to alternative scheduling are various forms of block scheduling and, learning from earlier lessons, they for the most part do not include any unstructured student time. In its simplest form block scheduling merely takes the traditional one-hour (usually less than one hour) per day per course Carnegie-type instructional periods and creates a longer block of time for fewer courses per day. Thus six 60-minute class periods per day might become four blocks of 90 minutes each. In some configurations the four classes might meet for the equivalent of a Carnegie year but obviously in fewer days. In other configurations a high school student might take six courses on a rotating schedule, with four courses meeting each day on the block schedule; total instructional minutes working out over the year would be equivalent to a traditional schedule. Joseph M. Carroll and other proponents of such plans maintain that high school teachers in block scheduling configurations meet with fewer students each day and thus can provide more individualized attention; opponents such as Reginald D. Wild counter with concerns about the spacing of instruction and retention rates.

Joseph M. Carroll

Block Scheduling

The Copernican Plan is not about "block scheduling." It is about the relationship between time and learning. My interest in this relationship began when I was assistant superintendent for research, budget, and legislation for the District of Columbia Public Schools in the mid-1960s. We initiated a remedial summer school for academically troubled students. For six weeks, these students studied math and English for four hours a day, five days a week—a typical summer program.

What was atypical was that we evaluated their progress carefully. Based upon traditional pre- and post-tests, average students' gains equalled the gains achieved in about two years in regular classes. The teachers' reports on the climate in the classroom, attendance, etc., were equally good. We were elated.

Then we asked if we can do this well in 30 four-hour summer classes in unairconditioned public schools, why can't we do better in our traditional 180-day regular programs? We thought of many possible reasons, but my only conclusion was we may know a lot more about teaching than we do about how students learn.

A Quiet Experiment

I followed up on this experience when I became superintendent of the Los Alamos Public Schools in New Mexico in the early 1970s. We offered students regular high school credit courses on a nonremedial basis as part of our summer school program. Each class met for four hours a day, five days a week, for six weeks, about 20 percent fewer total hours to complete a course than was provided under the school's traditional, 180-day schedule.

This disparity never surfaced, but it interested me greatly. The teachers were asked to use the same standards used during the regular year in grading their courses and to let us know whether the students could not meet the district's usual standards in this format.

Again the results were excellent and the teachers reported exceptionally good relations with the students. The "Coke breaks" were enjoyable and instructive. But what to do with this information? We seemed to have an answer looking for a problem!

The "problem" surfaced in the fall of 1982, when I was superintendent of the Masconomet Regional School District in Massachusetts. A tax limitation referendum passed in 1980 resulted in our district losing about one-sixth of its teaching staff. Keeping the program intact was a serious problem.

Necessity breeds invention, and I decided to try to put into practice this "macro scheduling," as I had come to call it. In the fall of 1983, I distributed a long concept paper that I called "The Copernican Plan."

Challenging Tradition

Four hundred years ago, the renaissance scholar Copernicus demonstrated the unsystematic movements of the planets could be systematically explained if one begins with the assumption that the sun, not the earth, is the center of the universe (as was then thought).

Unfortunately, this finding challenged basic, traditional teachings of the church and resulted in what was called the "Copernican Revolution." Indeed, the definition of "revolution" as social upheaval stems from the title of his book, *The Revolution of the Heavenly Orbs*.

Similarly, our Copernican Plan challenged tradition, the traditional organization of our secondary schools and particularly our high schools. Like Copernicus, the plan deals with facts and research that has been known for a long time, but which never seemed to make sense in the real world of schools. The Copernican problem was in the use of time, the daily and annual schedules.

What's wrong with the traditional secondary schedule? Plenty! The typical secondary school teacher must teach five classes a day for 180 days a year. Assuming an average class size of 25 students, a teacher typically deals with about 125 students each day in five classes, usually with three preparations and sometimes more than one discipline. A review of the research on effective instruction indicates the key concept is individualization. Teachers cannot deal meaningfully with every student every day under this traditional schedule.

Similarly, the student typically takes six classes each day, each packaged in periods of about 45 minutes, regardless of the subject. Assuming a seven-period day, a homeroom, and lunch, a typical student will be in nine locations pursuing nine different activities in a 6 1/2-hour school day. If the schedule includes physical education, he or she may have changed clothes twice and showered once.

This is a work schedule unlike any experienced either before or after high school or in the workplace. It produces a hectic, impersonal, inefficient instructional environment.

Nothing is wrong with the Carnegie-based schedule except that it prevents teachers from teaching well and students from learning well!

Time Redeployed

The Copernican Plan proposes many changes: interest/issues seminars; evaluation based on a mastery credit system; individual learning plans; multiple diplomas, a new credit system with two types of credits; and dejuvenilization of our high schools.

But the achievement of these changes—or any other of the many interesting changes proposed for our high schools—depends upon a fundamental change in the use of time. Classes can be taught in much longer periods—90 minutes, two or four hours a day—and which meet for only part of the school year—30 days, 45 days, 60 days, or 90 days. Students are enrolled in significantly fewer classes each day and teachers deal daily with significantly fewer classes and students.

The Copernican change in schedules is not an end; rather it is a means to several important ends. The most important of these are to improve vastly the relationships between teachers and students and to provide teachers and students with much more manageable workloads. In theory, improved teacher/student relationships and more manageable workloads should result in more successful schools.

Specific Findings

The Copernican Plan states: "Virtually every high school in this nation can decrease its average class size by 20 percent; increase its course offerings or number of sections by 20 percent; reduce the total number of students with whom a teacher works each day by 60 to 80 percent; provide students with regularly scheduled seminars dealing with complex issues; establish a flexible, productive instructional environment that allows effective mastery learning as well as other practices recommended by research; get students to master 25 to 30 percent more information in addition to what they learn in the seminars; and do all of this within approximately present levels of funding."

Most educators agree that to accomplish the above would be remarkable, particularly at the senior high school level. In 1983, when I first introduced the Copernican Plan, some research and a few nontraditional educational programs supported these concepts. The proposal generated many questions and much opposition at that time.

The critically important step I took was to arrange for a first-rate evaluation by a team from Harvard University that brought objectivity, competence, and credibility to our efforts. The evaluation addressed several key questions:

- Will students "burn out" in these much longer classes? (They won't.)
- Will teachers "burn out" under this type of schedule? (They don't.)
- Will students learn as much in about 25 percent less time per course? (They did, and they also completed many more courses.)
- Will students retain what they learned as well under a Copernican schedule as they do under a traditional schedule? (They do.)
- And by taking a course in a more intense schedule, will students develop the in-depth, problem-solving skills as well as they do (allegedly) in a traditional 180-day schedule? (They did significantly better.)

As a result, the Harvard team stated: "Implementing a Copernican-style schedule can be accomplished with the expectation of favorable pedagogical outcomes."

That statement now has been tested in an evaluation of seven quite different high schools in four states and one Canadian province. These seven schools use six different Copernican scheduling formats.

The common evaluations are all outcomes-based, measuring student conduct and academic mastery. The evaluative design compares the results achieved at each school with those achieved under a Copernican schedule. In every case, the results solidly favored the Copernican structure and the results were statistically significant at consistently high levels of confidence.

While significant differences occurred in the results under different Copernican formats, every school benefited from the change. Some formats are more effective than others. The orders of magnitude of these improvements in conduct and increases in academic mastery are educationally spectacular.

These results, however, are not really surprising. They are consistent with the research. The Harvard team was right. Any school can implement a Copernican-type schedule with the expectation of pedagogical gain.

The Change Process

Schools, particularly high schools, don't change much. Why? Many books and articles address that question. Most answers follow a pattern: strategic planning; beliefs analysis; district vision; school vision; scope and sequence, objectives, outcomes, authentic tasks, assessing authentic tasks. The total quality movement appears to undergird these efforts.

These are useful approaches. Certainly a common vision, a good plan, and strong support of all stakeholders are most desirable. A few messages from this decade of Copernican experiences add to this large body of professional literature concerning change. Interestingly, they differ considerably from the current conventional wisdom about how to change schools.

These messages include:

Process is not product.

Three of the seven schools evaluated plus Masconomet followed more traditional practices in achieving change. Nonetheless, all showed significant improvements in student performance; indeed they had the best total results. (And one is hard pressed to find evidence of even modest student improvement as a result of other current efforts at educational reform.)

Only two schools had special grants to develop their program. Six schools had only the normal district resources. Five of the seven schools and Masconomet had a solid majority of teachers supporting the proposed change. Three did not and their results were among the best of this group. The difference appears to be that change in all of these schools was far more "product" dominated than usual, and this emphasis directed the process.

Based on conversations over many years with hundreds of educators from schools planning to change, the change process itself dominates the scene far too often and there is an assumption that whatever is done or not done will improve the school.

Successful change must be research-based and systemic.

A surprise: The school with the poorest process and least preparation of staff had the best overall results. The school with the best staff development program, which used an inclusive, multi-year planning process, had the poorest results, although the school's total program improved over results achieved under its traditional structure. The differences were significant. Why?

The answer seems to come from W. Edwards Deming and the TQM [total quality management] concepts. Deming refers to the 85/15 rule; 85 percent of the problems are in the system and only 15 percent are in the people or subgroups. A Copernican change is systemic; it impacts all of the students and teachers in every class every day. However, the traditional schedule is also systemic. The difference is that no research supports continuing with the Carnegie unit; it actually impairs effective instruction. The Copernican structure is research-based and fosters more effective instruction.

The message: The process must be centered on developing a system that is based on sound instructional research and upon research-based evaluations of programs that demonstrated improved student performance.

Leadership is critical.

All of these schools had good leadership, leaders with a clear "feel" for the problems with the present system who were determined to make improvements. They seemed to understand that while it is possible to change without improving, it is impossible to improve without changing.

Too many schools and school districts are waiting for a "textbook process" to be completed. Too often the process becomes a vehicle to slow or avoid substantive change. Aristotle said: "In practical matters the end is not mere speculative knowledge of what is to be done, but rather the doing of it." The expectation of action to plan and also a plan of action based upon solid research is the major contribution the superintendent and other administrators can provide their staff.

Change the whole school at once.

The school is the productive unit in education. Avoid pilot programs and schools within a school. Schools, like people, seem to have an in-built rejection mechanism that is disruptive and subverts change. Pilot programs threaten those who do not want to be involved, and what threatens them most is that the program will be considered successful and they may have to change!

Evaluate, evaluate, evaluate.

The major problem in plans to change schools is the failure to plan the evaluation as an integral part of the program and to evaluate in terms of student outcomes. Use competent outside evaluators who can provide professional expertise not readily available in most schools. They have more credibility because they are not part of the school's administrative structure and appear more objective.

Change always generates critics. In a couple of years, critics will be looking for "solid data." Lacking this, the program could be terminated. Many good professionals will advise superintendents not to initiate academic evaluations until the new program is being implemented properly. This could take several years.

This experience does not support that position. The key political and professional question is whether the new program is improving the education of students, based on measures that the profession and the public will accept as "solid." That is a reasonable question. Be prepared to answer that question. Observe carefully: Nothing, absolutely nothing, has happened in education until it has happened to a student. Evaluate!

A caveat: Beware of the gifted opposition.

Teachers and parents associated with honors courses are usually pleased with the current program and see no reason to change. Consequently, the group that most often leads the opposition are teachers and parents associated with the higher-performing tracks, the honors students. For similar reasons, schools viewed locally as very good are harder to change than those that are viewed as troubled.

Two of the seven schools included in my studies, as well as Masconomet, encountered this source of opposition, and a number of other schools also have reported the honors parents as a source of opposition. Honors parents and teachers are stakeholders in the process, but they see their stake in retention of the program under which their children prosper. Try to improve their understanding. Able students do better under a Copernican structure. But remember, there are many more "gifted parents" than "gifted students!"

Determine how much change a school community can absorb.

Don't try to make several major changes at once. There is usually a logical sequence in pacing the changes you try to implement. Limit change, and sequence the changes carefully.

Ripe for Change

Schools are political entities. The nation has serious educational problems and depends upon about 15,000 school districts and 100,000 individual schools to identify these problems and implement improvements. This nonsystem is not capable of meeting the nation's requirements for improved student performance. Probably we will see little substantive improvement until schools can operate under a substantially different political structure. But lacking that change, a Copernican revolution in the nation's secondary schools financially is feasible and will do much to address our nation's educational problems. In doing that, it also will address the local school district's needs, Most importantly, it will result in something very good happening to students. Remember, nothing has happened in education until it happens to a student.

NO

Reginald D. Wild

Science Achievement and Block Schedules

Introduction

Achievement in science, mathematics and other subjects is only one of many considerations in making a scheduling change in a secondary school. School size, nature of the student population, the community, special programs, school goals, etc., all play a part in such a decision. Achievement, however, is pivotal to such a decision in many schools, especially those with a highly academic or a university/college bound student population. The decision to change a school schedule is often fraught with controversy as parents, newspapers, and other media get involved. School leaders often compound the issues by overusing rhetoric rather than evidence when promoting such a change.

Timetables/schedules come in almost as many variations as there are schools. These variations all have advantages and disadvantages. In the world of schools, elementary/primary through secondary through universities or colleges, timetables/schedules are, in general, *all-year* in organization. There are exceptions but until recently these were relatively uncommon.

Canada and the United States are countries with major secondary school timetable exceptions. Since the late 1960's a more intensive approach has been used in some of the secondary schools of British Columbia, Ontario and other Canadian provinces. The name used was "semester," or "4×4," or more recently, in the United States, ... "block" scheduling. A typical semester/block timetable might include 4 courses each semester, with 4 classes a day every day for half the school year with a duration of 75 to 90 minutes per class. ...

In September 1991, one secondary school in British Columbia implemented a somewhat radical timetable innovation—classes of about two and one-half hours in length, only two classes a day, and the same two courses every day for approximately 9 or 10 weeks. As of 1997, the number of schools on this timetable has increased to 20 schools or more. This timetable could be viewed as the logical next step beyond a semester/block approach in increased intensity of instruction. The 8 courses a year are completed in 4 "quarters" and the term often used to describe this timetable is "Copernican" quarter, in order to distinguish this system from other quarter timetable systems. Why "Copernican"? The idea for this timetable innovation came from an article titled *The Copernican Plan: Restructuring the American High School* (Carroll, 1990). This plan, with numerous components, included one key component— the "Copernican change" (Carroll, 1990), a timetabling change to more intensive approaches to secondary schooling. Both semester/block and "Copernican" quarters would constitute acceptable "Copernican" timetables according to the Carroll model. It is noteworthy that this intensive scheduling change proposal did not include music or physical education—they would continue all year. In British Columbia, music and physical education are often included in the regular "Copernican" quarter timetable, with somewhat disastrous results in music and very mixed results in physical education. Intensive approaches do appear to favor subject areas such as technical education and other project-oriented programs.

Since the beginning of [the 1990s], in the United States and Canada, it appears that there has been an increasing move towards a semester/block approach with, however, little indication of many schools moving towards a "Copernican" quarter timetable. The most recent estimate is that about 50% of American secondary schools are on some form of block scheduling, including alternate-day blocks of all-year scheduling (*NSTA Reports,* 1997). This percentage is similar to many parts of Canada. . . .

Claimed Benefits of Intensive Approaches

Claimed benefits of using more intensive approaches to timetabling are quite numerous and have included (Canady & Rettig, 1995; Carroll, J. M. 1990; and others):

- overall as good or higher achievement
- improved attendance
- fewer discipline problems
- improved school atmosphere
- fewer dropouts
- use of more effective teaching strategies—teachers can no longer lecture all the time
- reduced emphasis on memorization
- more attention to critical thinking and problem solving
- reduction in the amount of fragmented instruction
- higher grades
- lower fail rate
- less material covered but depth of coverage improves
- teachers get to know students better
- easier for teachers to manage fewer courses at a time
- easier for students to manage fewer courses at a time
- fewer final examinations at a time (Grade 12 in particular)
- better opportunity to repeat failed courses
- at-risk students benefit
- less time is spent on classroom administration

- improved achievement by some Grade 12's, as they have an opportunity or multiple opportunities to rewrite final examinations for higher standing
- etc., etc., etc.

As expected, research and time have proven some of these claims to be unsubstantiated (e.g., improved attendance, Kramer, 1997a), other claims supported in part by research (e.g., fewer dropouts—however, see the discussion of participation rate later in this [selection]), and the majority of these claims being very problematic (since when do excellent teachers lecture all the time!).

There is also the important question of the retention of achievement over time. Intensive approaches can lead to large gaps in time between related courses. For example, a student might do a course such as Chemistry 11 in the 1st quarter of Grade 11 and not do Chemistry 12 until the last quarter of the following year. . . .

Practice and Theory

Why are the *majority* of timetable and schedules in the world, Kindergarten to Post-secondary, mainly of an all-year format? Why would you have difficulty convincing Grade 5 teacher, Mr. Jones and his Principal, Ms. Smith, that mathematics is best taught in, for example, the first 10 weeks of the school year, mornings, $2\frac{1}{2}$ hours a day, every day and science left until the last 10 weeks of the school year? We cannot just say "Elementary schools are different." How does the usual all-year timetabling practice in Grade 5 suddenly become a poor idea in Grade 8 or Grade 12 as a school moves towards a more intensive approach? How do proponents of intensive practice like Carroll (1990) rationalize these approaches? . . .

It appears that the tendency to justify radical shifts in secondary school timetables is based on personal observation with little reference to the research literature and also by the use of somewhat banal slogans in the context of a "more individualized" approach to teaching. In a later article Carroll (1994) describes his evaluation of eight different high schools using some form of intensive timetabling and concludes:

> There is no professional reason to delay; in fact, continuing with the present Carnegie structure [*short classes, all-year*] raises serious questions of professional malpractice. . . . The change in structure—the systematic change—will get significantly better results than will be possible under the traditional structure. . . .

Again we have claims, based on very limited data, supporting very strong assertions.

In terms of theory supporting all-year timetable approaches, learning specialists in psychology refer to the *spacing effect*. This has been summarized in a review article as:

> The spacing effect—the tendency, given an amount of . . . time, for spaced [*or distributed*] presentations of a unit of information to yield much better learning than massed presentations—is one of the most remarkable phenomena to emerge from laboratory research on learning. (Dempster & Farris, 1990, p. 97)

The importance of the spacing effect is also summarized by Dempster & Farris (1990):

> 1st—The spacing effect is one of the most dependable and robust phenomena in experimental psychology.
>
> 2nd—The spacing effect is truly ubiquitous in scope. It had been observed in virtually every experimental learning paradigm, and with all sorts of traditional research material.
>
> 3rd—The spacing effect has the distinction of being one of the most venerable phenomena in psychological literature.

While it appears that theory matches . . . all-year timetables—is [the] theory supported by research on achievement?

Research on Achievement

While there have been numerous small-scale studies and school reports on achievement increases with intensive approaches, there have been relatively few large-scale studies, most of which have been completed in Canada. . . .

Large-scale studies tend to be much more consistent. The first of these studies was reported in 1986 by Raphael, Wahlstrom & McLean, who looked at the achievement of 5,280 all-year and semestered mathematics students in 250 Ontario classrooms as part of the Second International Mathematics Study. They reported:

> Suggestions reported in the literature of better student attitudes and achievement were not supported, and performance of grade 12 and 13 students in semestered classes was significantly lower than those in year-long classes. (p. 36)

In 1990 Bateson, as part of the Provincial Science Assessment in British Columbia, looked specifically at science achievement in Grade 10 classes. Similar to the Raphael et al. study (1986) he compared results between semester/block schools and all-year schools. His sample size was also large with 30,116 students completing the assessment instruments, with about 65% on an all-year format, 28% on a semester/block format, and the remaining on a variety of other timetable formats. He reported his results in *JRST* [Journal of Research in Science Teaching] as follows:

> "It was found that, contrary to reported teacher perceptions of semester versus all-year courses, students in the all-year course consistently outperformed both first- and second-semester students in the domains tested, and there were no significant differences in the affective domain." (Bateson, 1990, p. 233)

He also explored background components and found, except for a small difference in teacher experience, no difference in student, teacher, and school characteristics which could provide an alternative explanation of the achievement differences....

The work of Bateson (1990) was replicated in May 1995 as part of the British Columbia assessment of both science and mathematics in Grade 10. This was the first opportunity to compare Grade 10 achievement in schools timetabled in formats that were all-year, semester/block or quarter ("Copernican"). There was considerable interest in this data, because of the on-going timetable debates in British Columbia and elsewhere. The format involved multiple forms, sorted by goals, with large samples (3,000 to 4,000) for each form. The result:

> It appears that the hypothesized benefits of semester and quarter systems, in terms of student achievement, are not being realized in mathematics and science achievement in British Columbia. (Marshall et al., 1996, p. 163)

In both mathematics and science at the Grade 10 level, with almost complete consistency on different forms, all-year students outscored semester students who outscored quarter students....

In 1997, the Council of Ministers of Education, Canada, reported a country-wide assessment of Mathematics achievement at ages 13 and 16 (School Achievement Indicators Program). All 10 provinces and the Territories participated. In five of the provinces there were both French and English versions. Typical provincial samples were in the range of 500–1,000 participants. Results were reported from level 1 (lowest) to level five (highest). Results for semestered (block, 4×4's, etc.) schools were compared to full-year schools as [shown in *Table 1*].

Again we have achievement results which are consistent with previous studies: full-year students achieve at a higher level as compared to semester students. It should be noted that the Council also completed an assessment of Science Achievement in 1995, but did not gather data based on school organization....

Summary

While there are benefits to more intensive approaches to secondary school schedules, increased achievement in science and mathematics is not one of them. It also appears that the greater the intensity, the lower the achievement, that is, all-year students outperform semester/block students who outperform

Table 1

Age	Sample size	% of age group	% of those students at Level 3 or above
13	12,881	Full year 86%	30%
		Semestered 8%	24%
16	11,079	Full year 40%	71%

"Copernican" quarter students in science and mathematics. There [are] also serious questions as to the opportunity to excel (percentage of "A" grades) and the perceived opportunity for success as determined by the completion rate/participation rate. It appears that there are very large effects in some cases. Is this a typical case of data mirroring theory (the spacing effect)? With limited evidence available, is it possible to generalize these conclusions to other subjects including the development of writing skills (English) and foreign languages?

There are a number of questions to be considered—

- How will more intensive approaches affect success and participation rate in *Advanced Placement* programs?
- For avid proponents of intensive forms of secondary school timetables —would the maximum "benefits" occur if only one course were taught at a time, for 5/6 hours per day for 5 weeks?
- How does increased intensity of timetabling apply to an "at risk" population compared to an "academic" population? Borderline academic students appear to drop out of Grade 12 "hard" courses or not even try (participation rate). Do more intense approaches discourage students from taking "tough" courses and hence limit their future career choices? . . .
- In some schools the issue is change or rather the notion that a change is needed in order to provide stimulation and interest on the part of the staff, students and the community. Will a timetable change assist in meeting this perceived need?

. . . Lastly, in terms of any school change, it is important that a timetable change reflect the goals of the school. In general, successful schools have clear goals with a distinct understanding and commitment on the part of the teachers, students and the rest of the school community. The key question in making a timetable change:

> "How will this change reflect and enhance the goals and mission of the school?"

Note

1. Colour Ranking Inspection Trend Analysis System (CRITRA System)*
   *Reginald D. Wild 1998

References

Anderson, John O.; Muir, Walter; Bateson, David J.; Blackmore, David & Rogers, W. Todd (1990). *The Impact of Provincial Examinations on Education in British Columbia: General Report.* Victoria, B.C. British Columbia Ministry of Education.

Bateson, D. (1990). Science Achievement in Semester and All-year Courses. *Journal of Research in Science Teaching, 27,* 233–240.

Black, Susan (1998). Learning on the Block. *The American School Board Journal, 185,* 32–34.

British Columbia Ministry of Education. Victoria (1996). *Distribution of Letter Grades by Course and School Organization.*

British Columbia Ministry of Education. Victoria (1997). *Distribution of Letter Grades by Course and School Organization.*

British Columbia Ministry of Education. Victoria (1997). *Distribution of Letter Grades: Full Year Summary.*

Canady, R. L., & Rettig, M. D. (1995). The Power of Innovative Scheduling. *Educational Leadership 3,* 4–10.

Carroll, J. M. (1990). The Copernican Plan: Restructuring the American High School, *Phi Delta Kappan, 71,* 358–365.

Carroll, J. M. (1994). The Copernican Plan Evaluated: The Evolution of a Revolution. *Phi Delta Kappan, 75,* 105–13.

Dempster, Frank M., Farris R. (1990), The Spacing Effect: Research and Practice. *Journal of Research and Development in Education, 23,* 97–101.

Eineder, Dale V., Bishop, H. L. (1997). Block Scheduling the High School: The Effects on Achievement, Behaviour, and Student-Teacher Relationships. *National Association of Secondary School Principals Bulletin, 81,* 45–53.

Gore, Gordon (1997). Timetables and Academic Performance. *The Physics Teacher, 35,* 525–527.

Kramer, S. (1997a). What We Know About Block Scheduling and Its Effects On Math Instruction, Part I. *National Association of Secondary School Principals Bulletin, 81,* 18–42.

Kramer, S. (1997b). What We Know About Block Scheduling and Its Effects On Math Instruction, Part II. *National Association of Secondary School Principals Bulletin, 81,* 69–82.

Lockwood, Susan L. (1995). Semesterizing the High School Schedule: The Impact of Student Achievement in Algebra and Geometry. *National Association of Secondary School Principals Bulletin, 79,* 102–110.

Marshall, M.; Taylor, A.; Bateson, D.; & Brigden, S. (1996). *The British Columbia Assessment of Mathematics and Science: Technical Report.* British Columbia Ministry of Education, Victoria, B.C.

NSTA REPORTS! (1997). *Block period schedules.* National Science Teachers Association, Arlington, Virginia May/June, Vol. 8, No. 6, p5.

Powell, B. (1976). *Intensive Education: The Impact of Time on Learning,* Education Development Center, Inc. Boston.

Raphael, Dennis; Wahlstrom, Merlin; & McLean, L. D. (1986). Debunking the Semestering Myth. *Canadian Journal of Education* 11:1, 36–52.

School Achievement Indicators Program: Mathematics Assessment (1997), Council of Ministers of Education, Canada; Toronto, p97.

Wronkovich, M.; Hess, C. A.; Robinson, J. E. (1997). An Objective Look at Math Outcomes Based on New Research Into Block. *National Association of Secondary School Principals Bulletin, 81,* 32–41.

POSTSCRIPT

Is Block Scheduling Better Than Traditional Scheduling?

Given the glare of publicity related to the need for improvement of secondary school education (or at least the improvement of test scores) and the concomitant pressures on high school administrators and teachers to provide evidence of taking necessary action toward such improvement, it is no wonder that "highly visible" changes such as alternative scheduling have increased in popularity. Ideally, as stated by Carroll, such changes would flow from a careful analysis of "the relationship between time and learning," but that does not always seem to happen. Rather, the change to some form of alternative time configuration such as block scheduling often appears to be an end unto itself and is not accompanied or followed by any substantive changes or improvements in instruction.

However, the case can also be made that the traditional high school schedule of six daily periods of approximately one hour each did not develop from any careful analysis of time and instruction. The origin of the traditional or "Carnegie unit" schedule in the early 1900s was motivated by a desire for greater standardization of high school records and transcripts. A total of approximately 120 hours in one subject meeting daily for the "agrarian era school year" of approximately 36–40 weeks generated one Carnegie unit of credit. (Many school systems have abandoned the Carnegie unit and now equate any one-year course to 10 units of credit, but the principle remains the same.) As subjects were added to the high school curriculum, they were all built around this "one size fits all" record-keeping mechanism. The number and minutes of the daily class periods emerged from the number of units required in each content area and the overall requirements for graduation.

Other readings by block scheduling proponents include *Block Scheduling: A Catalyst for Change in High Schools,* by Robert Canady and Michael Rettig (Eye on Education, 1995); "The Power of Innovative Scheduling," by these same authors in *Educational Leadership* (November 1995); and in the same issue, "Finding Time to Learn," by John O'Neil. Readings from the opposing perspectives include "More Data Rebut Block Scheduling," by David Boldt in the *Philadelphia Inquirer* (September 24, 1996) and *Block Scheduling: Implications for Music Education,* by Larry Blocher and Richard Miles (Focus on Excellence, 1996).

ISSUE 14

Is Homework Beneficial to Students?

YES: Harris Cooper, from "Homework for All—in Moderation,"
Educational Leadership (April 2001)

NO: Etta Kralovec and John Buell, from "End Homework Now,"
Educational Leadership (April 2001)

ISSUE SUMMARY

YES: Harris Cooper, chair of the Department of Psychological Sciences at the University of Missouri–Columbus, argues that research supports the contention that for high school students more homework results in higher achievement levels.

NO: Etta Kralovec, vice president for learning at Training and Development Corporation, and John Buell, a freelance journalist, present three "myths" supporting homework that they maintain insulate that traditional practice from careful study and criticism.

Schooling in the United States involves many sacrosanct traditions that seem to successfully resist challenges regarding their efficacy in contributing to student learning. Certainly the practice of assigning and requiring the completion of homework can be listed as one of those traditions. Homework has long been employed as an instructional tool, with various rationales supporting its use. Such rationales include training to enhance academic discipline, practice and drill to exercise the intellect, providing an advanced organizer for upcoming classroom work, assessing student knowledge, and engaging parents in the student's schooling. Periodically some of those rationales are challenged or debunked, but the tradition itself lives on.

Many teachers report that a growing number of their students, especially at the secondary level, simply refuse to do required homework, thus not only losing any learning advantages that might have accrued to them, but also losing ground in terms of the credit ascribed to completing the homework. The net result is that something designed to help students becomes instead a factor in their lack of success in school.

Some might argue that a student's failure to complete or even attempt homework is symptomatic of a lack of motivation or self-discipline on the student's part and/or a lack of involvement or supervision by parents. For a given student, that may indeed be the case. Also the notion of having students use nonschool time to support and expand their learning seems to be logical and defensible.

But such arguments, as Etta Kralovec and John Buell would agree, may be overly simplistic when applied to all students. Factors related to family structure and responsibilities; family income and student employment; and access to instructional support and materials, such as libraries and computers, can either enhance or impede a student's opportunity and/or ability to do homework. Another concern relates to the availability of time and whether or not the time devoted to homework may detract from a student's opportunities to pursue other worthy, nonschool activities.

The tremendous range of diversity related to demographic factors and family circumstances makes the homework issue more complex than it may appear at first glance. Additionally, curriculum development and new requirements in areas such as community service learning, which involves nonschool time, will also have implications for secondary school students vis à vis homework. Some teachers are also beginning to voice concerns that the increased emphasis on accountability and high-stakes standardized testing may cause schools to use class time for review and test preparation purposes, thus forcing greater reliance on homework as a means to cover the regular curriculum.

Kalovec and Buell's selection is adapted from their book, *The End of Homework: How Homework Disrupts Families, Overburdens Children and Limits Learning* (Beacon Press, 2000).

Harris Cooper  **YES**

Homework for All—in Moderation

Almost like clockwork, the controversy regarding the value of homework has begun again. Homework controversies follow a 30-year cycle, with outcries for more homework or less homework occurring about 15 years apart.

At the start of the 20th century, scientists viewed the mind as a muscle that could be strengthened through mental exercise. People viewed homework favorably as an exercise that could be done at home. During the 1940s, the emphasis in education shifted from drill to problem solving. In the 1950 edition of the *Encyclopedia of Educational Research,* Professor H. J. Otto wrote, "Compulsory homework does not result in sufficiently improved academic accomplishments" (p. 380). The launch of Sputnik by the Russians in the mid-1950s, however, reversed this thinking. The public worried that education in the United States lacked rigor and that it left students unprepared for complex technologies. Homework might accelerate knowledge acquisition.

The 1960s witnessed yet another reversal, with homework perceived as a symptom of needless pressure on students. Educator P. R. Wildman (1968) wrote,

> Whenever homework crowds out social experience, outdoor recreation, and creative activities, and whenever it usurps time devoted to sleep, it is not meeting the basic needs of children and adolescents. (p. 203)

In the 1980s, homework again leapt back into favor. A primary stimulus was the report *A Nation at Risk* (National Commission on Excellence in Education, 1983), which cited homework as a defense against the rising tide of mediocrity in U.S. education. The push for more homework continued into the 1990s, fueled by educators who used it to meet increasingly rigorous state-mandated academic standards.

As the century turned, a predictable backlash set in, led by beleaguered parents concerned about their stressed-out children (Winerip, 1999). There is evidence, however, that the outcry results not from a widely held distress, but rather from a vocal minority. A recent national survey of 803 parents of public school students revealed that 64 percent of parents believed that their child was getting "about the right amount" of homework, 25 percent believed that their child was getting "too little" homework, and only 10 percent believed that their child was getting "too much homework" (Public Agenda, 2000, p. 6).

Research on the Effects of Homework

Policymakers have used research to muster a case for every possible position on homework. Advocates and opponents may refer to small portions of the literature or imprecisely weigh the accumulated evidence. When I received a grant from the National Science Foundation to examine the research on the effects of homework, I had no predisposition about whether homework was good or bad. I attempted to uncover the past evidence, both positive and negative (Cooper, 1989). After reviewing nearly 120 studies of homework's effects, I synthesized the information and discovered factors in the school and home environment that influence homework's impact (Cooper, 1998).

My task began with cataloging homework's positive and negative effects. Among the suggested positive effects of homework, the most obvious is that it will have an immediate impact on the retention and understanding of the material it covers. More indirectly, homework will improve students' study skills, improve their attitudes toward school, and teach them that learning can take place anywhere, not just in school buildings.

Homework has many potential nonacademic benefits as well, most of which relate to fostering independent and responsible character traits. Finally, homework can involve parents in the schooling process, enhancing their appreciation of education and allowing them to express positive attitudes toward their children's achievements and accomplishments.

The suggested negative effects of homework make more interesting reading. Some educators and parents worry that homework could lead to students feeling satiated with academic information. They suggest that any activity can remain rewarding for only so long. If students are required to spend too much time on academic material, they are bound to grow bored with it. Others say that homework denies access to leisure time and community activities. Children learn important lessons, both academic and nonacademic, from soccer and scouts. Another problem is that parental involvement can often turn into parental interference. For example, parents can confuse students if the instructional techniques they use differ from those used by teachers. Homework can also lead to the acquisition of undesirable character traits by promoting cheating, through either the direct copying of assignments or help with homework that goes beyond tutoring.

Finally, homework could accentuate existing social inequities. Students from low-income homes will have more difficulty completing assignments than their middle-class counterparts. Low-income students are more likely to work after school or may not have quiet, well-lighted places in which to complete their assignments. Homework, opponents argue, is not the great equalizer.

Does Homework Work?

Three kinds of studies focused on whether homework improves students' achievement (Cooper, 1989).

In the first set of studies, researchers simply compared the achievement of students given homework assignments with students not given homework or any other activity to compensate for their lack of home study. Of these 20 studies, 14 produced effects favoring homework and 6 favored no homework.

The most interesting result from these studies was the dramatic association between grade level and homework's effectiveness. Let us assume that a fictional teacher has two classes of 25 students, and, through some remarkable accident of nature, each student in one class has an exact counterpart in the other. Assume further that the teacher uses the same instructional methods in both classes, except that one class gets homework and the other class does not.

The studies revealed that if the teacher were teaching high school students, the average student in the homework class (50th percentile) would outperform 69 percent of the students in the no-homework class. Put differently, the student who ranked 13th in achievement in the homework class would rank 8th if he or she were shifted into the no-homework class just before the final exam. If the teacher teaches in junior high school, the 13th-ranked homework-doer would rank 10th in the no-homework class. In elementary school, however, homework would not help the student surpass other schoolmates.

The second set of evidence compared homework to in-class supervised study. In these investigations, students not receiving homework were required to engage in some other kind of activity. Most often, students did homework-like assignments while in school.

These studies were not as favorable toward homework as the first set. Overall, the positive effect of homework was about half of what it was when compared to no assignment for home study. This should not surprise us. There is no reason to believe that homework would be more effective than in-class study for improving test scores. Most important in these studies was the emergence once again of a strong grade-level effect. When homework and in-class study were compared in elementary schools, in-class study proved superior. In junior high, homework was superior, and in high school the superiority of homework was most impressive.

The third set of studies correlated the amount of time students reported spending on homework with their achievement levels. Many of the correlations in these 50 studies came from statewide surveys or national assessments. Of course, correlation does not mean causation; it is just as likely that high achievement causes students to do more homework as vice versa.

In all, 43 correlations indicated that students who did more homework had better achievement scores, whereas only 7 indicated that those who did more homework had lower achievement scores. Again, a strong grade-level qualifier appeared. For students in grades 3–5, the correlation between the amount of homework and achievement was nearly zero; for students in grades 6–9, the correlation was somewhat higher ($+ 0.07$); and for high school students, the correlation was highest ($+ 0.25$). The new evidence that has accumulated since my original review of the research more than a decade ago lends even more support to these findings (Cooper, Lindsay, Nye, & Greathouse, 1998).

In sum, homework has substantial positive effects on the achievement of high school students, and junior high students benefit about half as much. For elementary school students, the effect of homework on achievement is trivial, if it exists at all.

Cognitive and developmental psychology sheds light on the grade-level effect (Muhlenbruck, Cooper, Nye, & Lindsay, 2000). Studies indicate that younger students have limited attention spans, or more specifically, limited abilities to tune out distractions. Thus, the distractions at home more easily entice them away from the books spread out on the kitchen table. Also, younger students haven't yet learned proper study skills. They don't know how to apportion their time between easy and hard tasks or how to engage in effective self-testing. Each of these cognitive limitations suggests that homework should not be expected to impressively improve test scores and that expectations for homework assigned in primary grades should be aligned with other goals.

An Optimum Amount

Nine studies correlate time on homework with achievement, looking at how performance levels are a function of the amount of time spent on homework (Cooper, 1989). As we might expect, the line of progress is flat for younger students. For junior high school students, achievement continues to improve with more homework until assignments last between one and two hours a night, at which point achievement levels do not improve. For high school students, however, progress continues to go up to the largest number of hours spent on homework each night. Although common sense dictates that there is a point of diminishing returns, the more homework that high school students do, the higher their achievement levels.

Guidelines for Homework Policies

The following homework policy guidelines (Cooper, 2001) can make homework an effective teaching tool. The guidelines are general and should serve only as a starting point for discussions about homework.

Coordinate policies   Districts, schools, and classrooms should coordinate their policies. Some of the issues addressed at each level are unique, but others overlap.

State the rationale   Districts need to state clearly the broad rationale for homework, why it is often mandatory, and what the general time requirements ought to be. Schools need to further specify time requirements, coordinate assignments among classes (if desired), and set out the role of teachers and principals. Teachers need to adopt classroom policies that outline what is expected of students and why.

Assign homework   The amount and type of homework that students do should depend on their developmental level and the quality of their support at home. In a guide for parents, the National Parent Teacher Association and the National Education Association (2000) state,

> Most educators agree that for children in grades K–2, homework is most effective when it does not exceed 10–20 minutes each day; older children, in grades 3–6, can handle 30–60 minutes a day.

Educators often refer to this as the Ten Minute Rule, or 10 minutes multiplied by the student's grade level per night. My combined analyses of dozens of studies support these recommendations. If educators and parents expect homework far out of line with these recommendations to result in big gains in test scores, they are likely to be disappointed.

If homework for younger students bears no relation to achievement, why assign it at all? As I noted earlier, homework can have beneficial effects other than knowledge acquisition. In the primary grades, homework can help younger students develop good study habits and grow as their cognitive capacities mature. Homework can help students recognize that they can learn at home as well as at school. It can foster independent learning and responsible character traits. Homework can give parents an opportunity to see what's going on at school and express positive attitudes toward achievement. To obtain these outcomes, however, homework assignments in elementary grades should be short, employ materials commonly found in the home, and lead to successful experiences.

Use other approaches, too   Homework can be an effective instructional device, but it must serve different purposes at different grade levels. Our expectations for its effects, especially in the short term and in earlier grades, must be modest. Homework should be one of several approaches we use, along with soccer and scouts, to show our children that learning takes place everywhere.

The question for educators and parents is not whether homework has positive or negative effects. Either of these effects can occur. To avoid the negative effects, flexible homework policies should let individual schools and teachers take into account the unique needs and circumstances of their students. School districts, teachers, and parents should avoid the extremes.

References

Cooper, H. (1989). *Homework*. New York: Longman.

Cooper, H. (1998). *Synthesizing research: A guide for literature reviews* (3rd ed.). Thousand Oaks, CA: Sage.

Cooper, H. (2001). *The battle over homework: Common ground for administrators, teachers, and parents.* Newbury Park, CA: Corwin Press.

Cooper, H., Lindsay, J. J., Nye, B., & Greathouse, S. (1998). Relationships between attitudes about homework, the amount of homework assigned and completed, and student achievement. *Journal of Educational Psychology, 90,* 70–83.

Muhlenbruck, L., Cooper, H., Nye, B., & Lindsay, J. J. (2000). Homework and achievement: Explaining the different relations at the elementary and secondary school levels. *Social Psychology of Education, 4,* 295–317.

National Commission on Excellence in Education. (1983). *A nation at risk: The imperative for educational reform.* Washington, DC: U.S. Department of Education.

National Parent Teacher Association and National Education Association (2000). *Helping your student get the most out of homework* [Online]. Available: www.pta.org/programs/edulibr/homework.htm

Otto, H. J. (1950). Elementary education. In W. S. Monroe (Ed.), *Encyclopedia of Educational Research* (pp. 380–381). New York: Macmillan.

Public Agenda. (2000). *Survey finds little sign of backlash against academic standards or standardized tests* [Online]. New York: Author. Available: www.publicagenda.org/aboutpa/pdf/standards-backlash.pdf

Wildman, P. R. (1968). Homework pressures. *Peabody Journal of Education, 45,* 202–204.

Winerip, M. (1999, January 3). Homework bound. *New York Times: Education Life,* pp. 28–31.

 **NO**

End Homework Now

P arents say that teachers require it. Teachers say that parents demand more of it. Politicians call for grading parents on their ability to help with it. Citizens run for school board seats on no-homework platforms. The National Parent Teacher Association and the National Education Association set guidelines. Some dismiss the current anti-homework outcry as just the latest swing of the opinion pendulum. School boards and politicians dictate homework policies for political rather than pedagogical reasons. Teachers say that they are increasingly uncomfortable about handing over to parents the learning for which teachers are accountable. Welcome to the homework wars.

When the school board in Piscataway, New Jersey, voted [in 2000] to limit homework in the elementary grades to half an hour each night and high school homework to two hours a night, the *New York Times* ran a front-page article on the school (Zernike, 2000) and national television networks followed suit. Homework is controversial, not only because of legitimate questions about its efficacy. Concern about homework is also part of a growing apprehension in the United States about the time pressures that both adults and children now face. Unstructured family time is shrinking in the face of longer workweeks and more hours of homework than ever before (Hofferth & Sandberg, in press).

In the early 1990s, we discovered the impact of homework on students' lives when we helped conduct a study of alternative schools for Maine's Department of Education, aiming to find out why these schools had been so successful in helping former high school dropouts graduate from high school (Antonnuci & Mooser, 1993). We spoke with parents, school personnel, and school board members and conducted in-depth interviews with more than 45 at-risk students enrolled in these schools, asking them to identify when they had known they were going to drop out of school. Students told us about chaotic family lives, cramped living quarters, and parents who worked at night. They also kept mentioning their inability to complete homework as a factor in the decision to leave school.

Surprised that homework contributed so dramatically to students' dropping out of school, we analyzed research reports and talked with hundreds of teachers, parents, high school dropouts, and high school students. Instead of focusing narrowly on homework's impact on academic achievement or its presumed role in developing self-discipline and good work habits, we examined homework in the context of the lives of students, families, and communities. From this perspective, we found that homework often disrupts family life, interferes with what parents want to teach their children, and punishes students in poverty for being poor. Perhaps more significantly for educators are the serious limitations of homework's pedagogical prowess (Kralovec & Buell, 2000).

In the past 20 years, family life in the United States has undergone dramatic demographic and economic changes. More mothers work, more single parents run households, and more parents work longer—all contributing to a decrease in unstructured family time (Hofferth & Sandberg, in press). White middle-class parents in the past decade have increased their time at work by nearly six full-time weeks a year. African American middle-income families log an average of 4,278 hours per year, almost 500 hours per year more than white families (Mishel, Bernstein, & Schmitt, 2001).

Homework squeezes family life. All parents have educational agendas for their children. They want to pass on their cultural heritage, religious beliefs, and important life skills. They want to teach their children how to be good citizens and how to share in the responsibilities of running a home. More homework makes parents put their own agendas on hold even as they often struggle to help their children cope with homework assignments. Additionally, families need time to constitute themselves as families. According to a 1998 survey by Public Agenda, nearly 50 percent of parents reported having a serious argument with their children over homework, and 34 percent reported homework as a source of stress and struggle. Parents often have conflicting feelings about homework, viewing it as a way for their children to succeed but also as imposing serious limits on family time.

Homework reinforces the social inequities inherent in the unequal distribution of educational resources in the United States. Some students go home to well-educated parents and have easy access to computers with vast databases. Other students have family responsibilities, parents who work at night, and no educational resources in their homes. A principal once told us that he had solved the homework problem for students in poverty simply by not assigning them homework. This curious solution raises troubling questions: Either homework is of no educational value—in which case why is anyone doing it—or we are committing the worst form of educational discrimination by differentiating academic programs on the basis of economic class.

The poor person's version of the emblematic soccer mom is the burger mom—the mother who works nights in a fast food restaurant while her children sit in a booth waiting for her to help them with homework. Close to 20 percent of children in the United States live in poverty, and homework further exacerbates their academic problems. Well-meaning parents cannot overcome their lack of resources, including the time needed to make sure that their children complete school assignments.

Homework: The Black Hole

The call for greater accountability in education, with its increased focus on test scores and outcomes, puts homework on the line. When we leave a sizable portion of learning to parents, how can we hold schools and teachers responsible for meeting higher standards? To teach to standards means to teach in a more tightly controlled system, leaving no room for an unknown variable—the black hole of homework—in the education process. Moreover, how can teachers know the level of their students' learning if they don't know how students are getting their assignments done at home?

Cognitive scientists have contributed to a revolution in learning theory, building on the foundation laid by Jean Piaget and Lev Vygotsky. Educators accept that students have unique cognitive structures that determine their abilities to solve problems at different points in their development. We know that we must scaffold new learning onto existing mental frameworks to build new knowledge. Understanding students' mistakes is a crucial part of the teaching process. When work goes home, teachers have little understanding of the mistakes that students have made on the material and little control over who does the work. Teachers wonder, Did the students do their own work? Did they exchange answers with friends over the phone or before school? Did they send homework by e-mail to their grandparents, who did the work and returned it early the next morning? Did they download the paper they are handing in? Homework is a black hole in the learning process, leaving teachers unaware of each student's true educational level or progress and unable to scaffold new knowledge for the students.

Homework Myths

Three homework myths have persisted during the past century, making us unwilling to ask for solid evidence on the benefits of homework and acquiescent in accepting claims about its efficacy.

Myth: Homework increases academic achievement.

Even supporters of homework acknowledge the problems of research on homework. Homework supporter Harris Cooper acknowledges that "the conclusions of past reviewers of homework research show extraordinary variability.... the reviews often directly contradict one another" (1989, p. 28). Most researchers now concede that homework does not improve academic achievement for elementary students (Cooper, 1994). Recently, homework advocates have shifted their focus from homework's questionable impact on student achievement to homework's alleged importance in developing traits like self-discipline and time management. According to these views, developing homework habits early means that a student will be more disciplined about completing homework in high school and beyond.

According to Piaget, however, asking children to perform tasks before they are developmentally ready proves counterproductive to development. We need to ask ourselves whether homework falls into this category. Lacking solid evidence, homework supporters ask us to take on faith the notion that homework can instill desirable character traits.

Myth: If our students don't do lots of homework, their test scores will never be competitive internationally.

Comparisons of student test scores often pit U.S. students against students from other countries. Ironically, the 1995 Third International Math and Science Study (TIMSS) found that 8th graders in Japan and Germany are assigned less homework but still outperform U.S. students on tests (National Center for Educational Statistics, 2001). Japanese schools spend a greater portion of their budgets on professional development and organize their school days so that teachers can work collaboratively. Teachers in Japan are at school eight to nine hours a day, but they teach only four hours a day. In addition, the Japanese school calendar has longer school days, longer school years, longer lunches, and longer recess periods. The Japanese classroom is a sacred space that does not allow interruptions. We can learn many lessons from the Japanese system (Rohlen & LeTendre, 1995).

Myth: Those who call homework into question want to dilute the curriculum and kowtow to the inherent laziness of students.

By calling homework into question, we are not questioning the work of homework, but rather the value of students completing that work at home. Students need to complete long-term, independent projects as part of a rigorous academic program. They need to learn many skills through drill and practice. They need time to make new learning their own. Professional educators need to design rigorous academic work, scaffold new knowledge, and coach new study habits. The place for such work is in the school.

Focus on Genuine Reforms

Educators are under the gun as never before to improve student achievement. With national attention now focused on school reform, education leaders have a valuable opening for educating the public about how to improve schools in the United States. Rather than defending the practice of homework, educators should direct national discussion to more important issues.

- After close to 20 years of school reform measures, we now have some proven practices for increasing academic success. A recent RAND study of academic achievement compared 1993–1996 state test results and found that the states with higher test results shared three important characteristics: smaller class size, more pre-K education, and more resources for teachers (Grissmer, Flanagan, Kawata, & Williamson, 2000). A call for more school funding should be the mantra of our profession.

- The rush to fund and build after-school programs is now a major policy initiative with the potential to solve some of the homework problems we face (Miller, 2000). Education leaders should seek to ensure that after-school learning programs are academically rigorous and work closely with the community organizations that provide after-school services.

- Research on learning suggests the importance of physical movement in the learning process (Jensen, 2000). Beyond the back problems associated with heavy backpacks, students who sit all day in a classroom and then for hours to complete homework at night face a potential health threat. Turning up the pressure to achieve, instituting high-stakes testing programs, cutting physical activities, and piling on the homework are recipes for disaster. Educators should help parents and politicians understand how an overemphasis on testing will result in one-dimensional learning.

Piling on homework and arguing for its value are cheaper and less politically risky strategies, but educators need to inform the public about the real levers of school improvement. Do we have the courage to call for adequate school funding? Are we willing to declare an eight-hour workday for both students and teachers? Are we willing to commit ourselves to the professional development that teachers need to teach effectively in their classrooms? Are we willing to staff our after-school programs with professionals who can support student learning? Educators need to consider these questions before answering calls about homework from parents and the local news media.

References

Antonnuci, F., & Mooser, E. (1993). *Research report: Assessment of alternative programs.* Augusta: Maine State Department of Education.

Cooper, H. (1989). *Homework.* New York: Longman.

Cooper, H. (1994). *The battle over homework: An administrator's guide to setting sound and effective policies.* Thousand Oaks, CA: Corwin Press.

Grissmer, D., Flanagan, A., Kawata, J., & Williamson, S. (2000). *Improving student achievement: What the NAEP test scores tell us.* Santa Monica: RAND Corporation.

Hofferth, S., & Sandberg, J. (in press). Changes in American children's time, 1981–1997. In T. Owens & S. Hofferth (Eds.), *Children at the millennium: Where have we come from, Where are we going?* New York: Elsevier Science.

Jensen, E. (2000). Moving with the brain in mind. *Educational Leadership, 58*(3), 34–37.

Kralovec, E., & Buell, J. (2000). *The end of homework: How homework disrupts families, overburdens children, and limits learning.* Boston: Beacon Press.

Miller, B. (2000). The power of the hours: The changing context of after school. *School-Age Review, 2*(1), 18–23.

Mishel, L., Bernstein, J., & Schmitt, J. (2001). *The state of working America, 2000-2001.* New York: Cornell University Press.

National Center for Educational Statistics. (2001). *Pursuing excellence: Comparison of international 8th grade mathematics and science achievement from a U.S. perspective, 1995 and 1999* [Online]. Available: nces.ed.gov/pubs2001/2001028.pdf

Public Agenda. (1998). *Playing their parts: What parents and teachers really mean by parental involvement* [Online]. Available: www.publicagenda.org/specials/parent/parent.htm

Rohlen, T., & LeTendre, G. (1995). *Teaching and learning in Japan.* Boston: Cambridge University Press.

Zernike, K. (2000, October 10). Homework: What's enough? *New York Times,* pp. A1, A29.

POSTSCRIPT

Is Homework Beneficial to Students?

The enduring image of Abraham Lincoln reading and studying by candlelight in the family log cabin makes a compelling case for the virtues and values of homework. Indeed, the acceptability of employing homework as an instructional tool not only has history and tradition on its side but also strong parent support. As Cooper reports, a recent national survey of 803 parents of public school students showed that 64 percent of parents believed that their child was getting "about the right amount of homework," 25 percent felt that there was "too little homework," and only 10 percent believed that their child was getting "too much homework." Positive parental views regarding homework were also recorded in the annual Phi Delta Kappa/Gallup Poll of the Public's Attitudes Toward the Public Schools of 2000, wherein 68 percent of the respondents indicated that they believed that classroom work and homework provided the best way to measure student academic achievement whereas only 26 percent felt that test scores provided the best measure. Further evidence of parental belief in the importance of homework was reported in the 1997 edition of the Phi Delta Kappa/Gallup poll wherein only 13 percent of the respondents reported that they did not spend any time helping their child with homework. That is significantly down from 34 percent in 1986 who provided no help.

But tradition and positive parental perceptions are not always the best guides to effective educational practices. At one time caning and paddling of students was considered an appropriate and acceptable disciplinary technique (and some may still view it that way). Until recently denying school attendance to unwed expectant mothers was a common and widely supported policy in most school systems. Tracking and achievement level grouping remain widely prevalent practices in spite of some strong arguments and research findings against them.

Thus it is entirely appropriate and important that questions be asked and research conducted regarding the efficacy and other effects of homework on students in spite of the prevailing wisdom that supports its use.

A sidebar issue related to homework that teachers and school administrators are beginning to address is the proliferation of Internet sites and resources devoted to "homework assistance." Not only does this create greater disparity among students with respect to equity of access, but it also increases the potential for plagiarism and other forms of cheating. This type of electronic assistance may also eventually reduce the involvement of parents with their children's homework.

ISSUE 15

Does the Practice of Grading Students Serve Useful Purposes?

YES: Robert J. Marzano, from *Transforming Classroom Grading* (McREL Institute, 2000)

NO: Alfie Kohn, from "From Degrading to De-grading," *The High School Magazine* (March 1999)

ISSUE SUMMARY

YES: Robert J. Marzano, a senior fellow of Mid-continent Research for Education and Learning (McREL), argues that grading is useful for feedback purposes, which in turn enhance student learning.

NO: Alfie Kohn, an author and educational commentator, takes the position that grades reduce students' interest in learning, their willingness to choose challenging work, and the quality of their thinking.

T he practice of assigning a letter or numerical rating/ranking to individual students based upon some form of evaluation of their achievement is another of those perennial educational issues that seem impervious to change. Certainly the methods by which grading is done by teachers and the various permutations by which grades are reported to students and their parents undergo almost constant review and change, and yet the basic concept of providing some sort of evaluative rating of individual students has remained virtually unchanged over the years. We are now in the midst of a somewhat schizophrenic era vis à vis the grading of students. On the one hand, there are many adherents and advocates of the notion of authentic assessment, which fundamentally would avoid grading as it is traditionally done. Instead, assessment would consist of merely reporting on or providing exhibits of the actual artifacts or evidence of the performance of the individual student on a given learning task. But at the same time that this individualized, nonevaluative, and noncompetitive movement is gaining favor among educators, many states are fully committed to a standards-based curriculum and standardized testing program that can be translated into uniform criteria for classroom grading and also provide benchmarks for student promotion and graduation from high school. And in some states, such as

California, comparison of student achievement levels forms the basis for competition among schools and teachers for cash awards. An interesting example of this schizophrenia regarding grading can be seen in the Phi Delta Kappa/Gallup Poll of the Public's Attitudes Toward the Public Schools (1994), wherein the poll reported that parents felt that newer systems of reporting student progress, such as written descriptions, were more useful than the traditional A to F grading system. In the same poll, another question asked the parents to grade the public schools using the A to F format.

It is in the function of comparing and sorting students that grading plays a crucial, and to some an unsavory, role. For secondary school students, their grades in individual classes (even in classes prior to high school) may determine their eligibility for admission into college preparatory classes or the next class in a curricular sequence. Taken collectively, a student's grades in high school in aggregate form his or her grade point average, which in turn directly impacts eligibility for higher education and where that higher education might take place. Even with the student who does not aspire to higher education, grades can establish whether or not he or she will be allowed to participate in band, drama, or athletics. And as we all know, grades are often used by parents as criteria for determining whether or not their child will gain or lose certain privileges. Insurance companies even use a student's grades to set rates for car insurance.

In short, grading is a high-stakes tradition with many implications for both the present and the future of every student. As Robert J. Marzano and Alfie Kohn agree, that alone is good cause to study this issue very carefully. Marzano contends that research unquestionably supports the importance of feedback (grading) to specific learning while Kohn asserts that, while conventional grades persist, teachers and parents ought to do everything in their power to help students forget about them.

Robert J. Marzano  **YES**

Transforming Classroom Grading

What Are Grades For?...

Purposes of Grades

Measurement experts... explain that educators use grades primarily (1) for administrative purposes, (2) to give students feedback about their progress and achievement, (3) to provide guidance to students about future course work, (4) to provide guidance to teachers for instructional planning, and (5) to motivate students.

Administrative Purposes
For at least several decades, grades have served a variety of administrative functions, most dealing with district-level decisions about students, including

- Student matriculation and retention.
- Placement when students transfer from one school to another.
- Student entrance into college....

Feedback About Student Achievement
One of the more obvious purposes for grades is to provide feedback about student achievement. Studies have consistently shown support for this purpose. For example, in 1976, Simon and Bellanca reported that both educators and noneducators perceived providing information about student achievement as the primary purpose of grading. In a 1989 study of high school teachers, Stiggins, Frisbie, and Griswold reported that this grading function—which they refer to as the information function—was highly valued by teachers....

Guidance
When used for guidance purposes, grades help counselors provide direction for students. Specifically, counselors use grades to recommend to individual students courses they should or should not take and schools and occupations they might consider....

Instructional Planning

Teachers also use grades to make initial decisions about student strengths and weaknesses in order to group them for instruction. Grading as a tool for instructional planning is not commonly mentioned by measurement experts....

Motivation

Those who advocate using grades to motivate students assume that they encourage students to try harder both from negative and positive perspectives. On the negative side, receiving a low grade is believed to motivate students to try harder. On the positive side, it is assumed that receiving a high grade will motivate students to continue or renew their efforts....

The Issue of Reference

Another issue to address when developing a coherent grading system is the point of reference from which grades are interpreted. Three primary reference points are commonly used to interpret grades: (1) a predetermined distribution, (2) an established set of objectives, and (3) progress of individual students.

Reference to a Predetermined Distribution

Assigning grades based on a predetermined distribution can be thought of as a "norm-referenced" approach to grading. The concept of norm-referencing is so embedded in educational practice that it is worth discussing in some detail. Most educators are familiar with the term as it relates to standardized tests. For example, scores on tests like the *Iowa Tests of Basic Skills* commonly are reported as percentile ranks. Results for a particular student on the reading comprehension section of a standardized test might be reported as the 73rd percentile, meaning that the score the student received was higher than 73 percent of the scores received by other students. These "other students" to which the sample student's score is compared are referred to as the "norming group." With standardized tests, the norming group is usually assumed to be students across the country as the same age/grade level. Additionally, it is commonly assumed that the scores of the norming group, when arranged in order of magnitude, are distributed in a "bell curve."

The technical name for the "bell curve" is the "normal distribution." ... [T]he normal distribution is quite symmetrical, which allows mathematicians and statisticians to make a wide variety of predictions based on it. You might recall from statistics or measurement classes that about 68 percent of the scores in a normal distribution will fall within one standard deviation above and below the mean; about 95 percent of the scores will fall within two standard deviations above and below the mean, and almost 100 percent of the scores will fall within three standard deviations above and below the mean.

The concept of normal distribution has had a profound effect on educational practice—and, indeed, on Western society. The mathematical equation for the normal distribution was formulated as early as 1733 by Abraham de Moivre (1667–1754). Its critical importance to probability theory was later articulated by mathematicians Pierre de Laplace (1749–1827) and Carl Friedrich

Gauss (1777–1855). Today, Gauss is commonly thought of as the father of the normal distribution. In fact, so compelling were his writings about the characteristics and applications of the normal distribution, that it is frequently referred to as the "Gaussian distribution."

The wide use of the normal distribution in education stems from the fact that many physical and psychological phenomena adhere to it. . . .

Many characteristics do take the shape of a normal distribution when they are arranged in order of magnitude. Perhaps this is why many prominent researchers assume that the normal distribution can and should be used to describe student achievement. Among the most prominent are Arthur Jensen, Richard Herrnstein, and Charles Murray. Jensen is perhaps most well known for his book *Bias in Mental Testing* (1980). In it he argues that because aptitude is distributed normally, educators and psychologists should generally expect grades (or scores on any educational test) to conform to a normal distribution. Jensen notes that a tendency for scores to take the form of the normal distribution is so strong that it occurs even when tests are designed in such a way as to avoid a normal distribution. . . .

Richard Herrnstein and Charles Murray wrote the popular book *The Bell Curve* (1994). In this controversial work, the authors make a case not only that intelligence is distributed normally, but that it is a prime determinant of differences in factors such as income level, parenting ability, success in school, and virtually every social indicator of success. Of course, this position has rather strong negative implications for members of certain socioeconomic strata.

Because a teacher uses the normal distribution as a basis for grading does not necessarily mean that he or she agrees with the assertions of Jensen or Herrnstein and Murray. However, by using the bell curve as the reference point for grading, a teacher is implicitly assuming that the performance of students should or will approximate the bell curve. . . .

Reference to a Set of Learning Objectives

Specific learning objectives are another common point of reference for grades. Many measurement experts strongly endorse this approach. . . . This approach is commonly thought of as a "criterion-referenced" approach to grading, as opposed to the norm-referenced approach described previously.

Again, you are probably familiar with the term "criterion-referenced" as it relates to tests designed to assess student achievement on state standards. In such cases, the criterion is a specific score sometimes referred to as a "cut score." Students who do not obtain a score equal to or greater than the "cut score" are assumed not to have mastered the content at the requisite level. Of course, the key to designing such a test is to ensure that it contains items that students will answer correctly if they have a mastery of the content, but will answer incorrectly if they do not.

. . . The driving force behind criterion-referenced grading is to ascertain the extent to which students reach a specific level of knowledge or skill in a specific learning outcome at the end of a grading period.

Reference to Knowledge Gain

As the name implies, reference to knowledge gain uses individual student learning as the basis for grading. In this approach, the point of reference for each student is the level of skill or understanding at which the student begins the grading period. Stated differently, each student's entry level of knowledge is hie or her unique point of reference. Each student's grade, then, is based on how much he or she progresses beyond the initial level of knowledge or skill. The logic behind this approach is that students should not be compared to one another but, rather, to the amount of progress they can legitimately be expected to make. One challenge in this approach is to design a scale that can accommodate the different beginning points of reference for each student. Following is a sample of the types of scales that must be used in this approach.

- A = Exceptional effort and improvement in the student's ability
- B = Good effort; improvement exceeds expectations
- C = Adequate effort; improvement consistent with level of effort and ability
- D = Little improvement, but some evidence of effort
- F = Little or no improvement; no effort

As this example illustrates, when a student's entry-level knowledge is used as the reference point for grades, teachers commonly include these factors: (1) understanding of and skill in the content, (2) effort, and (3) aptitude. The highest grades are given to students who exhibit exceptional effort and improvement beyond what is expected of them (i.e., beyond what is expected for their level of aptitude).

The Position of This [Selection]

Although there is no right way or wrong way to design grades, there are ways that fit best with a given set of assumptions or beliefs. This [selection] is based on two assumptions:

1. The most important purpose of grades is to provide information or feedback to students and parents.
2. The best referencing system for grading is content-specific learning goals: a criterion-referenced approach.

Research unquestionably supports the importance of feedback to specific learning goals. To illustrate, after reviewing 7,827 studies on learning and instruction, researcher John Hattie (1992) reported that providing students with specific information about their standing in terms of particular objectives increased their achievement by 37 percentile points. To dramatize the implications of this research, assume that two students of equal ability are in the same class learning the same content. Also assume that they take a test on the content before beginning instruction and that both receive a score that puts their knowledge of the content at the 50th percentile. Four weeks go by and the students receive exactly the same instruction, the same assignments, and so on. However, one student receives systematic feedback in terms of specific learning goals; the other does not. After four weeks, the two students take another test. Everything else being equal, the student who received the systematic feedback obtained a score that was 34 percentile points higher than the score of the student who had not received feedback. It was this dramatic finding that led Hattie to remark: "The most powerful single innovation that enhances achievement is feedback. The simplest prescription for improving education must be 'dollops of feedback'" (p. 9).

The Case Against Having Any Grades at All

Before concluding this general discussion of grades, let's look at a final topic: doing away with any form of quantitative feedback. More specifically, the practice of providing students with quantitative feedback about their knowledge or skill has been strongly criticized by a few zealous and, unfortunately, persuasive individuals. Education writer Alfie Kohn is perhaps the most well known of this group. In a series of publications, Kohn asserts that almost all forms of grading should be abolished. His popular book *Punished by Rewards: The Trouble with Gold Stars, Incentive Plans, A's, Praise and Other Bribes* (1993) begins with an impassioned case against the use of rewards to motivate students. Kohn explains that American education is ostensibly trapped in a pattern of trying to bribe students into achievement.

> ... Regardless of the political persuasion or social class, whether a Fortune 500 CED, or a preschool teacher, we are immersed in this doctrine; it is as American as rewarding someone with apple pie.
>
> To induce students to learn, we present stickers, stars, certificates, awards, trophies, memberships in elite societies, and, above all, grades. (Kohn, 1993, p. 11)

Kohn blames this pattern of behavior on what he calls "pop behaviorism," which, he asserts, permeates our culture and our educational system: "pop behaviorism is perpetuated through the example of other significant individuals in our lives, too, including teachers and powerful people in the workplace" (p. 15). For Kohn, behaviorism so permeates the culture of education that we are literally unaware of it.

To counteract the negative influence of behaviorism on American education, Kohn cites a number of studies indicating that rewards do not positively influence behavior. For example, rewards are not good motivators in helping people lose weight, quit smoking, or use seat belts. He also cites research indicating that rewards do not improve performance on cognitive tasks. He places heavy emphasis on a dissertation by Louise Miller, who arranged a series of drawings of faces so pairs of identical and nearly identical images would be flashed on the screen. Nine-year-olds were then asked to differentiate between identical and nonidentical faces. Some of the students were paid when they succeeded; others were not. As Kohn explains, Miller

> brought 72 nine-year-olds into her laboratory one at a time and challenged them to tell the two faces apart. Some of the boys were paid when they succeeded, others were simply told each time whether or not they were correct. (1993, p. 42)

To the surprise of the researcher, the performance of the group that was paid was inferior to that of the group that was not.

In a later work entitled *Beyond Discipline: From Compliance to Community* (1996) Kohn summarizes the research on rewards:

> At least two dozen studies have shown that when people are promised a reward for doing a reasonably challenging task—or for doing it well—they tend to do inferior work compared with people who are given the same task without being promised any reward at all. Other research has shown that one of the least effective ways to get people to change their behavior (quit smoking, lose weight, use their seatbelts, and so on) is to offer them an incentive for doing so. The promise of a reward is sometimes not just ineffective but counterproductive—that is, worse than doing nothing at all. (p. 33)

Finally, in a 1999 article entitled "From Grading to Degrading," Kohn asserts that

- Grades tend to reduce students' interest in learning itself.
- Grades tend to reduce students' preference for challenging tasks.
- Grades tend to reduce the quality of students' thinking. (p. 39)

Based on his analysis of research on rewards—particularly monetary rewards—Kohn calls for significant changes in grading practices within education. Specifically, in *Punished by Rewards,* Kohn (1993, pp. 208–209) recommends that educators

1. Limit the number of assignments for which you give a letter grade.
2. Do not grade assignments using an A/B/C/D/F scale. Rather, use a scale like the following: check-plus/check/check-minus.
3. Reduce the number of possible grades to two: A and incomplete.
4. Never grade students when they are still learning something.
5. Never grade for effort.
6. Never grade on a curve.
7. Bring students in on the evaluation process as much as possible.

Some of Kohn's recommendations have merit—particularly 4, 6, and 7. Others, however, are questionable, at best, and downright dangerous, at worst. I believe Kohn's argument suffers from four primary weaknesses or misconceptions.

First, Kohn does not adequately address the complexities surrounding the issues of assessing and evaluating human learning. Stated differently, he ignores the research on the inappropriate and appropriate uses of assessment as a tool in the learning process. This [selection] is an attempt to articulate the very issues that Kohn has ignored.

Second, Kohn does not accurately interpret the influence of behaviorism on education today. Specifically, he interprets as behavioristic a wide variety of educational practices that have little or nothing to do with behaviorism. Psychologist John Anderson explains that this is a common trap:

> Modern educational writers assume that the behaviorist approach to education has been a failure, although little hard evidence has been cited. Recent writings have tended to generalize the perceived failure of the behaviorist program to the conclusion that any program that attempts to analyze a skill into components will fail. (1995, p. 396)

... Third, Kohn appears to misinterpret the research on grading, perhaps because he confuses rewards with feedback. Although it is true that tangible rewards have little effect on achievement, feedback has a strong and straightforward relationship to achievement. As mentioned previously, in a review of 7,827 studies in education, Hattie (1992) round that accurate feedback to students can increase their level of knowledge and understanding by 37 percentile points.

Finally, Kohn does not address the rather extensive body of research on rewards that contradicts his basic thesis. A basic premise for Kohn is that the rewards inhibit intrinsic motivation. However, in a review of 96 experimental studies, researchers Judy Cameron and W. David Pierce (1994) note: "Results indicate that, overall, reward does not decrease intrinsic motivation. When interaction effects are examined, findings show that verbal praise produces an increase in intrinsic motivation. The only negative effect appears when expected tangible rewards are given to individuals simply for doing a task. Under these conditions, there is a minimal negative effect on intrinsic motivation..." (p. 363). Speaking specifically about grades, researcher David Berliner explains:

> In fact, the evidence is persuasive that grades do motivate students to learn more in a given subject area.... The judicious use of grades that are tied to objective performance, as in mastery and some other instructional programs, appears to be related to increased achievement and positive student attitudes. (1984, p. 70)

Research offers strong support for grades and others forms of feedback (even rewards) as useful tools for learning. Unfortunately, because of a great many misconceptions about their use they have fallen out of favor with some educators.

NO

Alfie Kohn

From Degrading to De-grading

You can tell a lot about a teacher's values and personality just by asking how he or she feels about giving grades. Some defend the practice, claiming that grades are necessary to "motivate" students. Many of these teachers actually seem to enjoy keeping intricate records of students' marks. Such teachers periodically warn students that they're "going to have to know this for the test" as a way of compelling them to pay attention or do the assigned readings—and they may even use surprise quizzes for that purpose, keeping their gradebooks at the ready. Frankly, we ought to be worried for these teachers' students. In my experience, the most impressive teachers are those who despise the whole process of giving grades. Their aversion, as it turns out, is supported by solid evidence that raises questions about the very idea of traditional grading.

Three Main Effects of Grading

Researchers have found three consistent effects of using—and especially, emphasizing the importance of—letter or number grades:

1. Grades tend to reduce students' interest in the learning itself One of the best-researched findings in the field of motivational psychology is that the more people are rewarded for doing something, the more they tend to lose interest in whatever they had to do to get the reward (Kohn, 1993). Thus, it shouldn't be surprising that when students are told they'll need to know something for a test—or, more generally, that something they're about to do will count for a grade—they are likely to come to view that task (or book or idea) as a chore.

While it's not impossible for a student to be concerned about getting high marks and also to like what he or she is doing, the practical reality is that these two ways of thinking generally pull in opposite directions. Some research has explicitly demonstrated that a "grade orientation" and a "learning orientation" are inversely related (Beck, Rorrer-Woody, and Pierce, 1991; Milton, Pollio, and Eison, 1986). More strikingly, study after study has found that students—from elementary school to graduate school, and across cultures—demonstrate less interest in learning as a result of being graded (Benware and Deci, 1984;

From Alfie Kohn, "From Degrading to De-grading," *The High School Magazine*, vol. 6, no. 5 (March 1999). Copyright © 1999 by Alfie Kohn. Reprinted by permission of the author.

Butler, 1987; Butler and Nisan, 1986; Grolnick and Ryan, 1987; Harter and Guzman, 1986; Hughes, Sullivan, and Mosley, 1985; Kage, 1991; Salili et al., 1976). Thus, anyone who wants to see students get hooked on words and numbers and ideas already has reason to look for other ways of assessing and describing their achievement.

2. Grades tend to reduce students' preference for challenging tasks   Students of all ages who have been led to concentrate on getting a good grade are likely to pick the easiest possible assignment if given a choice (Harter, 1978; Harter and Guzman, 1986; Kage, 1991; Milton, Pollio, and Eison, 1986). The more pressure to get an A, the less inclination to truly challenge oneself. Thus, students who cut corners may not be lazy so much as rational; they are adapting to an environment where good grades, not intellectual exploration, are what count. They might well say to us, "Hey, you told me the point here is to bring up my GPA, to get on the honor roll. Well, I'm not stupid: the easier the assignment, the more likely that I can give you what you want. So don't blame me when I try to find the easiest thing to do and end up not learning anything."

3. Grades tend to reduce the quality of students' thinking   Given that students may lose interest in what they're learning as a result of grades, it makes sense that they're also apt to think less deeply. One series of studies, for example, found that students given numerical grades were significantly less creative than those who received qualitative feedback but no grades. The more the task required creative thinking, in fact, the worse the performance of students who knew they were going to be graded. Providing students with comments in addition to a grade didn't help: The highest achievement occurred only when comments were given *instead of* numerical scores (Butler, 1987; Butler, 1988; Butler and Nisan, 1986).

 In another experiment, students told they would be graded on how well they learned a social studies lesson had more trouble understanding the main point of the text than did students who were told that no grades would be involved. Even on a measure of rote recall, the graded group remembered fewer facts a week later (Grolnick and Ryan, 1987). A brand new study discovered that students who tended to think about current events in terms of what they'd need to know for a grade were less knowledgeable than their peers, even after taking other variables into account (Anderman and Johnston, 1998).

More Reasons to Just Say No to Grades

The preceding three results should be enough to cause any conscientious educator to rethink the practice of giving students grades. But there's more.

Grades aren't valid, reliable, or objective.   A "B" in English says nothing about what a student can do, what she understands, where she needs help. Moreover, the basis for that grade is as subjective as the result is uninformative. A teacher can meticulously record scores for one test or assignment after another, eventually calculating averages down to a hundredth of a percentage point, but that doesn't change the arbitrariness of each of these individual marks. Even the score on a math test is largely a reflection of how the test was written: what skills the teacher decided to assess, what kinds of questions happened to be left out, and how many points each section was "worth."

Moreover, research has long been available to confirm what all of us know: any given assignment may well be given two different grades by two equally qualified teachers. It may even be given two different grades by a single teacher who reads it at two different times (for example, see some of the early research reviewed in Kirschenbaum, Simon, and Napier, 1971). In short, what grades offer is spurious precision—a subjective rating masquerading as an objective evaluation.

Grades distort the curriculum. A school's use of letter or number grades may encourage what I like to call a "bunch o' facts" approach to instruction because that sort of learning is easier to score. The tail of assessment thus comes to wag the educational dog.

Grades waste a lot of time that could be spent on learning. Add up all the hours that teachers spend fussing with their gradebooks. Then factor in the (mostly unpleasant) conversations they have with students and their parents about grades. It's tempting to just roll our eyes when confronted with whining or wheedling, but the real problem rests with the practice of grading itself.

Grades encourage cheating. Again, we can continue to blame and punish all the students who cheat—or we can look for the structural reasons this keeps happening. Researchers have found that the more students are led to focus on getting good grades, the more likely they are to cheat, even if they themselves regard cheating as wrong (Anderman, Griesinger, and Westerfield, 1998; Milton, Pollio, and Elson, 1986).

Grades spoil teachers' relationships with students. Consider this lament, which could have been offered by a teacher in your district:

> I'm getting tired of running a classroom in which everything we do revolves around grades. I'm tired of being suspicious when students give me compliments, wondering whether or not they are just trying to raise their grade. I'm tired of spending so much time and energy grading your papers, when there are probably a dozen more productive and enjoyable ways for all of us to handle the evaluation of papers. I'm tired of hearing you ask me, "Does this count?" And, heaven knows, I'm certainly tired of all those little arguments and disagreements we get into concerning marks which take so much fun out of the teaching and the learning.... (Kirschenbaum, Simon, and Napier, 1971, p. 115).

Grades spoil students' relationships with each other. The quality of students' thinking has been shown to depend partly on the extent to which they are permitted to learn cooperatively (Johnson and Johnson, 1989; Kohn, 1992). Thus, the ill feelings, suspicion, and resentment generated by grades aren't just disagreeable in their own right; they interfere with learning.

The most destructive form of grading by far is that which is done "on a curve," such that the number of top grades is artificially limited: No matter how well all the students do, not all of them can get an A. Apart from the intrinsic unfairness of this arrangement, its practical effect is to teach students that others are potential obstacles to their own success. The kind of collaboration that can help all students to learn more effectively doesn't stand a chance in such an environment.

Sadly, even teachers who don't explicitly grade on a curve may assume, perhaps unconsciously, that the final grades "ought to" come out looking more or less this way: a few very good grades, a few very bad grades, and the majority somewhere in the middle. But as one group of researchers pointed out, "It is not a symbol of rigor to have grades fall into a 'normal' distribution; rather, it is a symbol of failure—failure to teach well, failure to test well, and failure to have any influence at all on the intellectual lives of students" (Milton, Pollio, and Elson, 1986, p. 225).

The competition that turns schooling into a quest for triumph and ruptures relationships among students doesn't just happen within classrooms, of course. The same effect is witnessed schoolwide when kids are not just rated but ranked, sending the message that the point isn't to learn, or even to perform well, but to defeat others. Some students might be motivated to improve their class rank, but that is completely different from being motivated to understand ideas. (Wise educators realize that it doesn't matter how motivated students are; what matters is how students are motivated. It is the type of motivation that counts, not the amount.)

Grade Inflation ... and Other Distractions

Most of us are directly acquainted with at least some of these disturbing consequences of grades, yet we continue to reduce students to letters or numbers on a regular basis. Perhaps we've become inured to these effects and take them for granted. This is the way it's always been, we assume, and the way it has to be. It's rather like people who have spent all their lives in a terribly polluted city and have come to assume that this is just the way air looks—and that it's natural to be coughing all the time.

Oddly, when educators are shown that it doesn't have to be this way, some react with suspicion instead of relief. They want to know why you're making trouble, or they assert that you're exaggerating the negative effects of grades (it's really not so bad—cough, cough), or they dismiss proven alternatives to grading on the grounds that our school could never do what other schools have done.

The practical difficulties of abolishing letter grades are real. But the key question is whether those difficulties are seen as problems to be solved or as excuses for perpetuating the status quo. The logical response to the arguments and data summarized here is to say: "Good heavens! If even half of this is true, then it's imperative we do whatever we can, as soon as we can, to phase out traditional grading." Yet, many people begin and end with the problems of implementation, responding to all this evidence by saying, in effect, "Yeah, yeah, yeah, but we'll never get rid of grades because...."

It is also striking how many educators never get beyond relatively insignificant questions, such as how many tests to give, or how often to send home grade reports, or what grade should be given for a specified level of achievement (e.g., what constitutes "B" work), or what number corresponds to what letter. Some even reserve their outrage for the possibility that too many students are ending up with good grades, a reaction that suggests stinginess with A's is being confused with intellectual rigor. The evidence indicates that the real problem isn't grade inflation, it's grades. The proper occasion for outrage is not that too many students are getting A's, but that too many students have accepted that getting A's is the point of going to school.

Common Objections

Let's consider the most frequently heard responses to the above arguments—which is to say, the most common objections to getting rid of grades.

First, it is said that students expect to receive grades and even seem addicted to them. This is often true; personally, I've taught high school students who reacted to the absence of grades with what I can only describe as existential vertigo. (*Who am I if not a B+?*) But as more elementary and even some middle schools move to replace grades with more informative (and less destructive) systems of assessment, the damage doesn't begin until students get to high school. Moreover, elementary and middle schools that *haven't* changed their practices often cite the local high school as the reason they must get students used to getting grades regardless of their damaging effects—just as high schools point the finger at colleges.

Even when students arrive in high school already accustomed to grades, already primed to ask teachers, "Do we have to know this?" or "What do I have to do to get an A?", this is a sign that something is very wrong. It's more an indictment of what has happened to them in the past than an argument to keep doing it in the future.

Perhaps because of this training, grades can succeed in getting students to show up on time, hand in their work, and otherwise do what they're told. Many teachers are loath to give up what is essentially an instrument of control. But even to the extent this instrument works (which is not always), we are obliged to reflect on whether mindless compliance is really our goal. The teacher who exclaims, "These kids would blow off my course in a minute if they weren't getting a grade for it!" may be issuing a powerful indictment of his or her course. Who would be more reluctant to give up grades than a teacher who spends the period slapping transparencies on the overhead projector and lecturing endlessly at students about Romantic poets or genetic codes? Without bribes (A's) and threats (F's), students would have no reason to do such assignments. To maintain that this proves something is wrong with the kids—or that grades are simply "necessary"—suggests a willful refusal to examine one's classroom practices and assumptions about teaching and learning.

MUST CONCERNS ABOUT COLLEGE DERAIL
HIGH SCHOOL LEARNING?

Here is the good news: College admissions is not as rigid and reactionary as many people think. Here is the better news: Even when that process doesn't seem to have its priorities straight, high schools don't have to be dragged down to that level.

Sometimes it is assumed that admissions officers at the best universities are 80-year-old fuddy-duddies peering over their spectacles and muttering about "highly irregular" applications. In truth, the people charged with making these decisions are often just a few years out of college themselves and, after making their way through a pile of interchangeable applications from 3.8-GPA, student-council-vice-president, musically-accomplished hopefuls from high-powered traditional suburban high schools, they are desperate for something unconventional. Given that the most selective colleges have been known to accept home-schooled children who have never set foot in a classroom, secondary schools have more latitude than they sometimes assume. It is not widely known, for example, that at least 280 colleges and universities don't require applicants to take either the SAT or the ACT ("ACT/SAT Optional," 1997).

Admittedly, large state universities are more resistant to unconventional applications than are small private colleges simply because of economics: it takes more time, and therefore more money, for admissions officers to read meaningful application materials than it does for them to glance at a GPA or an SAT score and plug it into a formula. But I have heard of high schools approaching the admissions directors of nearby universities and saying, in effect, "We'd like to improve our school by getting rid of grades. Here's why. Will you work with us to make sure our seniors aren't penalized?" This strategy may well be successful for the simple reason that not many high schools are requesting this at present and the added inconvenience for admissions offices is likely to be negligible. Of course, if more and more high schools abandon traditional grades, then the universities will have no choice but to adapt. This is a change that high schools will have to initiate rather than waiting for colleges to signal their readiness.

At the moment, plenty of admissions officers enjoy the convenience of class ranking, apparently because they have confused being better than one's peers with being good at something; they're looking for winners rather than learners. But relatively few colleges actually insist on this practice. When a 1993 NASSP survey asked 1,100 admissions officers what would happen if a high school stopped computing class rank, only 0.5 percent said the school's applicants would not be considered for admission, 4.5 percent said it would be a "great handicap," and 14.4 percent said it would be a "handicap" (Levy and Riordan, 1994). In other words, it appears that the absence of class ranks would not interfere at all with students' prospects for admission to four out of five colleges.

Even more impressive, some high schools not only refuse to rank their students but refuse to give any sort of letter or number grades. Courses are all taken pass/fail, sometimes with narrative assessments of the students' performance that become part of a college application. I have spoken to representatives of each of the five schools listed below, and all assure me that, year after year, their graduates are accepted into large state universities and small, highly selective colleges. *Even the complete absence of high school grades is not a barrier to college admission,* so we don't have that excuse for continuing to subject students to the harm done by traditional grading.

Any school considering the abolition of grades might want to submit a letter with each graduating student's transcript that explains why the school has chosen this course. In the meantime, feel free to contact any of these successful grade-free schools:

Metropolitan Learning Center
2033 NW Glisan
Portland, OR 97209
503/916-5737
www.pps.k12.or.us/schools/
profiles/?location_id=154
Contact: Sue Brent

Waring School
35 Standley St.
Beverly, MA 01915
978/927-8793
Contact: Peter Smick

Carolina Friends School
4809 Friends School Rd.
Durham, NC 27705
919/383-6602
Contact: Rocco Trisolini

Saint Ann's School
129 Pierrepont St.
Brooklyn Heights, NY 11201
718/522-1660
http://www.saintanns.k12.ny.us
Contact: Stanley Bosworth

Poughkeepsie Day School
39 New Hackensack Rd.
Poughkeepsie, NY 12603
914/462-7600
Contact: Tony Buccelli

"If I can't give a child a better reason for studying than a grade on a report card, I ought to lock my desk and go home and stay there." So wrote Dorothy De Zouche, a Missouri teacher, in an article published in February ... of 1945. But teachers who can give a child a better reason for studying don't need grades. Research substantiates this: When the curriculum is engaging—for example, when it involves hands-on, interactive learning activities—students who aren't graded at all perform just as well as those who are graded (Moeller and Reschke, 1993).

Another objection: it is sometimes argued that students must be given grades because colleges demand them. One might reply that "high schools have no responsibility to serve colleges by performing the sorting function for them" —particularly if that process undermines learning (Krumboltz and Yeh, 1996, p. 325). But in any case the premise of this argument is erroneous: Traditional grades are not mandatory for admission to colleges and universities. *(See box.)*

Making Change

A friend of mine likes to say that people don't resist change—they resist being changed. Even terrific ideas (like moving a school from a grade orientation to a learning orientation) are guaranteed to self-destruct if they are simply forced down people's throats. The first step for an administrator, therefore, is to open up a conversation—to spend perhaps a full year just encouraging people to think and talk about the effects of (and alternatives to) traditional grades. This can happen in individual classes, as teachers facilitate discussions about how students regard grades, as well as in evening meetings with parents, or on a website —all with the help of relevant books, articles, speakers, videos, and visits to neighboring schools that are farther along in this journey.

The actual process of "de-grading" can be done in stages. For example, a high school might start by freeing ninth grade classes from grades before doing the same for upperclassmen. (Even a school that never gets beyond the first stage will have done a considerable service, giving students one full year where they can think about what they're learning instead of their GPAs.)

Another route to gradual change is to begin by eliminating only the most pernicious practices, such as grading on a curve or ranking students. Although grades, per se, may continue for a while, at least the message will be sent from the beginning that all students can do well, and that the point is to succeed rather than to beat others.

Anyone who has heard the term "authentic assessment" knows that abolishing grades doesn't mean eliminating the process of gathering information about student performance—and communicating that information to students and parents. Rather, abolishing grades opens up possibilities that are far more meaningful and constructive. These include narratives (written comments), portfolios (carefully chosen collections of students' writings and projects that demonstrate their interests, achievement, and improvement over time), student-led parent-teacher conferences, exhibitions, and other opportunities for students to show what they can do.

Of course, it's harder for a teacher to do these kinds of assessments if he or she has 150 or more students and sees each of them for 45–55 minutes a day. But that's not an argument for continuing to use traditional grades; it's an argument for challenging these archaic remnants of a factory-oriented approach to instruction, structural aspects of high schools that are bad news for reasons that go well beyond the issue of assessment. It's an argument for looking into block scheduling, team teaching, interdisciplinary courses—and learning more about schools that have arranged things so each teacher can spend more time with fewer students (e.g., Meier, 1995).

Administrators should be prepared to respond to parental concerns, some of them completely reasonable, about the prospect of edging away from grades. "Don't you value excellence?" You bet—and here's the evidence that traditional grading *undermines* excellence. "Are you just trying to spare the self-esteem of students who do poorly?" We are concerned that grades may be making things worse for such students, yes, but the problem isn't just that some kids won't get A's and will have their feelings hurt. The real problem is that almost all kids (including yours) will come to focus on grades and, as a result, their learning will be hurt.

If parents worry that grades are the only window they have into the school, we need to assure them that alternative assessments provide a far better view.

But if parents don't seem to care about getting the most useful information or helping their children become more excited learners—if they demand grades for the purpose of documenting how much better their kids are than everyone else's—then we need to engage them in a discussion about whether this is a legitimate goal, and whether schools exist for the purpose of competitive credentialing or for the purpose of helping everyone to learn (Kohn, 1998; Labaree, 1997).

Above all, we need to make sure that objections and concerns about the details don't obscure the main message, which is the demonstrated harm of traditional grading on the quality of students' learning and their interest in exploring ideas.

High school administrators can do a world of good in their districts by actively supporting efforts to eliminate conventional grading in elementary and middle schools. Working with their colleagues in these schools can help pave the way for making such changes at the secondary school level.

In the Meantime

Finally, there is the question of what classroom teachers can do while grades continue to be required. The short answer is that they should do everything within their power to make grades as invisible as possible for as long as possible. Helping students forget about grades is the single best piece of advice for creating a learning-oriented classroom.

When I was teaching high school, I did a lot of things I now regret. But one policy that still seems sensible to me was saying to students on the first day of class that, while I was compelled to give them a grade at the end of the term, I could not in good conscience ever put a letter or number on anything they did during the term—and I would not do so. I would, however, write a comment—or, better, sit down and talk with them—as often as possible to give them feedback.

At this particular school I frequently faced students who had been prepared for admission to Harvard since their early childhood—a process I have come to call "Preparation H." I knew that my refusal to rate their learning might only cause some students to worry about their marks all the more, or to create suspense about what would appear on their final grade reports, which of course would defeat the whole purpose. So I said that anyone who absolutely had to know what grade a given paper would get could come see me and we would figure it out together. An amazing thing happened: as the days went by, fewer and fewer students felt the need to ask me about grades. They began to be more involved with what we were learning because I had taken responsibility as a teacher to stop pushing grades into their faces, so to speak, whenever they completed an assignment.

What I didn't do very well, however, was to get students involved in devising the criteria for excellence (what makes a math solution elegant, an experiment well-designed, an essay persuasive, a story compelling) as well as deciding how well their projects met those criteria. I'm afraid I unilaterally set the criteria and evaluated the students' efforts. But I have seen teachers who were more willing to give up control, more committed to helping students participate in assessment and turn that into part of the learning. Teachers who work with their students to design powerful alternatives to letter grades have a replacement ready to go when the school finally abandons traditional grading—and are able to minimize the harm of such grading in the meantime.

References

"ACT/SAT Optional Colleges List Soars to 280." *FairTest Examiner,* Summer 1997: 5. (Available at www.fairtest.org.)

Anderman, E. M., T. Griesinger, and G. Westerfield. "Motivation and Cheating During Early Adolescence." *Journal of Educational Psychology* 90 (1998): 84–93.

Anderman, E. M., and J. Johnston. "Television News in the Classroom: What Are Adolescents Learning?" *Journal of Adolescent Research* 13 (1998): 73–100.

Beck, H. P., S. Rorrer-Woody, and L. G. Pierce. "The Relations of Learning and Grade Orientations to Academic Performance." *Teaching of Psychology* 18 (1991): 35–37.

Benware, C. A., and E. L. Deci. "Quality of Learning With an Active Versus Passive Motivational Set." *American Educational Research Journal* 21 (1984): 755–65.

Butler, R. "Task-Involving and Ego-Involving Properties of Evaluation: Effects of Different Feedback Conditions on Motivational Perceptions, Interest, and Performance." *Journal of Educational Psychology* 79 (1987): 474–82.

Butler, R. "Enhancing and Undermining Intrinsic Motivation: The Effects of Task-Involving and Ego-Involving Evaluation on Interest and Performance." *British Journal of Educational Psychology* 58 (1988): 1–14.

Butler, R., and M. Nisan. "Effects of No Feedback, Task-Related Comments, and Grades on Intrinsic Motivation and Performance." *Journal of Educational Psychology* 78 (1986): 210–16.

De Zouche, D. " 'The Wound *Is* Mortal': Marks, Honors, Unsound Activities." *The Clearing House* 19 (1945): 339–44.

Grolnick, W. S., and R. M. Ryan. "Autonomy in Children's Learning: An Experimental and Individual Difference Investigation." *Journal of Personality and Social Psychology* 52 (1987): 890–98.

Harter, S. "Pleasure Derived from Challenge and the Effects of Receiving Grades on Children's Difficulty Level Choices." *Child Development* 49 (1978): 788–99.

Harter, S. and Guzman, M. E. *The Effect of Perceived Cognitive Competence and Anxiety on Children's Problem-Solving Performance, Difficulty Level Choices, and Preference for Challenge.* Unpublished manuscript, University of Denver. 1986.

Hughes, B., H. J. Sullivan, and M. L. Mosley. "External Evaluation, Task Difficulty, and Continuing Motivation." *Journal of Educational Research* 78 (1985): 210–15.

Johnson, D. W., and R. T. Johnson. *Cooperation and Competition: Theory and Research.* Edina, Minn.: Interaction Book Co., 1989.

Kage, M. "The Effects of Evaluation on Intrinsic Motivation." Paper presented at the meeting of the Japan Association of Educational Psychology, Joetsu, Japan, 1991.

Kirschenbaum, H., S. B. Simon, and R. W. Napier. *Wad-Ja-Get?: The Grading Game in American Education.* New York: Hart, 1971.

Kohn, A. *No Contest: The Case Against Competition.* Rev. ed. Boston: Houghton Mifflin, 1992.

Kohn, A. *Punished by Rewards: The Trouble with Gold Stars, Incentive Plans, A's, Praise, and Other Bribes.* Boston: Houghton Mifflin, 1993.

Kohn, A. "Only for *My* Kid: How Privileged Parents Undermine School Reform." *Phi Delta Kappan,* April 1998: 569–77.

Krumboltz, J. D., and C. J. Yeh. "Competitive Grading Sabotages Good Teaching." *Phi Delta Kappan,* December 1996: 324–26.

Labaree, D. F. *How to Succeed in School Without Really Learning: The Credentials Race in American Education.* New Haven, Conn.: Yale University Press, 1997.

Levy, J., and P. Riordan. *Rank-in-Class, Grade Point Average, and College Admission.* Reston, Va.: NASSP, 1994. (Available as ERIC Document 370988.)

Meier, D. *The Power of Their Ideas: Lessons for America from a Small School in Harlem.* Boston: Beacon, 1995.

Milton, O., H. R. Pollio, and J. A. Eison. *Making Sense of College Grades.* San Francisco: Jossey-Bass, 1986.

Moeller, A. J., and C. Reschke. "A Second Look at Grading and Classroom Performance: Report of a Research Study." *Modern Language Journal 77* (1993): 163-69.

Salili, F., M. L. Maehr, R. L. Sorensen, and L. J. Fyans, Jr. "A Further Consideration of the Effects of Evaluation on Motivation." *American Educational Research Journal 13* (1976): 85–102.

Does the Practice of Grading Students Serve Useful Purposes?

In many ways the contention and debate regarding grading revolves around the difference between assessment and evaluation. Neither Marzano nor Kohn nor the vast majority of researchers and teachers argue with the appropriateness and even the necessity of regularly assessing student progress. Marzano contends that "feedback" can be an important factor for the learner in terms of motivation, and it is also important to the teacher in terms of measuring whether or not certain instructional strategies are working.

What complicates the situation is when assessment data are used for evaluative purposes. Assessment is simply measurement, while evaluation involves making judgments about the value or worth of the measurement. For example, it is an assessment when measurement shows that someone has thrown a discus 15 feet. It only becomes evaluation when a judgment is rendered about the worthiness of the throw. Further complicating this issue is that the evaluation of the worthiness of the throw can focus on the fact that 15 feet is the thrower's personal best effort, or it can focus on a comparative judgment based on the records of other throwers.

Perhaps it is inevitable in America's competitive and capitalistic society that people are not generally satisfied with simple assessment or even with evidence of self-improvement. We usually want to know how our (or someone else's) achievement compares with that of others. Such is the case with grading practices. With some notable exceptions we generally will not settle for merely an exhibition or performance that shows what a given student can do, even if that performance is much better than the student has ever done before. We want to know how that performance compares with the performances of others and beyond that with preestablished standards or expectations.

Obviously in some endeavors it is altogether appropriate that we make evaluative judgments and ratings regarding the worthiness of comparative performances. We want and need to know the success rate of various surgeons on a given operation, the safety records of airline pilots, and the food critic's rating of chefs. And of course much of the popularity of spectator sports and sports heroes is centered around our desire to adjudge someone the "best" on the basis of competition. There is also some validity to the argument that in order to recognize and reward merit and achievement there must be competition, ratings, and grading.

It is somewhat ironic that as opposition to high-stakes standardized testing grows, the traditional A to F grading system may actually be strengthened.

For example, one of the oft-stated rationales against using the Scholastic Aptitude Test (SAT) for university admission purposes is that the best predictor of success in college is the high school grade point average, and thus the SAT is unnecessary.

Other works on this issue include J. D. Krumboltz and C. J. Yeh, "Competitive Grading Sabotages Good Teaching," *Phi Delta Kappan* (December 1996); two books by Kohn, *No Contest: The Case Against Competition* (Houghton Mifflin, 1992) and *Punished by Rewards: The Trouble With Gold Stars, Incentive Plans, A's, Praise and Other Bribes* (Houghton Mifflin, 1993); Linda Darling Hammond and Beverly Falk, "Using Standards and Assessments to Support Student Learning," *Phi Delta Kappan* (November 1997); J. Eric Bishop and Sharon Fransen, "Building Community: An Alternative Assessment," *Phi Delta Kappan* (September 1998); and Beverly Falk and Suzanna Ort, "Sitting Down to Score: Teacher Learning Through Assessment," *Phi Delta Kappan* (September 1998).

ISSUE 16

Can Technology Transform Education?

YES: Don Tapscott, from *Growing Up Digital: The Rise of the Net Generation* (McGraw-Hill, 1998)

NO: Todd Oppenheimer, from "The Computer Delusion," *The Atlantic Monthly* (July 1997)

ISSUE SUMMARY

YES: Author Don Tapscott posits that the "Net Generation" (N-Gen) requires and will demand an approach to teaching and learning built upon educational technology.

NO: Todd Oppenheimer, a freelance writer with a special interest in interactive media, presents a caveat with regard to the unexamined proliferation of electronic learning tools in America's classrooms.

James Burke and Robert Ornstein, in *The Axemaker's Gift* (Putnam, 1995), describe the historical development of technology (from the axe to the computer) and detail both the benefits and the downside that have accrued to humankind due to these "advancements." In describing the "double-edged" nature of technology, Burke and Ornstein suggest that technology has historically tended to concentrate power in the hands of those who master its use(s) but that modern computer technology has the potential to end this reductionism and help empower greater numbers of people.

Given the wide acceptance of the notion that we are in midst of the Information Age, it is understandable that schools are seen as being pivotal to whether or not our children will be beneficiaries or victims of this new age. The number of computers in U.S. schools has grown dramatically. In 1994 35 percent of schools and 3 percent of classrooms had Internet access; by 1999 those proportions were 95 percent and 63 percent, respectively. Former president Bill Clinton's goal of "a computer in every classroom" is rapidly being realized.

Given the momentum and pushing for increased use of computer technology in schools, there is considerable pressure on teachers and school administrators to increase such use. This pressure emanates from the belief that not only do all students need to be computer literate but that the application of technology can improve all areas of schooling and learning. In spite of what seems to be an inevitable movement toward increased use of computers in schools, there are those who urge a more cautious if not resistive stance.

Social critic and communications professor Neil Postman in a 1990 speech delivered to the German Informatics Society stated, "I believe that you will have to concede that what ails us, what causes us the most misery and pain ... has nothing to do with the sort of information made accessible by computers. The computer and its information cannot answer any of the fundamental questions we need to address to make our lives more meaningful and humane.... The computer is, in a sense a magnificent toy that distracts us from facing what we most needed to confront.... Does one blame the computer for this? Of course not. It is, after all, only a machine. But it is presented to us, with trumpets blaring ... as a technological messiah."

The selections that follow exemplify the widely divergent beliefs and values that accompany this controversy. Don Tapscott proposes that the new media enable—and the N-Gen needs for learning demand—a shift from broadcast learning to "interactive learning." This combination of a new generation and new digital tools will cause a rethinking of the nature of education in both content and delivery. Todd Oppenheimer cautions that there is no good evidence that most uses of computers significantly improve teaching and learning, yet school districts are cutting programs—music, art, physical education—that enrich children's lives to make room for this "dubious nostrum."

Don Tapscott

N-Gen Learning

Broadcast Learning

Historically, the field of education has been oriented toward models of learning which focus on instruction—what we can call *broadcast learning*. The term *teacher* implies approaches to learning where an expert who has information transmits or broadcasts it to students. Those students who are "tuned in" take the information they are "taught"—i.e., which is transmitted to them—into active working memory. The field of educational psychology is rich with research, theories, and lessons regarding what impedes such information from being received and stored for subsequent replay. It has long been thought that through repetition, rehearsal, and practice, facts and information can be stored in longer-term memory, which can be integrated to form larger knowledge structures. The product of this is certain outcomes and behaviors—which, in turn, can be measured during testing.

The lecture, textbook, homework assignment, and school are all analogies for the broadcast media—one-way, centralized, and with an emphasis on predefined structures that will work best for the mass audience.

This approach has been the foundation of authoritarian, top-down, teacher-centered approaches to education which go back centuries. At the extreme, reinforcement and punishment were said to enhance learning. I remember my father describing how he was hit with a ruler for giving the wrong answer to a question. More recently, a school of psychology called behaviorism, popular in the 1960s and 1970s (and still in vogue in some circles), emphasized the importance of reinforcement in learning. Positive reinforcement is said to result in certain outcomes. Similarly, negative reinforcement, or the lack of positive reinforcement, leads to the extinguishing of certain behaviors. So when a rat exhibits desired behaviors in a cage (called a Skinner box, after the founder of behaviorism B. F. Skinner), the animal is reinforced through receiving a food pellet. The rat has been taught the relationship between doing something and being reinforced. Behaviorism extrapolated from the experience with rats to humans and was an important influence in education for many years.

Today, teaching methods and even many computer-based instruction programs are largely based on this broadcast view of learning. The teacher is primarily a transmitter. Curricula are designed by experts who presumably know the best sequencing of material and how children can best learn math, acquire a new language, or understand Mesopotamia. Programs are not customized to each student, but rather designed to meet the needs of a grade—one-size-fits-all, like a broadcast.

Of course, many teachers have worked hard to be more than just transmitters of information, measures of retention, and judges of performance. Dating back to Sidney Poitier in *To Sir With Love,* Hollywood and the television networks have made a mini-industry of great teachers. Most of us can recall at least one teacher who inspired us to be our best; who jolted us into thinking differently; who enabled us to process and integrate information from different fields; who helped us acquire knowledge and values. I remember listening to my high-school music teacher take us through a vivid and passionate tale of Tchaikovsky's life. As a class, we imagined the anguish Tchaikovsky must have felt as we listened, enchanted, to the Symphony *Pathetique.* Not one of us stirred. We were enthralled and inspired to work hard on developing our musical abilities.

But, notwithstanding the noble and sometimes heroic efforts of teachers, working with large class sizes and limited resources, the delivery system of education is still very much designed around the broadcast model. This is especially true today, in a time of cutbacks in educational spending in many countries. When you have a class with 38 students and no technological tools for a different approach, broadcast not only makes sense, it is the only option.

The Crisis in Education

It has become cliché to say that the educational system in the United States and other developed countries is in crisis. True enough, some schools look more like war zones. Test results are not encouraging. Parents are not happy. There are cutbacks in funding in many advanced countries. And, overall, there is a feeling that, given all the improvements in technology and epistemology, we could be doing much better.

Further, the echo wave is crashing into a school system which is designed for fewer kids. United States school enrollments will continue to increase at least until the year 2006, with 54.6 million school-age children. The previous peak was set by the boomers in 1971, with 51.3 million attending American schools. And, unlike the previous boom in student population, this one is a "long, slow, rising wave and we see no immediate falloff," according to a U.S. Department of Education study entitled, *A Back to School Special Report: The Baby Boom Echo.* Between 1996 and 2006, public high school enrollment is expected to increase by 15 percent, the number of high school graduates will increase by 17 percent and college enrollment is projected to rise by 14 percent. The ethnic composition of the schools will continue to change as well, with Latino-Americans and Asian-Americans the fastest growing segments of the student population.

The implications of student growth are jarring. Assuming the current broadcast teaching model (as the Department of Education report does), 190,000 new teachers will be required. Add to this the 175,000 teachers who retire or change professions each year and need to be replaced. The report calculates that 6000 new schools will be needed, not including the replacement of older, badly out-of-date schools and facilities. There will be approximately $15 billion in additional annual operating expenditures. A myriad of concerned parents and well-intentioned educators are working to address the problem. There is growing appreciation that the old approach is ill-suited to the intellectual, social, motivational, and emotional needs of the new generation.

Six Truisms and Corresponding False Conclusions

In our research we have been impressed and sometimes amazed by how the digital media enable a new view of education and, more broadly, learning. Yet we also heard every conceivable argument against using the digital media to transform the model of learning. Many of these arguments start off with a true statement and then draw a conclusion which is unwarranted.

Truism 1: "The problems with the school system go far beyond the schools" True enough. By the time kids get to the schools, many have already been significantly damaged. The most critical period of brain development is the first three years of life. Because of the breakdown of the traditional family, many children are lacking good parental attention during this formative period. The number of single-parent families has grown from 10 percent in 1965 to 28 percent in 1996. Most children come from families where there is no stay-at-home parent. The percentage of families with both parents working has risen from 37 percent in 1975 to 62 percent in 1996. In most families, both parents must work to get by. This is a big change. Combine this with working single parents and we've got a whopping 64 percent of families where all parents are working. Overall, parents spend 40 percent less time with children than they did at the peak of boom families, and many of these hours are spent watching TV, where opportunities for meaningful interaction are reduced.

When children come to school hungry or from dysfunctional family situations, lacking motivation and seeing no hope to better their lot in life, then the schools will be troubled places. It is true that to really fix the schools we must fix much of what ails us as a society.

False conclusion: "We should not take dramatic steps to transform the schools." Of course the problem of the schools cannot be addressed in isolation, but this is not to say that we shouldn't take steps now to rethink the education system —both what is done at schools and how it is done. There are numerous examples of teachers, administrators, and parents who work together to create a school of the future. In so doing they change the context. A good example is the River Oaks School in Oakville, Ontario, which I described in *The Digital*

Economy. Most students have a desktop computer, used for interactive, self-paced learning. The curriculum has been changed significantly, as has the role of the teacher—all for the better according to everyone involved, including parents. The result was improved student learning and higher student motivation. The River Oaks project didn't solve the problems of the community, but it has helped change the community by improving community involvement in the welfare of children. It not only changed the children, but the attitudes of parents and local businesses, for the better.

The old saw "everything is connected to everything else" cuts both ways. Schools are a product of economic, social, and values structures. But, conversely, change a school and you change the world.

Truism 2: "We need to understand the purpose of the schools—the ends of education, not just the means"   The most articulate spokesman of this view is social critic and technology skeptic Neil Postman. "Should we privatize our schools? Should we have national standards of assessment? How should we use computers? How shall we teach reading? And so on.... These questions evade the issue of what the schools are for. It is as if we are a nation of technicians, consumed by our expertise of how something should be done, afraid and incapable of thinking about why."

Postman argues that the schools should serve several purposes: to help students understand that we are all stewards of the Earth, relying on each other and protecting our small planet; to cure the itch for absolute knowledge and certainty; to encourage critical thinking and the ability to disagree and argue; to encourage diversity while understanding that this does not negate standards; and to develop and use language, which is the basis of making us human, and which enables us to transform the world and in doing so to transform ourselves ("when we form a sentence we are creating a world").

False conclusion: "We should table any discussion of means until we have agreement on the ends."   Let us accept Postman's aspirations for education. While Postman's discussion of the ends of education may be laudable, he misses an important point: the means have become the ends. The broadcast approach to learning (which Postman does not appear to support) is becoming antithetical to the ends he espouses. The schools are not producing the language-rich critics, arguers, collaborators, and stewards he seeks—in part because the broadcast model of learning is an obstacle to such development.

Conversely, in adopting the new interactive model of learning, N-Geners are already assimilating the learning goals Postman espouses. They aren't just discussing such goals—they're achieving them. They rely on each other for learning. They debate everything online. They are critics. They are tolerant of diversity in their collaborations. And they communicate by forming sentences—they are creating their worlds. Through a new communications medium, N-Geners are already becoming what Postman aspires for them. McLuhan's words are ringing true through the N-Generation: Their medium has become the message. It's not a case of ends before means. The means are beginning to create new learning results. Postman's hostility toward technology is misdirected as he tilts at the windmills of the broadcast media.

What about the critics who say that e-mail and chatting are not improving communication skills because the spelling, punctuation and style are not proper? My observations tell me the critics are wrong. Time spent using these services is time spent reading. Time spent thinking about your response is time spent analyzing. And time spent composing a response is time spent writing. Such intense communications activity can be either very immediate with tight time pressures, such as on a chat line, or reflective, such as on a bulletin board or e-mail. Writing is like a muscle; it requires exercise. These kids are developing a powerful muscle that will serve them well in future work environments.

Says Allison Ellis of FreeZone, "The more chances that kids have to read and write, the better." In fact, on FreeZone, if sentence structure, grammar, or spelling inhibits the child's ability to communicate effectively, the FreeZone moderator will correct them by saying, "Hey, I didn't understand your point because you didn't complete your sentence." Moreover, language is something which evolves. The N-Generation is using the characters of the ASCII alphanumeric keyboard to add rich nonverbal elements to written communications. Their creativity in doing so seems infinite.

Truism 3: "The solution to the problem of education is not technology"
It seems that in every discussion I've had recently about United States government's efforts to get computers into the schools, someone will say that computers aren't the answer. "It won't help to just throw computers at the wall, hoping something will stick." "I've seen lots of computers sitting unused in classrooms. I've even seen them sitting for months in their packing boxes." "Isn't technology a solution in search of a problem?" Or, as David Shenk, author of the book *Data Smog*, says, "Let's be very skeptical when people like the President and Vice President say [computers and the Internet] are going to revolutionize education. I think that is absolute hogwash."

Theodore Roszak, who wrote *The Cult of Information: A Neo-Luddite Treatise on High Tech, Artificial Intelligence and the True Art of Thinking*, said in a recent article, "People who recommend more computers for the schools are like doctors who prescribe more medicine. What medicine? How much medicine? For what reason? The same questions apply to computers."

Of course, unloading millions of computers into school warehouses and classrooms will not cure what ails contemporary education, any more than dumping a random selection of books into schools 200 years ago or prescribing random medicine to a patient would. To rephrase an election slogan, "It's the curriculum, stupid."

False conclusion: "We should abandon or delay efforts to infuse schools with the digital media." Rather than "People who recommend more computers for the schools are like doctors who prescribe more medicine," it is more true that "People who oppose computers in the schools are like doctors who oppose the use of modern medicine." Unlike medicine, the use of the new media to transform education will not be determined or sanctioned in some educational equivalent of the FDA [Food and Drug Administration]. Rather, it will grow from the rich experience of students working with teachers, researchers, business people, and educators to forge, through actual experience, a new model of learning.

This is not to say that children should be guinea pigs. There is plenty of experience already to show that the new media can be a stimulus for change.

The digital media are a necessary but insufficient condition for reinvention of education. Computers and the Net are simply preconditions for moving to a new paradigm in learning. However, every project we investigated that introduced the Net and computer technology to students has been a stimulus for more far-reaching change. Such initiatives raise issues for teachers, parents, educators, and students to address. They encourage curiosity and experimentation. They enable the natural leaders for change to come forward and debunk old stereotypes. They pose questions raised by Roszak—but in real life, not academic debate. What is this new technology about? How can we use it? How might this affect the way we teach and the role of the teacher?

Most importantly, such initiatives provide the children themselves with the tools they need to learn and to catalyze the rethinking of education. Changes to a century-old system will not come about because of some top-down decree from educators. The schools need to become learning organizations themselves. Teachers, administrators, and students need to learn as organizations together. And I have become convinced that the most revolutionary force for change is the students themselves. Give children the tools they need and they will be the single most important source of guidance on how to make the schools relevant and effective.

Truism 4: "It's dumb to teach children how to use computers instead of teaching them math, science, reading, and writing" This statement was made to me by Michael Bloomberg in the previously mentioned debate at a recent conference of business leaders in Switzerland. Or, as Julianne Malveaux writes in a *USA Today* column entitled "Make Basics a Higher Priority than Internet," "Computer literacy is no substitute for basic literacy." We can certainly all agree that kids need to learn the basics, and if we must compare, then this is more important than learning the exec function in Windows 95. Furthermore, numerous studies have shown that teachers who approve of computers in the classroom seek, as a primary goal, to "teach computer literacy."

False conclusion: "We should abandon or delay efforts to get the digital media into the schools." Bloomberg and those like him have it wrong on three counts. First, use of technology does not inhibit learning about math, science, reading, and writing. The opposite is true. The research to date shows that when appropriately integrated into a curriculum, the new media improve student performance, not to mention motivation, collaboration, and communication skills. Even when it is not part of the curriculum, use of the new technology helps in learning basic abilities. Chat groups involve reading and writing. Compare this to television.

Second, fluency with the new media is required for productive life in the new economy and effective citizenship in the digital age. It is important that children know not only how to keyboard, search the Net, participate in a virtual community, or use important software applications (all learned effortlessly by children), but that they understand the underlying assumptions behind technology. ... [C]hildren don't need to become geeks, but they do need to know about software and how it works and to feel empowered to change their online world and the rules of the game.

Third, children acquire fluency with the media not just by studying these media but by using them to do other things. Comments like Bloomberg's are ironic in that they paint a picture of a teacher explaining to students how to use computers. The opposite is more likely to be true in many classrooms because of the generation gap. The students teach themselves. While they're at it they can probably teach their teachers as well. This has been the experience to date.

These new-breed teachers know that they are not just teaching children about computers but rather using computers to help children learn. "I teach cyber arts, but I don't teach computer courses. I teach extended media. I teach video production. I teach imaging. I teach photography and a lot of it uses computers.... But it is not a computer class," says Kathy Yamashita, cyber arts teacher, Northview Heights Secondary School, North York, Ontario. While Yamashita's comment is insightful, in reality students are also acquiring computer fluency. Says Alliance for Converging Technologies president David Ticoll, commenting on this case, "If she's teaching techniques for image enhancement on a computer, she's teaching a computer skill, just like teaching photography involves camera and lighting skills." Learning about anything in the digital age should enhance fluency with the digital media as a by-product—just like learning in the age of the printing press also enhanced reading and writing skills.

Truism 5: "Learning is social"   Most understanding is socially constructed. Through conversation and dialogue, children come to their own understanding of an experience. This is true for adults as well. Learning organization theorist Peter Senge argues forcefully that learning within organizations tends to occur in teams.

False conclusion: "Computers are used individually, therefore they inhibit learning, which is done socially."   The computer has shifted from a tool to automate and manage information to something broader—a communications tool. Anyone with experience using the Net, even in its current, relatively primitive form, can grasp this concept. E-mail, chat sessions, bulletin-board-type forums, video conferencing, and shared digital workspaces are all communications tools. This is true for Web sites, which increasingly involve interaction with people. For example, children's personal Web sites are used as a way to share information and opinions with others—interactively.

Furthermore, much Net-based activity in homes and schools involves face-to-face interaction. When children cluster around computers at River Oaks School you can hear their excitement—literally—by the buzz and laughter in the room. The same was true when my son and I searched the Net for his project on fish. True, to get the photos he needed we had to look at a lot of snapshots taken of fish in personal aquariums around the world, not to mention the products of assorted trout-fishing expeditions. But the experience was a very social one.

Truism 6: "Teachers are skilled, motivated professionals dedicated to the advancement of their students" Both my parents were teachers. They cared deeply about their students. They took it personally when a student failed or could not learn. Society has made a huge investment in teachers—there are currently 3,092,000 teachers in the United States. Increasingly, teachers work under very difficult conditions. It would be wrong to place the blame for the crisis in education at the feet of teachers. Further, there are many examples of teachers who enthusiastically support the new view of learning and the role of the digital media.

False conclusion: "Teachers are not an obstacle." It shouldn't surprise us that many teachers resist change. When a shift like this occurs, leaders of the old are often the last to embrace the new. Old paradigms, if I may use that word, die hard. Teachers have been schooled in the broadcast mode of pedagogy. As evidence, a 1997 survey of 6000 United States teachers, computer coordinators, and school librarians found that 87 percent believe that Internet usage by students in grades 3 to 12 does not help improve classroom performance. This is an amazing number, perhaps explained by the sad reality that most of these teachers have not attempted to use the Internet to change the way learning is imparted.

"Everything they learn from day one reinforces their role as the sage on the stage," says Michael Dore, director of the Hacienda/La Puente Unified School District in Southern California. "So when they get computers in the classroom they use them for drill and kill—practice and testing. By training, teachers reject the discovery model of learning." Education and technology specialist Bob Beatty is involved in a project to get 40,000 students wired in the city of London. Referring to the role of teachers as maintaining discipline and order, he says. "It's strange, but there are never discipline problems when the kids are using their computers. The only problem is peeling them off the screen."

Teachers have legitimate concerns about their role as the learning model changes to interactive from broadcast. The irony here is that if they don't change and transform their classrooms and themselves to the new model, they face even greater threats to their job security. Society will find other ways to deliver learning and bypass them.

Todd Oppenheimer

 **NO**

The Computer Delusion

In 1922 Thomas Edison predicted that "the motion picture is destined to revolutionize our educational system and . . . in a few years it will supplant largely, if not entirely, the use of textbooks." Twenty-three years later, in 1945, William Levenson, the director of the Cleveland public schools' radio station, claimed that "the time may come when a portable radio receiver will be as common in the classroom as is the blackboard." Forty years after that the noted psychologist B. F. Skinner, referring to the first days of his "teaching machines," in the late 1950s and early 1960s, wrote, "I was soon saying that, with the help of teaching machines and programmed instruction, students could learn twice as much in the same time and with the same effort as in a standard classroom." Ten years after Skinner's recollections were published, President Bill Clinton campaigned for "a bridge to the twenty-first century . . . where computers are as much a part of the classroom as blackboards." . . .

If history really is repeating itself, the schools are in serious trouble. In *Teachers and Machines: The Classroom Use of Technology Since 1920* (1986), Larry Cuban, a professor of education at Stanford University and a former school superintendent, observed that as successive rounds of new technology failed their promoters' expectations, a pattern emerged. The cycle began with big promises backed by the technology developers' research. In the classroom, however, teachers never really embraced the new tools, and no significant academic improvement occurred. This provoked consistent responses: the problem was money, spokespeople argued, or teacher resistance, or the paralyzing school bureaucracy. Meanwhile, few people questioned the technology advocates' claims. As results continued to lag, the blame was finally laid on the machines. Soon schools were sold on the next generation of technology, and the lucrative cycle started all over again.

Today's technology evangels argue that we've learned our lesson from past mistakes. As in each previous round, they say that when our new hot technology —the computer—is compared with yesterday's, today's is better. "It can do the same things, plus," Richard Riley, the U.S. Secretary of Education, told me. . . .

How much better is it, really?

The promoters of computers in schools again offer prodigious research showing improved academic achievement after using their technology. The research has again come under occasional attack, but this time quite a number of teachers seem to be backing classroom technology. In a poll taken [in] early [1996] U.S. teachers ranked computer skills and media technology as more "essential" than the study of European history, biology, chemistry, and physics; than dealing with social problems such as drugs and family breakdown; than learning practical job skills; and than reading modern American writers such as Steinbeck and Hemingway or classic ones such as Plato and Shakespeare.

In keeping with these views New Jersey cut state aid to a number of school districts [in 1996] and then spent $10 million on classroom computers. In Union City, California, a single school district is spending $27 million to buy new gear for a mere eleven schools. The Kittridge Street Elementary School, in Los Angeles, killed its music program [in 1996] to hire a technology coordinator; in Mansfield, Massachusetts, administrators dropped proposed teaching positions in art, music, and physical education, and then spent $333,000 on computers; in one Virginia school the art room was turned into a computer laboratory. (Ironically, a half dozen preliminary studies recently suggested that music and art classes may build the physical size of a child's brain, and its powers for subjects such as language, math, science, and engineering—in one case far more than computer work did.) Meanwhile, months after a New Technology High School opened in Napa, California, where computers sit on every student's desk and all academic classes use computers, some students were complaining of headaches, sore eyes, and wrist pain.

Throughout the country, as spending on technology increases, school book purchases are stagnant. Shop classes, with their tradition of teaching children building skills with wood and metal, have been almost entirely replaced by new "technology education programs." In San Francisco only one public school still offers a full shop program—the lone vocational high school. "We get kids who don't know the difference between a screwdriver and a ball peen hammer," James Dahlman, the school's vocational-department chair, told me recently. "How are they going to make a career choice? Administrators are stuck in this mindset that all kids will go to a four-year college and become a doctor or a lawyer, and that's not true. I know some who went to college, graduated, and then had to go back to technical school to get a job." [In 1996] the school superintendent in Great Neck, Long Island, proposed replacing elementary school shop classes with computer classes and training the shop teachers as computer coaches. Rather than being greeted with enthusiasm, the proposal provoked a backlash.

Interestingly, shop classes and field trips are two programs that the National Information Infrastructure Advisory Council, the Clinton Administration's technology task force, suggest[ed] reducing in order to shift resources into computers. But are these results what technology promoters really intend? "You need to apply common sense," Esther Dyson, the president of EDventure Holdings and one of the task force's leading school advocates, told me recently. "Shop with a good teacher probably is worth more than computers with a lousy teacher. But if it's a poor program, this may provide a good excuse for cutting it. There will be a lot of trials and errors with this. And I don't know how to prevent those errors."

The issue, perhaps, is the magnitude of the errors. Alan Lesgold, a professor of psychology and the associate director of the Learning Research and Development Center at the University of Pittsburgh, calls the computer an "amplifier," because it encourages both enlightened study practices and thoughtless ones. There's a real risk, though, that the thoughtless practices will dominate, slowly dumbing down huge numbers of tomorrow's adults. As Sherry Turkle, a professor of the sociology of science at the Massachusetts Institute of Technology and a longtime observer of children's use of computers, told me, "The possibilities of using this thing poorly so outweigh the chance of using it well, it makes people like us, who are fundamentally optimistic about computers, very reticent."

Perhaps the best way to separate fact from fantasy is to take supporters' claims about computerized learning one by one and compare them with the evidence in the academic literature and in the everyday experiences I have observed or heard about in a variety of classrooms.

Five main arguments underlie the campaign to computerize our nation's schools.

- Computers improve both teaching practices and student achievement.
- Computer literacy should be taught as early as possible; otherwise students will be left behind.
- To make tomorrow's work force competitive in an increasingly high-tech world, learning computer skills must be a priority.
- Technology programs leverage support from the business community—badly needed today because schools are increasingly starved for funds.
- Work with computers—particularly using the Internet—brings students valuable connections with teachers, other schools and students, and a wide network of professionals around the globe. These connections spice the school day with a sense of real-world relevance, and broaden the educational community.

"The Filmstrips of the 1990s"

Clinton's vision of computerized classrooms arose partly out of the findings of the presidential task force—thirty-six leaders from industry, education, and several interest groups who have guided the Administration's push to get computers into the schools. The report of the task force, "Connecting K-12 Schools to the Information Superhighway" (produced by the consulting firm McKinsey & Co.), begins by citing numerous studies that have apparently proved that computers enhance student achievement significantly. One "meta-analysis" (a study that reviews other studies—in this case 130 of them) reported that computers had improved performance in "a wide range of subjects, including language arts, math, social studies and science." Another found improved organization and focus in students' writing. A third cited twice the normal gains in math skills. Several schools boasted of greatly improved attendance.

Unfortunately, many of these studies are more anecdotal than conclusive. Some, including a giant, oft-cited meta-analysis of 254 studies, lack the necessary scientific controls to make solid conclusions possible. The circumstances are artificial and not easily repeated, results aren't statistically reliable, or, most frequently, the studies did not control for other influences, such as differences between teaching methods. This last factor is critical, because computerized learning inevitably forces teachers to adjust their style—only sometimes for the better. Some studies were industry-funded, and thus tended to publicize mostly positive findings. "The research is set up in a way to find benefits that aren't really there," Edward Miller, a former editor of the *Harvard Education Letter,* says. "Most knowledgeable people agree that most of the research isn't valid. It's so flawed it shouldn't even be called research. Essentially, it's just worthless." Once the faulty studies are weeded out, Miller says, the ones that remain "are inconclusive"—that is, they show no significant change in either direction. Even Esther Dyson admits the studies are undependable. "I don't think those studies amount to much either way," she says. "In this area there is little proof."

... "Computers in classrooms are the filmstrips of the 1990s," Clifford Stoll, the author of *Silicon Snake Oil: Second Thoughts on the Information Highway* (1995), told *The New York Times* [in 1996], recalling his own school days in the 1960s. "We loved them because we didn't have to think for an hour, teachers loved them because they didn't have to teach, and parents loved them because it showed their schools were high-tech. But no learning happened." ...

During recent visits to some San Francisco-area schools I could see what it takes for students to use computers properly, and why most don't.

On a bluff south of downtown San Francisco, in the middle of one of the city's lower-income neighborhoods, Claudia Schaffner, a tenth-grader, tapped away at a multimedia machine in a computer lab at Thurgood Marshall Academic High School, one of half a dozen special technology schools in the city. Schaffner was using a physics program to simulate the trajectory of a marble on a small roller coaster. "It helps to visualize it first, like 'A is for Apple' with kindergartners," Schaffner told me, while mousing up and down the virtual roller coaster. "I can see how the numbers go into action." This was lunch hour, and the students' excitement about what they can do in this lab was palpable. Schaffner could barely tear herself away. "I need to go eat some food," she finally said, returning within minutes to eat a rice dish at the keyboard.

Schaffner's teacher is Dennis Frezzo, an electrical-engineering graduate from the University of California at Berkeley. Despite his considerable knowledge of computer programming, Frezzo tries to keep classwork focused on physical projects. For a mere $8,000, for example, several teachers put together a multifaceted robotics lab, consisting of an advanced Lego engineering kit and twenty-four old 386-generation computers. Frezzo's students used these materials to build a tiny electric car, whose motion was to be triggered by a light sensor. When the light sensor didn't work, the students figured out why. "That's a real problem—what you'd encounter in the real world," Frezzo told me. "I prefer they get stuck on small real-world problems instead of big fake problems"— like the simulated natural disasters that fill one popular educational game. "It's sort of the Zen approach to education," Frezzo said. "It's not the big problems. Isaac Newton already solved those. What come up in life are the little ones."

It's one thing to confront technology's complexity at a high school— especially one that's blessed with four different computer labs and some highly skilled teachers like Frezzo, who know enough, as he put it, "to keep computers in their place." It's quite another to grapple with a high-tech future in the lower grades, especially at everyday schools that lack special funding or technical support. As evidence, when *U.S. News & World Report* published a cover story [during the fall of 1996] on schools that make computers work, five of the six were high schools—among them Thurgood Marshall. Although the sixth was an elementary school, the featured program involved children with disabilities—the one group that does show consistent benefits from computerized instruction.

Artificial Experience

... What about hard sciences, which seem so well suited to computer study? Logo, the high-profile programming language refined by Seymour Papert and widely used in middle and high schools, fostered huge hopes of expanding children's cognitive skills. As students directed the computer to build things, such as geometric shapes, Papert believed, they would learn "procedural thinking," similar to the way a computer processes information. According to a number of studies, however, Logo has generally failed to deliver on its promises. Judah Schwartz, a professor of education at Harvard and a codirector of the school's Educational Technology Center, told me that a few newer applications, when used properly, can dramatically expand children's math and science thinking by giving them new tools to "make and explore conjectures." Still, Schwartz acknowledges that perhaps "ninety-nine percent" of the educational programs are "terrible, really terrible."

Even in success stories important caveats continually pop up. The best educational software is usually complex—most suited to older students and sophisticated teachers. In other cases the schools have been blessed with abundance—fancy equipment, generous financial support, or extra teachers—that is difficult if not impossible to duplicate in the average school. Even if it could be duplicated, the literature suggests, many teachers would still struggle with technology. Computers suffer frequent breakdowns; when they do work, their seductive images often distract students from the lessons at hand—which many teachers say makes it difficult to build meaningful rapport with their students....

"Hypertext Minds"

Today's parents, knowing firsthand how families were burned by television's false promises, may want some objective advice about the age at which their children should become computer literate. Although there are no real guidelines, computer boosters send continual messages that if children don't begin early, they'll be left behind. Linda Roberts [Clinton administration lead technology advisor in the Department of Education] thinks that there's no particular minimum age—and no maximum number of hours that children should spend at a terminal. Are there examples of excess? "I haven't seen it yet," Roberts told me with a laugh. In schools throughout the country administrators and teachers demonstrate the same excitement, boasting about the wondrous things that children of five or six can do on computers: drawing, typing, playing with elementary science simulations and other programs called "educational games."

The schools' enthusiasm for these activities is not universally shared by specialists in childhood development. The doubters' greatest concern is for the very young—preschool through third grade, when a child is most impressionable. Their apprehension involves two main issues.

First, they consider it important to give children a broad base—emotionally, intellectually, and in the five senses—before introducing something as technical and one-dimensional as a computer. Second, they believe that the human and physical world holds greater learning potential.

The importance of a broad base for a child may be most apparent when it's missing. In *Endangered Minds,* Jane Healy wrote of an English teacher who could readily tell which of her students' essays were conceived on a computer. "They don't link ideas," the teacher says. "They just write one thing, and then they write another one, and they don't seem to see or develop the relationships between them." The problem, Healy argued, is that the pizzazz of computerized schoolwork may hide these analytical gaps, which "won't become apparent until [the student] can't organize herself around a homework assignment or a job that requires initiative. More commonplace activities, such as figuring out how to nail two boards together, organizing a game . . . may actually form a better basis for real-world intelligence."

Others believe they have seen computer games expand children's imaginations. High-tech children "think differently from the rest of us," William D. Winn, the director of the Learning Center at the University of Washington's Human Interface Technology Laboratory, told *Business Week* in a . . . cover story on the benefits of computer games. "They develop hypertext minds. They leap around. It's as though their cognitive strategies were parallel, not sequential." Healy argues the opposite. She and other psychologists think that the computer screen flattens information into narrow, sequential data. This kind of material, they believe, exercises mostly one half of the brain—the left hemisphere, where primarily sequential thinking occurs. The "right brain" meanwhile gets short shrift—yet this is the hemisphere that works on different kinds of information simultaneously. It shapes our multifaceted impressions, and serves as the engine of creative analysis.

Opinions diverge in part because research on the brain is still so sketchy, and computers are so new, that the effect of computers on the brain remains a great mystery. "I don't think we know anything about it," Harry Chugani, a pediatric neurobiologist at Wayne State University, told me. This very ignorance makes skeptics wary. "Nobody knows how kids' internal wiring works," Clifford Stoll wrote in *Silicon Snake Oil,* "but anyone who's directed away from social interactions has a head start on turning out weird.... No computer can teach what a walk through a pine forest feels like. Sensation has no substitute."

This points to the conservative developmentalists' second concern: the danger that even if hours in front of the screen are limited, unabashed enthusiasm for the computer sends the wrong message: that the mediated world is more significant than the real one. "It's like TV commercials," Barbara Scales, the head teacher at the Child Study Center at the University of California at Berkeley, told me. "Kids get so hyped up, it can change their expectations about stimulation, versus what they generate themselves." In *Silicon Snake Oil*, Michael Fellows, a computer scientist at the University of Victoria, in British Columbia, was even blunter. "Most schools would probably be better off if they threw their computers into the Dumpster."

Faced with such sharply contrasting viewpoints, which are based on such uncertain ground, how is a responsible policymaker to proceed? "A prudent society controls its own infatuation with 'progress' when planning for its young," Healy argued in *Endangered Minds*.

> Unproven technologies ... may offer lively visions, but they can also be detrimental to the development of the young plastic brain. The cerebral cortex is a wondrously well-buffered mechanism that can withstand a good bit of well-intentioned bungling. Yet there is a point at which fundamental neural substrates for reasoning may be jeopardized for children who lack proper physical, intellectual, or emotional nurturance. Childhood—and the brain—have their own imperatives. In development, missed opportunities may be difficult to recapture.

The problem is that technology leaders rarely include these or other warnings in their recommendations....

The Schools That Business Built

Newspaper financial sections carry almost daily pronouncements from the computer industry and other businesses about their high-tech hopes for America's schoolchildren. Many of these are joined to philanthropic commitments to helping schools make curriculum changes. This sometimes gets businesspeople involved in schools, where they've begun to understand and work with the many daunting problems that are unrelated to technology. But if business gains too much influence over the curriculum, the schools can become a kind of corporate training center—largely at taxpayer expense.

For more than a decade scholars and government commissions ... criticized the increasing professionalization of the college years—frowning at the way traditional liberal arts are being edged out by hot topics of the moment or strictly business-oriented studies. The schools' real job, the technology critic Neil Postman argued in his book *The End of Education* (1995), is to focus on "how to make a life, which is quite different from how to make a living." Some see the arrival of boxes of computer hardware and software in the schools as taking the commercial trend one step further, down into high school and elementary grades. "Should you be choosing a career in kindergarten?" asks

Helen Sloss Luey, a social worker and a former president of San Francisco's Parent Teacher Association. "People need to be trained to learn and change, while education seems to be getting more specific."

Indeed it does. The New Technology High School in Napa (the school where a computer sits on every student's desk) was started by the school district and a consortium of more than forty businesses. "We want to be the school that business built," Robert Nolan, a founder of the school, told me [recently]. "We wanted to create an environment that mimicked what exists in the high-tech business world." Increasingly, Nolan explained, business leaders want to hire people specifically trained in the skill they need. One of Nolan's partners, Ted Fujimoto, of the Landmark Consulting Group, told me that instead of just asking the business community for financial support, the school will now undertake a trade: in return for donating funds, businesses can specify what kinds of employees they want—"a two-way street." Sometimes the traffic is a bit heavy in one direction. In January [1997], *The New York Times* published a lengthy education supplement describing numerous examples of how business is increasingly dominating school software and other curriculum materials, and not always toward purely educational goals....

The business community also offers tangible financial support, usually by donating equipment. Welcome as this is, it can foster a high-tech habit. Once a school's computer system is set up, the companies often drop their support. This saddles the school with heavy long-term responsibilities: maintenance of the computer network and the need for constant software upgrades and constant teacher training—the full burden of which can cost far more than the initial hardware and software combined....

School administrators may be outwardly excited about computerized instruction, but they're also shrewdly aware of these financial challenges. In March of [1996], for instance, when California launched its highly promoted "NetDay '96" (a campaign to wire 12,000 California schools to the Internet in one day), school participation was far below expectations, even in technology-conscious San Francisco. In the city papers school officials wondered how they were supposed to support an Internet program when they didn't even have the money to repair crumbling buildings, install electrical outlets, and hire the dozens of new teachers recently required so as to reduce class size.

One way around the donation maze is to simplify: use inexpensive, basic software and hardware, much of which is available through recycling programs. Such frugality can offer real value in the elementary grades, especially since basic word-processing tools are most helpful to children just learning to write. Yet schools, like the rest of us, can't resist the latest toys. "A lot of people will spend all their money on fancy new equipment that can do great things, and sometimes it just gets used for typing classes," Ray Porter, a computer resource teacher for the San Francisco schools, told me recently. "Parents, school boards, and the reporters want to see only razzle-dazzle state-of-the-art."

Internet Isolation

It is hard to visit a high-tech school without being led by a teacher into a room where students are communicating with people hundreds or thousands of miles away—over the Internet or sometimes through video-conferencing systems (two-way TV sets that broadcast live from each room). Video conferences, although fun, are an expensive way to create classroom thrills. But the Internet, when used carefully, offers exciting academic prospects—most dependably, once again, for older students. In one case schools in different states have tracked bird migrations and then posted their findings on the World Wide Web, using it as their own national notebook. In San Francisco eighth-grade economics students have E-mailed Chinese and Japanese businessmen to fulfill an assignment on what it would take to build an industrial plant overseas. Schools frequently use the Web to publish student writing. While thousands of self-published materials like these have turned the Web into a worldwide vanity press, the network sometimes gives young writers their first real audience.

The free nature of Internet information also means that students are confronted with chaos, and real dangers. "The Net's beauty is that it's uncontrolled," Stephen Kerr, a professor at the College of Education at the University of Washington and the editor of *Technology in the Future of Schooling* (1996), told me. "It's information by anyone, for anyone. There's racist stuff, bigoted, hate-group stuff, filled with paranoia; bomb recipes; how to engage in various kinds of crimes, electronic and otherwise; scams and swindles. It's all there. It's all available." Older students may be sophisticated enough to separate the Net's good food from its poisons, but even the savvy can be misled. On almost any subject the Net offers a plethora of seemingly sound "research." But under close inspection much of it proves to be ill informed, or just superficial. "That's the antithesis of what classroom kids should be exposed to," Kerr said.

This makes traditionalists emphasize the enduring value of printed books, vetted as most are by editing. In many schools, however, libraries are fairly limited. I now volunteer at a San Francisco high school where the library shelves are so bare that I can see how the Internet's ever-growing number of research documents, with all their shortcomings, can sometimes be a blessing.

Even computer enthusiasts give the Net tepid reviews. "Most of the content on the Net is total garbage," Esther Dyson acknowledges. "But if you find one good thing you can use it a million times." Kerr believes that Dyson is being unrealistic. "If you find a useful site one day, it may not be there the next day, or the information is different. Teachers are being asked to jump in and figure out if what they find on the Net is worthwhile. They don't have the skill or time to do that." Especially when students rely on the Internet's much-vaunted search software. Although these tools deliver hundreds or thousands of sources within seconds, students may not realize that search engines, and the Net itself, miss important information all the time.

"We need *less* surfing in the schools, not more," David Gelernter, a professor of computer science at Yale, wrote [in 1996] in *The Weekly Standard*. "Couldn't we teach them to use what they've got before favoring them with three orders of magnitude *more*?" In my conversations with Larry Cuban, of

Stanford, he argued, "Schooling is not about information. It's getting kids to think about information. It's about understanding and knowledge and wisdom." ...

Just a Glamorous Tool

It would be easy to characterize the battle over computers as merely another chapter in the world's oldest story: humanity's natural resistance to change. But that does an injustice to the forces at work in this transformation. This is not just the future versus the past, uncertainty versus nostalgia; it is about encouraging a fundamental shift in personal priorities—a minimizing of the real, physical world in favor of an unreal "virtual" world. It is about teaching youngsters that exploring what's on a two-dimensional screen is more important than playing with real objects, or sitting down to an attentive conversation with a friend, a parent, or a teacher. By extension, it means downplaying the importance of conversation, of careful listening, and of expressing oneself in person with acuity and individuality. In the process, it may also limit the development of children's imaginations.

Perhaps this is why Steven Jobs, one of the founders of Apple Computer and a man who claims to have "spearheaded giving away more computer equipment to schools than anybody else on the planet," has come to a grim conclusion: "What's wrong with education cannot be fixed with technology," he told *Wired* magazine [in 1996]. "No amount of technology will make a dent.... You're not going to solve the problems by putting all knowledge onto CD-ROMs. We can put a Web site in every school—none of this is bad. It's bad only if it lulls us into thinking we're doing something to solve the problem with education." Jane David, the consultant to Apple, concurs, with a commonly heard caveat. "There are real dangers," she told me, "in looking to technology to be the savior of education. But it won't survive without the technology."

Arguments like David's remind Clifford Stoll of yesteryear's promises about television. He wrote in *Silicon Snake Oil,*

> "Sesame Street" ... has been around for twenty years. Indeed, its idea of making learning relevant to all was as widely promoted in the seventies as the Internet is today.
>
> So where's that demographic wave of creative and brilliant students now entering college? Did kids really need to learn how to watch television? Did we inflate their expectations that learning would always be colorful and fun?

Computer enthusiasts insist that the computer's "interactivity" and multimedia features make this machine far superior to television. Nonetheless, Stoll wrote,

> I see a parallel between the goals of "Sesame Street" and those of children's computing. Both are pervasive, expensive and encourage children to sit still. Both display animated cartoons, gaudy numbers and weird, random noises.... Both give the sensation that by merely watching a screen, you can acquire information without work and without discipline.

As the technology critic Neil Postman put it to a Harvard electronic-media conference, "I thought that television would be the last great technology that people would go into with their eyes closed. Now you have the computer."

The solution is not to ban computers from classrooms altogether. But it may be to ban federal spending on what is fast becoming an overheated campaign. After all, the private sector, with its constant supply of used computers and the computer industry's vigorous competition for new customers, seems well equipped to handle the situation. In fact, if schools can impose some limits—on technology donors and on themselves—rather than indulging in a consumer frenzy, most will probably find themselves with more electronic gear than they need. That could free the billions that [might be devoted] to technology and make it available for impoverished fundamentals: teaching solid skills in reading, thinking, listening, and talking; organizing inventive field trips and other rich hands-on experiences; and, of course, building up the nation's core of knowledgeable, inspiring teachers. These notions are considerably less glamorous than computers are, but their worth is firmly proved through a long history.

[In the fall of 1996], after the school administrators in Mansfield, Massachusetts, had eliminated proposed art, music, and physical-education positions in favor of buying computers, Michael Bellino, an electrical engineer at Boston University's Center for Space Physics, appeared before the Massachusetts Board of Education to protest. "The purpose of the schools [is] to, as one teacher argues, 'Teach carpentry, not hammer,'" he testified. "We need to teach the whys and ways of the world. Tools come and tools go. Teaching our children tools limits their knowledge to these tools and hence limits their futures."

POSTSCRIPT

Can Technology Transform Education?

The phrase *boon or bane* is an apt description of the widely divergent views regarding the potential impact of technology, especially computer technology, on education. Schools, as is often their wont, are caught up in this controversy, and because this issue deals with our children, the controversy is often emotional and contentious.

Peter Stokes, in an article entitled "How E-Learning Will Transform Education," *Education Week* (September 13, 2000) states that because e-learning represents a powerful convergence of technological opportunity and economic necessity, its emergence presents a unique occasion to undertake a considered reevaluation of the role and function of education. Further, the work accomplished so far suggests that e-learning can play a substantive role in developing a new breed of literate citizens for the global economy of the twenty-first century.

The opposite perspective is captured by Lowell Monke in his article "The Web and the Plow," *Teacher Magazine* (October 1997). He asks, As the computer's role in education expands and lowers the floodgates to data, will the wisdom that grows out of making meaning from experience and ideas give way to the accumulation of information as the highest goal of our schools? Furthermore, will quiet contemplation give way to "hyper" net-surfing as the most esteemed intellectual process?

There is an abundance of literature and information on this issue. Seminal works on making meaning versus accumulating information include Marshall McLuhan's *Understanding Media: The Extensions of Man* (MIT Press, 1994), originally published in 1964, and, with Quentin Fiore, *The Medium Is the Message: An Inventory of Effects* (Wired Books, 1996), originally published in 1967. Neil Postman's cautionary works include *Amusing Ourselves to Death: Public Discourse in the Age of Show Business* (Viking, 1985) and *Technopoly: The Surrender of Culture to Technology* (Knopf, 1992). Books that speak to the promise and value of educational technology include *Technology and Education Reform,* by Barbara Means (Jossey-Bass, 1994); *Brave New Schools: Challenging Cultural Illiteracy Through Global Learning Networks,* by Jim Cummins and Dennis Sayers (St. Martin's Press, 1995); and *Electronic Collaborators,* by Curtis Bonk and Kira S. King (L. Erlbaum Associates, 1998).

A number of popular educational journals have devoted entire volumes to issues related to computers and technology: *Educational Leadership* (vol. 57, no. 2, 1999); *Phi Delta Kappan* (vol. 70, no. 1, 1988; vol. 73, no. 1, 1991; and vol. 77, no. 6, 1996); and the *NASSP Bulletin* (vol. 80, no. 582, 1996).

Should Service Learning Be a High School Graduation Requirement?

YES: Sheldon Berman, from "Integrating Community Service Learning With School Culture," *Service-Learning Network* (Spring 1999)

NO: Chester E. Finn, Jr. and Gregg Vanourek, from "Charity Begins at School," http://www.edexcellence.net/issuespl/subject/service/charity.html (April 9, 2001)

ISSUE SUMMARY

YES: Sheldon Berman, superintendent of schools in Hudson, Massachusetts, posits that both the academic content of the school curriculum and the ethics of young people can be positively impacted by student engagement in community service learning (CSL).

NO: Educational and social commentators Chester E. Finn, Jr. and Gregg Vanourek argue that "service learning," a euphemism for mandatory volunteerism, is not only an oxymoron but also fosters a left-of-center approach to political activism.

Community service learning (CSL) has been gaining acceptance as part of the K–12 curriculum since it was endorsed as part of school reform strategies proposed during the administrations of former presidents George Bush and Bill Clinton. A study conducted by the National Center of Educational Statistics indicates that 83 percent of high schools now offer some form of community service curriculum compared with 27 percent in 1984. And with this proliferation has come a growing number of school systems that now make some form of community service a requirement for graduation. Large systems such as Atlanta; Washington, D.C.; and Chicago, along with the entire state of Maryland, now have graduation requirements linked to community service. In many other school systems where community service has not been explicitly adopted as a graduation requirement, it is often found in the assignments of a required course, such as American government or English.

In part this rapid growth in community service curricula and requirements reflects the fact that historically there has been little argument with the notion that citizenship/civic education is a fundamental and legitimate purpose of public education. And a good case can be made that personal activities such as community service and volunteerism support the achievement of that purpose. Consistent with that theme, Sheldon Berman says, "We want students to be active citizens, concerned about the world around them and engaged in its improvement." He believes that CSL is central to this kind of systemic change in every area of the curriculum.

But agreement and consensus regarding the virtues of community service and volunteerism begin to erode when school encouragement of such personal activities evolves into school direction and requirements. Some educators are concerned that simple acts of decency or service to others, while commendable at a personal level, may cause students to confuse such acts with more substantive remedies for social problems, which can only be achieved through collective and systemic acts. For their part Chester E. Finn, Jr. and Gregg Vanourek state their belief that mandatory volunteerism runs the risk of degrading the virtue of service itself, while politicizing the school curriculum and recruiting impressionable youths for causes "dear to the hearts of graying activists."

Sheldon Berman  **YES**

Integrating Community Service Learning With School Culture

In an era of standards, accountability, and testing, community service learning (CSL) may seem distant from the mainstream of education reform. However, American education faces a challenge equal to that of student performance. Issues of civility, character, and respect have taken center stage in many schools and communities. Apathy about and disengagement from the social and political arena are at an all-time high among young people. In addition to raising performance standards that compare favorably with other countries, we need to develop in young people the concepts, skills, and sense of commitment that will revitalize our communities and our democracy.

Students benefit academically and socially from an education that integrates challenging academics with a commitment to creating a caring and civil community. This is not an either-or choice. By making community service learning an integral part of school culture, we can enrich our academic content and nurture an ethic of care and service in young people.

Community service learning tends to be relegated to second-class status in education reform because it is not implemented systemically. Too often, CSL is the private interest of one teacher or a group of teachers who create wonderful student projects that are disjointed from the larger improvement efforts pursued by their school or district. Alternatively, a school may become involved in a once-a-year fundraiser or activity in support of a good cause. These efforts are often fragmentary, and although they are beneficial in their own right, they reside on the fringe of education reform.

Community service learning is more than a singular event or activity. It is more than older children tutoring or assisting younger children and more than students raising money for a local food pantry or entertaining seniors during the holiday season. Although these are a part of the culture of service that must be present, true CSL means helping students make the connections between the subject material they are studying and issues in the larger world. It means tying CSL directly to the curriculum frameworks in each subject area. It means engaging students in action and reflection on important community, social, political, and environmental issues. It means thinking of students not as future citizens but as active members of their community. It means having students live the democratic process rather than simply teaching about democracy. Finally, it means providing CSL experiences marked by continuity, depth, and meaningfulness that are embedded in the curriculum and culture of the school.

We have learned a great deal from the systemic education reform efforts in mathematics and science. In these subject areas, reform has meant a deep rethinking of our goals, content, and instructional strategies in order to develop depth in understanding and reasoning. In mathematics, we now direct our attention to helping young people develop number sense and understand the power of mathematical thinking. In science, we direct our attention to active engagement in scientific investigations so that students come to understand natural systems and the methods of scientific problem solving.

Like reform in mathematics and science, reform in social studies and in education in general means rethinking our goals. No matter what discipline, the central motivation for reform is that we want to enable young people to be powerful thinkers and to think with clarity, precision, and depth. We want to help them develop the knowledge, skills, and habits of mind to recognize and discover patterns in the natural and social world, and make reasoned judgments based on evidence. We want students to be active citizens, concerned about the world around them and engaged in its improvement. CSL is central to this kind of systemic change in every area of the curriculum.

The overall goal of integrating CSL into the curriculum must be to foster the development of a socially conscious and socially responsible citizenry, i.e., to help students develop a personal investment in the well-being of others and of the planet. To accomplish this, we must begin in kindergarten and continue involving students in CSL activities throughout all the grades. But in order for these CSL activities to be viewed as integral to education reform, they must be consistent with the long-term improvement efforts pursued by the school or district and seen as an essential strategy for systemic change.

Community Service Learning and Education Reform

Community service learning can provide a key strategy in education reform and the long-term improvement efforts of a school district. Service learning provides teachers with an important instructional tool for enhancing student understanding. The movement toward inquiry-oriented, project-based, and thematically-organized forms of instruction that engage students in using real-world applications is central to education reform. By enhancing project-based, student-active instruction that focuses on real-world problems, CSL enables teachers to make the content more meaningful and understandable to students while enhancing their ownership for learning. In addition, CSL serves as an excellent vehicle for performance assessment by providing students with an opportunity to demonstrate their learning in the context of a situation in which their efforts have meaning and potency.

The research on service learning (Brandeis, 1997; Hedin & Conrad, 1990) shows that students engaged in service-learning activities strengthen their academic skills, civic attitudes, and skills for active citizenship. There is also growing evidence of the positive relationship between resiliency and service-learning in at- and high-risk students. Sagor (1997) points out that the key experiences that lead to resiliency include those practices that provide a sense of competence, belonging, usefulness, and potency. Service learning provides those conditions. In addition, the research in the development of social responsibility (Berman, 1997) shows that interest in civic participation and actual activism are stimulated by the unity of one's sense of self and one's morality, the sense of connectedness to others, and the sense of meaning that one derives from contributing to something larger than oneself. Prosocial action and service promote all these elements.

Additionally, Hodgkinson and Weitzman (1992) found that young people who participated in volunteer work in their childhood were more likely to continue volunteer activity into their teenage years. Therefore, we can expect that young people involved in service learning from an early age will do better academically and develop an ethic of care and service that fosters responsible civic participation.

Linking CSL to standards or curriculum frameworks in ways that clearly advance student performance is key to achieving these results. For example, the fourth-grade science program at Hudson [Massachusetts] Public Schools focuses on a variety of environmental, earth, and life science concepts. As part of our science program, we have initiated a year-long study of wetlands areas near each of our elementary schools. Students take water samples, collect data on plant variety, and collect "species ambassadors" who spend a short period of time in class and are then returned to their natural environment. This program has enriched student learning by focusing on significant content over an extended period using a hands-on, student-active methodology. Integrated into the unit is the study of the fragility of the wetlands and the need to preserve and promote the quality of the environment.

As part of their study, students clean up wetland areas, develop nature trails to educate others about the value of wetlands, and work to certify the vernal pools in their area. These CSL activities have deepened students' understanding of the material by connecting the content to a larger sense of meaning and purpose. These fourth graders, drawn from a wide range of socio-economic and cultural backgrounds, not only loved what they did and what they learned, but scored in the top 20 percent of all fourth graders on the new high-standards Massachusetts curriculum assessment test. Community service learning was not an add-on to the curriculum, but deeply integrated in and consistent with the rest of the content.

Similarly, in Hudson's ninth-grade program, English and Social Studies teachers collaborate on a year-long course with the essential question of "What is a just society and an individual's responsibility to creating a just society?" In this course, students study the Holocaust and other acts of genocide using the *Facing History and Ourselves* curriculum. Central to the course is the discussion of one's "universe of obligation," that is, the degree to which one is responsible for others. As part of expanding this universe of obligation, they are required to find a way to help create a more just society through a service-learning project.

Again, this CSL experience is integral to the course material and gives meaning to the subject matter.

However, systemic reform is more than just one or two powerful units of instruction integrated into the curriculum. If CSL is to be a systemic reform strategy, it must comprehensively and consistently cut across all curricular areas and grades.

Implementing Systemic Reform

Over the past five years, teachers and administrators in the Hudson Public Schools have worked to create a comprehensive K–12 CSL program. We are committed to integrating CSL into all classes and grade levels in a way that enhances the effectiveness of our instructional program. This is not an easy task. It involves ongoing professional development, collaborative planning, institutionalized teacher leadership, and strong administrative support.

The entire faculty has been engaged in professional development experiences in CSL. Several times a year we use our monthly curriculum coordination meetings to build consistency across schools and grade levels, ensure our CSL programs include adequate student preparation and reflection, and address key standards within the curriculum frameworks. To encourage the expansion of CSL initiatives, we used teacher mini-grants to support new initiatives as well as summer curriculum funds to support curriculum development.

In addition to providing professional development and curriculum planning time, teacher initiative and leadership has been essential to building the program. From the early stages, our CSL program was nurtured and promoted by a team of teachers representing each of our schools. This CSL Leadership Team planned the inservice programs, developed the mini-grant program, pursued and won grants to fund CSL in the district, and provided the planning and oversight for the effort. In addition, they developed an introductory CSL packet for each teacher that contains guidelines for CSL projects, a list of 100 good CSL ideas, and a resource list of organizations; created CSL reference and resource kits that have been placed in each school library; and served as consultants to teachers pursuing new initiatives.

Through these efforts, we have been able to develop a consistent and comprehensive program that enhances our instructional program. In 1997, we set a district goal of having the majority of students at all grade levels involved in some form of service learning. We have had remarkable success. Over 80 percent of our student body was involved in some form of service learning with 100 percent participation at the elementary level.

Administrative Commitment

This level of progress could not have been accomplished without administrative support. The superintendent of Hudson Public Schools has played a central role in the effort. He personally chaired the CSL Committee in the early years and continues to serve on the committee now that teachers have assumed the chairperson's role. He made it clear to principals that he expected all teachers to find a way to integrate CSL into their class. He supported the use of curriculum time for system-wide CSL planning. He also secured the support of Hudson's School Committee (school boards in Massachusetts are known as School Committees).

To highlight the importance of service learning in the district, the Hudson School Committee sets aside one of its meetings for a service-learning exposition in which all CSL projects are displayed and parents and the community are invited to learn about our students' efforts. In addition, the Superintendent has authorized special Superintendent's Award for Service for students at each school. These awards are presented to middle- and high-school recipients at the Hudson High School graduation to highlight their importance. This type of recognition demonstrates publicly the district's commitment to CSL.

The development of a systemic CSL initiative can take place in many ways in a district. However, systemic integration of CSL cannot take place without the support of principals, curriculum directors, and the superintendent. It is for this reason that the Education Commission of the States has formed a new organization to provide administrators with the tools and support necessary to take leadership in this area and to advocate for systemic integration of CSL nationally.

Supporting Administrators Nationally

The pressure to increase test scores and other indicators of student performance make it more challenging for administrators to support systemic community service-learning efforts. Although they may value CSL, they must have some degree of confidence that their investment will provide both social and academic results. In order to provide administrators with the tools and support they need to take a leadership role in developing systemic CSL programs, a group of chief state school officers and superintendents created an organization titled The Compact for Learning and Citizenship (CLC) under the auspices of the Education Commission of the States.

CLC provides a voice for educational leaders to advocate for quality service-learning opportunities that enhance academic achievement and civic engagement. The individual and collective efforts of CLC members are beginning to provide the leadership necessary to help schools make service-learning opportunities available to K–12 students and effectively use volunteers to help students improve their academic knowledge and skills.

CLC develops and disseminates resources on service learning, volunteers in schools, and policy; provides technical assistance to educational leaders and key decision-makers; organizes state, regional, and national conferences and meetings; and provides a collective public voice in support of service learning and the contribution volunteers make to improve student learning.

CLC is currently engaged in a national K–12 service-learning initiative supported by the W. K. Kellogg Foundation. CLC will work with five states and selected districts and schools to deepen service-learning practice and enhance policy development. The project will provide greater understanding of the conditions necessary for successful service-learning integration of the strategies necessary to overcome impediments.

As an organization of school leaders, CLC has the potential to widen the base of support for community service learning among school administrators and significantly advance the national effort to promote service learning.

Building Community Support for the Schools

Community service learning can form an important bridge between the community and the schools. We are living in a time when adults are suspicious of our youth and have very low opinions of them. Similarly, as declining civic participation among young adults shows, young people feel alienated and disaffected from our social and political community and often withdraw from participating in this arena. Service learning provides a bridge between young people and their community, giving young people a sense of hope, an experience of community, and a belief in their own personal effectiveness. In addition, service learning helps members of the community understand the contribution students can make to community improvement and brings them in direct contact with students and the instructional program of the school.

Community service learning can play a critical role in reclaiming our pride and confidence in public education. It can provide young people with experiences of community and connection that give them meaning and direction. It can enrich our academic program and improve student performance. Our challenge is to think of community service learning as we would any other systemic reform initiative and bring together the resources necessary to create broad-based implementation in our public schools.

References

Berman, S. (1997). *Children's Social Consciousness and the Development of Social Responsibility.* Albany, NY: SUNY Press.

Brandeis University (1997). Draft Interim Report: National Evaluation of Learn and Serve America School and Community-Based Programs. Center for Human Resources, Brandeis University and Abt Associates Inc. Waltham, MA.

Hedin, D. and Conrad, D. (1990). The impact of experiential education on youth development. In J. Kendall and Associates (eds.), *Combining Service and Learning: A Resource Book for Community and Public Service, Volume 1* (pp. 119–129). Raleigh, NC: National Society for Internships and Experiential Education.

Hodgkinson, V., and Weitzman, M. (1992). *Giving and Volunteering in the United States, 1992 Edition.* Washington, DC: The Independent Sector.

Sagor, R. (1996, September). Building resiliency in students. *Educational Leadership* 54(1), 38–43.

Chester E. Finn, Jr. and
Gregg Vanourek

 **NO**

Charity Begins at School

In 1989, with much fanfare, President [George] Bush convened the governors in Charlottesville, Virginia for a summit meeting on the nation's education woes. The primary accomplishment of their gathering was agreement on six broad goals to be achieved by century's end, goals that became the foundation of Mr. Bush's "America 2000" school reform strategy and, in altered form, of President Clinton's controversial "Goals 2000" program. Tucked away in the sweeping language of these goals were some highly specific objectives, one of which promised that by the year 2000 "[a]ll students will be involved in activities that promote and demonstrate good citizenship, community service, and personal responsibility." In plain words, America's children would all be expected to work as volunteers in programs organized by their schools.

Though this was the first time that mandatory volunteer work—an oxymoron known variously as "experiential education", "character education", "community service" and "service-learning"—received the federal government's stamp of approval, support for it had long been growing among professional educators. How better to tie students' textbook learning to the real world, imbue them with the habit of serving others, strengthen their character, and assist the needy, all in the name of sound civic education?

Such "volunteer" work is now under way in every state. According to a 1994 survey, 37 percent of U.S. high schools are either operating or planning programs in which students are "required to perform a specific number of hours of community service in order to graduate."

Service-learning, as educators usually term it, is located at the intersection of three familiar roads. The oldest of these, stretching to Aristotle and the Founders, is the belief that preparing the next generation for citizenship is a vital mission of any democratic society and that schools should habituate their students to what [Benjamin] Franklin termed the "publick religion." Today's enthusiasm for "character education" adds to this ancient rationale the mandate that schools should equip youngsters with ethical and behavioral norms that family and church no longer supply.

The second route to service-learning is the ineradicable conviction of "progressive" educators that the schools have an obligation to "build a new social order" (in the 1932 phrase of Columbia professor George S. Counts).

Educators of this persuasion have scant regard for "academic" knowledge and basic skills such as reading and writing. Knowing when the Civil War was fought, where the planet's major rivers flow, or how to distinguish Bach from Beowulf is derided by avant garde professionals as brain clutter. Far better, in their view, to arm the young with "critical thinking skills" and provide them with opportunities to right the wrongs perpetrated by adult society.

The third avenue is the American practice of channeling idealism into government-approved places via government-sponsored volunteer programs. Little is considered beyond the purview of bureaucratic management—not even the institutions of the "independent sector." If service is a good thing, so goes this reasoning, it will be even better if government mandates, shapes, and subsidizes it. Thus today's federal AmeriCorps and Learn & Serve America programs follow much the same route as yesterday's Civilian Conservation Corps, Peace Corps and VISTA.

Until the past few years, however, government-style voluntarism had little place in the schools and colleges. Picking up where Bush left off, Bill Clinton began his tenure in office by speaking eagerly of a Citizens Corps, with college-tuition aid offered to those who enlisted in it. A trial project was launched: a federally-funded "summer of service" that put some 1,500 young adults to work. By the autumn of 1993 the White House duly pronounced the trial a success, and by winter a new government body, the Corporation for National and Community Service (CNCS), was created to extend the "summer of service" into a year-round affair involving primary, secondary, and higher education. President Clinton declared that "[I]t is a very good thing for the states or local school districts to mandate community service for kids. . . . I think that every state should include community service as part of the curriculum."

The government structures that track progress toward the national education goals press in the same direction. In its 1994 report, for example, the National Education Goals Panel disclosed that 44 percent of high school seniors had engaged in community service within the two previous years. Were adults being surveyed, even a cheerleader for voluntarism might deem this a solid participation rate. But once one has embraced the objective that *all* students should be so engaged, less than half is a poor showing. Hence redoubled efforts to boost participation rates were demanded. This inevitably led back to Uncle Sam's doorstep. And he, of course, was glad to oblige. Thus a close reading of the 1200-page 1994 reauthorization of the Elementary and Secondary Education Act, by far the largest source of federal school aid, discloses almost twenty separate programs that encourage or underwrite "service-learning."

Many communities and states have responded. (Indeed, many of their programs antedate the federal initiatives, which may be said to have percolated from the bottom up.) In the District of Columbia, students are compelled to perform 100 hours of community service to graduate. Atlanta has required 75 hours of service for more than a decade. A number of smaller communities have similar requirements. At the state level, Maryland has been in the vanguard; it now boasts the only statewide service-learning requirement in the nation. In 1985, Maryland's board of education mandated that all school systems offer *elective* courses and programs involving volunteer work and community service. Seven years later, prodded by the energetic Kathleen Kennedy Townsend (now the state's lieutenant governor) but over objections from all but two of its 24 county school systems, Maryland made volunteer work a *requirement* for students in the ninth grade and above. Today, an elaborate service-learning infrastructure is in place across the state.

In some Maryland schools it is difficult to distinguish service-learning from ordinary classroom activity. Local school systems can opt to award service-learning credit for certain kinds of class projects. Thus, according to a recent state report, students in a seventh-grade language-arts class in Carroll County have met their volunteer-work requirement by "research[ing] disabilities and chronic illnesses . . . and then report[ing] their findings to their classmates." In Prince George's County, students in English classes have satisfied service-learning requirements by "penning letters to sick children or senior citizens in hospitals."

In other locations, the volunteering is somewhat more arduous and must be done outside of school. Baltimore students held "a party for the senior citizens at a nearby nursing home. They prepared the food, made the decorations, organized the entertainment and conducted the games." In Calvert County, students earned credit by recycling paper, cans, and plastic. In Frederick County, service-learning students "painted 'Chesapeake Bay Drainage' on all of the storm drains surrounding Thomas Johnson High School," with the goal of increasing "public awareness of local impact on the Bay." Other programs around the state involve fire prevention, food drives for the homeless, and cleaning up old cemeteries.

In some Maryland communities, students have fulfilled their service requirements by engaging in activities with a political tinge. In Cecil County, for example, they "wrote numerous letters to the county commissioners when the county abolished recycling due to expense. The students convincingly persuaded the commissioners to continue the project for the environmental benefits, despite the cost to the county."

In Harford County, students earned credit by "writing advocacy letters to affect legislation on a seat-belt law for school buses." And in Howard County, eighth graders at Patapsco Middle School kept a historic cemetery from being destroyed by developers.

As these examples suggest, much of what passes for service-learning has a bias toward political activism. That is because, in the eyes of its advocates, political activity is the most desirable form of service, and we should not be surprised that the causes they favor turn out to be the ones they are keenest for students to take up.

The Maryland Student Service Alliance (MSSA), long headed by Ms. Townsend, is the organization that administers the state's program of volunteer activities. One of the posters it uses to promote its own good work depicts a mountain showing various levels of community service. Halfway up the slope are activities like ladling hot food in a soup kitchen. At the pinnacle lies the loftiest form of voluntarism: lobbying.

MSSA also distributes a revealing service-learning handbook. It sets forth a "progression" of activities from "personal contact" (such as coaching children for the Special Olympics), to "indirect services" (such as recruiting others to a cause), and on to "advocacy," which in turn ranges from "writing a letter to the editor, to lobbying for a cause, to engaging in a political campaign." When a journalist asked MSSA's current director, Maggie O'Neill, whether her program crosses the line between community service and political action, she replied: "How would you differentiate between the two?"

The desire to entice children into political activism is also illustrated in prominent guidebooks for educators in the burgeoning learning-by-volunteering field. The premier such guide is *Civitas* (1991), a "framework for civic education" produced by the California-based Center for Civic Education. According to its authors, voluntarism will not fulfill its educational promise if students work in private agencies, because these provide "little sense of . . . public policy, or the power relationships of the modern service world." For *Civitas,* volunteer work should be seen less as an opportunity to expose students to homeless shelters and hospitals than as an opportunity to enhance "student competence to monitor and influence public policy in diverse arenas."

Another influential text in the service-learning field is Ralph Nader's *Civics for Democracy* (1992), published by The Center for Study of Responsive Law. Among its 75 "student-activity ideas" are: "investigate hospitals' Boards of Trustees to determine adequacy of consumer/patient/employee representation"; "survey companies for illegal tax avoidance"; "evaluate toxic and hazardous materials used in school chemistry labs"; and "test [repair shops'] honesty and competence. Follow up with programs to license repair shops or pressure businesses."

Civics for Democracy has been greeted enthusiastically in some quarters. Eleanor Smeal, former president of the National Organization for Women [NOW], hailed it as "a textbook that empowers students to become activists and leaders." The writer Studs Terkel predicted that its use will build "far more hip and active citizens." Jesse Jackson praised the book for recognizing that "people learn in different ways." Some, he continues, "think themselves into a way of acting while others act themselves into a way of thinking. *Civics for Democracy* allows students to do both."

Even if school-based volunteer programs steered completely clear of politics, which most of them do not, their compulsory nature would raise another set of concerns. Having an agency of government decide what does and does not qualify as volunteer work is a recipe for conflict; already dissenters have been punished, and court challenges are in the works.

A fourteen-year-old Boy Scout in Chapel Hill, North Carolina was told that his volunteer work for a local thrift shop and nature trail did not qualify for service-learning credit because the merit badges he earned meant he had received "compensation," and was therefore not a genuine volunteer. At Liberty High School in Bethlehem, Pennsylvania, another student—a Girl Scout volunteering on her own in a nursing home and for Meals on Wheels—forfeited her diploma when she refused to perform 60 hours of *school*-directed community service.

At Rye Neck High School in Mamaroneck, New York, a student who is a Jehovah's Witness had his proposed project rejected on the grounds that it violated the establishment clause of the First Amendment. Another Rye Neck student took the school to court, claiming that his paid work as a lifeguard helped his family cover its living expenses, and he could not spare the time to work as a volunteer. His parents added a philosophical objection of their own; as they explained to the Second Circuit Court of Appeals,

> We have taught our children through both word and example that to do good for others, without being asked or told and without compensation, is its own reward. . . . But never have we told our children that they must, or are obligated, to help others. That would defeat all we have tried to impart to them over the years about serving others and consequently destroy any moral value in serving others.

As such cases illustrate, mandatory voluntarism runs the risk of degrading the virtue of service itself, while politicizing the school curriculum and recruiting impressionable youths for causes dear to the hearts of graying activists. These issues would be vexing enough if individual schools and communities were working them out separately and families could choose the versions that suited them best, or simply opt out. But responsibility for decisions about student voluntarism is now increasingly being shifted to the state and federal levels.

In offices throughout Washington, people are now crafting rules for programs, conditions for grants, and measures by which progress toward national goals and objectives will be gauged. Sooner or later, every touchy issue will be resolved by a federal regulation. It will undoubtedly be said that these federal programs are voluntary and that states and communities are free to chart their own course, but three decades of experience reveals a familiar pattern: once a federal program addresses a topic, all that subsequently happens in that field is powerfully influenced by rules laid down in the nation's capital.

Schools and students will likely find themselves caught in a pincer, consisting on one side of federal financial support and on the other of national curriculum standards and annual reports of progress toward national education goals. It's a familiar tale, this creeping federalization of a fashionable and politically well-connected education issue. Anyone acquainted with the past quarter-century of federal bilingual or "special" education programs, for example, knows how powerful Uncle Sam's grip can be. Nobody associated with these activities makes a move today without consulting the federal regulations and figuring out how to get Washington to pay for it. It will be a special pity to see this fate befall service-learning, which does not merely affect the education of a defined sub-population, but potentially all 50 million schoolchildren in the United States.

The lessons our children are likely to learn from being compelled to "volunteer" are worth worrying about, but children are not the only cause for concern. Giving service to others, with no government coercion or expectation of compensation, is a deeply-rooted American tradition. By far the largest beneficiaries of philanthropic and volunteer impulses are churches, which absorb 62 percent of charitable contributions and the uncompensated services of

52 million people. It is unimaginable that this priority on church-based service can long co-exist with mandatory government-based service. Moreover, one wonders how much of the character-shaping benefits of voluntarism in church and community will survive the combination of compulsion and dilution that school-based service-learning entails. Are not young people likely to begin to view voluntarism through the same lens as a required lab report, a history paper, or laps around the track? Service projects required by schools as a condition of graduation run the risk of trivializing one of mankind's more admirable impulses while channeling volunteer energies into activities favored by government.

Most troubling of all, however, is that our schools, which have been botching their core mission of transmitting basic skills and essential knowledge, are now diverting time, energy, and money to non-academic matters. In Maryland, where service-learning has made so much headway, only 22 percent of fourth graders were "proficient" readers on the latest national assessment and, on the state's own tests, fewer than half of the eighth graders perform satisfactorily in math. Schools that can barely teach the fundamental skills and information needed by every citizen are now being co-opted by government and adult activists to shape students' attitudes and assumptions about citizenship itself. This may be a legitimate goal for individual schools and communities, but is arguably the last thing that should be tampered with by a government that is supposed to be the creation of its citizens, not the other way around.

POSTSCRIPT

Should Service Learning Be a High School Graduation Requirement?

The selections by Berman and Finn and Vanourek provide an excellent example of the volatility of certain educational issues when competing/conflicting philosophies and values collide. School curricula, which may have wide support when described in very general terms such as *character education* or *community service learning,* quickly become sources of controversy and contention when they are fleshed out through content and assignments. Whose views of "good character" will be used for selecting instructional materials? Whose notion of what qualifies—or does not qualify—as "community service" will prevail?

Such issues reveal two truths about educational decision making, one is that "the devil is indeed in the details," and the other is that there is no such thing as "the public" in terms of unanimity of opinion on controversial issues.

There are a number of difficult questions that need to be addressed with respect to community service learning, and there is no lack of individuals and groups willing to provide their own answers to those questions. Such questions include:

- Should paid work qualify as meeting community service requirements?
- Should involvement with "causes" and political activism be considered community service?
- Should school authorities encourage certain types of community service activities and discourage others? If so, then on what basis?
- Should involvement in religious activities such as proselytizing or recruiting qualify as meeting community service requirements?
- Does requiring involvement in community service devalue volunteerism? Does it violate constitutional issues?
- Should community service be integrated into the existing curriculum or exist as a "stand-alone" program?

One of the ongoing criticisms of public education, especially at the secondary level, is captured in the pejorative phrase "the shopping mall high school." This phrase refers to the ever-expanding proliferation of "special interest" courses and requirements in high school, which according to critics, has resulted in a watered-down curriculum. Whether community service learning proves to be a course contributing to such criticism or emerges as an important and fundamental component of the secondary school curriculum may depend on how questions such as those noted earlier are eventually answered.

308

A final note of both promise and caution regarding the focus of such programs is offered by Joel Westheimer and Joseph Kahne in "Service Learning Required," *Education Week* (January 26, 2000), wherein they state that if the focus on service learning downplays or distracts attention from systemic causes and solutions, then we risk teaching students that need is inevitable, that alleviating momentary suffering but not its origins is the only expression of responsible citizenship. The authors then describe some programs where student participants engage in social and political analysis of the issues related to their service. Westheimer and Kahne conclude that when this combination of service and analysis is present students do develop the attitudes, skills, and knowledge necessary to respond in productive ways.

ISSUE 18

Is the Emphasis on Globalization in the Study of World History Appropriate?

YES: National Center for History in the Schools, from *National Standards for History: Basic Edition, 1996* (National Center for History in the Schools, 1996)

NO: Gilbert T. Sewall, from "The Classroom Conquest of World History: Leveling the Cross-Cultural Playing Field," *Education Week* (June 13, 2001)

ISSUE SUMMARY

YES: The National Center for History in the Schools advocates courses that are "genuinely global in scope."

NO: Gilbert T. Sewall, director of the American Textbook Council, warns that a world history that slights the achievements of the West and concocts a "pseudohistory calculated to please contemporary multiculturalists" seems destined to become the rule in U.S. classrooms.

The widespread adoption of educational accountability systems based on standards-driven curricula, with accompanying "high-stakes" standardized testing, emphasizes the importance of understanding how curriculum standards come into being and the responses they evoke. The development of curriculum standards in all subject matter areas involves the selection of topics and content to be covered, the extent of that coverage, and, by implication, what will not be covered. In the past, textbook publishers tended to make such curricular decisions, but now with legally adopted curriculum standards becoming part of state approaches to assessment and accountability, the textbook (and test) publishers must respond to content prescribed by those adopted standards. Today's standards generally emanate from projects commissioned by the state or national agencies or by professional subject area organizations representing teachers of a given subject area, such as the National Council for the Teaching of Mathematics or the National Council for the Social Studies.

In short, the development of curriculum standards is a vital process impacting what students are expected to learn (and therefore what teachers are expected to teach), what is to be included in textbooks, and what is to be tested. Obviously the development and adoption of standards can become a source of controversy since certain themes will be emphasized to the diminution of others. That selection process leads naturally to questions such as not only "what standards?" but "whose standards?"

Such controversy certainly has been the case with the development of the National Standards for History by the National Center for History in the Schools. A highly emotional and publicized controversy arose over the first iteration of the Center's history standards when they were initially issued in 1994. The furor basically involved what critics alleged was an overemphasis on a multicultural, "every person" theme, which in turn deemphasized the more traditional "great man" approach to the study of history. Much of the debate and discussion involved the contents of the American history standards, but similar concerns were expressed about the world history standards. Eventually the standards were revised with assistance of groups such as the Council on Basic Education, and they were reissued in 1996.

But the controversy has not gone away. Within the National Center for History in the Schools selection about the history standards, a phrase such as "a grasp of the complexities of global independence today requires a knowledge of how the world economy arose" provides an example of the emphasis on globalism found in the document and engenders reactions such as Gilbert T. Sewall's statement that academic revisionists entertain radical ambitions for the world history curriculum:

National Standards for History

Contents of World History Standards

Approaches to World History

These guidelines call for a minimum of three years of World History instruction between grades 5 and 12. They also advocate courses that are genuinely global in scope. The Standards set forth [here] are intended as a guide and resource for schools in developing or improving World History courses.... The Standards presented here are compatible with and will support a variety of curricular frameworks....

Era 1
The Beginnings of Human Society

- Standard 1: The biological and cultural processes that gave rise to the earliest human communities
- Standard 2: The processes that led to the emergence of agricultural societies around the world

Overview

The Beginnings of Human Society—Giving Shape to World History
So far as we know, humanity's story began in Africa. For millions of years it was mainly a story of biological change. Then some hundreds of thousands of years ago our early ancestors began to form and manipulate useful tools. Eventually they mastered speech. Unlike most other species, early humans gained the capacity to learn from one another and transmit knowledge from one generation to the next. The first great experiments in creating culture were underway. Among early hunter-gatherers cultural change occurred at an imperceptible speed. But as human populations rose and new ideas and techniques appeared, the pace of change accelerated. Moreover, human history became global at a very early date....

Why Study This Era?

To understand how the human species fully emerged out of biological evolution and cultural development is to understand in some measure what it means to be human. The common past that all students share begins with the peopling of our planet and the spread of settled societies around the world.

The cultural forms, social institutions, and practical techniques that emerged in the Neolithic age laid the foundations for the emergence of all early civilizations.

Study of human beginnings throws into relief fundamental problems of history that pertain to all eras: the possibilities and limitations of human control over their environment; why human groups accept, modify, or reject innovations; the variety of social and cultural paths that different societies may take; and the acceleration of social change through time.

Era 2
Early Civilizations and the Emergence of Pastoral Peoples, 4000–1000 BCE

- Standard 1: The major characteristics of civilizations emerged in Mesopotamia, Egypt, and the Indus valley
- Standard 2: How agrarian societies spread and new states emerged in the third and second millennia BCE
- Standard 3: The political, social, and cultural consequences of population movements and militarization in Eurasia in the second millennium BCE
- Standard 4: Major trends in Eurasia and Africa from 4000 to 1000 BCE

Overview

Giving Shape to World History

When farmers began to grow crops on the irrigated floodplain of Mesopotamia in Southwest Asia, they had no consciousness that they were embarking on a radically new experiment in human organization. The nearly rainless but abundantly watered valley of the lower Tigris and Euphrates rivers was an environment capable of supporting far larger concentrations of population and much greater cultural complexity than could the hill country where agriculture first emerged. Shortly after 4000 BCE, a rich culture and economy based on walled cities was appearing along the banks of the two rivers. The rise of civilization in Mesopotamia marked the beginning of 3,000 years of far-reaching transformations that affected peoples across wide areas of Eurasia and Africa....

Why Study This Era?

This is the period when civilizations appeared, shaping all subsequent eras of history. Students must consider the nature of civilization as both a particular way of organizing society and a historical phenomenon subject to transformation and collapse.

In this era many of the world's most fundamental inventions, discoveries, institutions, and techniques appeared. All subsequent civilizations would be built on these achievements.

Early civilizations were not self-contained but developed their distinctive characteristics partly as a result of interactions with other peoples. In this era students will learn about the deep roots of encounter and exchange among societies.

The era introduces students to one of the most enduring themes in history, the dynamic interplay, for good or ill, between the agrarian civilizations and pastoral peoples of the great grasslands. . . .

Era 3
Classical Traditions, Major Religions, and Giant Empires, 1000 BCE–300 CE

- Standard 1: Innovation and change from 1000–600 BCE: horses, ships, iron, and monotheistic faith
- Standard 2: The emergence of Aegean civilization and how interrelations developed among peoples of the eastern Mediterranean and Southwest Asia, 600–200 BCE
- Standard 3: How major religions and large-scale empires arose in the Mediterranean basin, China, and India, 500 BCE–300 CE
- Standard 4: The development of early agrarian civilizations in Mesoamerica
- Standard 5: Major global trends from 1000 BCE–300 CE

Overview

By 1000 BCE urban civilizations of the Eastern Hemisphere were no longer confined to a few irrigated river plains. World population was growing, interregional trade networks were expanding, and towns and cities were appearing where only farming villages or nomad camps had existed before. Iron-making technology had increasing impact on economy and society. Contacts among diverse societies of Eurasia and Africa were intensifying, and these had profound consequences in the period from 1000 BCE to 300 CE. The pace of change was quickening in the Americas as well. If we stand back far enough to take in the global scene, three large-scale patterns of change stand out. These developments can be woven through the study of particular regions and societies as presented in Standards 1–5. . . .

Why Study This Era?

The classical civilizations of this age established institutions and defined values and styles that endured for many centuries and that continue to influence our lives today.

Six of the world's major faiths and ethical systems emerged in this period and set forth their fundamental teachings. Africa and Eurasia together moved in the direction of forming a single world of human interchange in this era as a result of trade, migrations, empire-building, missionary activity, and the diffusion of skills and ideas. These interactions had profound consequences for all the major civilizations and all subsequent periods of world history.

This was a formative era for many fundamental institutions and ideas in world history, such as universalist religion, monotheism, the bureaucratic empire, the city-state, and the relation of technology to social change. Students' explorations in the social sciences, literature, and contemporary affairs will be enriched by understanding such basic concepts as these.

Era 4
Expanding Zones of Exchange and Encounter, 300–1000 CE

- Standard 1: Imperial crises and their aftermath, 300–700 CE
- Standard 2: Causes and consequences of the rise of Islamic civilization in the 7th–10th centuries
- Standard 3: Major developments in East Asia and Southeast Asia in the era of the Tang dynasty, 600–900 CE
- Standard 4: The search for political, social, and cultural redefinition in Europe, 500–1000 CE
- Standard 5: The development of agricultural societies and new states in tropical Africa and Oceania
- Standard 6: The rise of centers of civilization in Mesoamerica and Andean South America in the first millennium CE
- Standard 7: Major global trends from 300–1000 CE

Overview

Beginning about 3000 CE almost the entire region of Eurasia and northern Africa experienced severe disturbances. By the 7th century, however, peoples of Eurasia and Africa entered a new period of more intensive interchange and cultural creativity. Underlying these developments was the growing sophistication of systems for moving people and goods here and there throughout the hemisphere—China's canals, trans-Saharan camel caravans, high-masted ships plying the Indian Ocean. These networks tied diverse peoples together across great distances. In Eurasia and Africa a single region of intercommunication was taking shape that ran from the Mediterranean to the China seas. A widening zone of interchange also characterized Mesoamerica. . . .

Why Study This Era?

In these seven centuries Buddhism, Christianity, Hinduism, and Islam spread far and wide beyond their lands of origin. These religions became established in regions where today they command the faith of millions. In this era the configuration of empires and kingdoms in the world changed dramatically. Why giant empires have fallen and others risen rapidly to take their place is an enduring question for all eras.

In the early centuries of this era Christian Europe was marginal to the dense centers of population, production, and urban life of Eurasia and northern Africa. Students should understand this perspective but at the same time investigate the developments that made possible the rise of a new civilization in Europe after 1000 CE.

In this era no sustained contact existed between the Eastern Hemisphere and the Americas. Peoples of the Americas did not share in the exchange and borrowing that stimulated innovations of all kinds in Eurasia and Africa. Therefore, students need to explore the conditions under which weighty urban civilizations arose in Mesoamerica in the first millennium CE. . . .

Era 5
Intensified Hemispheric Interactions, 1000–1500 CE

- Standard 1: The maturing of an interregional system of communication, trade, and cultural exchange in an era of Chinese economic power and Islamic expansion
- Standard 2: The redefining of European society and culture, 1000–1300 CE
- Standard 3: The rise of the Mongol empire and its consequences for Eurasian peoples, 1200–1350
- Standard 4: The growth of states, towns, and trade in Sub-Saharan Africa between the 11th and 15th centuries
- Standard 5: Patterns of crisis and recovery in Afro-Eurasia, 1300–1450
- Standard 6: The expansion of states and civilizations in the Americas, 1000–1500
- Standard 7: Major global trends from 1000–1500 CE

Overview

Intensified Hemispheric Interactions, 1000–1500 CE—Giving Shape to World History

In this era the various regions of Eurasia and Africa became more firmly interconnected than at any earlier time in history. The sailing ships that crossed the wide sea basins of the Eastern Hemisphere carried a greater volume and variety of goods than ever before. In fact, the chain of seas extending across the hemisphere—China seas, Indian Ocean, Persian Gulf, Red Sea, Black Sea, Mediterranean, and Baltic—came to form a single interlocking network of maritime trade. In the same centuries caravan traffic crossed the Inner Asian steppes and the Sahara Desert more frequently. As trade and travel intensified so did cultural exchanges and encounters, presenting local societies with a profusion of new opportunities and dangers. By the time of the transoceanic voyages of the Portuguese and Spanish, the Eastern Hemisphere already constituted a single zone of intercommunication possessing a unified history of its own.

A global view reveals four "big stories" that give shape to the entire era:

- China and Europe—Two Centers of Growth...
- The Long Reach of Islam...
- The Age of Mongol Dominance...
- Empires of the Americas...

Why Study This Era?

The civilizations that flourished in this era—Chinese, Japanese, Indian, Islamic, European, West Africa, Mesoamerican, and others—created a legacy of cultural and social achievements of continuing significance today. To understand how cultural traditions affect social change or international relations in the contemporary world requires study of the specific historical contexts in which those traditions took form. The modern world with all its unique complexities did not emerge suddenly in the past 500 years but had its roots in the developments of the 1000–1500 era, notably the maturing of long-distance trade and the economic and social institutions connected with it. To understand both the history of modern Europe and the United States requires a grasp of the variety of institutions, ideas, and styles that took shape in western Christendom during this era of expansion and innovation....

Era 6
The Emergence of the First Global Age, 1450–1770

- Standard 1: How the transoceanic interlinking of all major regions of the world from 1450 to 1600 led to global transformations
- Standard 2: How European society experienced political, economic, and cultural transformations in an age of global intercommunication, 1450–1750
- Standard 3: How large territorial empires dominated much of Eurasia between the 16th and 18th centuries
- Standard 4: Economic, political, and cultural interrelations among peoples of Africa, Europe, and the Americas, 1500–1750
- Standard 5: Transformations in Asian societies in the era of European expansion
- Standard 6: Major global trends from 1450 to 1770

Overview

Giving Shape to World History

The Iberian voyages of the late 15th and early 16th centuries linked not only Europe with the Americas but laid down a communications net that ultimately joined every region of the world with every other region. As the era progressed ships became safer, bigger, and faster, and the volume of world commerce soared. The web of overland roads and trails expanded as well to carry goods and people in and out of the interior regions of Eurasia, Africa, and the American continents. The demographic, social, and cultural consequences of this great global link-up were immense. . . .

Why Study This Era?

All the forces that have made the world of the past 500 years "modern" were activated during this era. A grasp of the complexities of global interdependence today requires a knowledge of how the world economy arose and the ways in which it produced both enormous material advances and wider social and political inequalities.

The founding of the British colonies in North America in the 17th century took place within a much wider context of events: the catastrophic decline of American Indian populations, the rise of the Spanish empire, the African slave trade, and the trans-Atlantic trade and migration of Europeans. The history of colonial America makes sense only in relation to this larger scene. Any useful understanding of American political institutions and cultural values depends on a critical grasp of the European heritage of this era.

The great empires of Eurasia—Ottoman, Persian, Mughal, and Ming/Qing—all experienced cultural flowerings that paralleled the Renaissance in Europe. These achievements are an important part of our contemporary global heritage. . . .

Era 7
An Age of Revolutions, 1750–1914

- Standard 1: The causes and consequences of political revolutions in the late 18th and early 19th centuries
- Standard 2: The causes and consequences of the agricultural and industrial revolutions, 1700–1850
- Standard 3: The transformation of Eurasian societies in an era of global trade and rising European power, 1750–1870
- Standard 4: Patterns of nationalism, state-building, and social reform in Europe and the Americas, 1830–1914
- Standard 5: Patterns of global change in the era of Western military and economic domination, 1800–1914
- Standard 6: Major global trends from 1750–1914

Overview

Giving Shape to World History

The invention of the railway locomotive, the steamship, and, later the telegraph and telephone transformed global communications in this era. The time it took and the money it cost to move goods, messages, or armies across oceans and continents were drastically cut. People moved, or were forced to move, from one part of the world to another in record numbers. In the early part of the era African slaves continued to be transported across the Atlantic in large numbers; European migrants created new frontiers of colonial settlement in both the Northern and Southern Hemispheres; and Chinese, Indian, and other Asians migrated to Southeast Asia and the Americas. International commerce mushroomed, and virtually no society anywhere in the world stayed clear of the global market. Underlying these surges in communication, migration, and trade was the growth of world population, forcing men and women almost everywhere to experiment with new ways of organizing collective life.

This was an era of bewildering change in a thousand different arenas. One way to make sense of the whole is to focus on three world-encompassing and interrelated developments: the democratic revolution, the industrial revolution, and the establishment of European dominance over most of the world....

Why Study This Era?

The global forces unleashed in the second half of the 18th century continue to play themselves out at the end of the 20th century. Students will understand the "isms" that have absorbed contemporary society—industrialism, capitalism, nationalism, liberalism, socialism, communism, imperialism, colonialism and so on—by investigating them within the historical context of the 18th and 19th centuries.

At the beginning of the 20th century, Western nations enjoyed a dominance in world affairs that they no longer possess. By studying this era students may address some of the fundamental questions of the modern age: How did a relatively few states achieve such hegemony over most of the world? In what ways was Western domination limited or inconsequential? Why was it not to endure?

The history of the United States, in this era, was not self-contained but fully embedded in the context of global change. To understand the role of the United States on the global scene, students must be able to relate it to world history....

Era 8
A Half-Century of Crisis and Achievement, 1900–1945

- Standard 1: Reform, revolution, and social change in the world economy of the early century
- Standard 2: The causes and global consequences of World War I
- Standard 3: The search for peace and stability in the 1920s and 1930s
- Standard 4: The causes and global consequences of World War II
- Standard 5: Major global trends from 1900 to the end of World War II

Overview

Giving Shape to World History

On a winter's day in 1903 the "Kitty Hawk," Orville and Wilbur Wright's experimental flying machine, lifted off the ground for twelve seconds. In the decades that followed air travel was perfected, and all the physical barriers that had obstructed long-distance communication among human groups virtually disappeared. Oceans, deserts, and mountain ranges no longer mattered much when people living thousands of miles apart were determined to meet, talk, negotiate, or do business. For the first time in history the north polar region became a crossroads of international travel as air pilots sought the shortest routes between countries of the Northern Hemisphere. Radio and, at mid-century, television revolutionized communication in another way. Long-distance messages no longer had to be transported from one point to another by boat or train or even transmitted along wires or cables. Now messages, whether designed to inform, entertain, persuade, or deceive, could be broadcast from a single point to millions of listeners or watchers simultaneously.

These and other technological wonders both expressed and contributed to the growing complexity and unpredictability of human affairs. In some ways peoples of the world became more tightly knit than ever before. Global economic integration moved ahead. Literacy spread more widely. Research and knowledge networks reached round the world. However, in other respects division and conflict multiplied. Economic and territorial rivalries among nations became harsher. Laboratories and factories turned out more lethal weapons and in greater quantities than ever before. People rose up against autocratic governments on every continent....

Why Study This Era?

Exploration of the first half of the 20th century is of special importance if students are to understand the responsibilities they face at the close of the millennium. The two world wars were destructive beyond anything human society had ever experienced. If students are to grasp both the toll of such violence and the price that has sometimes been paid in the quest for peace, they must understand the causes and costs of these world-altering struggles.

In this era the ideologies of communism and fascism, both rooted in the 19th century, were put into practice on a large scale in Russia, Italy, Germany, and Japan. Both movements challenged liberal democratic traditions and involved elaborate forms of authoritarian repression. The fascist cause was discredited in 1945, communism by the early 1990s. Even so, assessing the progress of our own democratic values and institutions in this century requires parallel study of these two alternative political visions. What did they promise? How did they work as social and economic experiments? In what conditions might they find new adherents in the future?

Active citizens must continually re-examine the role of the United States in contemporary world affairs. Between 1900 and 1945 this country rose to international leadership; at the end of the period it stood astride the globe. How did we attain such a position? How has it changed since mid-century? Any informed judgment of our foreign policies and programs requires an understanding of our place among nations since the beginning of the century.

In both scientific and cultural life this era ushered in the "modern." The scientific theories as well as aesthetic and literary movements that humanity found so exhilarating and disturbing in the first half of the century continue to have an immense impact on how we see the world around us. . . .

Era 9 The 20th Century Since 1945: Promises and Paradoxes

- Standard 1: How post-World War II reconstruction occurred, new international power relations took shape, and colonial empires broke up
- Standard 2: The search for community, stability, and peace in an interdependent world
- Standard 3: Major global trends since World War II

Overview

Giving Shape to World History
The closer we get to the present the more difficult it becomes to distinguish between the large forces of change and the small. Surveying the long sweep of history from early hominid times to the end of World War II, we might reach at least partial consensus about what is important to the development of the whole human community and what is not. The multifarious trends of the past half-century, however, are for the most part still working themselves out. Therefore, we cannot know what history students one or two hundred years from now will think was worth remembering about the decades after World War II. Clearly, the era has been one of tensions, paradoxes, and contradictory trends. Some of these countercurrents provide students with a framework for investigation and analysis. . . .

Why Study This Era?
The economic and social forces moving in our contemporary world will make sense to students only in relation to the rush of events since 1945. Historical perspectives—the Cold War, the breakup of empires, the population explosion, the rise of the Pacific rim, and the other sweeping developments of the era—are indispensable for unraveling the causes and perhaps even discerning the likely consequences of events now unfolding. Students in school today are going to be responsible for addressing the promises and paradoxes of the age. They will not be able to do this by reading headlines or picking bits of "background" from the past. They must gain some sense of the whole flow of developments and build a mental architecture for understanding the history of the world.

Gilbert T. Sewall  **NO**

The Classroom Conquest
of World History

Because of its unique role in civic education, U.S. history receives more curricular attention than any other area of the social studies. But World History is the fastest-growing course title in the field. In content and viewpoint, this new World History should not be confused with European History or Western Civilization, courses of study that it seeks not to embellish but to replace.

World history can be original and stimulating, providing insights and perspectives that inform far better or are more illuminating than the much-caricatured old history of European dynasties and wars. Spurred by historians of the caliber of Henri Pirenne, Fernand Braudel, and William H. McNeill, cross-cultural and global perspectives have enriched the thinking and writing of all historians for nearly half a century, long before some academic historians in the 1990s claimed a paradigm shift as their own.

The new world history is a different animal. For more than a decade, social studies educators and curriculum specialists have pushed multiculturalism, non-Western history, and globalism in countless conferences, workshops, and in-service teacher-training sessions. To make all cultures equally significant and consequential, new topics, heretofore unknown golden ages, unnoticed epochal events, and pressing identity themes have not only become dominant in world history. They are becoming the *only* world history.

Textbook publishers and curriculum developers often adhere to a doctrine of cultural equivalency. Thus, for example, the achievements of Classical Greece, the Abbasid caliphate, and Kush receive equal weight and consideration. As a result, some world-history lessons are barely recognizable, and in some cases, not even credible.

Adding content to an already overstuffed course of study requires some heavy pruning. So what goes? The political, constitutional, intellectual, military, and diplomatic history of the West—that is, the origins of the American nation and the modern world.

Why is this not the benign corrective and overdue change in emphasis that the new world history's votaries claim it is? Because without the lives, institutions, and ideas that constitute Western civilization, "American history

From Gilbert T. Sewall, "The Classroom Conquest of World History: Leveling the Cross-Cultural Playing Field," *Education Week*, vol. 20, no. 40 (June 13, 2001). Copyright © 2001 by Gilbert T. Sewall. Reprinted by permission of *Education Week* and the author.

and ideas, and the vision and fate of democracy on earth, are not intelligible," as the Boston University historian Paul Gagnon has said.

National standards commissioned by the U.S. Department of Education and the National Endowment for the Humanities [NEH] and published in 1994 signaled the hegemony of academic historians committed to "demythologizing" and "deprivileging" Western ideas and achievements. During the last seven years, these world-history standards have had a powerful effect on state requirements and textbook development.

◆

Today's world-history advocates have a focused viewpoint. World history's exponents are eager to "correct" history's content and overhaul its basic themes from the bottom up. "The time has come to redistribute the nation's historical capital," declared Gary B. Nash, the University of California, Los Angeles, history professor and the chief architect of the 1994 national history standards, shortly before their publication.

Academic revisionists, whose careers have moved forward, pulled by the intellectual troika of race, class, and gender, entertain radical ambitions for the world-history curriculum. Mr. Nash and other historians want to correct what they believe to be a "triumphal," "monocultural," and "ethnocentric" view of the West that is incomplete or false. Their buzzwords are inclusion, diversity, globalism, and empathy, concepts that classroom teachers embrace as much out of naiveté and workshop hectoring as conviction.

Not surprisingly, new personalities are appearing. Master narratives are shifting.

In order to make room for new people and subjects, erstwhile heroes such as Hannibal and the Duke of Wellington have disappeared from classrooms. So have their epic stories. Julius Caesar and Marcus Aurelius, Augustine and Thomas Aquinas, Martin Luther and John Calvin, Copernicus and Magellan, Charles V and Louis XIV, the Romanovs and the Hapsburgs, Napoleon, Gladstone and Disraeli, Charles Darwin, Woodrow Wilson, and many other figures are also being written out of narrative, no longer considered commanding figures of their ages.

◆

As Western history has shrunk, its content has also undergone a transformation. Non-Western topics compete for space with women's history, which runs like a thread through entire textbook and standards narratives. In the world-history textbook that is probably the single most widely used in junior high schools across the nation, Houghton Mifflin's *To See a World,* written by UCLA's Mr. Nash, Galileo is absent. Instead, students encounter Isabella D'Este and Christine de Pizan as exemplars of the Renaissance.

In the new world-history narratives, arcane, exotic, and trivial topics abound. In the new curriculum, much is made of Great Zimbabwe. Medieval Bantu migrations and the glories of the 12th-century Timbuktu assume major significance. Not much is made of the Magna Carta or the Enlightenment, or, for that matter, any political or constitutional history that helps students understand liberty and democracy.

The College Board's recently unveiled World History Advanced Placement course tells students explicitly that they are expected to know about Mamluks but not Almohads, Indian Ocean traders but not Gujarati merchants, Muhammad Ali but not Isma'il, European exploration but not the explorers, the World Wars but not the battles.

Two aspects of the AP World History course outline indicate where the subject is headed. First, it ordains that European history will make up no more than 30 percent of the test. Astonishingly, its "foundations" section does not include Greek antiquity at all, while it does include Mayan civilization and Bantu migrations.

Secondly, the new world-history curriculum officially commences in the year 1000 C.E. (that stands for "common era," as A.D. is now considered to be an obsolete and politically incorrect designation).

Why start with 1000? The AP World History course-description booklet declares, as though its logic were indisputable and crystal-pure, that this is because it "is generally recognized in the field as a chronological break point centering on the intensification of international contacts."

This trendy new baseline elides the origins of several civilizations, including Western civilization, and this elision is not accidental. It is trying to level the cross-cultural playing field.

World History's interests and angles are manifest in the three sample essay questions in the College Board's course description, published as models for all teachers and students who are considering the course of study. Of an infinite number of thematic possibilities, a document-based essay question chooses the impact of nationalism and the nation-state on women's rights.

A second essay on "change over time" asks students to describe world trading systems since 1000 ("explain how alterations in the framework of international trade interacted with regional factors to produce the changes and continuities throughout the period"). Student can choose one of four regions: China, Latin America, sub-Saharan Africa, or the Middle East. They cannot choose Europe or North America.

The third sample essay question is a better one than the first two, even though it provides additional evidence of the test-makers' fixation on race and social class. It asks students to compare and contrast the rise of slavery in the New World with Russian serfdom from 1450 to 1750.

Powered by the multicultural imperative that has swept through schools and the social studies curriculum during the past decade, this World History AP program dooms the long-established European History AP curriculum to extinction. The program and outlook that have brought it into being are sure to influence the way world history is taught in all high school courses, especially honors courses.

The new world history's advocates court public opinion, declaring multiculturalism to be the American way. Historians who reject the curriculum overhaul are labeled "defensive" or "fearful." Psychologizing traditional history, multiculturalists claim that resistance "projects a lack of faith in the very institutions and ideas that are being championed." This is a neat, modern ploy that avoids the counter-view, one presented by such discerning historians as the University of Pennsylvania's Walter A. McDougall.

In order to serve diversity, the new world history ignores the cause, effect, significance, and meaning of seminal events and ideas that matter to Americans of all ages. It warps the most valuable lessons that history can offer.

Assisted by such powerful agencies as the Department of Education, the NEH, and the College Board—public and private agencies that should know better—a world history that slights the achievements of the West and concocts a pseudohistory calculated to please contemporary multiculturalists seems destined to become the rule in U.S. classrooms.

If the new world history's classroom conquest is complete, the losers will be civic education and genuine global understanding. Sooner or later, the new narrative will affect how voters think about themselves, their country, and its relationship to the world. In this respect, the new world history could have painful and lasting consequences for the nation's foreign policy and international relations.

POSTSCRIPT

Is the Emphasis on Globalization in the Study of World History Appropriate?

Although this controversy involves curriculum standards for the study of history, similar scenarios are being played out in other subject matter areas, such as mathematics, where debates over "new" math, "drill and kill," and the use of calculators go unresolved. The same is true in science, wherein the ongoing controversy over evolution versus creationism always seems to be present in any discussion of curriculum standards. The same intense controversy is present when dealing with the type of literature found in the English curriculum. Cutting across subject matter content areas are other curricular controversies related to too much or too little multiculturalism and/or ethnocentrism.

It has been suggested that the very nature of these debates and the subsequent compromises that usually follow have resulted in a very irenic curriculum in the public schools—one that aims at not offending anyone or any group. But countering that point is the contention that the public schools are charged with educating "all of the children of all the people" and thus the public school curriculum should not reflect a particular point of view. Many say that parents who want their beliefs emphasized in the school curriculum can send their children to a private or parochial school where those beliefs are operant. That is the viewpoint of David Remes, a lawyer specializing in First Amendment matters. He argued against allowing parents to "opt" their children out of curriculum with which they disagree by stating, "public education is not 'public' just because it is free. It is 'public' because it is a kind of education—an education that instructs children as Justice William J. Brennan has put it, in 'a heritage common to all American groups and religions.' Public education is not and cannot be an education that instructs children in the orthodoxies of their parents."

It is true that the selection of curriculum standards often leads to controversy, but in fact controversies that arise over curriculum content can be viewed as healthy in that they are evidence of public interest and awareness. Speaking to that view, the National Council for the Social Studies in the executive summary to their 1994 *Curriculum Standards for Social Studies* states, "The importance of social studies ensures that policymakers, educators, parents, and citizens of all kinds will want to know what students should be taught, how they will be taught, and how student achievement will be evaluated." It can be said that the only thing wrong with that statement is that it seems to belie a professional inclination to assume that the named groups do not already have their own beliefs with regard to curriculum, teaching, and assessment. Perhaps that is why on this crucial topic the best decision making will result from a combination of professional input and public approval, which is the general process followed when a state formally adopts curriculum standards.

Other literature dealing with this issue includes Paul R. Gross, *Politicizing Science Education* (The Thomas B. Fordham Foundation, 2000), and from the same Foundation, a series on *The State of State Standards.* Also see *Closing the Gap* (Council for Basic Education, 2000); *Standards for Excellence in Education* (Council for Basic Education, 1998); and several articles in the March 1995 issue of *Educational Leadership* and the February 1999 issue of *Phi Delta Kappan.*

ISSUE 19

Should Classical Works Be the Emphasis of the High School Literature Curriculum?

YES: Carol Jago, from *With Rigor for All: Teaching the Classics to Contemporary Students* (Calendar Islands Publishers, 2000)

NO: Donald R. Gallo, from "How Classics Create an Aliterate Society," *English Journal* (January 2001)

ISSUE SUMMARY

YES: Carol Jago, a high school English teacher and director of the California Reading and Literature Project at the University of California–Los Angeles, states that a critical reading of classical literature results in a deep literacy that she believes is an essential skill for anyone who wants to attempt to make sense of the world.

NO: Donald R. Gallo, a former professor of English who writes and edits books for teachers and teenagers, posits that the United States is a nation that teaches its children how to read in the early grades, then forces them during their teenage years to read literary works that most of them dislike so much that they have no desire whatsoever to continue those experiences into adulthood.

Woe be it to today's high school English teacher, who must not only struggle against the traditional antipathy that many adolescents feel toward any activity that is not immediately "relevant" to their interests and experiences but now must compete with the vast array of expertly marketed entertainment venues available at the push of a button or the click of a mouse.

Motivation is considered a cornerstone of learning, and thus trying to capture the interest of students is one of the fundamental challenges for the effective teacher. Indeed, the proliferation of elective courses in the high school curriculum is partially the result of an attempt to provide students with content that they might find to be of greater interest than the traditional "3 Rs." Critics have suggested that this infusion of alleged high-interest subjects has resulted in a diluted "shopping mall" curriculum, which delivers little of substance and lasting value. The "back-to-basics" movement is a direct reflection of this criticism.

Among English teachers there is general agreement that trying to get students to read and perhaps even come to enjoy reading is a daunting task but one that is well worth the effort. However, where there is significant disagreement is in whether or not the content of the material being presented needs, in itself, to be of high interest and thus hopefully enjoyable to the students. Some, like Carol Jago, would argue that classical literature should not be sacrificed on the altar of "relevance and learning needs to be fun," but rather, through hard work and creative teaching, these works can be brought to all students. Jago contends that "all books are not created equal" in terms of the great writing and the insights and profundities these books can bring to students. Others, such as Donald R. Gallo, suggest that reading and the enjoyment of reading must be carefully cultivated. Moreover, requiring unsophisticated and reluctant readers to tackle the classics is incompatible with learning theory and developmental readiness and thus is ultimately a self-defeating task.

Carol Jago

With Rigor for All

Introduction

Rushed as I always am to get out of the house and on the road to school, I could not resist the morning paper's headline: "Something Is Rotund in Denmark." The story that followed was a rather dull article about poor eating habits in Denmark that was not a subject I typically found myself much drawn to. I began to wonder if the editor had created the headline in order to catch readers just like me.

While there weren't likely to be many *Los Angeles Times* readers who would be teaching *Hamlet* later in the day, it did seem that the editor counted on the fact that most people scanning the headlines would vaguely remember the ghost of Hamlet's murdered father and Marcellus proclaiming at the end of act 1, scene 4, that "Something is rotten in the state of Denmark."

I was eager to show the newspaper to my students. Here was one more bit of evidence proving that reading classical literature is not a punishment but a reward.

As an English teacher in a public urban high school, I know first-hand the challenges involved in teaching classical literature to today's students. One third of the 3,200 students at Santa Monica High School do not speak English at home. More than twenty different languages are spoken on campus. Our student body includes teenagers who live in million-dollar homes and others who reside in homeless shelters.

Without powerful stories to engage them, many of these students will never acquire the literacy skills they need. I believe that the most potent stories are those that have weathered the test of time: the "classics."

Though most high school course descriptions still call for a heavy dose of classical literature, teachers (particularly teachers who care a great deal about making school meaningful) seem increasingly reluctant to tackle these works. Thinking that contemporary novels will be more accessible and less daunting for reluctant readers, they abandon *Great Expectations* for more contemporary stories. They wheel out the VCR and show Leonardo DiCaprio as Romeo rather than have students read and listen to Shakespeare's lines and perform the role for themselves. While young adult literature and big-screen adaptations most certainly have a place in the reading and viewing lives of today's teenagers, the work of a literature classroom should be the careful and joyful reading of challenging texts.

It seems criminal to me that schools should reserve the classics for honor students. Ignoring the elitism that such a curricular decision betrays, teachers defend a watered-down reading list for "regular" students by explaining to themselves and others that most teenagers simply can't understand the difficult vocabulary. Besides, they argue, today's kids won't read anything that is old. If Shakespeare or Dickens had operated from such an elitist stance, neither would have been the popular success he was. "Regular" people loved Shakespeare's and Dickens' works. Their contemporary audiences did so for the very same reasons that readers today laugh with Falstaff and cry with Little Nell. Shakespeare and Dickens make characters come alive. While caught up in the spell of the story, readers care about them the way they care about real people, worrying when the characters are in trouble, celebrating when they triumph.

I worry that in our determination to provide students with literature they can "relate to" we sometimes end up teaching works that students actually don't need much help with at the expense of teaching classics that they most certainly do need assistance negotiating. This is not to suggest that we stop putting contemporary literature into students' hands, but only to remind ourselves that we should be teaching in what Lev Vygotsky (1962) calls the zone of proximal development. He has written that "the only good kind of instruction is that which marches ahead of development and leads it." If students can read a book on their own, it probably isn't the best choice for classroom study. Classroom texts should pose intellectual challenges to young readers. These texts should be books that will make students stronger readers—and stronger people.

When former students come to visit, I often see reflected in their eyes the question, "How could you still be doing the same old things after all this time?" Too polite to ask, they hint in subtle ways, fingering my ratty copy of *The Odyssey*, recognizing familiar assignments on the board. They can't quite believe that during all the time their lives have been changing so dramatically, mine has stayed the same. Or so they assume.

What I find impossible to explain to them is that while external things might remain the same, the students make it different every time around. . . .

I feel sorry for people who don't get to be English teachers. Each new group of students makes familiar texts come alive for me in new ways. Like Miranda when she first saw the likes of young men, I cannot help but exclaim, "Oh, brave new world that has such people in 't" (*The Tempest*, act 5, scene 1).

Apart from a rare few, the young people I teach do not pick up classic literature with much enthusiasm. At first they groan, "Three hundred pages of poetry!" Then they moan, "I can't do it. Not one word of what I read last night makes sense." They always hope that if they complain enough, I will abandon the text for something simpler. Instead I assure them that over the next few weeks I am going to show them how to unlock this book for themselves. I let students know that the satisfaction they will feel at meeting this textual challenge is an intellectual reward that I would not for the world deny them. Does every student experience this reward with every book? Of course not.

But many students who never expected to be able to negotiate classical literature find that with a little help from their teacher and classmates, the book isn't as impossible as they first thought. This dawning realization is an important instructional goal. Students are learning not to fear complicated syntax or unfamiliar vocabulary. As a result their literacy is enhanced.

Another goal I consciously pursue is love and respect for literature. In her provocative essay "I Know Why the Caged Bird Cannot Read," Francine Prose (1999) argues that:

> Traditionally, the love of reading has been born and nurtured in high school English class—the last time many students will find themselves in a roomful of people who have all read the same text and are, in theory, prepared to discuss it. High school—even more than college—is where literary tastes and allegiances are formed; what we read in adolescence is imprinted on our brains as the dreamy notions of childhood crystallize into hard data.

Who knows but that without determined high school English teachers, love and respect for literature would die out. Not many students stumble upon the works of Thomas Hardy on their parents' bookshelves or choose to peek between the covers if they do. But for as long as teachers continue to make enduring stories come to life for young readers, the study of literature will remain a vital pursuit.

My definition of a classic is both vague and generous. A classic is an enduring story. As a result, the texts I use in my classroom include both works from antiquity and contemporary novels. I see no contradiction with placing Zora Neale Hurston's heroine Janie Crawford side by side with Homer's hero Odysseus. Both embark on journeys that lead to self-discovery. Both return home to tell those they have left behind what they learned. It is important that students don't mistakenly come to believe that "classic" is synonymous with "ancient." Classics are stories that tell the truth about human experience across both time and culture.

Given so many teenagers' reluctance to read at all, handing out a Shakespeare play or Homer's epic poem (let alone *Moby Dick* or *Crime and Punishment*) may seem like folly for both teacher and student. Living as we do in an age that glorifies the screen rather than the printed page, it can be very hard work to persuade young people to turn off MTV and pick up a book. What follows will attempt to dispel the fear of teaching classical texts to contemporary kids and offer ideas for helping young people learn to read these enduring stories.

Creating a Context for the Study of Classical Literature

All books are not created equal. Some have the power to transport us to unexplored worlds and allow us—at least for as long as the book lasts—to become other than who we are. Others only ever attempt to offer us chicken soup for our teenage or middle-aged souls. While there is no question that it is easier to persuade students to pick up the second kind of novel, a critical reading of classical literature results in a deep literacy that I believe is an essential skill for anyone who wants to attempt to make sense of the world.

Marshall Gregory (1997), Harry Ice Professor of English at Butler University, Indiana, posits six contributions that the study of literature makes to student development:

1. Students develop *intellectually* as the content of great works of literature offers them the ways and means of delving into stories, and, through these stories, of having a vicarious experience of the human condition far greater than any of them could ever acquire on the basis of luck and firsthand encounters.
2. Students develop *cognitive skills* through the study of literature that support the critical reading of all texts, the precise use of language, and the creation of sound arguments.
3. Students develop an *aesthetic sensitivity* that helps them recognize and respond to art.
4. Students develop both an *intra and intercultural awareness* by reading texts both from their own culture and from cultures other than their own.
5. Students develop an *ethical sensitivity* that includes both the ability to regulate conduct according to principles and the ability to deliberate about issues both in their own heads and in dialogue with others.
6. Students develop an *existential maturity* that allows them to behave as civilized human beings in a world where others are not always so inclined. According to Gregory, existential maturity "is more easily defined by what it is not than by what it is. It is not self-centeredness; it is not unkindness; it is not pettiness; it is not petulance; it is not callousness to the suffering of others; it is not back-biting or violent competitiveness; it is not mean-spiritedness; it is not dogmatism or fanaticism; it is not a lack of self-control; it is not the inability ever to be detached or ironic; it is not the refusal to engage in give-and-take learning from others; it is not the assumption that what we personally desire and value is what everyone else desires and values." (57)

Literature Versus Workplace Documents

When the study of literature can accomplish so much (and so much that law enforcement and social services struggle in vain to accomplish), it seems foolhardy for schools to shortchange this essential element of a child's education. Yet all over this country curriculum experts are recommending that teachers focus on what they are calling workplace documents, influenced no doubt by a business community fed up with employees who need intensive and therefore expensive training before they can be put to work. Business leaders want schools to guarantee that graduates have workplace literacy, and in fact most state standards recommend that students learn to read with comprehension instruction manuals, consumer documents, and business memos. Standardized assessment instruments increasingly reflect these standards, and as assessment increasingly drives instruction, I fear there will be little time left in the curriculum for literature.

The cost of such a shift would be catastrophic. Elite private and suburban schools are not likely to replace *The Scarlet Letter* with workplace documents. The sons and daughters of the privileged will continue to read *The Odyssey* and *Beowulf* while urban public school kids are handed instruction manuals and consumer reports. A democracy isn't supposed to work this way.

Odysseus's adventures offer all teenage readers a useful map for internal navigation. If informational texts come to replace the classics in our curriculum, high schools will graduate young people who have never seen Circe turn men into swine, who have never sailed past Scylla and Charybdis, and who have no knowledge of the dangers lurking in the Land of the Lotus Eaters. If they never read the classics, students will truly be at sea.

And what is more "real world" than the story of *Beowulf*? A king is hounded by a seemingly all-powerful enemy and has no idea why this monster has singled out his land for destruction. Every night the evil beast creeps into his hall and slaughters the best and brightest of his men. To survive, the men must abandon their leader and find safety in hiding. Despair reigns throughout the land until the arrival of—you guessed it—Beowulf.

Luring Students to the Text

One of the worst mistakes a teacher can make when introducing a classic like *The Odyssey* or *Beowulf* to students is to take the cod liver oil approach: "Drink this. It tastes bad, but it's good for you. You'll thank me later." Abandon all hope of instructional success if you pursue this course. First, the concept of suffering now for later pleasure is lost on most teenagers. And second, most kids I know are very good at just saying, "No."

Before I ever put *Beowulf* in students' hands, I tell them about Grendel and his penchant for human flesh. I paint them a picture of the egomaniac Beowulf —a man able to swim in the North Sea for nine days without rest, dressed in full chain mail and carrying a large sword. Swimmers in class become particularly intrigued. Their experience with the ocean tells them that this is simply impossible. Who is this guy? Or, who does this guy Beowulf think he is? . . .

Marshall Gregory's Defense for the Study of Literature

Thinking about Marshall Gregory's defense of the study of literature, I saw that in their reading of *Beowulf* my students really had developed intellectually. Many had never before met a hero like Beowulf, so utterly sure of himself and his mission. Unlike a modern hero, Beowulf admits to no weaknesses nor does he succumb to the temptations of ordinary life. While this made him an unrealistic character for some students, most were able to see how Beowulf's exploits were not meant to be realistic, not for the epic poet's listeners any more than for readers like us. At the same time, students were able to experience vicariously what it felt like to do battle with a series of monsters: Grendel, Grendel's mother, and finally (fatally) the dragon without ever giving up or giving in to self-doubt.

As they compared the epic poem to rap lyrics, these students developed cognitive skills. [Tenth grader] Dannell and others could tell that I was reluctant to accept the comparison and so had to examine carefully the ways in which both texts used language in order to support their claim. While I remain convinced that *Beowulf* is the artistically superior poem, a great deal of powerful classroom discussion was triggered by the inclusion of Tupac Shakur's lyrics in our lesson. And though it had not been Dannell's intention to do so, he had developed in the rest of us a sense of what it means to be an outsider in Hrothgar's land and in our own society. He helped us begin to understand the rage that such a position can engender.

Aesthetic and ethical sensitivity is hard to measure. So is ethical maturity. But I believe that these tenth graders are well on their way to developing the habits of mind Marshall Gregory describes. *Beowulf* taught them things they didn't know they knew. Great books will do that if you only give them a chance. Lesser books, while excellent fare for pleasure reading, seldom have this kind of impact. . . .

Warning Students of the Obstacles in Reading Classics

In his 1987 Nobel Prize acceptance speech, Joseph Brodsky explained that

> In the history of our species, the book is an anthropological development, similar essentially to the invention of the wheel. Having emerged in order to give us some idea not so much of our origins as of what the Sapiens is capable of, a book constitutes a means of transportation through the space of experience, at the speed of turning a page.

The challenge for most teachers as they contemplate assigning a classic is how to help students operate this curious means of transportation and how to get them turning those pages. Judging from their commitment to literature, English teachers seem to agree that taking the textual trip through "the space of experience" is essential. What we struggle with is figuring out how to keep young readers moving. . . .

Even excellent teenage readers are daunted by the textual challenges posed by a Jane Austen or Joseph Conrad novel. It is easy for English teachers to forget this. Often we know a text so well that it is hard to imagine what students might find confusing. Can you remember the first Shakespeare play you tried to read on your own? Do you recall your first time through *The Sound and the Fury* or *Lord Jim*? . . .

How Teachers' Rereadings Can Interfere

. . . It makes good sense to let students know how a book is likely to challenge them as readers. Why let them think that there is something somehow wrong with them that is causing the book to be so difficult to read and the first chapter to seem so long? Why invite students to jump to the conclusion that *Frankenstein* is "Boring!" before they give the story a chance. When tackling a classic, students need to be prepared to adjust their recreational reading habits to a different kind of text. Which brings up another common obstacle to reading the classics: the belief that learning must be fun.

Does Learning Have to Be Fun?

One of the great fallacies about student achievement is that successful students love school. The real difference between successful and unsuccessful students has little to do with their proclivity for scholarly pursuits. The difference is in their willingness to do schoolwork.

What irks students is the work: paying attention, doing the reading, taking notes, studying for tests, writing papers. I don't blame them. But students who fail to discipline themselves to these onerous tasks learn very little. I wish it were otherwise. I wish that learning were as natural as breathing. It isn't. Reading a classic, like learning a language, takes applied effort.

Where educators have gone wrong is in promoting the idea that learning is fun. What follows from this faulty premise is the assumption that anything that isn't fun need not be completed. If the assignment feels like work, there must be something wrong with the book, or with the teacher, or maybe with the whole school. In fact learning can be enormous fun and with a good teacher often is, but fun is not the goal. The goal is learning.

No teacher with any sense would expect teenagers to love *Crime and Punishment* at first sight. A cursory glance at the 629-page novel sends the fainthearted scurrying. For this reason, I always warn students that they are going to have to struggle a bit before they can enter Dostoevski's fictional world. I promise to be there to help and answer questions, but I explain that I can't do the work for them. If they want to know Raskolnikov, it is going to take effort. The "fun" comes later when students realize how much this extraordinary character has taught them about themselves.

NO

Donald R. Gallo

How Classics Create an Aliterate Society

Were you an avid reader as a teenager? Did you love *Wuthering Heights* and *The Scarlet Letter* in high school? Good for you! At the same time, that could be a problem for you, because it may be impossible for you to understand why so many students in your school do not feel the same way about the classics.

It seems to be part of human nature for us to think that everyone has had experiences similar to ours and that they share our perspective on things. Thus, as a lover of classical literature, it seems logical for you to conclude that there is something wrong with today's students if they don't share your passion. You may never consider how the required literature in your school's curriculum affects kids who are not like you.

I've been able to see things differently, for I was not an avid reader as a teenager. I read my assignments—I was an obedient student. But I almost never read for pleasure. Books were dull. Adults who are avid readers say that reading is active because readers use their imagination, as opposed to watching television, which is a passive activity. HA! For me, playing baseball and stickball and football was active! Hiking and camping were active! Building forts in the woods, deep sea fishing, climbing trees ... those were active! Sitting in a chair to read a book, in comparison, was about as passive as anyone could get!

There were also no books in my home, except for a dictionary and a couple of Bibles. My father read the New York *Daily News* every day, and my family subscribed to *LIFE* magazine. And when I was a Boy Scout, I subscribed to *Boy's Life* and read it thoroughly each month. But that was about it.

Like many teens today, because I did not read much I had a weak vocabulary, and I did not write very effectively. That was doubly bad, because not only was I not *interested* in reading books like *Great Expectations, A Tale of Two Cities, Hamlet* and *Silas Marner*, I had to struggle to understand them when they were assigned.

Moreover, I did not see any connections between my life and the lives of the characters in those novels and plays. There's a character in Mel Glenn's poetry book, *Class Dismissed II*, whose viewpoint I shared. In that poem, Paul Hewitt says he can't identify with Huck Finn or care about Willie Loman. He asks if the teacher has any books that "deal with real life" (18). Why was I supposed to care about a Puritan woman who got pregnant from having sex with

From Donald R. Gallo, "How Classics Create an Aliterate Society," *English Journal*, vol. 90, no. 3 (January 2001). Copyright © 2001 by The National Council of Teachers of English. Reprinted by permission.

a minister? What did I have in common with a crazed old king who alienated the only daughter who really loved him and then didn't have enough sense to come in out of the rain? I did enjoy the witches and bloody stuff in *Macbeth*, and I found the riots and beheadings in *A Tale of Two Cities* interesting, but all that knitting by Madame DeFarge was boring.

Many of my classmates and I could never figure out what we were supposed to get out of those assigned stories and poems. Like most students, we relied on the teacher to tell us what they meant. One of my former college students defined a classic this way: a classic is a book that "requires a teacher to figure out a glimmer of what it says."

Nevertheless, I did read the required books, as I said; I listened in class most of the time, and I passed quizzes and tests on the material, usually with Bs and Cs because I was a fairly intelligent kid. (As a matter of fact, I and my parents were often told by school counselors and teachers that I was "not working up to my potential." You know the type.) My classmates Marjorie and Elizabeth, on the other hand, always earned As—they were smart and they loved to read. My less intelligent classmates did not fare as well: Roy, Richard, Vincent, Tony —the guys. Like the irradiated marigolds in Paul Zindel's Pulitzer Prize-winning play, *The Effect of Gamma Rays on Man-in-the-Moon Marigolds*, Marjorie and Elizabeth had mutated and flourished (they probably grew up to become teachers), while Richard and Tony and others like them, badly burned by their experiences, shriveled up and swore never to read another book in their lives.

Like too many students, I never learned much from those classics then, never developed a love of reading from them. Fortunately my life turned around halfway through college when my roommates Stu Wilson and Al Fassler, who loved to read, introduced me to Holden Caulfield and Immanual Kant, as well as to classical music. I also had several excellent English teachers, especially Dr. Jim Prins, who helped me see the relevance of the issues in classical literature. More significantly, my interest level caught up with the level at which classical literature has always existed. What interested me in real life was suddenly what all those books were about!

When I look back at that phenomenon now, it all makes perfect sense to me. I wasn't READY for classical literature when I was 13, 14... 17, 18. Even though I was more physically mature than most of my peers (I was shaving weekly before my twelfth birthday), I was still a typical teenager interested in teenage things. *The classics are not about TEENAGE concerns!* They are about ADULT issues. Moreover, they were written for EDUCATED adults who had the LEISURE time to read them. They were also, not incidentally, written to be ENJOYED—not DISSECTED, not ANALYZED, and certainly not TESTED. When I became an adult, I became interested in adult things, and so the classics finally had meaning for me, and I could finally appreciate them.

Now you can see why I understand and sympathize with the tenth grade boy who told me that his required literature books "...have nothing to do with me." And the tenth grade girl who defined literature as "keeping in touch with the dead." Or the teenager who said, "I'm tired of reading this boring stuff. I want to read something with a pulse!" One of my former graduate students put it this way: "My experience in high school with the classics was similar to dissecting a frog: it was tedious and it stunk."

Such negative experiences and their resulting attitudes have created over the last half century an aliterate society in America. We are a nation that teaches its children *how* to read in the early grades, then forces them during their teenage years to read literary works that most of them dislike so much that they have no desire whatsoever to continue those experiences into adulthood. Daniel Pennac, a French author, in his book *Better Than Life*, first published in French in 1992, describes the role of the typical school this way:

> ... it looks as though school, no matter the age or nation, has had only one role. And that's to teach the mastery of technique and critical commentary and to cut off spontaneous contact with books by discouraging the pleasure of reading. It's written in stone in every land: pleasure has no business in school, and knowledge gained must be the fruit of deliberate suffering. A defensible position, of course. No lack of arguments in its favor. School cannot be a place of pleasure, with all the freedom that would imply. School is a factory, and we need to know which workers are up to snuff. (91–92)

Pennac continues the factory metaphor, with teacher as bosses, subjects as tools, and competition as the model of the workaday world. He concludes his chapter with this:

> It is the nature of living beings to love life.... But vitality has never been listed on a school curriculum. Here, function is everything. Life is elsewhere. You learn how to read at school. But what about the love of reading? (92–93)

What About the Love of Reading?

I'd like to see "the love of reading" listed as the number one goal of the English curriculum at every grade in all school systems. What a revolutionary idea! Of course, those who advocate the teaching of classics have always said that loving and appreciating literature *is* their goal. The opposite, however, has been the result of those good intentions, as G. Robert Carlsen and Anne Sherrill show clearly in *Voices of Readers: How We Come to Love Books*. After studying the randomly selected autobiographical essays of 1,000 undergraduate and graduate students written over a thirty-year span, they conclude:

> ... [T]eachers profess that by presenting the classics, they are really increasing reading enthusiasm or teaching appreciation of great works or both. It is disturbing that the protocols indicate that exactly the opposite is happening to many of the young. (136)

In the early 1980s I asked students in a number of Connecticut schools how the books they chose to read on their own compare with the assigned readings in their English classes. Several students wrote: "Teacher books are boring." Several said the obvious: "The books I like are interesting." "Mine have a lot of action..." One student said: "The books I read sometimes are the same as to what is going on around me" (implying that assigned books are not connected with the real life of teenagers). Similarly, another student wrote, "[My books] talk and use the same language as me." Another said, "The books

I read on my own, you never want to put them down; the ones assigned, you never want to pick up" (Gallo "Reactions" 7–9).

In that same survey, 40 percent of junior high school boys and 35 percent of girls said they seldom or never liked the books they were required to read in school. In senior high schools, the percentages were 41 for boys and 23 for girls. In contrast, only 20 percent of the students said they usually or always liked the assigned books (8).

So, what do most teenagers today want from a book? Whatever the type of reading, almost all kids will be more attracted to a book that grabs their attention immediately—which right away leaves out most classical literature. Consider this opening from George Eliot's *Silas Marner*:

> In the days when the spinning wheels hummed busily in the farmhouses— and even great ladies, clothed in silk and thread-lace, had their toy spinning wheels of polished oak—there might be seen in districts far away among the lanes or deep in the bosom of the hills, certain pallid undersized men, who, by the side of the brawny country folk, looked like the remnants of a disinherited race.(1)

And that's only the first sentence! The first page of *Great Expectations, Pride and Prejudice, The Good Earth,* or *The Scarlet Letter* (if you consider "The Custom-House" as the opening chapter) aren't much better, especially when you consider them from the point of view of an Internet-savvy, TV-literate, MTV-viewing contemporary teenager.

Compare the opening of *Silas Marner* quoted above with this opening paragraph from Walter Dean Myers's recent award-winning *Monster*:

> The best time to cry is at night, when the lights are out and someone is being beaten up and screaming for help. That way even if you sniffle a little they won't hear you. If anybody knows that you are crying, they'll start talking about it and soon it'll be your turn to get beat up when the lights go out.(1)

Or these opening sentences from a short story by Will Weaver titled "The Photograph":

> "Naked?"
>   "Yes."
> "Ms. Jenson? Our beloved phys ed teacher and girls' track coach?"
> "Skinny-dipping. Absolutely. She was in the lake totally naked."(3)

I can't imagine any high school student not wanting to read more of that story.

Middle school kids, especially boys, want action, adventure, suspense. A seventh grader writing to his pen pal, one of my graduate students, a couple years back explained his tastes bluntly: "I like horror with a lot of killing and suspense." The writing also has to be vivid so that readers, as one boy said, can "get a clear picture of what is happening." Another seventh grade boy, in a class taught by a friend of mine, says he enjoyed a novel by Raymond Feist called *Shadow of a Dark Queen* because "it had great detail" so that "when he decapitated a guy because he killed a girl that he liked, I could visualize the picture in my mind." Maybe that's not quite the kind of interest we would like to see, but these seventh graders are very clear about their likes and dislikes.

What teens want more than anything else from novels is entertainment. And that's exactly what I want—and what I suspect most readers want—from a novel. That's also primarily what writers say they want readers to get from their books. If readers learn something along the way, that's even better. But once the lesson becomes the primary reason for using a book, the act of reading becomes a chore. So it makes good sense to find teachable novels whose stories are lively, interesting, enjoyable, hopefully humorous, too, from which we can also learn something—about how people deal with their problems, how other people interact, possibly how other cultures function (though younger teens, being basically self-centered, prefer to read about people as much like themselves as possible), and so forth.

One of my former university students recalled her early adolescent experiences with books: "As a teenager, I was able to be myself when I was reading, while the rest of the time I was fitting in. Because a lot of the novels I read dealt with teenagers with similar problems, I felt comfortable."

Another student, this one a seventh grade girl, when asked to analyze what makes a book interesting, wrote this:

> Most of my favorite books have all had one thing in common. That is the main characters in the books were young kids, or teens. I think that books with kids in them are very interesting to me because I can sort of relate to them, and I like reading about things that could happen to people my age. Also, sometimes when I read books that have older characters in them, they are dealing with problems that I can't relate to or don't understand.

One of the most valuable qualities of contemporary teenage fiction is that it helps students feel normal, comfortable, understood. In many school systems, teenage fiction is limited to middle school classes or to remedial level classes in the high school, mainly because those books are easier to read than classics. Older and more advanced readers can handle the classics—true. But even our brightest students are still teenagers with typical teenage problems and needs, and by limiting those more advanced students to classics, our curricula fail to meet their social and emotional needs. Everyone knows there are easy teen novels for younger and less able readers, but there are also some superb novels in this genre that are more complex—sophisticated enough for even AP readers. (On that topic, check out an article by Patricia Spencer in the November 1989 *English Journal.*)

But, you may ask, if we stop teaching classics, or at least decrease our reliance on them, how would we teach the reading and analytical skills with less challenging literary works? Significant question. The answer is easy: teach the newer books basically the same way. Well, let me qualify that. I mean teach the same literary concepts and develop the same analytical skills, but perhaps in a better way. There are still too many teachers who kill *any* book by the way they teach it, asking students to recall picky and insignificant details, testing every day, removing whatever joy a kid might have had in reading the book in the first place.

Like classics, contemporary books for teenagers have plots that can be charted, settings that play significant roles, and characters whose personalities, actions, and interactions can be analyzed. There are figurative language, foreshadowing, irony, and other literary elements in the best of the newer works. The symbolism, however, usually isn't as heavy as in most classics, and the vocabulary is usually less difficult, but no young adult reader will object to those things: in fact, many teachers I know will be relieved by that as well.

The only two elements common in the classics that some contemporary young adult novels lack are plot complexity and dull, lengthy descriptions. This doesn't mean that no contemporary novels for teens have complex plots: the works of Robert Cormier, M. E. Keer, Chris Crutcher, and Chris Lynch, for example, are quite complex. The most appealing characteristic of young adult novels, of course, is their high interest level. In short, we can teach high school students literary skills with YA [Young Adult] books while everyone enjoys the reading activity. (If you want research proof, go way back to 1965 and read Nathan S. Blount's report in the *Journal of Educational Research* and Bruce Appleby's 1967 dissertation.)

It bothers me a great deal when high school English teachers or university professors condemn young adult books because they believe they are shallow and poorly written. Those people are ignorant elitists who haven't done their homework, haven't read even an adequate sampling of the novels, short stories, nonfiction, and poetry for teens that is available for classroom use and independent reading. Those critics seem to think that young adult books mean shallow romances, Sweet Valley High, transparent mysteries, or supernatural thrillers like those by R. L. Stine. They equate simplicity with lack of quality. And they are partly right, because those kinds of books are part of what some kids are interested in, especially in middle school. But there is so much more....

There are literally hundreds of great books ... written by sensitive, knowledgeable, and insightful writers who understand teenage readers. Along with the well-established writers in this field, such as Richard Peck, Robert Cormier, Chris Crutcher, Norma Fox Mazer, Caroline Cooney, Bruce Brooks, M. E. Keer, Alden R. Carter, Will Hobbs, and Walter Dean Myers, there are many talented newer writers such as Ellen Wittlinger, Rob Thomas, Han Nolan, Adam Rapp, Trudy Krisher, Margaret Peterson Haddix, and Laurie Halse Anderson. You need to read their works and experience them for yourselves. Then, you need to tell your students about them, even if you never teach these books in your classroom, because there is no other way your students will ever hear about these books or others like them.

How else will your kids know about them? They don't see ads for these books on television. They don't hear them discussed on the radio. Their parents and grandparents can't recommend these books because most of them weren't written when those older folks were teenagers. In too many schools, library/ media specialists do not get a chance to recommend these books to kids because most teachers, especially in high school, never invite the librarians to their classrooms. Worse, many librarians who work with teenagers—in both school libraries and public libraries—were never trained in the field of books for young people, so they don't know as much about these books as they should.

Who is left? The only people in the whole universe who can talk to students about books—other than their peers—is us! Unfortunately, the evidence shows that most teachers DON'T talk with their teenage students about books that will interest them. In fact, 35 percent of the seventh grade students in a survey that one of my former students conducted said that they couldn't recall a single teacher ever recommending a book of any kind to them, and 60 percent recalled only one teacher who had ever done so (Cararini). And if their teachers did recommend books, it was usually classics that the teachers had read in college, books that were written for well-educated, leisured adults and that don't have a single teenage character in them. In that same survey of kids in a medium size city middle school, only three out of the fifty-seven eighth graders surveyed checked the statement, "Teachers know what books students like." How sad. In fact, that's almost criminal.

One of the best ways I've found to introduce teens to good books is to have an extensive classroom library—most paperbacks because they are easier for kids to handle and carry. Every classroom should contain dozens of them, nonfiction as well as fiction, and poetry too. Even picture books. Add to your collection frequently. Booktalk a few of them each week. (Of course, to do that, you will need to read them first.)

If you can't completely change the curriculum so that you can replace some of the classics with contemporary books, especially books with teenage main characters, then consider pairing teen novels with one or more of your classics. In *From Hinton to Hamlet*, Sarah Herz and I explain how you can do that quite efficiently. In four separate volumes of *Adolescent Literature as a Complement to the Classics*, edited by Joan Kaywell, you can find teaching ideas and even some daily lesson plans for doing that with several classics.

Another way to incorporate more teen lit into your classroom is to introduce your students to some of the numerous short stories with teenage characters that are now available. Twenty years ago there were five collections of stories written for teenagers. Today there are more than 100 collections. You can find an extensive list of many of those short story titles and how to use them in a text called *Into Focus: Understanding and Creating Middle School Readers*, edited by Kyleen Beers and Barbara Samuels (340–45).

Providing a block of time each week, or even each day, when kids can read whatever they choose for pleasure will increase reading interest and experience. Consider it practice. Athletes practice; musicians practice; our students need to practice reading, too. It would be even better if the entire school set aside 15–20 minutes every day for silent reading. School reading assignments are not allowed. No homework. Just pleasure reading. And *you* get to read as well.

You might even start your program by reading *to* your classes. Read the opening chapter or a particularly vivid scene from a novel and then stop. If the story and your lively reading of it have done their job, at least one of the students in your class will ask to borrow the book so she or he can read the whole thing. Don't be surprised if they do so in one night. And if one student is enthused about a book, that will influence others to try it. Good experiences are addictive. . . .

One final word: please do not conclude that I am against reading and teaching classics. But knowing that our traditional classical literature curricula have done more harm than good to so many students over the years, I urge you to also consider using some of the wonderful contemporary books that are available to meet the reading needs and interests of today's students. Not only will your students appreciate them, but I guarantee that YOU also will enjoy them.

Here's to the joy of reading!

Works Cited

Abelove, Joan. *Go and Come Back.* New York, DK Inc., 1998.

Anderson, Laurie Halse. *Speak.* New York: Farrar, Straus & Giroux, 1999.

Appleby, Bruce D. "The Effect of Individualized Reading on Certain Aspects of Litera-ture Study with High School Seniors." *Dissertation Abstracts* 28 (1967):2592.

Bauer, Joan. *Rules of the Road.* New York: Putnam, 1998.

Beers, Kylene, and Barbara G. Samuels, eds. *Into Focus: Understanding and Creating Middle School Readers.* Norwood, MA: Christopher-Gordon, 1998.

Blount, Nathan S. "The Effect of Selected Junior Novels and Selected Adult Novels on Student Attitudes Toward the 'Ideal Novel.'" *The Journal of Educational Research* 59.4 (1965): 179–82.

Cararini, Michael. "Reading Survey." Unpublished report, 1989.

Carlsen, G. Robert, and Anne Sherrill. *Voices of Readers: How We Come to Love Books.* Urbana, IL: NCTE, 1988.

Cochran, Thomas. *Roughnecks.* San Diego: Harcourt Brace, 1997.

Cormier, Robert. *After the First Death.* New York: Pantheon, 1979.

Crane, Stephen. *The Red Badge of Courage.* New York: D. Appleton-Century Co., 1925.

Crutcher, Chris. *Ironman.* New York: Greenwillow, 1995.

Eliot, George. *Silas Marner.* Boston: Houghton, Mifflin and Co., 1899.

Feist, Raymond E. *Shadow of a Dark Queen: A Novel.* New York: Morrow, 1995.

Gallo, Donald R. "Reactions to Required Reading: Some Implications from a Study of Connecticut Students." *Connecticut English Journal* 15.2 (1984): 7–11.

_____. ed. *Time Capsule: Short Stories About Teenagers throughout the Twentieth Cen-tury.* New York: Delacorte, 1999.

Glenn, Mel. *Class Dismissed II: More High School Poems.* New York: Clarion, 1986.

Herz, Sarah K., with Donald R. Gallo. *From Hinton to Hamlet: Building Bridges between Young Adult Literature and the Classics.* Westport, CT: Greenwood, 1996.

Hipple, Ted, ed. *Writers for Young Adults,* 4 volumes. New York: Scribner's 1997–2000.

Hobbs, Will. *Jason's Gold.* New York: Morrow, 1999.

_____. *The Maze.* New York: Morrow, 1998.

Kaywell, Joan, ed. *Adolescent Literature as a Complement to the Classics,* 4 volumes. Norwood, MA: Christopher-Gordon, 1993–1999.

Klause, Annette Curtis. *Blood and Chocolate.* New York: Delacorte, 1997.

Lynch, Chris. *Whitechurch.* New York: HarperCollins, 1999.

Mazer, Harry, ed. *Twelve Shots: Outstanding Stories About Guns.* New York: Delacorte, 1997.

McDonald, Joyce. *Swallowing Stones.* New York: Delacorte, 1997.

Myers, Walter Dean. *Monster.* New York: Scholastic, 1999.

Nolan, Han. *Dancing on the Edge.* San Diego: Harcourt Brace, 1997.

Paulsen, Gary. *Soldier's Heart: A Novel of the Civil War.* New York: Delacorte, 1998.

Pennac, Daniel. *Better Than Life.* Trans. David Homel. York, ME: Stenhouse/Pembroke, 1999.

Spencer, Patricia. "YA Novels in the AP Classroom: Crutcher Meets Camus." *English Journal* 78:7 (1989): 44–46.

Spinelli, Jerry. *Stargirl*. New York: Knopf, 2000.
Thomas, Rob. *Doing Time: Notes from the Undergrad*. New York: Simon & Schuster, 1997.
Wallace, Rich. *Playing Without the Ball*. New York: Knopf, 2000.
Weaver, Will. "The Photograph." *No Easy Answers: Short Stories about Teenagers Making Tough Choices*. Ed. Donald R. Gallo. New York: Delacorte 1997. 3–24.
Werlin, Nancy. *The Killer's Cousin*. New York: Delacorte, 1998.
———. *Locked Inside*. New York: Delacorte, 2000.
Wittlinger, Ellen. *Hard Love*. New York: Simon & Schuster, 1999.
Woodson, Jacqueline. *I Hadn't Meant to Tell You This*. New York: Delacorte, 1994.
Zindel, Paul. *The Effect of Gamma Rays on Man-in-the-Moon Marigolds*. New York: Harper, 1971.

POSTSCRIPT

Should Classical Works Be the Emphasis of the High School Literature Curriculum?

$\mathbf{O}$bviously the competing values underscoring this issue transcend the choice of literature in the secondary school English curriculum. Similar debates with regard to appropriateness of subject matter content are occurring in history, the sciences, and even mathematics, as teachers struggle with questions related to depth of coverage versus breadth; traditional, "basic" content versus new, more "multicultural" content; and "great men" approaches to history versus "everyman" approaches.

Many ask whether or not specific curriculum that is determined to be of great value is only of great value to some students. The diametrically opposite answers to this question illustrate the philosophical and political dimensions of this issue. At one end of the spectrum are advocates of a basic "liberal" education for all students. Opponents of such all-inclusive requirements argue that secondary school students are better served by a curriculum that is tailored to their individual needs, interests, and goals. They support curricular concepts such as school-to-work, vocational training, and Advanced Placement (AP) courses and alternative organizational structures such as magnet schools, charter schools, and schools-within-schools. It is somewhat ironic that these "student-centered" attempts at individualizing the curriculum have often resulted in controversial practices such as grouping and tracking. Concomitantly, even when all students must take a certain subject such as English or algebra to graduate, in practice there are often "different" courses of English and algebra.

So thus it is with this specific issue—there are different layers of contention with opposing viewpoints at each level. Fundamentally, some would argue that fairness and equity require that all students be allowed to benefit from a study of the classics. They further argue that for some students high school education will be their last experience with formal education, and thus if students are not exposed to great literature in high school they will never experience it. Opponents counter that "force feeding" the classics to all students simply will not work; instead, it will alienate and frustrate many. Further, they state that using more "reader-friendly" material is not only motivational but also allows the teacher to find material that represents a broader spectrum of cultural/ethnic authorship than that offered by the classics.

Regardless of the position that one takes on this issue it is indisputable that schools, especially public schools, are charged with the responsibility to transmit the culture and the heritage of the nation. The argument can certainly be made that there is no one specific culture or one heritage. But after all such arguments are made the fact remains that there is a body of indisputably great and lasting literature that is available to young people, and to the extent that they have the opportunity to explore and experience it they will be benefited.

Other articles and books dealing with this topic include Harold Bloom's *The Western Canon: The Books and School of the Ages* (Harcourt Brace, 1994); Louise Rosenblatt, *Literature as Exploration* (Modern Language Association, 1983); Francine Prose, "I Know Why the Caged Bird Cannot Read," *Harper's Magazine* (September 1999); John Kaywell, ed., *Adolescent Literature as a Complement to the Classics* (Christopher-Gordon, 1993–1999); Robert Probst, "Adolescent Literature and the English Curriculum," *English Journal* (vol. 76, no. 3, 1987); and Ben Nelms, "Adolescent Literature as Literature," *Iowa English Bulletin* (vol. 29, no. 2, 1980).

ISSUE 20

Should We Be Cheering for High School Sports Programs?

YES: Arkansas Activities Association, from "The Case for High School Activities," http://www.ahsaa.org/case_for_high_school_activities.htm (October 12, 2000)

NO: Jay J. Coakley, from *Sport in Society: Issues and Controversies*, 6th ed. (McGraw-Hill, 1997)

ISSUE SUMMARY

YES: The Arkansas Activities Association, which serves as the rule-making body for Arkansas high school athletic programs, points to criteria such as grades, discipline referrals, drop-out rates, attendance, and graduation rates wherein high school athletes outperform nonathletes.

NO: Jay J. Coakley, professor at the University of Colorado, contends that students who choose to participate in activities, including athletics, are different to begin with, and thus differences on simple statistics between participants and nonparticipants do not establish cause for concluding that participation in sports is the reason for increased academic success.

High school extracurricular activities, and specifically school sports programs, seemingly exist in the category of "apple pie, flag, and motherhood" with respect to their acceptance by the general public. This notion of school activities and sports is not new; indeed the National Education Association (NEA) Commission on the Reorganization of Secondary Education in 1918 included as part of its *Cardinal Principles of Secondary Education* a commitment to "health, ethical development, and the worthy use of leisure time." A revealing piece of data related to the high regard held for these programs was included as part of the 1996 Phi Delta Kappa/Gallup Poll of the Public's Attitudes Toward the Public Schools. The poll asked parents the question, "Which one of the following would you prefer of an oldest child—that the child get A grades or that he or she make average grades and be active in extracurricular activities?" The results showed that 60 percent of the respondents came down on the side of average grades combined with extracurricular activities; and 9 percent replied "both." In the 2000 edition of the Phi Delta Kappa/Gallup Poll, 46 percent of the respondents with children in the public schools said that extracurricular activities were as important as academic subjects.

While there are numerous programs that fall under the heading of high school cocurricular/extracurricular activities, in most schools it is the athletic program that has the greatest number of student participants and receives the greatest amount of publicity and public support. A strong case for the value of such participation, especially in high school sports, is made by the rules-making body for all high school sports, the National Federation of State High School Associations (NFHS), in "The Case for High School Activities." In many states high school sports programs culminate in state championships and national exposure for schools and student athletes. Participation in high school activities and, in particular, high school athletics receives explicit endorsement from colleges and universities by virtue of admissions criteria that usually rate such participation as a key element in acceptance and/or the awarding of scholarships.

But there are also some disquieting elements about the high status afforded to high school athletic programs and participants. An alleged motivational factor in the tragedy at Littleton, Colorado's Columbine High School recently was the reported perception of the perpetrators that certain athletes in the school had somehow mistreated them. In Long Beach, California, male high school athletes were allegedly involved in organized sexual exploitation of underage female students. It is true that such perversions are not characteristic of most programs, but that they exist anywhere is cause for concern.

Obviously high school athletic programs are founded on competition. Alfie Kohn, in his article "The Case Against Competition," *The Working Mother* (September 1987), states, "When it comes to competition, we Americans typically recognize only two legitimate positions: enthusiastic support and qualified support." He goes on to posit that the pressures and publicity attendant to an overemphasis on competition and winning can lead to inordinate demands being placed on young people as well as to ill-advised actions by adults. Speaking to the same argument, Jay J. Coakley in his selection warns, "But if varsity sports are organized in ways that lead young people to think that adults are controlling them for their purposes, interscholastic programs become developmental dead ends and students become cynical about school and society."

The Case for High School Activities

At a cost of only one to three percent (or less in many cases) of an overall school's budget, high school activity programs are one of the best bargains around. It is in these vital programs—sports, music, speech, drama, debate—where young people learn lifelong lessons as important as those taught in the classroom.

Unfortunately, there appears to be a creeping indifference toward support for high school activity programs by the general public. This neglect undermines the educational mission of our schools and the potential prosperity of our communities.

There is no better time than today to assert "The Case for High School Activities." Education and community leaders across the nation must be made aware of the facts contained in this material. From interscholastic sports to music, theatre and debate, activities enrich a student's high school experience, and the programs must be kept alive.

The National Federation of State High School Associations (NFHS) and its membership believe that interscholastic sports and fine arts activities promote citizenship and sportsmanship. They instill a sense of pride in community, teach lifelong lessons of teamwork and self-discipline and facilitate the physical and emotional development of our nation's youth.

The NFHS supports extracurricular endeavors through many avenues, including:

- The Citizenship Through Sports and Fine Arts curriculum—The curriculum is designed to help coaches and advisers use teachable moments to create better young people through extracurricular activities.
- National High School Activities Week—The nation's high schools are encouraged to promote the values inherent in high school athletics and other activities such as speech, music, theatre, band and spirit squads during this week-long celebration the third week in October.
- Student Activities: An Integral Part of Education—This presentation documents the value of high school athletic and activity programs and includes a slide presentation and video.

Benefits of extracurricular activities

- Activities Support the Academic Mission of Schools. They are not a diversion but rather an extension of a good educational program. Students who participate in activity programs tend to have higher grade-point averages [GPA], better attendance records, lower dropout rates and fewer discipline problems than students generally.
- Activities are Inherently Educational. Activity programs provide valuable lessons for practical situations—teamwork, sportsmanship, winning and losing, and hard work. Through participation in activity programs, students learn self-discipline, build self-confidence and develop skills to handle competitive situations. These are qualities the public expects schools to produce in students so that they become responsible adults and productive citizens.
- Activities Foster Success in Later Life. Participation in high school activities is often a predictor of later success—in college, a career and becoming a contributing member of society.

Following are some of those benefits, with case studies, where applicable, listed to document the benefits:

Participation in high school activities is a valuable part of the overall high school experience.

- Of the 60 students listed in the May 14, 1998, *USA Today's* All-USA High School Academic First, Second and Third Teams and the 51 who earned honorable mention, 75 percent were involved in sports, speech, music or debate.
- The 29th annual Phi Delta Kappa/Gallup Poll of the Public's Attitudes Toward the Public Schools of September 1997 reflects an increase in perceptions about the value of extracurricular activities. In 1978, 45 percent of the public judged extracurricular activities to be very important. That figure fell to 31 percent in 1984. In 1985, the figure was 39 percent and jumped to 63 percent in the 1997 poll. The 1997 poll also asked about the emphasis placed on such sports as football and basketball. Fifty-three percent of the respondents believed the current emphasis was about right.
- The Role of Sports in Youth Development, Carnegie Corporation, New York, in a report of a meeting in March 1996, found that evidence showed that the involvement of young people in sports produces multiple benefits for them. At their best, sports programs promote responsible social behaviors and greater academic success, confidence in one's physical abilities, an appreciation of personal health and fitness, and strong social bonds with individuals and institutions. Teachers attribute these results to the discipline and work ethic that sports require.

- In a survey of 4,800 high school students in March 1995, the Minnesota State High School League found that 91 percent of them said students who participate in school activities tend to be school leaders and role models; 92 percent said that participation in school activities provides an opportunity not found in a regular classroom setting to develop self-discipline.

- *Adolescent Time Use, Risky Behavior, and Outcomes: An Analysis of National Data*, issued in September 1995, by the Department of Health and Human Services found that students who spend no time in extracurricular activities are 57 percent more likely to have dropped out of school by the time they would have been seniors; 49 percent more likely to have used drugs; 37 percent more likely to have become teen parents; 35 percent more likely to have smoked cigarettes; and 27 percent more likely to have been arrested than those who spend one to four hours per week in extracurricular activities. . . .

- Research conducted in 1991 by Skip Dane of Hardiness Research, Casper, Wyoming, revealed the following about participation in high school sports: 1) By a 2-to-1 ratio, boys who participate in sports do better in school, do not drop out and have a better chance to get through college. 2) The ratio for girls who participate in sports and do well in school is three to one. 3) About 92 percent of sports participants do not use drugs. 4) School athletes are more self-assured. 5) Sports participants take average and above-average classes. 6) Sports participants receive above-average grades and do above average on skills tests. 7) Those involved in sports have knowledge of and use financial aid and have a chance to finish college. 8) Student-athletes appear to have more parental involvement than other students. 9) Students involved in athletics appear to change focus from cars and money to life accomplishments during the process.

- A 1989 nationwide study by the Women's Sport Foundation indicated that athletes do better in the classroom, are more involved in school activity programs and stay involved in the community after graduation. The study also revealed that high school athletic participation has a positive educational and social impact on many minority and female students. The study, based on an analysis of data collected by the U.S. Department of Education's High School and Beyond Study, indicated that: 1) Girls receive as many benefits from sports as boys. 2) The "dumb jock" stereotype is a myth. 3) Sports involvement was significantly related to a lower dropout rate in some school settings. 4) Minority athletes are more socially involved than non-athletes.

- In 1985, the NFHS sponsored a national survey of high school principals and nearly 7,000 high school students in all 50 states. The survey, funded by a grant from the Lilly Endowment in Indianapolis, was conducted by Indiana University in cooperation with the National Association of Secondary School Principals. Following are the results of that survey.

- 95 percent believed that participation in activities teaches valuable lessons to students that cannot be learned in a regular class routine.
- 99 percent agreed that participation in activities promotes citizenship.
- 95 percent agreed that activity programs contribute to the development of "school spirit" among the student body.
- 76 percent said they believe the demand made on students' time by activities is not excessive.
- 72 percent said there is strong support for school activity programs from parents and the community at large.

Students who compete in high school activity programs make higher grades and have better attendance.

- In a comprehensive, statewide study of the academic performance of high school student-athletes in North Carolina over a three-year period, the North Carolina High School Athletic Association found significant differences between athletes and non-athletes. Five criteria were used, including grade-point average, attendance rate, discipline referrals, dropout rate and graduation rate, for the 1994–95 academic year.

Table 1

	Athletes	Non-Athletes
Grade-point average	2.86	1.96
Average number of absences per 180 school year	6.52 days	12.57 days
Discipline referrals	30.51%	40.29%
Dropout Rate	0.7%	8.98%
Graduation Rate	99.56%	94.66%

- Findings from the National Center for Education Statistics, Extracurricular Participation and Student Engagement, June 1995, revealed that during the first semester of their senior year, participants reported better attendance than their non-participating classmates. Half of them had no unexcused absences from school and half had never skipped a class, compared with one-third and two-fifths of non-participants, respectively. Students who participated were three times as likely to perform in the top quartile on a composite math and reading assessment compared with non-participants. Participants also were more likely than non-participants to aspire to higher education; two-thirds of participants expected to complete at least a bachelor's degree while about half of non-participants expected to do so.

- A 1992 study by the Colorado High School Activities Association and the Colorado Department of Education revealed that Colorado high school students who participate in some form of interscholastic activity have "significantly higher" grade-point averages and better attendance. Of the students surveyed, the average participant's GPA was 2.96 (on a 4.0 scale), compared to 2.35 for the non-participant. In one school, participants had an average reading test score of 76.30, compared to 58.91 for non-participants. In another school, participants scored 16.17 on the math standardized test, compared to 13.31 for non-participants. A participant missed school an average of 3.59 days a year, while a non-participant missed 5.92 days. The survey showed that the larger the school, the more pronounced the differences in participant and non-participant test scores and attendance results.
- High school students who compete in activity programs in New Mexico had a 2.80 grade-point average, compared to 2.00 for non-participants, according to a 1992 survey by the New Mexico Activities Association. The survey also indicated that more than 60 percent of the state's principals found that GPAs of at-risk students improved by being active in interscholastic activities.
- 1990–91 study in the Randolph (North Carolina) County school system showed a strong correlation between participation in athletics and positives such as improved grades and increased attendance rates. Athletes in grades 9 through 12 in the school system's four high schools recorded an 86 average, compared to 79 for the general population. Athletes averaged four absences, while the general population averaged seven. Eleven percent of the athletes had discipline referrals, compared to 25 percent of the general population. None of the athletes dropped out, while 3.7 percent of the general population were dropouts.
- In a 1988 survey, John Chevrette and Kenneth Patranella concluded from an investigation in San Antonio, Texas, that educational outcomes related to scholastic performance are enhanced for those secondary students who participate in activity programs. A study of a high school population of 3,536 students found that secondary pupils who participated in more than one activity during a semester tended to experience higher academic performance levels than other participants and non-participants.
- Students participating in a number of activities not only achieve better academically but also express greater satisfaction with the total high school experience than students who do not participate, according to a 1985 survey conducted for the NFHS by Indiana University. The grade-point average for "high activity" students was 3.05 on a 4.0 scale, compared to a GPA of 2.54 for "low activity" students. Researchers defined high activity as involvement in four or more activities, while low activity students were involved in one activity or none.

Participation in activity programs yields positive results after high school as well.

- Admission officers at Harvard, Yale and 70 percent of the nation's other major universities have stated that high school credit and achievement in the arts are significant considerations for admission to their institutions. This finding was from *Can Colleges Help School Fine Arts Programs?* in a 1992 article in *Connecticut Music Educators Association News.*
- Results of a 1987 survey of individuals at the executive vice-president level or above in 75 Fortune 500 companies indicated that 95 percent of those corporate executives participated in sports during high school. In addition, 54 percent were involved in student government, 43 percent in the National Honor Society, 37 percent in music, 35 percent in scouts and 18 percent in the school's publication.
- The American College Testing Service compared the value of four factors in predicting success after high school. "Success" was defined as self-satisfaction and participation in a variety of community activities two years after college. The one yardstick that could be used to predict later success in life was achievement in school activities. Not useful as predictors were high grades in high school, high grades in college or high ACT [American College Test] scores.
- The College Entrance Examination Board's Scholastic Aptitude Test (SAT) was examined in much the same way. It was found that having a high SAT score did not necessarily indicate success in a chosen career. The best predictor of later success, the study showed, was a person's independent, self-sustained ventures. Teens who were active in school activities, had hobbies or jobs, were found to be most likely to succeed at their chosen profession and make creative contributions to their community.

From a cost standpoint, activity programs are an exceptional bargain when matched against the overall school district's education budget.

Generally speaking, the NFHS has determined through information received across the country that activity programs make up only one to three percent of the overall education budget in a school. In Chicago, that figure is even less. In 1992, the overall budget for the Chicago Board of Education was $2.6 billion, and activity programs received only $2.9 million, a minuscule one-tenth of one percent (.001).

Activity programs fulfill students' basic needs, help in students' attitudes toward self and school and minimize dropout and discipline problems.

- A report on *The Condition of Education*, United States Department of Education, National Center for Education Statistics in 1995 found that participation in extracurricular activities may affect academic performance, attachment to school and social development. The report further stated that almost every high school in the United States offers some type of extracurricular activity, such as music, academic clubs and sports. These activities provide opportunities for students to learn the values of teamwork, a channel for reinforcing skills and the opportunity to apply academic skills in other arenas as a part of a well-rounded education.

- American Youth and Sports Participation, a survey of 10,000 students by the Sporting Goods Manufacturers Association (1990) revealed that the No. 1 reason that girls and boys participate in high school sports is to have fun. Conversely, lack of fun was the leading reason for dropping out of participation. Winning was not seen as a major benefit of sports by young people who participate—it was ranked No. 8 by boys and No. 12 by girls. Skill development was considered a crucial aspect of fun—it was considered more important than winning even among the best athletes. Another finding: The most rewarding challenges of sports are those that lead to self-knowledge. Finally, intrinsic rewards (self-knowledge that grows out of self-competition) are more important in creating lifelong athletes than extrinsic rewards (victory or attention from others).

- A Wyoming High School Activities Association [WHSAA] Statewide Student Activities Survey compiled in the summer of 1998 points out addiction dangers of tobacco use. Yearly, monthly and weekly reported use of tobacco by high school students is low when compared to the high percentage of daily users. Approximately 25 percent of those involved in athletics or activities report daily tobacco use, compared to 40 percent for non-participants. For students involved in both athletics and activities, that percentage drops to 13 percent. A focus of future WHSAA surveys will explore the reasons for this outcome.

In light of these findings, the WHSAA encourages coaches and activity sponsors to continue (or begin) an emphasis on teaching the addictive dangers of tobacco and make solutions known and available to all students.

Extracurricular activities teach lessons that lead to better citizens.

- The Alberta Schools' Athletic Association (ASAA), in conjunction with the Metro Edmonton High School Athletic Association and the Alberta Centre for Well-Being, completed a survey of 883 students. The survey, completed in November 1997, was undertaken to assess the potential impact that high school athletics has on the lives and attitudes of students in Alberta.

Findings showed student-athletes are less likely to smoke (30 percent versus 44 percent), and if they do smoke, they are less likely to smoke heavily. Overall, 35 percent of students reported they currently smoke cigarettes. The survey findings indicated student-athletes (9 percent) are less likely to report drinking more than once a week in comparison to non-athletic students (20 percent).

"The results of this survey suggest that students who participate in school-based sport programs are good school citizens and may be even better school citizens than their non-sport peers," said John Paton, executive director, ASAA. "School athletes demonstrate positive lifestyle behaviors, such as less smoking and less drug use when compared to non-sport students."

Paton also indicated that if administrators, teachers or parents are concerned that school sport programs compete for students' attention and participation with other extracurricular activities, the study disputes these concerns. Student-athletes tend to participate at a greater rate in other school activities, and they have a more positive perception of their school.

- A study conducted by Public Agenda released in June 1997 (*Kids These Days: What Americans Really Think About the Next Generation*) found that more than six in 10 adults, or 61 percent, said youngsters' failure to learn such values as honesty, respect and responsibility is a very serious problem. Only 37 percent believe today's children, once they're grown, will make the United States a better place. Those polled also said greater availability and use of school programs and volunteer groups would be an effective way to help children.
- Consider the captain at a track championship who had won the long jump and was the leader in the triple jump when he reported to the start of the 100-meter dash. Upon his arrival, he discovered another runner from a rival school had forgotten his spikes. This young man was the only person in the league with a chance to defeat him. Without hesitating, he gave the boy his backup pair of spikes. The young man with the borrowed spikes won in the final while setting a league record in the event. The same scenario played itself out in the finals of the 200-meter dash. The boy who lent the spikes indicated, "It never occurred to me to do anything else."
- Early in a soccer championship game, a forward and defender both jumped to head the ball. Their heads collided, and one player was injured but did not drop to the ground—the signal to the referee to stop play. The coach on the opposing team recognized the distress of the player and despite his team having the opportunity to clear the ball and take the advantage in play, he directed his team to kick the ball out of bounds. He gave up possession of the ball near his goal to stop play and allow the player to be assisted.

Jay J. Coakley  **NO**

Sports in High School and College: Do Varsity Sports Programs Contribute to Education?

Arguments for and Against Interscholastic Sports

Most people in the U.S. take interscholastic sport programs for granted; they have been an expected part of life at school. However, recent budget cutbacks and highly publicized problems in certain high school and college sports programs have raised questions about how sports are related to educational goals and to the overall development of young people. Similar questions are being raised about interscholastic sports in Canadian schools. Responses to these questions are varied. Program supporters claim that interscholastic sports support the educational mission of schools; critics claim that they interfere with that mission....

Although interscholastic sport programs have been studied frequently, the debate about their educational relevance continues today. When people enter this debate they often exaggerate the benefits or the problems associated with varsity sport programs. Supporters emphasize glowing success stories, and critics emphasize shocking cases of excess and abuse, but the most accurate descriptions probably lie somewhere in between. Nonetheless, both the supporters and the critics call attention to many of the important issues in the relationship between sports and education. This [selection] will focus on some of those issues.

Interscholastic Sports and the Experiences of High School Students

Do varsity sports programs affect the educational and developmental experiences of high school students? This question is difficult to answer. Education and development occur in connection with many activities and relationships. Even though varsity sport programs are very important in some schools and for some students, they constitute only one of many sources of potentially influential experiences. Research on this issue has focused primarily on the characteristics of student-athletes, although some social scientists have tried to study how sports are connected with the overall school-based culture that exists among high school students.

High School Student-Athletes

Studies have shown consistently that when compared with students who do not play varsity sports, high school athletes, *as a group,* generally have better grade point averages, more positive attitudes towards school, more interest in continuing their education after graduation, and a slightly better educational achievement rate (see Miracle and Rees, 1994). These differences usually have been modest, and it has been difficult for researchers to separate the effects of sport participation from the effects of family backgrounds, support from friends, and other factors related to educational attitudes and performance. However, membership on a varsity team is a valued source of status in most U.S. schools, and it seems to go hand in hand with positive educational experiences for some students (Marsh, 1993). But research has not told us what it is about sport participation that might cause those positive experiences.

Of course, the most logical explanation for differences between varsity athletes and other students is that interscholastic sports, like other extracurricular activities, attract students who already have characteristics associated with academic and social success in high school. Most studies have not been able to test this explanation, because they don't actually follow students throughout their high school careers to keep track of how and why changes occur in their lives. Usually, the studies simply report information collected from students at one point in time and then compare those on sport teams with those who are not on teams. This makes it impossible for researchers to say whether playing varsity sports really changes people, or whether students who try out for varsity teams, get selected for teams, and continue as team members are simply different from other students *before* they become varsity athletes.

Even when researchers think that young people do change while playing varsity sports, they are unable to say anything about specific aspects of sport participation that account for the changes. The mere fact that young people grow and develop during the same years they play on varsity teams does not mean that sport participation *causes* the growth and development. After all, fourteen to eighteen-year-olds grow and develop in many ways, whether they play varsity sports or do other things. Most studies do not distinguish among all the different factors that might explain growth and development.

Fortunately, there are a few studies that follow students over time and measure changes that occur in their lives. For example, Elmer Spreitzer, a sociologist from Bowling Green State University, did a study in which he analyzed data from a national probability sample of 12,000 young men and women from 1,100 public and private schools around the United States. Spreitzer collected information from high school sophomores and seniors in 1980, and then gathered follow-up information from the same students in 1982, 1984, and 1986.

This enabled him to track students who played on varsity sport teams, and to compare them with other students as they got older. Spreitzer found that compared with other students, young people who played on varsity sport teams were more likely to come from *economically privileged* backgrounds, and have *above-average* cognitive abilities, self-esteem, and academic performance records (grades and test scores). In other words, students who tried out for teams, made teams, and stayed on them were different in certain ways from other students *before* they became high school athletes.

Spreitzer found that this type of "selection" pattern was common to nearly all extracurricular activities, not just varsity sports. In other words, students who choose to participate in official, school-sponsored activities tend to be slightly different from other students. These differences are greatest in those activities in which student self-selection is combined with formal tryouts in which teachers or coaches choose students for participation. In the case of varsity sports, this self-selection and choice process is especially powerful, because it begins in youth sports and continues through junior high school....

Spreitzer also tracked changes during the six-year period after students left high school. He found that those who played varsity sports as seniors were no different on a number of traits from those who did not play. The traits included psychological adjustment, patterns of alcohol use, level of self-esteem, age at marriage, and age at birth of first child. There was a slight difference in educational achievement, but playing varsity sports was not nearly as important as other factors affecting college attendance and degree completion.... So what does this research tell us about interscholastic sports?

- *First,* it tells us that we should be very careful when generalizing about the educational value of interscholastic sports. Playing varsity sports does not produce negative effects, but neither does it automatically change high school students in positive ways—indeed, in any ways that make them significantly different from other high school students. Usually those who try out for teams, get selected by coaches, and stay on teams for more than one year are somewhat different from other students to begin with. Therefore, simple statistical comparisons between the two types of students don't prove anything about the value of sport participation itself.
- *Second,* the research suggests that if we want to learn more about the effect of interscholastic sports in the lives of high school students, we must do long-term studies enabling us to look at the overall lives of students, not just their sport lives. Growth and development occur in connection with many different experiences—some outside the school and some inside the school. Unless we know something about young people's lives in general, we can't claim that varsity sport participation is more influential than working at a part-time job, joining the debate team, writing for the school newspaper, or caring for younger brothers and sisters.
- *Third,* the research suggests that we should examine how the educational lives of student-athletes might be different from those of other

students. Do those who play sports take courses in which high grades are characteristic? Do they receive more academic help? Do teachers evaluate them differently? Do they make different academic decisions than other students do, and if so, how does the issue of eligibility affect those decisions?

- *Fourth,* the research also suggests that we should study the effect of varsity sports on the larger student culture that exists in high schools. It may be that the social importance of sports rests in how they are connected with gender, class, and race and ethnic relations in an entire school. It would seem to be a higher priority to study this possibility than to focus only on the students who try out for and make teams....

Student Culture in High Schools

... **Sports and ideology**   Interscholastic sport programs do more than simply affect the status structures of high school students. H. G. Bissinger clearly illustrated this in his book *Friday Night Lights* (1990). Bissinger, a noted Pulitzer Prize–winning author, wrote about a football team in a Texas high school known for its emphasis on football. His account was deliberately dramatic, and he made the case that in Odessa, Texas, as in many other American towns,

> football stood at the very core of what the town was about.... It had nothing to do with entertainment and everything to do with how people felt about themselves (p. 237).

As Bissinger described events through the football season, he noted that football was important because it celebrated a male cult of toughness and sacrifice and a female cult of nurturance and servitude. When the team lost, people accused the coaches of not being tough enough and the players of being undisciplined. Women stayed on the sidelines and faithfully tried to support and please the men who battled on behalf of the school and town. Students and townspeople could go to football games and have their ideas about "natural differences" between men and women reaffirmed. Young men who couldn't hit hard, physically intimidate opponents, or play with pain were described as "pussies." "Gay bashing" was considered an approved weekend social activity by many of the athletes. And a player's willingness to sacrifice his body for the team was taken as a sign of commitment and character.

Bissinger also noted that high school sports were closely tied to a long history of racism in the town, and football itself was organized and played in ways that reaffirmed traditional racial ideology among whites and produced racial resentment among African Americans. Many Anglo townspeople in 1988 still referred to blacks as "niggers," and they blamed blacks and Mexicans for most of the town's problems. They had accepted racial desegregation in 1980 because they thought it could be used to strengthen their school's football team. The irony associated with a situation in which young black males worked hard to benefit whites who wanted a successful team was noted by a local black minister when he observed that "Today, instead of the cotton field, it's the sports arena." ...

Additional Consequences of High School Sports

... **Getting noticed and rewarded**   Research on interscholastic sports has led me to conclude that in and of themselves, sports are not educational. However, if sports are organized and played in certain ways, they can be used to meet educational goals. For example, when varsity sports are organized so that young people are taken seriously as human beings and valued by those who are important in their lives, sport participation can contribute to their educational development. But if varsity sports are organized in ways that lead young people to think that adults are controlling them for their own purposes, interscholastic programs become developmental dead ends and students become cynical about school and society....

Do Schools Benefit From Varsity Sports Programs?

The influence of high school and college varsity sport programs extends well beyond the athletes who play on teams. In this section we will look at the effect of these programs on school spirit... and relations between a school and the larger community.

School Spirit

Anyone who has attended a well-staged student pep rally or watched the student cheering section at a well-attended high school or college game realizes that sports can generate impressive displays of energy and spirit. Of course, this does not happen with all sport teams in a school, nor does it happen in all schools. Teams in low-profile sports usually play games without student spectators, and teams with long histories of losing records seldom create a spirited response among more than a few students. However, in many cases, varsity sport events do provide the basis for spirited social occasions. And students frequently use those occasions to express their feelings about themselves, their teams, and their schools.

Proponents of varsity sports say that displays of school spirit at sport events strengthen student identification with their schools and create the feelings of togetherness needed to achieve educational goals. Critics say the spirit created by sports is temporary, superficial, and unrelated to the achievement of educational goals. What we know at this point is that being a part of any group or organization is more enjoyable when there are feelings of togetherness that accompany the achievement of goals. In the United States—and to an increasing extent in Canada and Japan—sports are one of the ways these feelings of togetherness are created in schools (Miracle, 1980; Rees and Miracle, 1997). But there is nothing magical about sports. Schools in other countries have used other methods to bring students together and provide them with enjoyable, educational experiences revolving around recreation and community service.

People outside the U.S. often see varsity sports in U.S. schools as elitist activities that involve most students in the passive role of spectator, which produces little in the way of educational experiences. They note that the resources devoted to sports might be used to fund other integrative activities that would involve more than cheering for teams, while providing experiences making young people feel valued as contributing members of their communities. In response to the belief that sports "keep kids off the streets," they say that instead of varsity sports, there should be programs through which young people can make the streets better places to be.

In summary, we can acknowledge that varsity sports often create school spirit. However, for that spirit to take on educational significance, it must be part of an overall school program in which students are treated as valued participants and given a sense of ownership in the school and its programs. Unless students are actively involved in what happens every day at school, their cheering at weekly games is simply a superficial display of youthful energy having nothing much to do with education. . . .

Varsity High School Sports: Problems and Recommendations

Existing high school and college sport programs generally enjoy widespread support; many people have vested interests in keeping them the way they are. However, reforms are needed in many programs. Some high school programs are doing an excellent job; others have not only lost direct connections with education, but have subverted the educational process for some students. Problems vary from one high school program to the next. But the most serious problems include the following: (1) an overemphasis on "sports development" and "big-time" program models, (2) limited participation access for students, and (3) too many coaches who emphasize conformity and obedience rather than responsibility and autonomy.

Overemphasis on "Sports Development" and "Big-Time" Program Models

Some high school administrators, athletic directors, and coaches seem to think that the best way to organize high school sports is to model them after big-time intercollegiate programs. When this happens, people involved with varsity sports become overconcerned with winning records and presenting tightly organized, high-profile programs to the community at large; these programs often highlight football or men's basketball. In the process of trying to build high-profile sports programs, they often overlook the educational needs of all students in their schools. Their goal is to be "ranked" rather than to respond to the needs of students.

People who focus on "sports development" often give lip service to the idea that sports must be "kept in proper perspective," but many forget their own words when it comes to the programs at their schools. In fact, they may even encourage students to specialize in a single sport for twelve months a year, instead of encouraging them to develop a wide range of skills in different sports. They set up sport camps or identify camps that they strongly encourage "their athletes" to attend during summer break. They sometimes forbid their athletes to play other sports and then recommend that they join community clubs where they can continue playing through the off-season. And they continually tell students that they must sacrifice to achieve excellence in the future. This, of course, turns off many students who want to have fun with a sport right now, and who want to enjoy participation even if they do not plan on being all-American athletes in the future.

People who adhere to a "sports development" model hire and fire coaches on the basis of win-loss records rather than teaching abilities. They even may describe coaches as good teachers when teams have winning records, and as bad teachers when teams lose. Their goal is to build a "winning tradition" without ever critically examining how such a tradition is connected to the education of students; they just assume that "winning" is educational. This orientation has led an increasing number of high schools to recruit seventh- and eighth-grade athletes in certain sports to build big-time teams that will be highly ranked on the national or state level. They want to use the public relations generated by popular spectator sports to increase their visibility and status; private schools want to use the public relations to recruit more tuition-paying students.

These big-time sports programs have created an atmosphere in which many high school students mistakenly believe that athletics are a better route to rewards and college scholarships than academics. This is just one of the ways that some varsity sport programs can subvert the achievement of educational goals.

POSTSCRIPT

Should We Be Cheering for High School Sports Programs?

M ost offerings within the secondary school curriculum have, at one time or another, come under careful scrutiny and even severe criticism. Over the past decade we have seen academic areas in the core curriculum challenged in terms of their emphases and their efficacy. Approaches and standards related to the study of mathematics, science, history, reading, and writing have been altered, amended, and in some cases abrogated because of such challenges. But there is one programmatic area that, for the most part, has escaped such evaluation. High school extracurricular activities and most especially high school sports programs have enjoyed uncritical acceptance and support.

Often times this advocacy is tempered by references to the importance of sportsmanship and ethical behavior. Endorsement of athletics as a means of character building is the focus of an essay by former Olympian John Naber entitled "Accepting the Rules of the Game," *The Power of Character* (Jossey-Bass, 1998). The Citizenship Through Sports Alliance (CTSA) links several organizations, such as the National Collegiate Athletic Association (NCAA), Major League Baseball, the NFHS, and the U.S. Olympic Committee, which are interested in promoting the value of sport activities. A similar endorsement for sports competition based on sportsmanship is presented in Russell Gough's *Character Is Everything: Promoting Ethical Excellence in Sports* (Harcourt Brace, 1997). While it is obvious that all high school sports programs are founded on competition, there are many other extracurricular activities that are also characterized by competition. The National Association of Secondary Principals (NASSP) has issued a publication devoted entirely to approved regional and national high school contests and competitions in activities such as music, drama, cheerleading, speech, journalism, science, mathematics, foreign languages, and chess.

In *No Contest: The Case Against Competition* (Houghton Mifflin, 1986), Alfie Kohn suggests that, in spite of widespread popularity, competition among young people—especially in school activities such as organized sports—does not build ethical character and instead causes damage to the participants and ultimately to society. While Kohn focuses on the psychic damage to young people caused by excessive competition, there is also the real danger of physical injury. The National SafeKids Campaign reports that there are 1,000,000 injuries each year to school-age children directly attributable to sports competition. A unique approach to sports and games without competition can be found in *The Cooperative Sports and Games Book,* by Terry Orlick (Pantheon, 1978).

Contributors to This Volume

EDITOR

DENNIS L. EVANS is director of educational leadership development and codirector of the Ed.D. program in educational administration in the Department of Education at the University of California–Irvine. He also teaches in the department's secondary education and administrative services credential programs. Prior to coming to the University in 1992, he served as a high school principal for 21 years with his school receiving the U.S. Department of Education's Exemplary Secondary School Recognition Award in 1985. He received a B.A. in political science from Whittier College, an M.Ed. from Whittier College, and an Ed.D. from the University of Southern California. His articles and essays have appeared in numerous educational journals and books. He has served as an expert witness in several court cases dealing with issues such as administrative supervision, teacher dismissal, and school uniforms. He serves as a member of the Board of Institutional Reviewers for the California Commission on Teacher Credentialing and has chaired several accreditation review teams for that body.

STAFF

Theodore Knight   List Manager
David Brackley   Senior Developmental Editor
Juliana Gribbins   Developmental Editor
Rose Gleich   Administrative Assistant
Brenda S. Filley   Director of Production/Design
Juliana Arbo   Typesetting Supervisor
Diane Barker   Proofreader
Richard Tietjen   Publishing Systems Manager
Larry Killian   Copier Coordinator

AUTHORS

ARKANSAS ACTIVITIES ASSOCIATION serves as the rule-making body for Arkansas high school athletic programs.

MOLEFI KETE ASANTE is a professor of African American studies at Temple University in Philadelphia. He is the author of a number of books and scholarly papers including *Malcolm X as Cultural Hero and Other Afrocentric Essays* (Africa World Press, 1993) and was the founding editor of the *Journal of Black Studies*. He also founded the Afrocentric philosophical movement and The National Afrocentric Institute.

SHELDON BERMAN is superintendent of the Hudson Public Schools in Hudson, Massachusetts. He has been active in his school district and the state with respect to innovative uses of technology in the schools. He is also an advocate of character education and service education.

PAUL V. BREDESON is professor of educational administration at the University of Wisconsin–Madison. His research interests and publications focus on instructional leadership and the principalship.

DAVID L. BRUNSMA is a professor of sociology at the University of Alabama–Huntsville. His research interests include school uniforms and parent involvement strategies in the schools. He teaches courses in sociology of education, sociology of music, and mass media.

JOHN BUELL is freelance journalist who has taught at the College of the Atlantic. He is a former associate editor of *The Progressive* and his books include *Democracy by Other Means: The Politics of Work, Leisure and Environment* (University of Illinois Press, 1995) and, with Thomas S. DeLuca, Jr., *Sustainable Democracy: Individuality and the Politics of Growth* (Sage Publications, 1996). His selection, coauthored with Etta Kralovec, is adapted from *The End of Homework: How Homework Disrupts Families, Overburdens Children and Limits Learning* (Beacon Press, 2000).

JOSEPH M. CARROLL is a former school superintendent who has authored two books entitled *The Copernican Plan: Restructuring the American High School* (Regional Laboratory for Educational Improvement of the Northeast and Islands, 1989) and *The Copernican Plan Evaluated: The Evolution of Revaluation* (Copernican Associates, 1994).

RICHARD R. CHAPLEAU is the 1995 winner of the California Milken Teacher of the Year Award. He teaches chemistry at Lancaster High School and also works with student teachers at Chapman University.

JAY J. COAKLEY is a professor of sociology at the University of Colorado. His publications include *Sport in Society: Issues and Controversies,* 7th ed. (McGraw-Hill, 2001) and, with Eric Dunning, *Handbook of Sports Studies* (Sage Publications, 2000).

HARRIS COOPER is chair of the department of psychological sciences at the University of Missouri–Columbus. He is the author of *Synthesizing Research: A Guide for Literature Reviews,* 3rd ed. (Sage Publications, 1998). He is also the editor, with Larry Hedges, of *The Handbook of Research Synthesis* (Russell Sage Foundation, 1993).

CHESTER E. FINN, Jr. is the president of the Thomas B. Fordham Foundation and John M. Olin Fellow at the Manhattan Institute. He is also a Distinguished Visiting Fellow at Stanford's Hoover Institution. He is the author of 13 books and his most recent, coauthored with Bruno V. Manno and Gregg Vanourek, is entitled *Charter Schools in Action: Renewing Public Education* (Princeton University Press, 2000). His primary focus is the reform of primary and secondary education.

DONALD R. GALLO is a former university professor, a trainer of English teachers, and an authority on books for teenagers. He has edited a number of award-winning collections of short stories for teen readers, chief among them *Sixteen: Short Stories by Outstanding Writers for Young Adults* (Listening Library Incorporated), which is considered by the American Library Association as one of the one hundred Best of the Best Books for Young Adults published during the last four decades.

ANNIE LAURIE GAYLOR is the editor of *Women Without Superstition: No God, No Master* (Freedom From Religion Foundation, 1997), an anthology of women freethinkers and *Freethought Today*, a newspaper published by the Freedom From Religion Foundation in Madison, Wisconsin.

JOHN I. GOODLAD is codirector of the Center for Educational Renewal at the University of Washington. He has authored, coauthored, or edited over 30 books and has had more than 200 articles appear in professional journals. He received the American Educational Research Association Award for Distinguished Contributions to Educational Research in 1993.

ANN WEAVER HART is provost and vice president for academic affairs at Claremont Graduate University. She has written extensively on the principalship and its importance to school administration. She is also editor of *The International Journal of Graduate Education*.

JOHN HOLT (1923–1985) was an educator and commentator/critic of public schooling. His books on education include *How Children Fail* (Perseus Books, 2000); *What Do I Do Monday?* (Boynton/Cook Publishers, 1995); and *Freedom and Beyond* (Boynton/Cook Publishers, 1995). His focus was on children's rights and a child-centered, individualized approach to education.

ROBERT M. HUTCHINS (1879–1977) served at the University of Chicago from 1929 until 1951, the last six years as chancellor. He served as associate director of the Ford Foundation and in 1959 founded the Center for the Study of Democratic Institutions. From 1943 to 1974 he was chairman of the Board of Editors of Encyclopaedia Britannica. He also was editor, with Mortimer J. Adler, of the 54-volume *Great Books of the Western World* (Ayer Company Publishers, 1977). His authored works include *The Higher Learning in America*, 2d ed. (Transaction Publishers, 1999) and *The Conflict in Education in a Democratic Society* (Greenwood Publishing Group, 1972).

CAROL JAGO is a high school English teacher and director of the California Reading and Literature Project at the University of California–Los Angeles. Her books include *Beyond Standards: Excellence in the High School English Classroom* (Boynton/Cook Publishers, 2001) and *With Rigor for All: Teaching the Classics to Contemporary Students* (Calendar Islands Publishers, 2000). She is also a regular contributor to the *Los Angeles Times.*

ALFIE KOHN is a writer and lecturer who comments on human behavior, education, and social theory. His eight books include *Punished by Rewards: The Trouble With Gold Stars, Incentive Plans, A's, Praise and Other Bribes* (Houghton Mifflin, 1999); *No Contest: The Case Against Competition,* rev. ed. (Houghton Mifflin, 1992); *The Schools Our Children Deserve: Moving Beyond Traditional Classrooms and "Tougher Standards"* (Houghton Mifflin, 2000); and *The Case Against Standardized Testing: Raising the Scores, Ruining the Schools* (Heinemann, 2000).

ETTA KRALOVEC is vice president for learning with the Training and Development Corporation in Maine. She was a teacher for 12 years and also served as professor of education and director of teacher education at the College of the Atlantic. Her selection, coauthored with John Buell, is adapted from *The End of Homework: How Homework Disrupts Families, Overburdens Children and Limits Learning* (Beacon Press, 2000).

TOM LOVELESS is senior fellow of governmental studies and director of the Brown Center on Education Policy at the Brookings Institution. He is a former associate professor of public policy at Harvard University with expertise in education policy, K–12 schools, and education reform.

HORACE MANN (1796–1859) was a national leader in the common school movement to bring publicly-funded education to all children. He served as secretary of the Massachusetts State Board of Education for 12 years. He was instrumental in making Massachusetts, in 1852, the first state to make education compulsory. Under his leadership, Massachusetts also took the lead in bringing public secondary education into the mainstream of American life.

ROBERT J. MARZANO is a senior fellow at Mid-continent Research for Education and Learning (McREL). He recently headed a team of authors in developing *Dimensions of Learning Teacher's Manual and Trainer's Manual,* 2d ed. (Association for Supervision and Curriculum Development, 1997). His most recent book is entitled *Transforming Classroom Grading* (Association for Supervision and Curriculum Development, 2000).

MICHAEL W. McCONNELL is a professor in the School of Law at the University of Utah and previously taught at the University of Chicago. His specialty is constitutional law and theory, with a focus on the religion clauses of the First Amendment. He is widely published in the field of church-state relations.

NATIONAL ASSOCIATION OF SECONDARY SCHOOL PRINCIPALS is a national professional advocacy organization for secondary school administrators.

NATIONAL CENTER FOR HISTORY IN THE SCHOOLS is the source for the major United States and European history standards projects.

JEANNIE S. OAKES is a professor of education and director of the Institute for Democracy, Education, and Access at the University of California–Los Angeles. Her research examines inequalities in U.S. schools. In her book, *Keeping Track: How Schools Structure Inequality* (Yale University Press, 1986), she focuses attention on how tracking and ability grouping limit the school experiences of low-income students and students of color. She has also coauthored, with Karen Hunter Quartz, Steve Ryan, and Martin Lipton, *Becoming Good American Schools: The Struggle for Civic Virtue in Education Reform* (Jossey-Bass, 2002).

TODD OPPENHEIMER, a writer based in San Francisco, is a former associate editor of *Newsweek Interactive.* He is expanding his selection, which received the 1998 National Magazine Award for public interest journalism, into a book to be published by W. W. Norton & Company.

REECE PETERSON is an associate professor of special education at the University of Nebraska–Lincoln. His research interests include identification of and interventions for students with emotional and behavioral disorders and student discipline. He recently served as president of the Council for Children With Behavioral Disorders.

RICHARD P. PHELPS is an educational researcher and author of the Test Bashing series for *Education News.* He has conducted research for the Indiana Department of Education, the General Accounting Office, and the American Institutes of Research. He also served on the staff of the Organization for Economic Co-operation and Development in Paris.

MICHAEL J. PODGURSKY is a professor and chair of the Department of Economics at the University of Missouri–Columbia. His recent publications include "Regulation Versus Markets: The Case for Greater Flexibility in the Market for Public School Teachers," Paper presented at the New Teachers for a New Century Conference (November 17–19, 1999) and "Do We Need Schools of Education?" Paper presented at the Education Writers Association Annual Meeting (April 14, 2000).

DIANE RAVITCH is a senior fellow at the Brookings Institution, a visiting fellow at the Hoover Institution at Stanford, and a member of the Koret Task Force on K–12 Education. She is also a member of the Society of American Historians. Among the books she has authored are *Left Back: A Century of Battles Over School Reform* (Simon & Schuster, 2001) and *National Standards in American Education: A Citizen's Guide* (Brookings Institution Press, 1996).

DIANE STARK RENTNER is associate director of the Center on Education Policy. She served as legislative associate for the U.S. House of Representatives' Committee on Education and Labor from 1988 to 1994. She has also worked for the National PTA and the Council of Chief State School Officers in their government relations offices.

KERRY A. ROCKQUEMORE is an assistant professor of family studies at the University of Connecticut. She specializes in race and ethnic relations, urban sociology, and the sociology of education.

DONAL SACKEN is a professor of education at Texas Christian University. His research interests include the development of school leaders and legal and ethical issues in educational institutions.

PETER SACKS is a journalist and essayist. His essays on education and American culture have appeared in *Change, Thought and Action, American Enterprise,* and the *New York Times.* His most recent book is *Standardized Minds: The High Price of America's Testing* (Perseus Books Group, 1999).

ROSEMARY C. SALOMONE is a professor law at St. John's University School of Law and a fellow of the Open Society Institute. She is the author of *Visions of Schooling: Conscience, Community, and Common Education* (Yale University Press, 2000).

THE SECRETARY'S COMMISSION ON ACHIEVING NECESSARY SKILLS (SCANS) was established in 1990 by the secretary of labor to determine the skills young people need to succeed in the world of work.

GILBERT T. SEWALL is director of the American Textbook Council and editor of *The Eighties: A Reader* (Perseus Books Group, 2000). He writes frequently on educational issues.

THEODORE R. SIZER is Professor Emeritus at Brown University and chairman of the Coalition of Essential Schools, founded in 1983. He served as dean of the Graduate School of Education at Harvard and as headmaster of Phillips Academy in Andover, Massachusetts. He is the founding director of the Annenberg Institute for School Reform. His publications include *Horace's Compromise: The Dilemma of the American High School,* rev. ed. (Houghton Mifflin, 1997); *Horace's School: Redesigning the American High School,* rev. ed. (Houghton Mifflin, 1997); *Horace's Hope: What Works for the American High School* (Houghton Mifflin, 1997); and, with Nancy Faust Sizer, *The Students Are Watching: Schools and the Moral Contract* (Beacon Press, 1999).

RUSS SKIBA is director of the Institute for Child Study and associate professor in the Department of Counseling and Psychology at Indiana University. He is project director of the Building Safe and Responsive Schools Program jointly conducted with Reece Peterson at the University of Nebraska.

LEWIS C. SOLMON is senior vice president and senior scholar of the Milken Foundation. From 1985–1991 he served as dean of the University of California–Los Angeles's Graduate School of Education, where he is now a professor emeritus.

DON TAPSCOTT is the author of several books related to technology in education and business. His *Growing Up Digital: The Rise of the Net Generation* (McGraw-Hill, 2000) won the Amazon.com Bestseller Award in 1998. He is chairman of Digital 4Sight, a think tank dealing with the Internet and new media.

UNITED STATES DEPARTMENT OF EDUCATION is the federal cabinet level office dealing with educational matters.

GREGG VANOUREK has served as vice president for programs at the Thomas B. Fordham Foundation and as research fellow at the Hudson Institute.

REGINALD D. WILD is a professor in the Department of Curriculum Studies at the University of British Columbia. His research interests include the evolving secondary science curricula and science teachers' attitudes about the quarter system school schedule.

WELLFORD W. WILMS is a professor of education and faculty director of the Educational Leadership program at the University of California–Los Angeles. His current research deals with how service organizations (higher education, teacher unions, and police agencies in particular) adjust to rapid changes in the environment and the implications for education and policy.

Index